David Friedrich Strauss

A New Life of Jesus for the People

Vol. II.

David Friedrich Strauss

A New Life of Jesus for the People
Vol. II.

ISBN/EAN: 9783337054328

Printed in Europe, USA, Canada, Australia, Japan

Cover: Foto ©Lupo / pixelio.de

More available books at **www.hansebooks.com**

THE
LIFE OF JESUS

FOR THE PEOPLE.

BY

DAVID FRIEDRICH STRAUSS.

Authorized Translation.

IN TWO VOLUMES.

VOL. II.

SECOND EDITION.

WILLIAMS AND NORGATE,
14, HENRIETTA STREET, COVENT GARDEN, LONDON;
AND 20, SOUTH FREDERICK STREET, EDINBURGH.

1879.

LONDON:
PRINTED BY C. GREEN AND SON,
178, STRAND.

CONTENTS OF VOL. II.

SECOND BOOK.
MYTHICAL HISTORY OF JESUS.

SEC.		PAGE
51.	Arrangement	3

First Chapter.—Prefatory Mythical History of Jesus.

52.	Subdivision	5
	FIRST GROUP OF MYTHS. JESUS, THE SON OF DAVID	6— 39
53, 54.	The Two Genealogies	6
55.	His Birth in the City of David	19
56.	As Messiah dedicated like David	28
	SECOND GROUP OF MYTHS	39— 68
57.	Begotten of the Holy Ghost	39
58.	Annunciation and Birth of the Forerunner	46
59.	Birth of Jesus	52
60, 61.	Jesus, the Creative Word of God, Incarnate	55
	THIRD GROUP OF MYTHS	69—115
62, 63.	His Life endangered and preserved by the Star	69
64.	His Presentation in the Temple	87
65.	Dedicated like Moses and Samuel	95
66.	The Messiah withstands Temptation in the Desert	100

Second Chapter.—Mythical History of the Public Life of Jesus.

67.		116
	FIRST GROUP OF MYTHS	117—126
68.	Jesus and his Precursor	117
	SECOND GROUP OF MYTHS	126—149
69, 70.	Jesus and his Disciples	126
	THIRD GROUP OF MYTHS. JESUS AS A PERFORMER OF MIRACLES	149—280
71.	Cures of the Blind	149
72.	Cures of Cripples	160
73.	Cures of Lepers, and of the Deaf and Dumb	172
74.	Cures of Persons possessed by Devils	179
75.	Cures involuntary and at a distance	192

SEC.		PAGE
76.	Cases of the Raising of the Dead	204
77.	Raising of Lazarus	213
78.	Sea Anecdotes	237
79.	Miracle of the Loaves and Fishes	252
80.	Miracle at Cana	266
81.	Cursing of the Fig-tree	276
	FOURTH GROUP OF MYTHS. TRANSFIGURATION AND ENTRANCE OF JESUS INTO JERUSALEM	281—295
82.	The Transfiguration	281
83.	His Entrance into Jerusalem	290

Third Chapter.—Mythical History of the Passion, Death and Resurrection of Jesus.

	FIRST GROUP OF MYTHS	296—324
84.	The Meal at Bethany and the Anointing	296
85.	The Passover and the Last Supper	304
86.	The Feet-washing, the Treason, and Denial	316
	SECOND GROUP OF MYTHS. THE AGONY AND ARREST OF JESUS	324—341
87.	The Agony at Gethsemane	324
88.	Arrest of Jesus	336
	THIRD GROUP OF MYTHS. TRIAL AND CONDEMNATION OF JESUS	342—365
89.	Trial before the High-priest	342
90.	Death of the Traitor	348
91.	Trial before Pilate and Herod	355
	FOURTH GROUP OF MYTHS. CRUCIFIXION, DEATH, AND BURIAL OF JESUS	365—402
92.	The Crucifixion	365
93.	The Words on the Cross	376
94.	The Miracles at his Death	381
95.	The Spear-stab in his Side	387
96.	His Burial	395
	FIFTH GROUP OF MYTHS. HIS RESURRECTION AND ASCENSION	402—430
97.	History of the Resurrection	402
98.	The Ascension	417
99, 100.	Conclusion	430

Second Book.

MYTHICAL HISTORY OF JESUS,

ITS ORIGIN AND FORMATION.

Second Book.
MYTHICAL HISTORY OF JESUS.

51. Arrangement.

So far we have drawn the rough outlines of a real Biography of Jesus, have endeavoured to make him as intelligible to us as is possible in the case of a figure which we view not merely at so remote a distance, but, in the main, through a medium so dim, and one which interrupts the light in a manner so peculiar. We now proceed to decompose the medium itself, *i.e.* to analyse the images visible in it, by pointing out the conditions under which they have originated.

For performing these processes we may adopt more than one method of arrangement. We might take each of our four Gospels by itself, according to the epoch which it marks in the course of the development of Christian ideas and conceptions, and shew how, at this epoch, such and such efforts being made by the Church, such and such dogmatical principles being assumed, the Life of Jesus did and must necessarily have presented itself to men's apprehension; or, looking to the closer relation of the three first Evangelists and the connection of different tendencies in them, we might combine these together, contrast them with the fourth, and develop first the Synoptic, then the Johannine circle of myths, according to their respective origin, so that we should have to go through the course of the Life of Jesus, in the first case four times, in the second at least twice. The first of these processes would certainly be tedious, the second would be somewhat violent. Notwithstanding all the discrepancy between the synoptic Gospels and that of John, still the fundamental principles of the former are in close connection with those of the latter; even in the case of particular narratives they are assumed by the latter, and stand in the same relation of degree to those of the Synoptics as the superlative does to the positive and comparative. A criticism, therefore, whose highest problem it is to make the Gospels intelligible as literary and historical products, might find it convenient to take each by itself, and to develop connectedly its description of the Life of Jesus; we, whose object it is to answer the question, whether in the evangelical narratives we have historical accounts of Jesus, or, if not, what, must take another road.

We shall take, not exactly separate narratives, but separate groups of them—for instance, the narratives of the genealogy, the procreation, the baptism, the miracles of Jesus, and pursue them in their development through all four Gospels; and in doing this we shall, as far as is practicable, take as a clue the chronology of the Life of Jesus.

The materials for the first section are, naturally, the prefatory mythical history of Jesus, containing the accounts, on the one hand, of the coming of the forerunner—on the other, that of his introduction by that forerunner, the history of the baptism and of the temptation, as being inseparable from it.

FIRST CHAPTER.

PREFATORY MYTHICAL HISTORY OF JESUS.

52. Subdivision.

The whole prefatory history of Jesus, in the form in which it lies before us in the Gospels, assuming the historical notices of his domestication in Nazareth, his subsequent relation to John the Baptist, his own name, and perhaps also the names of his parents, was developed from the simple proposition of the new faith, that Jesus was the Messiah.

Jesus was the Messiah, *i.e.* the Son of David, the Son of God, the second Moses, the last, greater Saviour of his people, and of so many of mankind as faithfully turn to him.

He was the Son of David, *i.e.* in the first place, he was descended from his family. Efforts were made to prove this on different sides, and from different points of view. Hence the two genealogies in Matthew and Luke. He was the Son of David, *i.e.* in the next place, he was born in the city of David. But as he was notoriously "the Nazarene," the one Evangelist made use of a particular machinery in order to bring the parents of Jesus from Nazareth, the other to bring them away from Bethlehem to Nazareth. He was the Son of David, *i.e.* in the third place, he was, like David, anointed by a man of a prophetical character, filled, by this anointing, with the Holy Spirit, and prepared to undertake his high calling.

As the Messiah, Jesus was also the Son of God, and in the most literal acceptation of the phrase. This meant, in the view of the authors of the first and third Gospels, that he was begotten in the womb of his mother by the Holy Ghost without the co-operation of a human father, announced and welcomed by angels. In the view of the author of the fourth Gospel, it meant that Jesus was the Creative Word of God become incarnate, a dignity in comparison with which not only the descent from David and the birth in the city of David, but also the pastoral scenes of the occasion of his announcement and birth, vanished, as petty and insignificant.

As the Messiah, lastly, Jesus was the second Moses; *i.e.* had been miraculously preserved from the same dangers as once threatened, in like manner, the infancy of the first Saviour, dangers produced by the fact that the Star out of Jacob promised in the books of Moses had shewn itself on the occasion of his birth, that those who brought gifts from Saba had attended to do homage to the Messianic Infant; the second Moses, who, like the first and like Samuel, having been even as a child dedicated to his high calling, was the Teacher of the learned; who, lastly, withstood the temptations to which the people, under the guidance of Moses, had succumbed, and thus proved himself to be the Restorer and the Regenerator.

FIRST GROUP OF MYTHS.

JESUS, THE SON OF DAVID.

I. JESUS, THE MESSIAH, OF THE FAMILY OF DAVID. THE TWO GENEALOGIES.

53.

THE object being to prove the descent from David, which, according to the conceptions of his countrymen, was a necessary attribute of Jesus if he was the Messiah (John vii. 42; Rom. i. 3), this task was facilitated on both sides by two opposite circumstances. The first was, that the genealogy of David was known both upwards and downwards; that of Jesus was, unquestionably, unknown.

The pedigree of David might be read by all men in the list of Jewish kings down to the captivity, as given at length in historical narrative by the Books of the Kings and Chronicles; it might be read in the form of a pedigree, as given by the introduction to the first Book of the Chronicles, coming down to Scrubabel, the leader of those who returned from the captivity, and his immediate posterity. It was a matter of course that he who was descended from David was, at the same time, a descendant of the national patriarch Abraham. But as not only the Son of David was seen in the Messiah, but also that seed promised to Abraham in whom all nations of the earth were to be blessed (1 Mos. xxii. 18; Galat. iii. 15), it might appear appropriate to trace the family of David upwards to Abraham, implied as it was already partly in the first book of Moses, partly at the end of the little Book of Ruth, and in the introduction to the Chronicles. Nay, if it was wished to take a step upwards from Abraham to Adam, the first created man, there was no difficulty in doing so. What was wanted was found in the fifth and eleventh chapter of Genesis, and again in the introduction to the Chronicles.

Consequently the genealogical thread, as given in the Old Testament, ran down from Adam to Scrubabel and his immediate successors; here it came to an end and hung suspended in the air, being about 500 years shorter than it ought to be, and requiring to be lengthened by so much if it was to be taken as the genealogy of Jesus. This might be done in two ways; best naturally, if the descent of Jesus could be known so far up, and supported by original records. But it will be admitted that there is but little probability that this could be done. We do not even require the information of Julius Africanus, that Herod, ashamed of his own ignoble descent, destroyed the Jewish genealogical registers,*

---

* Quoted in Eusebius, Ecclesiastical History, i. 7, 13.

to make it extremely doubtful that after the stormy periods, first of the Macedonian rule, then of that of the Maccabees, and finally of the beginning of that of the Romans, the obscure family of a Galilean carpenter should have had genealogical trees reaching so far up. It may well, indeed, be believed that at a later period, after a Christian Church had sprung up, the relatives of "The Lord" busied themselves much with the genealogy of their family, as the same Julius Africanus tells us they did; and such efforts, in which the members of the family were certainly assisted by other members of the Church, may be supposed to have given rise to our two genealogical tables in Matthew (i. 1—17) and Luke (iii. 23—28); but the fact that these writers fill up the gap already mentioned with totally different names, confirms our supposition that they had not at their disposal any original records for doing so, but depended upon their own surmise and conjecture. The son of Serubabel, through whom the pedigree of Jesus runs, is called by Matthew Abiud, by Luke Resa (both, in this, differing from 1 Chron. iii.), while the father of Joseph, through whom Jesus is supposed to come from Serubabel and David, is called by Matthew Jacob, by Luke Eli, and, between the two, the names are different as well as the number of generations, of which, in Matthew, including Serubabel and excluding Joseph, we find ten, in Luke nearly as many again, namely nineteen.

This discrepancy was, as we said, very natural when the authors of the two genealogies were thrown back upon their own invention in the filling up of that gap, and neither knew anything of the attempt of the other. But even if the author of the genealogy in Luke was acquainted with that of Matthew, he might have his own reasons for differing from it. For he differs from him even as to the members from David down to Serubabel, which he, as well as the composer of the other genealogy, had before him in the Old Testament. From David downwards, the genealogy given in Matthew makes the pedigree of Jesus run through Solomon and the well-known series of the kings of Judah; while that in Luke selects Nathan from among the sons of David. Now Nathan, in 1 Chron. iii. 5, is named immediately before Solomon, but his posterity is nowhere spoken of in the Old Testament, so that the compiler of the genealogy in Luke, finding no list of them elsewhere, had to invent their names himself. Different reasons may be thought of for his deviating from the royal line, as given in the Old Testament. Naturally, it was not, in his opinion, too eminent and too good for his Christ. Consequently it must, in some way or other, have been too mean and unworthy. It is well known that, as is often the case in dynasties merely hereditary, that of David also had degenerated in later times. With regard to the last scion of it, that Jechoniah or Jehoiachin, who was carried away to Babylon, the prophet Jeremiah (xxii. 30) had delivered judgment in the name of Jehovah: "No man of his seed shall prosper, sitting upon the throne of David, and ruling any more in Judah." It is impossible that any one remembering these words of Jehovah could represent as descending from an ancestor thus rejected, him to whom the Lord should give the throne of his father David, and who should "reign over the house of Jacob for ever" (Luke i. 32 ff.). But in fact that degenerate member of the royal line was not the first that had gone astray, but already Rehoboam, nay even Solomon himself with his licentiousness and his idolatry, might be considered as degenerate also; so that we cannot be surprised that, according to one ancient account,* there was already a party among the Jews who expected the Messiah, not from this, the ruling line of the posterity of David, tainted as it was with crimes, but from a line that in its obscurity had continued pure. It was as obvious for the author of the third Gospel, educated as he

---

Comp. Credner's Introduction to the New Testament, i. 68 ff.

was in the school of Paul, to adopt into his work a genealogy sketched from this point of view, as it was for the composer of the first, with his more Jewish-Christian spirit, to prefer the other. For the Jewish Christian was as regards his Messiah naturally a legitimist. On the other hand, the Pauline, possessed, so to say, with an Orleanistic spirit, might prefer a Messiah who, descended from a non-reigning line, appeared* at the same time less as a Jewish King. For the same reason the author of the third Gospel welcomed in the genealogy adopted by him the continuation beyond Abraham up to Adam and God himself, or he himself made that continuation, through which Jesus, in the character of the second Adam (1 Cor. xv. 45, 47), was placed outside of the limits of Judaism in a relation to the whole of mankind.

But it is not merely in the discrepancy between these two genealogies, but also in the character of each of them separately, that we recognise less the results of historical investigation than the products of dogmatic assumption. That in Matthew divides itself into three portions, containing each an equal number of members, of which the first reaches from Abraham to David, the second from David to the Babylonian captivity, the third from this last to Jesus. It is clear from the title which he gives it, "Book of the generation of Jesus Christ," that the compiler had in view the bipartite register of the primeval generation in Genesis (1 Mos. v. 1 ff., xi. 10 ff.), that in Genesis being called, according to the Alexandrian translation, "Book of the generation of men."† Now this latter gives, first, from Adam to Noah ten generations, and then, certainly not without a meaning and a purpose, the same number from Shem to Abraham. In this correspondence of the periods within which the great historical epochs succeeded each other, as in this case the first

---

* Comp. Hilgenfeld, The Gospels, p. 165.

† 1 Mos. v. 1: αὕτη ἡ βίβλος γενέσεως ἀνθρώπων. Matt. i. 1: βίβλος γενέσεως Ἰησοῦ Χριστοῦ.

Patriarch of mankind was succeeded by the second, and he by the Father of the faithful, the Rhythm of History was supposed to be discovered, the key-note, as it were, of the divine government of the world—the character of which, however, is not quite so simple as that. Now when our evangelical genealogist combined with the accounts in Genesis the genealogy at the conclusion of the Book of Ruth, he found from Abraham to David, both included, fourteen members. Whether there were ten, as in Genesis, or fourteen, was indifferent to him; nay, the number fourteen, as the double of seven, was a particularly sacred number; only as the number ten was repeated in the one case, so must the fourteen be repeated here. And as one more group of fourteen, even taking the numerous Jewish kings into the genealogy, did not reach to Christ, it was necessary to have two more groups of fourteen—three, therefore, altogether, so that again a sacred number resulted in the number three. Moreover, as the first fourteen ended with David, the third with the Messiah, so also it was necessary that the conclusion of the second should coincide with a historical epoch. Now for this there was, this time, no great personage, or favourite of God, but the grand execution of God's judgment in the Babylonish captivity naturally presented itself.

Now with the exception of the name of Serubabel and that of his father, with which the compiler of the genealogy wished to embellish it, there were no other names at hand to enable him to make the third portion uniform with the first. But this was no obstacle to him. Again, thirteen generations were not enough for the six hundred years, or nearly so, from Jechoniah to Jesus (not counting in the latter), seeing that, on the average, each son must have been born when his father was 64 years old. But this gave him little trouble. The case of the middle portion was more difficult. For from Solomon to the end of the kingdom, there were twenty Jewish kings, or, not counting Joash and Zedekiah, who did not carry on the generation, still eighteen; if, therefore, the number fourteen was to prevail, four had to be rejected. It cannot be said that, in doing so, the genealogist fixed on the worst, for Joas and Amaziah, whom he passes over, were, in the estimation of the Old Testament historians, praiseworthy princes, and in any case better than Joram and many others, whom nevertheless he thought worthy to occupy a place in his list. But when we see how, before Jechoniah or Jehoiachin, he passes over his father Jehoiachim, one might suppose a mistake to have been committed from the similarity of sound, especially as he gives Jehoiachin brothers, which not he but his father Jehoiachim had. But when we find further on that, instead of passing from Joram to Ahaziah, or, in Greek, Ochoziah (omitting three names, Ahaziah, Joas, and Amaziah), he goes to Usia, in Greek, Ozias, we are almost inclined to suspect that he had selected for his omissions, intentionally, those passages in which a resemblance in the sound of the names might to a certain extent conceal those omissions. Only he did in reality too much; for, after those omissions, the second group of fourteen only has its full complement by counting over again, at the beginning of it, the name of David, which had been already counted in the first, and then ending with Josiah. Or if we begin with Solomon, then Jechoniah must be taken in at the end, and, as without him the third division has only thirteen members, he, instead of David, must be counted twice over, being, as he is, named both before and after the Babylonian captivity that defines the section. By these means the object of the compiler is certainly attained: the pedigree of Jesus the Messiah is not merely derived in a general way from Abraham and David, but runs down to him in three uniform cascades of fourteen steps each, a sign, in the mind of the writer, that it was not blind chance that was here at work, but a higher power, ordering the destiny of man; in ours, that the result was not that of certain historical investigation, but of arbitrary and dogmatizing compilation.

The genealogy in Luke has no such subdivisions of numbers. The sum-total, therefore, assumes greater importance. This is not brought into relief as it is in Matthew, but it is, reckoning the name of God at the head of it seventy-seven, consequently eleven times the sacred number seven. Some trouble, however, was required to extend it to this number. At the point where it leaves the Old Testament, we may see this from the numerous repetitions of the same names, that of Joseph occurring four times, of Judah twice, of Levi, Melchi, Matthat, Mattathias, the same, and one Mattatha besides. Names like these do indeed occur in historical genealogies, but, thus accumulated, they point rather to the exhausted imagination of a writer who, when he could think of no new names, kept repeating those he had already used.

It is clear, besides, that the compiler of this list was not the author of the third Gospel, but that the latter found the genealogy ready-made as a separate portion, and incorporated it into his work as well as he could (perhaps with the extension alluded to above). This is clear from the way in which, in the Gospel, it appears, according to Schleiermacher's striking expression, wedged in between the two accounts, so closely connected together, of the Baptism and Temptation of Jesus. In Matthew it stands at the beginning of the Gospel, and very appropriately, as the history of the birth of Jesus is in close connection with it. So far it might be supposed that the Evangelist had himself completed the list with a view to introducing it in this very place. But this assumption is rendered impossible, both in the case of Matthew and of Luke, by a reason involved in the contents of the genealogy. In their accounts of the birth, both Evangelists exclude Joseph from all participation in the procreation of Jesus, but the genealogies deduce the pedigree of Jesus from David through Joseph. Both do indeed in their genealogies describe Joseph only as the supposed father of Jesus, or as the husband of Mary, his mother; but these are obviously only interpolations and alterations, made by them in order to bring the genealogies into harmony with their accounts of the birth. Whoever, in order to prove Jesus to be the Son of David, *i. e.* the Messiah, planned a genealogy representing Joseph to be a descendant of David, must necessarily have considered this Joseph to have been the real father of Jesus. The two genealogies in the first and third Gospels are memorials of a time and a circle when Jesus was considered a human being naturally begotten. Whoever conceived of him as having been called into existence without male co-operation by the operation of Deity in Mary, had no resource, supposing him also to wish to prove him to be the Son of David, but to keep to the mother's side, and to derive her from the family of David. Our Evangelists exhibit genealogies of Joseph which they did not wish to be lost, but could not use them in the form in which they were, giving Jesus as the real son of Joseph. So by these additions they cut off the natural connection between Jesus and Joseph, without noticing that they had thus cut the vital nerve, and the power of proof contained in those genealogies.

54.

Thus we have considered the genealogies from the natural point of view. From this point they are easily and simply explained, with all their discrepancies from each other, and from the history and the sequel of the evangelical narrative: so easily and simply, that it is almost inconceivable how from any other point of view difficulties so desperate can be found in them, and, *a priori*, that point of view may be considered as the wrong one from which such difficulties result. But what they do result from is the supposition that not only in these genealogies, and indeed in both of them, we have genuine historical records, but also in the history of the infancy of Jesus an account of historical value.

Can it, in the first place, be explained on this supposition how Matthew, or whoever is the compiler of the genealogy given by him, came to omit out of it four well-known Jewish kings, and to maintain the absolutely false proposition that from David to the Babylonish captivity only fourteen generations succeeded each other? In the case of an inspired writer, a mistake is not to be thought of, and even one writing independently of inspiration could at the most only take Jehoiachim and Jehoiachin as one and the same person. But that, besides this, he omits three other kings, that is, exactly the number that was necessary in order to bring out his second group of fourteen, cannot have been accidental, but must have been intentional. We say then that the intention was not to get more than fourteen members, but we find in the manner in which the author proceeded an instance of unhistorical caprice. The theologians of the modern Church, on the contrary, as many Fathers of the Church had done before them, find in this something deeply significant. That is, in the omission of the three kings between Joram and Usia, they find an inculcation of the divine prohibition against idolatry (2 Mos. xx. 5); Joram, they say,* had in marriage Athalia, the idolatrous daughter of Ahab and Jezebel, whose descendants were unworthy of succeeding to the theocratic throne, and were, therefore, omitted from the genealogy of Christ. But, as all the succeeding kings and ancestors of Jesus were descendants of this married couple, the whole genealogical list, on this supposition, should have been broken off at this place. No! says the theologian, it is only to the third and fourth generation that Jehovah threatens in that passage of the law to punish the sin of idolatrous men;

* Krafft, Chronology and Harmony of the Four Gospels, p. 55. Ebrard, Scientific Criticism of the Evangelical History, p. 192 of the 2nd edition.

consequently it was only for the son, grandson, and great-grandson of that couple, exactly as we find it in Matthew, that the right to figure in the genealogy of Jesus was destroyed. Madness, we see, has here its method; hence the wrong application of reasonable grounds.

In the second place, if the genealogies are taken as historical records, the discrepancy between them requires, above everything, to be explained. How can Joseph have been at the same time a son of Jacob and of Heli, how have descended from David at the same time through Solomon and the kings, and again through Nathan and a line not royal? At first sight, the answer does not appear so difficult. If we had genealogies of Scipio Africanus the younger, one might give the line of the Scipios, the other that of the Æmilii, and still both be historical, as the author of the one might have kept to the natural, the other to the adòptive father of the hero. Thus the father of the Church Augustin* considered the Jacob of Matthew to be the natural, the Heli of Luke to be the adoptive, father of Jesus. In the law of Moses it was provided, in order to prevent families dying out, that when a married man had died childless, his brother, if he had one, should marry the widow, and that their first-born son should be entered in the register of the family in the name of the deceased brother (5 Mos. xxv. 5 ff.). Accordingly, even before the time of Augustin, the learned Christian,† Julius Africanus, thought to explain the discrepancy between the genealogies by supposing that Joseph's mother had been first married to Heli, by whom she had no son, and that then, after his death, his brother Jacob married her, and had by her Joseph in his own name. Consequently Matthew is as correct in saying that Jacob begot Joseph,

---

* De Consensu Evangelistaram, ii. 3.

† Quoted in Eusebius, Ecclesiastical History, i. 7, and afterwards corroborated by Augustin in the Retractations, ii. 7.

inasmuch as he was his natural father, as Luke in calling Joseph the son of Heli, in whose name he was registered according to the law.

But if Jacob and Heli were brothers-german, then they both had the same father, and the two genealogies must have coincided above them, which is by no means the case. Therefore Africanus assumed that Jacob and Heli were only brothers on the mother's side, and that their mother had two husbands in succession, one of whom belonged to the line of Solomon, the other to that of Nathan, in the family of David, and that of these husbands one was the father of Jacob, the other of Heli. This solution would be indeed far-fetched, but still good in so far as it is not impossible, provided the thing was settled by it. But exactly as Joseph in this case, so, higher up, Scrubabel's father Salathiel, in which two names both genealogies, in the midst of clear discrepancies, unfortunately coincide, has in both two different fathers and lines of descent, in Matthew Jechoniah of the royal, in Luke Neri of the other line. So that again the same double hypothesis becomes necessary, first that Jechoniah and Neri were brothers, and the one the natural, the other, according to the Levitical law, the lawful father of Salathiel, and then that the two were only half-brothers on the mother's side, consequently that these two fathers married successively the same woman, and that moreover, exactly as before, the one genealogy took the legal, the other, in opposition to the Mosaic ordinance, the natural father. But this is too much even for many theologians, so they prefer either the simple relation of adoption, or explain* Salathiel and Scrubabel in Luke to be different persons from those in Matthew—or, and this is the favourite solution, they consider one genealogy as that of Mary.

We cannot but be curious to know to which of the two genealogies the last explanation is to apply, as in the one of

* As Schmid, Biblical Theology, i. 45.

them Mary is not named at all, in the other only as the wife of Joseph, the descendant of David. And yet it is in this very genealogy, which at all events does name her, that the reference of it to her by the expression, "Jacob begot Joseph, the husband of Mary," is so specifically excluded, that the genealogy in which her name is wanting altogether, *i.e.* that of Luke, might with more confidence be considered as hers.* In that case, when it is said (ver. 23 ff.), Jesus was (as it was believed) a son of Joseph, the (son) of Heli, the (son) of Matthat, &c., the word son, in the first, third and following places, is supposed to mean a real son, and only in the second place, between Joseph and Heli, a son-in-law;† or it is explained, Jesus was believed to be a son of Joseph, (going higher up, a son, *i.e.* through Mary a grandson) of Heli, (still higher up, a son, *i.e.* a great-grandson) of Matthat, &c.;‡ two modes of explanation between which we might hesitate, if it were necessary to award the prize to the most unnatural, which we should choose. Besides this, different Fathers of the Church and the apocryphal Gospels assign a descent from David to Mary also.§ Not so the Gospel of Luke; otherwise, on the occasion of the taxing (ii. 4), it would not say that Joseph also went with Mary to be registered because *he* was of the family of David, but because they both were.

In the third place, it has to be explained, if not only the genealogies but the account of the Infancy, which we shall discuss further on, are to be taken historically—if therefore Joseph was indeed a descendant of David, but not the father of Jesus, what, as far as Jesus is concerned, the genealogy is intended to prove. The answer is, that they, or at least

* Thus Krafft, Chronology and Harmony of the Gospels, p. 56 ff. Ebrard, Scientific Criticism, p. 195.
† Paulus, in the Commentary on the passage.
‡ Krafft, as quoted, p. 58.
§ Protevang. Jacobi, c. 1, 2, 10. Evang. de Nativ. Mariæ, i. 13. Justin, Dial. cum Tryph. 23, 43, 100.

the genealogy in Matthew, if we appropriate that in Luke to Mary, is intended to shew, not the natural pedigree of Jesus, but the entailing upon him of the theocratic right to the dignity of the Messiah from David through the husband of his mother. Thus it would be not a genealogical but a juridical pedigree.* But according to the notions both of the Jews and the original Christians (Rom. i. 3; John vii. 42), the two things were inseparable, as they clearly were also in the original sketch of our genealogies; the Messianic claim was considered to be a claim inherited with the blood of David, and it was only a change in their view of the person of Jesus, according to which the genealogies could no longer have maintained their ground, at all events as those of Joseph, but only as those of Mary, that caused the Evangelists, not wishing to lose these old and valued documents, to introduce the break above mentioned, and to make them harmless indeed as far as the new dogma, but at the same time unmeaning as far as the genealogies themselves were concerned.

II. JESUS, AS THE MESSIAH, IS BORN IN THE CITY OF DAVID.

55.

It was out of Bethlehem, according to the text in the Prophet (Micah v. 1), that the desired Shepherd of the people of God, *i.e.* the Messiah, was to come. This was understood of his being born in Bethlehem (Matt. ii. 4 ff.); and thus, if Jesus was the Messiah, he must of course be born in the city of David (John vii. 42).

It was not quite so easy to bring this about as it was to trace the descent of Jesus from David. Of the parents of Jesus it was not known that they were of the line of David, but as no one knew the contrary, any one might boldly maintain upon this point whatever he thought fit. With the

* Ebrard, as quoted, p. 191.

home of Jesus, the dwelling-place of his parents, the case was otherwise. Of this, on the contrary, every one knew that it had been, as far as could be remembered, Nazareth, not Bethlehem. But, as a home and a birthplace do not necessarily coincide, the prophecy might still maintain its right. Jesus might possibly have been born on the road, or his parents might have changed their dwelling in his earliest childhood. In the first case, they had always lived in Nazareth, and had only once, on an accidental occasion, sojourned temporarily in Bethlehem. In the other case, Bethlehem had originally been their dwelling-place, but they had subsequently had a motive for changing it to Nazareth. So in this the narrators had their choice of the mode in which they would represent the story, and we may still recognise the motive which might induce one to decide in favour of one statement, the other in favour of another.

The stronger the spirit of Jewish dogmatism was in one, the greater the importance he attributed to the prophecy with its Bethlehem: the stronger that of Greek pragmatism in the other, the more he was inclined to the relation with Nazareth, which was historically known. To the one, accordingly, Bethlehem appeared not only as the birthplace of Jesus, but also as the immemorial home of his parents; to the other, Nazareth, as the town in which Jesus was not only brought up, but would also have been born, if it had not been necessary for him to be born elsewhere in compliance with the prophecy. We see at once that the first was the case of Matthew, the latter of Luke.

Matthew begins his narrative with the parents of Jesus, the pregnancy of his mother, the doubts of Joseph and the pacifying of them by the angel in a dream, without saying where all this took place (i. 18—25). But immediately afterwards, and without further prefatory remark, he represents Jesus as being born in Bethlehem (ii. 1). We must therefore assume that what has been already recounted took place there, consequently that that was the home of the parents of Jesus, but that the Evangelist does not name Bethlehem until it was of importance for his dogmatic purpose, that is on the occasion of the birth of Jesus, who could not have been the Messiah if he had not been born in the city of David. Here the parents of Jesus receive the visit of the wise men from the East, and would not have thought of quitting the place if they had not been warned by an angel in the dream to take flight into Egypt to avoid the threatened murder of the infants (ii. 14); nay, even from there they were on the point of returning again at once to Bethlehem, after the death of the murderer, had not his successor in Judea, not a much better man than he, caused them alarm: and now the honest angel of the dream makes them settle in the Galilean Nazareth (ii. 22 ff.). Here he who runs may read: the Evangelist assumes as a given fact that the parents of Jesus lived in Bethlehem. He represents them as having been there always, and therefore makes use of no sort of arrangement to take them there for the purpose of the birth of Jesus; on the contrary, his problem is to bring them away from the place after it has happened, and to explain how it came to pass that they are, at a later period, to be found, with Jesus, in Nazareth.

Luke, on the contrary, as soon as he begins to speak of the parents of Jesus, mentions Nazareth as their dwelling-place. Here he represents the angel Gabriel as announcing to Mary her miraculous pregnancy (i. 20 ff.); here Mary's household must be supposed to have been, to which she returns after the visit to Elizabeth (i. 56); hither, after their temporary sojourn in Bethlehem, the parents of Jesus come back with the child, and on this occasion Nazareth is described expressly as their own city, *i.e.* their dwelling-place (ii. 39). In Luke, therefore, the parents of Jesus are not at home in Bethlehem, as Matthew says, but exactly the converse is assumed, namely, Nazareth. The whole object, therefore, of the narrator must be to bring them to Bethlehem at the proper time. Their return thence to Nazareth, being their home, results naturally.

Let us, in the presence of this problem, transport ourselves still more definitely into the position of the third Evangelist. He was confronted, on the one hand, by Jesus as the native of Nazareth, as he lived in historical tradition—on the other, by Jesus as the Messiah, and who, consequently, in accordance with a dogmatic hypothesis, must be born in Bethlehem. We know not whether he was acquainted with Matthew's account of the birth and infancy of Jesus; but even if he was, he might be of opinion that his older colleague had made the matter too easy. How came the parents of Jesus to Bethlehem? This was the question he proposed to himself; and the answer of Matthew that they had always been there, must have appeared to him an assumption of a fact for which a cause ought to be assigned. As he is not more economical of his angelic appearances than Matthew, he might possibly have brought about a visit to Bethlehem by such an appearance. It might have plainly directed Joseph to travel to Bethlehem with his betrothed in order to fulfil the prophecy of Micah. But this proceeding would have been a little abrupt, and consequently not to be applied except in case of necessity. Moreover, an angel had been already used on occasion of the annunciation of Jesus and his forerunner, and angels had to be brought in subsequently on the occasion of his birth. So it seemed a more delicate process to explain that change of locality by natural causes, by the historical circumstances of the period. And in doing so, arrangements of a higher order were not excluded.

Especially was an opportunity given to the author of shewing that he knew many things of which other Evangelists were ignorant, that he was no stranger to history and antiquities, not merely Jewish, but also Roman. He is fond of bringing forward pieces of information of this kind. We see this not only from the narrative here in question, but from the mode in which he endeavours to define, chronologically, the appearance of the Baptist (iii. 1), and from the historical allusions in the speech of Gamaliel in the Acts of the Apostles (v. 36 ff.). We see, indeed, at the same time, from these very proofs of historical knowledge on the part of our Evangelist, that it was not very accurate. In the first passage he represents a Lysanias as being in office thirty years after the birth of Christ, whereas he had undoubtedly been dead thirty years before that epoch;* in the next passage he makes a member of the High Council in Jerusalem speak of an "uprising" as an event of the past, which did not take place until ten years after the time of the speech, and represents another "uprising" as having occurred after the former, which falls thirty odd years earlier. "Before these days," says Gamaliel in the reign of Tiberius, "rose up Theudas;" and then he goes on to describe his insurrection in the same terms as Josephus,† from whom we know that it occurred during the governorship of Cuspius Fadus, whom Claudius had sent to Judea. "After this man," continues Gamaliel, "rose up Judas of Galilee in the days of the taxing;" and this was the well-known taxing of Quirinus after the deposition of Archelaus by Augustus. But theologians are as indulgent to their authors as markers to great men in rifle-shooting; the latter may have gone as wide of the mark as they pleased, still they hit the gold. So in this case, a later Lysanias and an earlier Theudas have been made out of nothing, in order to maintain in due honour the historical knowledge of Luke, or rather of the Holy Spirit. But when an author, employed upon historical learning, makes three mistakes (for we shall find immediately that in

* See the question more accurately examined in my Life of Jesus critically discussed, p. 341 ff. of the second edition, to which I refer the reader generally in this section. † Jewish Antiquities, xx. 5, 1.

this passage, with which we are now engaged, a similar case occurs), I say makes three mistakes of such a kind that his interpreters have their hands full to set the matter tolerably straight, all is not on this head exactly as it should be.

But however this may be, the author knew, at any rate, many things in history; he knew in particular of the taxing, or the Roman census, the execution of which had before caused among the Jews so much ill blood and occasioned the insurrection of Judas the Galilean. When he was working out the problem how to bring to Bethlehem the parents of Jesus who were living in Nazareth, for the purposes of his birth, was it extraordinary that in doing so the taxing occurred to him? As this taxing had been the cause of so much besides, might it not have also caused the parents of Jesus to undertake the journey which the writer so much required? Taxings or registerings had it certainly in their power to cause journeys; chronologically, that taxing might appear to him all the better adapted for the purpose of the Evangelist, the less clearly he knew anything about the time of it. When, in the passage in the Acts, he represents it as succeeding an event that happened some thirty years later, he made a mistake about one occurrence or the other, probably about both. He knew, indeed, of several other points in connection with this taxing, as he shews, as well as he can, in the passage in the Acts. He knew (ii. 1 ff.) what is corroborated by history, that it was the first Roman taxing in Judea, and that this was the very reason that the insurrection of Judas had been connected with it. He knew, moreover, that it had been undertaken by Quirinus, as Governor of Syria, as Josephus also tells us. He knew, lastly, that it had been set on foot in obedience to a command that had gone out from the Emperor Augustus Cæsar, that the whole inhabited world, *i.e.* the whole Roman Empire, should be taxed.

On this point he certainly knows more than history does; for no more ancient writer, standing nearer to the time of

Augustus, mentions a general census of the Empire commanded by this Emperor, and neither Suetonius, or Dio Cassius, or the Monument of Ancyra, are acquainted with anything but repeated registerings and taxings of the *people*, *i.e.* the Roman citizens, nor are there any records, excepting those of a much later date, from the end of the fifth century of the Christian era downwards, which speak of an enumeration or registering of the whole kingdom, doing so in words which betray their dependency upon the passage in Luke. Meanwhile we might overlook the Evangelist having here taken rather too much in hand, whether from a notion that only an universal decree of this sort was suitable for the Roman ruler of the world, or that what summoned the parents of the world's Saviour to Bethlehem must have been something that set the whole world in motion,* provided only the account of this census in Judea at that time were correct.

Now this is indeed the case to this extent, that, as has been mentioned above, after Archelaus had been appointed to the Ethnarchy over Judea and Samaria, and his district had been incorporated with the province of Syria, Quirinus as governor of the province did, in accordance with an imperial decree, direct the requisite register to be made of the inhabitants and their property for the purposes of taxation.† But at that time, according to our Christian chronology, Jesus was

---

* Very lately a Christian Jurist (Huschke, "On the Census taken at the Time of the Birth of Christ," 1840, p. 35), speaks of the "internal historical necessity," not only of the introduction of the census of the Empire under Augustus, but also of that of the coincidence of the birth of Christ with it, in so far as it was necessary that "the Saviour of the world as the second Adam from heaven" should be born exactly at the moment when Augustus, as "the new earthly Adam," was occupied with the census of the Empire. "Is it," adds the author in a spirit of the stanchest faith, "is it to create any anxiety in us that this general census is not mentioned in any source of history, either contemporaneous or otherwise, deserving of entire confidence?" Certainly not, especially if, with the clear-sighted Jurist, we suppose such a source to be found in the gaps of Dio Cassius, and the hiatus of the Monument of Ancyra.

† See Josephus, Jewish Antiquities, xvii. 13, 5; xviii. 1, 1.

a child of six or seven years old, and according to Matthew (ii. 1), and probably also according to Luke (i. 5—26), he must, as having been born under Herod the Great, have been even a couple of years older; so that this taxing of Quirinus came in any case too late to bring his mother to Bethlehem for the purpose of his birth.

But might not something like a census have been undertaken in Judea ten years earlier, and the like effect have been produced by it? Possibly. Only we would premise the remark that according to this Luke would, in the first place, have confounded a provincial census with a census of the world, *i.e.* a census of the kingdom, and, in the second, an earlier census with a later. Of these two mistakes, the latter would be not merely a mistake in chronology, but that earlier census could not, as Luke states, have been undertaken by Quirinus as governor of Syria, as it was not until several years after Herod's death that Quirinus undertook the governorship of Syria. Moreover, Josephus, who is very explicit in the affairs of this period, says not a word of such census, nor was it the Roman custom to introduce anything of the kind until a country had been entirely deprived of its native rulers and placed immediately under the Roman dominion; and, above all, the census of Quirinus, after the deposition of Archelaus, by the commotion which it excited among the people, appears to be marked out as the first that had ever taken place among the Jewish people. But supposing even that for some cause or other—such as is supposed to be found in a passage of Josephus,* exceptionally, and it is supposed to be possible to point out a similar exception in a notice in Tacitus †—supposing that even before the conversion of Judea into a Roman province, a Roman census had been undertaken there, still it must have been carried out in the manner usual in such cases and in accordance with the object in view. Now, according to Luke (ii. 3 ff.), every one, in

---

* Jewish Antiquities, xvi. 9, 3.   † Annal. vi. 41.

obedience to the imperial decree, every one travelled to his own city, *i.e.* as is afterwards explained with reference to Joseph, to the place from which his family originally descended—Joseph therefore to Bethlehem, because, a thousand years before, David, the ancestor of his race, had been born there. Now this, according to the common supposition, was the custom in the Jewish registerings, as the Jewish political system, at least in ancient times, rested upon the basis of family and race; the Romans, on the contrary, whose object was entirely statistic and financial, in the provincial census had no such object, but, according to the most credible accounts,* the country-people were summoned into the chief town of the circle, and generally every one to the place of which his real or adoptive father had been a citizen. Now there cannot be the least probability in the supposition that the surviving descendants of David (even supposing that Joseph was one of them), if they had settled too in a distant country, should, after all the revolutions of a period of a thousand years, have still been considered as citizens of Bethlehem. And if it is suggested that the Romans in their foreign taxings adopted the usages of the subject countries, they would only have done so in so far as the operation did not tend to defeat their objects, which would manifestly have been the case had they moved a man for the purpose of entering his own name and that of his family, together with an account of his property, from the distant Galilee to Bethlehem, where they could have very little power of checking the entries he might make. But Luke represents Joseph as not only travelling to Bethlehem himself, but also as taking with him his betrothed, Mary, in order that she might be registered with him (ver. 5). But this joint journey of Mary was superfluous, not only according to the Roman, but also the Jewish custom. It is known from the Old Testament that no account was taken of women in

---

* Proofs are found in Paulus, Manual of Exegesis, on the passage in Luke, and in Huschke, in the treatise quoted, p. 116 ff.

the Jewish registerings; and, moreover, according to the law of Servius Tullius, neither had the Roman citizens on the occasion of the census to bring with them their wives and children in person, but only to give in their names, nor in the case of the provincials can the necessity of the personal appearance of women, according to the Roman law, be proved.* If, therefore, Mary travelled to Bethlehem, it must have been by Joseph's free will or her own; nay, the whole journey appears on the part of both to have been voluntary, everything having disappeared that, according to Luke, could have compelled them to it. It cannot have been the census of Quirinus, for that did not take place until ten years later; it cannot have been one so much earlier, for nothing is known of anything of the sort, and it would be in contradiction to the circumstances; not a Roman census, for that would not have summoned a Galilean to Bethlehem; quite as little a Jewish registering, for on such an occasion, as on that of a Roman one, Mary might have stayed at home.

The parents of Jesus had, therefore, no visible cause for undertaking that journey just at a moment the most inconvenient possible for a pregnant woman. On the other hand, the Evangelist had so much the more reason to represent them as undertaking it, and for him that inconvenient time was just the only convenient one, in order to make his Jesus be born in the city of David, and thus an important characteristic of the Messiah adhere to his person.

III. Jesus, as Messiah, like David, consecrated like David to his Office by a Prophet.

56.

In order to represent the greater David in all points, it was necessary for the Messiah not only to be descended of

* Not even from Lacant. de Mort. Persecutor. 23, to which Huschke appeals, admitting at the same time that the occurrence was not only 300 years later, but also a case of extraordinary severity.

David's line, and be born in David's city, but also, as in the case of David, for a man of prophetic order to consecrate him to his regal office by divine commission. In the case of David, Samuel performed this task, and it consisted of an anointing with oil, such as the Seer had already executed upon the first king, Saul. But in reference to David, the divine command issued in the despatch of Samuel to Jesse at Bethlehem, where God had promised him to point out to him from among the sons of that personage the one whom he had chosen (1 Sam. xvi. 1 ff.); on the other hand, God had sent Saul to Samuel, and told Samuel on the entrance of Saul that Saul was the man whom he was to anoint (1 Sam. ix. 15 ff.).

Now this antitype in David of the consecration of the Messiah, had been crossed in the time after the captivity by another conception. The degenerate people was threatened with a terrible day of judgment to be held by Jehovah; but before this came upon them, the prophet Malachi promised (iii. 23 ff.), that Jehovah would make a last attempt to purify and save his people, by sending to them the prophet Elijah, who, by means of his powerful preaching, would prepare their minds as much as possible for the reception of the God of judgment (Luke i. 17). He was the messenger who was to prepare the way of the Lord (Mal. iii. 1), and to him was referred the voice which at the end of the captivity was heard to call by the second Isaiah, to make straight in the desert a highway for the God of Israel. This time of the return of Elijah, of this restorer of all that was degenerated and perverted, was waited for by the pious Israelite with longing, and they were called happy who should live to see it (Sirach xlviii. 11 ff.); and as he for whose coming Elijah was to prepare men was subsequently considered, instead of the Jehovah, to be the Messiah, Elijah was expected as the forerunner of the Messiah (Matt. xvii. 11). But he was, in reference to the latter, to undertake at the same time the character which Samuel had had with David, to anoint him, and thus, as Samuel had made David, to make him known to others in his exalted destination.*

Now no human being knew of Elijah having returned to life, and having anointed Jesus, and it would have been dangerous to maintain it; if therefore this mark of the Messiah was not to be lost, it was necessary, among the real persons with whom Jesus had come into contact, to find one who had some resemblance to Elijah, and had done something to Jesus which might be so strained as to be considered an anointing. Such a resemblance was offered by John the Baptist, who had been popular shortly before the coming of Jesus. He had appeared in the wilderness of Judea, was therefore the voice in the desert spoken of by Isaiah; he called men to repentance because the kingdom of heaven was near, was therefore the preparer of the way for the Lord; he was a stern ascetic, was therefore in this respect to be compared to the Tishbite. He had not anointed Jesus, but baptized him; this might be considered an anointing, if the object of the ceremony in the case of Jesus was not, as in the case of every one else, considered, not as an obligation to repentance, but the dedication to his Messianic office, and the preparation for it.†

The Baptist, who was bound by his calling to the Jordan, could not, like Samuel on the previous occasion of the anointing of David, be sent to the house of Jesus, but it was necessary for the latter, as was undoubtedly done, to go to the Baptist at the Jordan. In order to undertake the baptism of Jesus (Matt. iii. 13—17; Mark i. 9—11; Luke iii. 21 ff.; John i. 32—34), John did not, like Samuel for the anointing,

---

* The Jew Trypho, in the Dialogue with Justin, viii. 49, states this as the expectation spread among the Jewish people.

† Even the baptism of Christians was sometimes described as an anointing, in virtue of the imparting of the Spirit which was included in it. 1 John ii. 20—27.

require a special divine commission, as he conferred it upon all without distinction; but it was necessary that in the case of Jesus a particular importance should attach to it; it was necessary that the powers requisite for the exercise of his Messianic office should be imparted to him, if not by means of, but contemporaneously with, the baptism which was to represent his anointing. The essence of these divine powers, or more accurately the bearer and distributor of them to men, was, according to the conception of the Jews, the Spirit of God. When Samuel had anointed David in the midst of his brethren (1 Sam. xvi. 13), it is said that from that selfsame day the Spirit of Jehovah fell upon David. And of the branch from the root of Jesse, the Messiah, Isaiah (xi. 1 ff.) had prophesied that there shall rest upon him the Spirit of Jehovah, the spirit of wisdom and understanding, the spirit of counsel and might, the spirit of knowledge and of the fear of the Lord.

Now in the Old Testament the pre-eminence of men of God in especial favour, as Kings and Prophets (Isaiah lxi. 1), had been, that the Spirit of God came upon them, and was observable in consequence of the effects of a higher inspiration. This, in the new Church of the Messiah, had become common property, inasmuch as (according to the prophecy of Joel, iii. 1 ff.) the communication of the Holy Spirit was supposed to be connected with baptism in the name of Jesus, and the laying on of hands by the Apostles (Acts ii. 38, viii. 17, xix. 5 ff.; Rom. viii. 9, 11, 15; Gal. iii. 2). It was supposed that the communication to Christ himself must have been antecedent to this derived communication to the Christians; it must, it was thought, be perceptible not merely in its extraordinary operations, but it must itself have been a miraculous external occurrence. A natural symbol of the Spirit was always found in fire. John had predicted that he who should come after him would baptize with the Holy Ghost and with fire. And thus, in fact, when

Christ had ascended, the first communication from heaven by him of the Spirit to the Apostles was distinguished from that subsequently effected by their laying on of hands, as reported in the narrative in the Acts of the Apostles (ii. 3), by the visible appearance of tongues of fire, and a Gospel used by Justin represented a fire as being kindled on the occasion of the baptism of Jesus, as he stepped down into the water.* But altogether with fire there was, in the expressions which the Old Testament used about the Holy Spirit, another symbol also introduced. It was to "rest" upon the branch of David, to "descend" upon it. Before the beginning of creation it had "moved upon the face" of the primeval water (1 Mos. i. 2): "like a dove," was added by the ancient Jewish interpreters, a dove which "moves" or hovers over her young without touching them.† Moreover, in the time of Noah a dove had again appeared (1 Mos. viii. 8—12), and as the saving water of baptism was looked upon in Christendom as the counter-type of this destroying water (1 Peter iii. 21), and the former, with its regenerating power, was moreover a parallel to the water of the creation, how obvious it was, when the baptismal water appeared for the first time in its exalted significance, *i.e.* on occasion of the baptism of the Messiah, again to represent the dove as appearing. The symbolism of the Dove as well as of the Lamb was, besides, familiar to Christianity (Matt. x. 16), and might appear even more suitable than consuming fire to indicate the mildness of its spirit.

The Gospel of the Hebrews represented this Holy Spirit not merely as descending upon Jesus in the form of a dove, but also as passing into him;‡ it was natural that to the

---

* Dial. c. Tryph. 88. Similarly the Prædicatio Pauli; according to the Tractatus de non iterando bapt. in Cyprian's Works, p. 142, ed. Rigalt.

† See these and other passages in my Life of Jesus critically discussed, i. 116 ff.

‡ Quoted in Epiphanius, Hæres. xxx. 13, comp. 29.

Ebionites, who, in opposition to the later doctrine of the Church, maintained the original human nature of Jesus, it should be of importance to bring out in the most palpable manner his subsequent higher preparation. In the three first Gospels also the narrative of the baptism of Jesus, in its original plan, belongs, like the genealogy, to that point of view which saw in Jesus a human being naturally begotten; but even from this point of view they might keep themselves aloof from the extravagant feature of the entering of the dove —without doubt into the mouth of Jesus—as the remaining, *i.e.* the continuance of the dove over him, expressly, indeed, stated only by John, but unquestionably assumed by the others, equally well answered the same purpose for them, that, namely, of indicating, if not the immanence, at any rate the permanence, of the effect of the divine principle upon Jesus.

The heavens opened, and the dove came out of them. This, indeed, even without the great light which according to the Gospel is said to have shone around the place, shewed that it was not a common dove, but a being of a higher order; still, up to this point the whole proceeding was but dumb-show, requiring an explanation. This explanation the Baptist could give; it must be to the effect that Jesus, by this communication of the Spirit, was prepared to be the Messiah, and was accredited as such by the visible portion of it. Such an explanation was supposed to be found in a famous passage of the Old Testament, but it was put into the mouth of Jehovah himself, in the words of the Psalm (ii. 7), "Thou art my Son, this day have I begotten thee." That this speech refers to some Israelitish king, who is thus declared to be the representative of God, may be seen as certainly as it is uncertain and of no consequence to us what king may be alluded to in it.* In the New Testa-

---

* Comp. besides, C. Meier, The Three Royal Psalms, &c., in Zeller's Theological Annual, 1846, p. 334 ff., and Hitzig's Commentary on the passage.

ment, on the other hand, the text is thrice repeated (Heb. i. 5, v. 5; Acts xiii. 33), referred to Jesus and applied to the declaration of him as the Messiah or the Son of God in the higher sense. In the Psalm it was probably given through David (comp. Acts iv. 25) by divine commission; what then more obvious now that it was to be verified than to represent it as being solemnly repeated by God himself? Already was heaven opened for the descent of the Holy Spirit as a dove; thus from the heaven so opened the voice of God also might issue down, in order, by the well known divine address to the Messiah, to bring out into full expression the significance of the whole scene.

In all this it is assumed that the voice from heaven originally expressed itself in the form in which Justin quotes it from the Memorabilia of the Apostles,* that is, exactly in the words of Psalm ii. 7: "Thou art my Son, this day have I begotten thee." In this form the passage was read by several Fathers of the Church of a later age, and this also is the reading given us by one of the MSS. of our Gospels in the passage of Luke.† In the Gospel of the Hebrews of Epiphanius, this form is combined with that known to us in our own Gospels. There, the voice from heaven says first, as we now find it in Mark and Luke, "Thou art my beloved Son, in thee I am well pleased;" then, again, "This day have I begotten thee."

Then, when the flash of light appears, the Baptist asks Jesus, "Who art thou, Lord?" whereupon the voice from heaven says in answer what we read in Matthew, "This is my beloved Son, in whom I am well pleased." We learn clearly from the mode in which Justin attempts to smooth over the difficulty, what the reason was for first putting in the background, and then entirely removing, the words, "This day have I begotten thee." He says that it does not

* Dial. c. Tryph. 88, 103.
† Comp. Hilgenfeld, The Gospels of Justin, &c., p. 169 ff.

follow from these words that Jesus had not, until that moment, been begotten as the Son of God; that it was not objectively his Sonship with regard to God that commenced with his baptism by John, but only, subjectively, the knowledge of it on the part of man that did so. The words in question harmonised indeed very well with the view which, as we have pointed out above, lies at the foundation of the genealogies in Matthew and Luke, and which we find at a later period in Cerinthus and among the Ebionites, that Jesus had been a naturally-begotten human being, to whom the higher principle was not imparted until his baptism; but when Jesus came to be looked upon as having been from the first begotten by the Holy Spirit, which we shall soon see more clearly to have been the case with the authors of our three first Gospels, and as Justin also does, then these words created a difficulty, and had either to be explained artificially or to be entirely removed. But as in the latter case the voice from heaven would have been entirely lost, and this was undesirable, other words of God, also interpreted in a Messianic sense, were seized upon from Isaiah xlii. 1. Matthew, applying these words to Jesus in another passage (xii. 18), gives them thus: "Behold, my servant, whom I have chosen; my beloved, in whom my soul is well pleased." This text must have appeared the more suitable to the baptismal scene, as in the sequel to it Jehovah declares that he has put his Spirit on this beloved one (who, indeed, according to the historical sense of the passage in the prophet, is no other than the people of Israel). The harmony with the passage in the prophet is most obvious in the form in Matthew, "THIS is my beloved Son:" in Mark and Luke in the address, "THOU ART MY BELOVED SON," &c. &c., the sound is still heard of the rejected passage in the Psalm.

Accurately speaking, indeed, it was not this passage in the Psalm only that would not agree with the change of view of the person of Jesus. If Jesus had been originally begotten by the Holy Spirit, then what need was there for that Spirit to descend upon him? Was it then possible that over and above that physical Sonship, to say nothing of the indwelling of the divine Logos, there should be a higher, more perfect communication of the Divinity? And was it, generally, befitting that the Son of God should submit himself to the baptism of repentance by John? To remove the latter difficulty, the author of our first Gospel (Matt. iii. 14 ff.) introduced the scene which represents that when Jesus came to the baptism of John, the Baptist endeavoured to divert him from his purpose by the words, "I have need to be baptized of thee, and comest thou to me?" To which Jesus replies, "Suffer it to be so now: for thus it becometh us to fulfil all righteousness;" *i.e.* without doubt, to satisfy the expectation, founded upon supposed types and prophecies, that another Elijah would anoint the Messiah.

But while all impropriety in the act of baptism appeared to be removed, there still remained the contradiction between the supplementary communication of the Holy Spirit and the original procreation by it; indeed it came out all the more glaringly. If the Baptist made that objection before the baptism of Jesus, consequently before he had seen the miraculous signs which followed upon it, then he must already have known Jesus as one superior to him, and, as he confesses himself to have need of the baptism of Jesus by the Holy Spirit and fire, as the Messiah himself; consequently those signs could not have been intended for him, the Baptist, but they must have had reference to Jesus himself or to the people. The baptismal miracle referred to Jesus, according to the original meaning of the narrative, in the very literal sense that it was on this occasion that the Spirit of God was first communicated to him; but this sense was excluded by the higher view of his person, and therefore Matthew and Mark represent the occurrence to us as a spectacle granted to Jesus (we cannot indeed say with what object) and perhaps (for the language is doubtful) also to the Baptist; while Luke, who also expressly embodies the dove, makes all the bystanders witnesses of it. It was impossible that this mode of representation should satisfy the fourth Evangelist, who could be but little inclined to admit that on this occasion his Christ had gained anything which had not, with the Logos, already dwelt within him; it was necessary that the purpose of the appearance should be decidedly transferred from Jesus to the Baptist, to whom it was to serve as a token whereby to recognise the Son of God. But he could only require this if he had not already known Jesus to be the Messiah; and it is therefore expressly stated by the fourth Evangelist, that he had not, in contradiction and probably with definite reference to the first. And so from this point of view the voice from heaven was also dropped out, being changed into a statement that God had on a previous occasion pointed out to the Baptist the sign that was to be expected.

By thus understanding the evangelical narrative of the miraculous appearances at the baptism of Jesus historically, that is, in the spirit of the narrators and their time, and for this very reason accepting them non-historically, we escape a series of difficulties to which the theological explanation of them, in the attempt to maintain the historical character of the occurrence, must be subject. Thus one interpreter, in order to make the miracle more acceptable, considers everything as a vision, produced indeed by God, but only in the mind of Jesus and the Baptist; another makes a real but still a natural dove hover over Jesus; another prefers imagining a meteoric phenomenon, a flash of lightning and a clap of thunder, which at the same time helps him to explain the voice from heaven. Explanations such as these would be the least of what we should have to encounter. But the question recurs as to what could be the object of a supplementary communication of the Spirit to him who was born the Son of God? In order to answer this question, which from our point of view solves itself, theologians hatched a whole nest of artifices and evasions, one more absurd than the other. The Spirit of God says one,* dwelt in Jesus from eternity; but now the Holy Ghost, the third person of the Godhead, came into a new relation with him, a relation different from the identity of the essence of the Spirit with Son and Father. The Holy Spirit, says another,† was innate in Jesus as the spirit of life, but at his baptism it was imparted to him as the spirit of his office; or he is said to have had from eternity the consciousness of Sonship as the Son of God, but he has received now for the first time the power of proving himself as such to the world—mere miserable sophistries and unmeaning abstractions, in which even the very authors of them can hardly have imagined or intended anything definite.

Thus the evangelical narrative of the occurrences at the baptism of Jesus, notwithstanding all the additions which it has received from other conceptions, may, in its main features, be derived from the attempt to provide for Jesus as the Son of David an anointing, and, combined with it, a communication of the Spirit, of the same character as was imparted through Samuel to his ancestor. And we find this effort, in the case of one of our Evangelists, carried still further up. The Books of Samuel, of which David is properly the hero, begin not with the history of David's birth, but with that of Samuel. Similarly Luke prefaces the history of the annunciation and conception of Jesus with that of his forerunner, and in such a manner that the imitation is not to be mistaken. So far as this goes, this would be the place for tracing the origin and rise of the history of the infancy of the Baptist; but that history is so closely connected with that of the announcement and infancy of Jesus, that it can

---

* Ebrard, Scientific Criticism, 261.

† Luthardt, The Gospel of John in its Peculiarity, &c., p. 238.

only be considered in connection with the latter. And this, being sketched from the point of view which considered Jesus, not as the Son of David, but the Son of God, must begin a new section.

SECOND GROUP OF MYTHS.

JESUS, THE SON OF GOD.

I. JESUS BEGOTTEN OF THE HOLY GHOST.

57.

According to all that has been said so far, it appears that Christianity, in its moral and religious aspect, issued out of Judaism, but could not have issued out of Judaism until the latter had been penetrated with all kinds of foreign matter, tending to modify its form, and more especially matter of Greek origin. This is also true of a conception which does not indeed belong to the spiritual basis of Christianity, but has contributed to define its form, the conception of Jesus as the Son of God. This appellation, applied to Jesus considered as the Messiah, had its origin in the most ancient Judaism, but had in this, as we saw above, a merely figurative sense, not excluding mere human sonship. As applied to Jesus, the expression was taken literally—Jesus was considered as the Son of God, with no human father. In this we cannot fail to see heathen notions acting upon the earliest circle of Christianity.

The passage in the Psalm about the Son of God this day begotten, was, as we have seen, applied to Jesus, in the first instance, by those who nevertheless considered him as Joseph's son, and understood that divine procreation and Sonship in the traditional theocratic sense, *i.e.* that Jesus, like the best of the kings of David's line before him, was to be considered as a favourite and representative of God, only in an incomparably higher degree than they. It is true, indeed, that in reference to Jesus, the belief in his resurrection, in his glorified and continuous existence with God, contributed not a little to the exaggeration of this idea, without, however, immediately destroying the natural view of his origin. The Apostle Paul, as we read in the introduction to the Epistle to the Romans (i. 3), says of Jesus, "which was made of the seed of David according to the flesh, and declared to be the Son of God with power, according to the Spirit of holiness, by the resurrection from the dead"—and thus we see how little these two points of view excluded each other.

There is, moreover, even within the limits of Judaism itself, a tendency observable to oppose to one another the natural and religious points of view, in such a manner that in the birth of personages of importance the share of the natural parents is limited as much as possible in favour of the Divine co-operation. The Hebrew legend is fond of describing individuals, upon whom in the scheme of God with his chosen people very much depended, as the children of old parents or mothers who had been long barren. Abraham, says the Apostle Paul (Rom. iv. 17 ff.), trusted in God, who quickeneth the dead and calleth those things which be not as though they were; therefore he considered not his own body, now dead, when he was about an hundred years old, neither yet the deadness of Sarah's womb, but staggered not at the promise of God through unbelief, but was strong in faith giving glory to God, and being fully persuaded that what he had promised he was able also to perform —that is, in their old age to give them Isaac as a son. Again, Joseph, Jacob's wise and favourite son and the saviour of his family, is the child of a mother who had been long barren; so also Samson, the strong hero, and Samuel, the restorer of the people and the pure worship of God; in the case of the two last, their birth, which had become improbable, is announced by heavenly messengers, as that of Isaac by Jehovah himself. The fact that the history of the Baptist's birth in Luke has the same outline has been already alluded to, and in the apocryphal Gospels Mary also, the mother of Jesus, is represented as a late-born child, and on this occasion one of these apocryphal writers thus instructively discloses the idea that lies at the bottom of such representations. "God," he remarks, "if he closes the womb of a woman, only does so in "order the more miraculously to open it again, and to shew "that what is there born is not the fruit of human passion, "but a gift of God."* If in the case of such late births it was considered necessary that God should have the greater share, it was obvious enough, in a case the issue of which was to be especially distinguished, to represent him as the sole agent, *i.e.* as the share of the female, when the origination of a human being was in question, could not at all events be dispensed with, as taking entirely and exclusively the place of the male.

This supposition, however, involved something calculated to repel the strictly orthodox Jew. God, as the Creator and Preserver of the world and the operative powers in it, might open a womb that had long been closed, revive the dead powers of generation of old married people, without trenching on the purity of his supersensuous nature; but to represent his agency as absolutely taking the place of the absent male, as the generative principle, was demurred to, because it appeared to degrade him into sensuality, to assimilate him to the philoprogenitive gods of the heathen. There was, indeed, in the Old Testament a passage which lent itself to such a theory, and which has even by Christians been long interpreted in this sense, the passage of the virgin who is

* Evangel. de Nativ. Mariæ, c. 3, in Thilo. Cod. apocr. N. T. i. 322. Comp. my Life of Jesus, i. 130, Rem. 2.

to conceive, Isaiah vii. 14. When, in the time of king Ahaz, the kings of Syria and Israel advanced against Judah, and the trembling king sued for the support of Assyria, the prophet gave him the tranquillizing sign: Circumstances, says he, shall change for the better so rapidly, that a young woman,* now becoming pregnant (the wife, probably, of the prophet himself, comp. viii. 3, 8), will be able to call her son, born within the proper period, Emmanuel, *i.e.* God with us. In this passage, in point of fact, neither the Messiah nor a birth from a virgin, is spoken of; but with the fantastic mode of interpretation prevalent among the Jews, this would have as little prevented them from accepting the passage as an allusion to the Messiah, as the Christians would have been prevented by the same reason from considering it as a prophecy applying to their Christ, if the conception of such an origin of the Messiah had been in existence among the Jews. But we have not succeeded in tracing this interpretation to pre-Christian times.

On the other hand, no proof is wanted to shew that in the province of the Greco-Roman religion the idea of Sons of God was currently in vogue. It referred not merely to the demigods of the mythical period, but was also applied to historical personages of the later times. In many cases it may have been the vanity of rulers or the flattery of subjects; in others it was undeniably a real faith of a narrower or wider circle, and this faith sometimes appears very early, almost before personages so worshipped have departed this life. To say nothing of Pythagoras, whom, at a later period, his enthusiastic adherents represented as a son of Apollo,† there was a legend current about Plato in Athens, even in the lifetime of his nephew Speusippus, that Apollo had had

---

* For the Hebrew word means a young marriageable woman, whether married or single, not an absolute virgin : like the virgines nuptæ, and the puellæ jam virum expertæ in Horace, Carm. ii. 8, 22; iii. 14, 10.

† Iamblich. Vita Pythag. 2.

intercourse with his mother Perictione,* in reference to which a learned Father of the Christian Church makes the remark that people could only conceive of the prince of philosophy as the son of a virgin (and of the God of Wisdom, he might have added).† Alexander the Great may, indeed, have himself originated the report that he was begotten by Zeus with his mother Olympias; Livy,‡ also, insinuates that the elder Scipio favoured the rise of a similar legend that was current about him among the Roman people; still less was Augustus too good for this, as Suetonius and Dio Cassius§ give us, from ancient sources, an account of his procreation, obviously an imitation of that of Alexander; how, that is to say, his mother Atia fell asleep in the temple, on occasion of a midnight festival held in honour of Apollo, and a snake had intercourse with her, and then after ten months she had a son who was considered the offspring of Apollo. But, however they may have arisen, histories of this kind were believed under many forms at a time, with the impulse of which towards contact with the supernatural world they corresponded, and thus we cannot be surprised if the Christians sought to give to their Messiah a birth of equal rank with these teachers of philosophy and rulers of the world of divine origin. In doing so, it was natural that everything of a sensuous character, everything relating to human intercourse, carefully removed as it was from the Greco-Roman narratives, should also be struck out from those of the Christians; it was no God in a human or serpent form that had enjoyed the intimacy of his mother, but it was the Holy Spirit, the supersensual creative power of God, which in the womb of the pure virgin had called the divine fruit into life.

In this form the conception might be acceptable even to the Jewish-Christian; he found a prophecy of this mode of generation in the son of the virgin mentioned in Isaiah, ap-

* Diog. Suet. iii. 1, 2. † Hieron. adv. Jovin. i. 26.
‡ Book xxvi. 19. § Sueton. Octav. 94. Dio Cass. Hist. 45.

proximating types in the men of God of the Old Testament, born late and contrary to human expectation; and withdrawing himself at the same time from the old Jewish prejudices by the unsensual form in which the idea was clothed, he had, by the pre-eminence which an origin of this kind assured to Christ above Moses and all Jewish prophets, gained a strong weapon in the conflict with Judaism.

But this conception, once attained, had now to be properly brought upon the scene, to be put forward in a regular narrative. For doing this, the most appropriate means, as in the case of most of those Old Testament births at an advanced period of the parents' lives, was a supernatural announcement previous to the event. Then the natural father was in existence upon whom the genealogy had built so much, and who now must be set aside. Finally, it was necessary to prepare for the heavenly scion a fitting reception upon earth.

With regard to the two first points, we have in our Gospels a twofold account, one in the first and one in the third Gospel (Matt. i. 18—25; Luke i. 26—38), of which, if we consider them without prejudice, the first will appear the earliest and most original. It is both sterner and more simple than the other. Sterner in so far as it puts forward the repulsive fact of the pregnancy of a bride without the agency of the bridegroom, and, so far as the reader is concerned, immediately removes the difficulty by the addition that the pregnancy was caused by the Holy Ghost, but represents Joseph, the bridegroom, as really taking offence, and only becoming subsequently pacified by an angel in a dream. In this account we do not learn whether even Mary had been previously made acquainted with the cause of her pregnancy. That she should not have been so, appeared to the author of the corresponding narrative in Luke, even if he were otherwise acquainted with that of Matthew, altogether too abrupt. Still, in the case of Mary, violence could not be supposed to have been offered to her, as by heathen gods in heathen story, but she must, according to Luke, have come to an understanding about the matter. So an angel is sent to Mary. And this angel is not a common nameless one, but the angel known from the Old Testament (Dan. viii. 16, ix. 21; comp. Tob. xii. 25) as one of the highest dignitaries in the court of God. And he is deputed to announce to her that she is favoured by God so far as to become pregnant and to be the mother of the Messiah, and moreover that all this, as the angel adds in answer to her doubting question, is effected by the Holy Ghost, and that therefore the holy offspring of her womb shall be called, in the full sense of the words, the Son of God. Mary acquiescing in the Divine pleasure, the author considers it superfluous to add anything by way of explanation as to Joseph's conduct in the matter; and, conversely, Matthew thinks it superfluous to state at all how Mary was informed of what was to happen to her.

These discrepancies are caused by the difference in the plan of the two narratives. But they have two main features in common. They are these: first, that a heavenly messenger announces the miraculous conception of the Messianic infant; and, secondly, that he fixes beforehand on the name, Jesus. Instances of this were already furnished by the Old Testament types, in the histories of Isaac and Ishmael, of Samson and Samuel. As in Matthew the angel says to Joseph, She, thy wife, shall (or in Luke, to Mary, Thou wilt) bear a Son, and thou shalt call his name Jesus, exactly in the same manner had Jehovah (1 Mos. xvii. 19) spoken to Abraham, Thy wife shall bear to thee a son, and thou shalt call his name Isaac: as the latter name is derived from the laughter, at one time of Abraham himself (xvii. 17), at another time of Sarah (xviii. 12—15), then of the people (xxi. 6), so in Matthew the name of Jesus is derived from the destination of the infant to save the people from their sins. And this, again, is done in words which remind us of the announcement of Samson's destination to save Israel from the hand of the Philistines (Judges xiii. 5). This imitation of Old Testament narratives points to an origin in a Jewish-Christian circle. Agreeable to it also is the Jewish view of the destiny of Jesus, especially in Luke, where the throne of David, endless dominion over the house of Jacob, is spoken of (i. 32 ff.); though in Matthew also, not only the sins are alluded to, from which the child, miraculously conceived, shall redeem his people (i. 21), but also, in the Jewish sense, the consequences of them, that is, subjugation to, and maltreatment by, the people of the Heathen.

58. Annunciation and Birth of the Forerunner.

The history of the birth of Jesus is more artificially sketched in Luke than in Matthew. This, indeed, appears in the characteristics already considered, but is still more decisively shewn by the fact, that while Matthew is satisfied with making us acquainted with the beginning of the life of Jesus, Luke draws that of his precursor, John, within the range of his description (i. 5—25, 36, 39—80). So far, as has been already remarked, the beginning of his Gospel resembles that of the first Book of Samuel, which also starts from the history of the birth, not of king Saul or king David, but of the Seer Samuel, who was destined to anoint them, without, however, connecting the accounts of the nativity of these kings with that of Samuel, in the manner in which the author of the first chapter of the Gospel of Luke connects that of Jesus the Messiah and his forerunner John.

Samuel's parents live on Mount Ephraim. So, likewise, those of the Baptist in the hill-country of Judea (i. 39). Samuel, the king-maker, was looked upon, at least in the later Jewish tradition, as a branch of the stem of Levi (1 Chron. vii. 26 ff.), probably because the anointing of kings was, according to the latest ordinance, performed by a priest (1 Kings i. 39). So also in Luke, the man who was to anoint the Messiah was, on the father's side, descended from Levites, while his mother is even made a descendant of Aaron and namesake of his wife (2 Mos. vi. 23). And by this, perhaps, as the mother of Jesus is called a cousin of the mother of his precursor (i. 36), a further point was supposed to be attained, that, namely, of deriving the royal Son of David through his mother from a priestly line, and consequently of representing him as a Priest and King, after the order of Melchizedek (Ps. cx. 4).* Samuel's mother had been long barren; so also is that of John. But the former, like Rachel and Leah, is associated as the barren but beloved wife with another who bears children to her husband. The mother of the Baptist, on the other hand, is made a second Sarah; that is, according to the custom of that time, she is represented as the only wife, having grown old in barrenness, of a husband equally advanced in years. And the similar expression in both cases, "they both were well stricken in years" (Luke i. 7; 1 Mos. xviii. 11), leaves no doubt as to the imitation. Then, again, it is in accordance with the type of Samuel that the promise of the Son is connected with a religious journey; in the case of Samuel, with the annual journey of his parents to Shiloh, to offer a sacrifice to Jehovah; in that of John, with the journey of his father to perform the duties of his priestly office. The wish to have issue in the parents of Samuel, as the father had children by the other wife, was particularly strong on the part of the barren wife. It is, therefore, she who prays Jehovah for a son, and receives from the High-priest the assurance that her prayers are heard (1 Sam. i. 10 ff.). But in the parents of the Baptist the wish is supposed to be equally strong on both sides; but, as the wife in this instance

* As he appears in the Testament of the Twelve Patriarchs; comp. Hilgenfeld, The Gospel of Justin, &c., p. 265, Remark.

does not accompany the husband, we must assume it to have been made known to God by him alone during the offering of incense in the sanctuary, and the angel Gabriel to have appeared and signified to him the assent of the Almighty. The angelic appearance, which is not found in the history of Samuel, was borrowed by the evangelical accounts from the history of Samson, who was likewise a son of parents advanced in years (Judges xiii.); to the parents of Samson the angel appears in some undefined place in the country, to Zachariah in the Temple. The cause of this difference is the difference in the position of the parents in each case; but the name of the angel, which is peculiar to the narrative of Luke, and is taken from the mythology of the Jews subsequent to the Captivity, was to a certain extent already given in Samson's history, where indeed the angel refuses to give his name (ver. 18), but is repeatedly designated as a "man of God," which is just the meaning of Gabriel.

In the history of Samson, no doubt whatever is expressed as to the fulfilment of the promise given by the messenger of God. Quite as little in that of Samuel as to the assurance of the High-priest. The parents are not represented as being old in either of these cases, and consequently the result is not considered as improbable. But the narrative of Luke makes the parents of the Baptist an old married couple, like Abraham and Sarah, and therefore borrowed also the feature of the word of the angel appearing, at first, incredible to Zachariah. As in that case the parents in succession insist upon the objection arising from their old age (1 Mos. xvii. 17, xviii. 12), so in this Zachariah insists upon it on his own behalf and that of his wife (i. 18); and as Abraham, on receiving the first promise that he, through his descendants, shall possess the land of Canaan, asks the question, how he is to know this (1 Mos. xv. 8), so, and in the same words also, Zachariah expresses his doubt to the angel (ver. 18). Thus the unbelief of Abraham and Sarah passed away;

but they had as yet before them no similar example of the effect of miraculous power; on the other hand, Zachariah, who in the history of his people had several instances of this sort before him, was struck dumb, as a sign of punishment, until the fulfilment of the promise (ver. 20), as Paul, according to the narrative in the Acts, was struck blind for a time after the reproachful apparition of Christ, and as Daniel became dumb after the appearance of the angel (not indeed by way of punishment, but at the majesty of the figure), until he touched the lips of the prophet, and thus restored his speech (Dan. x. 15 ff.).

The name of the promised child is fixed beforehand, and this is a feature borrowed from the history of Ishmael and Isaac (1 Mos. xvi. 11, xvii. 19). The precepts, again, as to his future mode of life, how he is to avoid wine and strong drink, are word for word the same that were given to the mother of Samson for her observance during her pregnancy (Judges xiii. 4, vii. 14); moreover, the dedication of both infants to higher objects from their mothers' womb, and their waxing in the spirit, is in both cases expressed in similar words (Judges xiii. 5, 24 ff.; Luke i. 15, 80). On the other hand, the hymns of praise interwoven with the narrative in Luke, are taken from the history of Samuel. His mother, on bringing to the High-priest the son that had been given to her (1 Sam. ii. 1 ff.), broke out into a hymn of praise. So likewise does the father of the Baptist, when on the circumcision of the latter his tongue is again loosened (Luke i. 67 ff.); although in particular points the hymn of Mary (Luke i. 64 ff.) resembles that of the mother of Samuel more than that of Zachariah does.

Thus the author of this prefatory history in the third Gospel compounded his narrative like a mosaic out of different antitypes in the Old Testament. And the process can only appear improbable to one who has no conception of the form of thought and authorship of the later Jews. The Jew of that period of the Epigoni lived so entirely in the earlier history of his people, and in the sacred books in which that history was laid down, that he found in them everything that subsequently took place prefigured, everywhere prophecies and symbols of following events; and the poet likewise who wished to glorify the birth of a man of God of a later period could imagine nothing but that all had taken place in connection with it as in the corresponding cases of sacred history in primeval times.

Otherwise the composer of the prefatory history is no spiritless imitator, but, when the object he has in view requires it, can, without binding himself to matter already given, exercise independent invention. This is shewn by the original manner in which he brings about a meeting between the mother of the Messiah and that of his precursor. In the arrangement of this meeting, his object was no other but that of glorifying Jesus by putting the Baptist as early as possible into a relation with him, and making that relation one of subordination. This object could not be attained better than by bringing together, not the sons in the first instance, but the mothers, with the embryos of the sons already in the womb, and by representing something to take place significantly prefiguring the subsequent relative position of the two men. In order to give probability to their meeting, it was necessary that the women should be connected: their actual meeting was brought about by a hint of the angel, who in order to make the fulfilment of the promise given to Mary credible to her, referred her to what God had done in the case of her cousin Elizabeth, and which was scarcely less incredible. The author indeed puts a prognostic of the relation between the two sons into the words with which he represents the mother of the precursor as saluting the mother of the Messiah (i. 43): "And whence is this to me that the mother of my Lord should come to me?" *i.e.* how am I so honoured that, &c. And this, only referring to the mothers, implies the same as is implied in the words put by Matthew (iii. 14) into the mouth of the Baptist on the approach of Jesus: "I have need to be baptized of thee, and comest thou to me?" But the prognostic was incomparably more striking if the embryo Baptist himself also took part in this homage. And the writer had before him an analogous instance in the Old Testament history. Rebecca, the wife of the patriarch Isaac, was also at first barren, and it was not until after the prayer of her husband that Jehovah bestowed upon her those twins who were to be the progenitors of two nations, the Edomites and the Israelites (1 Mos. xxv. 21). The subsequent relation between these nations had, according to the Hebrew legend, been already typified in the relation between the two children in the womb of their mother. First, their hostile position to each other by the fact that the two children struggled in the womb of their mother (xxv. 22); next, the spiritual superiority of the versatile but weaker Israel over the uncultivated strength of Edom, in the circumstance that on the occasion of the birth Jacob took hold of the heel of his first-born brother (xxv. 26; comp. xxvii. 36). But as the Baptist was not to be the twin brother of Jesus, there was nothing else possible but that he should make in the womb of his mother a significant movement. Abraham had rejoiced that he should see the day of the appearing of Christ, and had been glad when (in Paradise) he had really lived to see it (John x. 56). In like manner, the forerunner of Christ, while even in his mother's womb, expressed his joy at the coming of him whom he was afterwards to announce, by making a movement indicative of joy on occasion of the salutation given by Mary on her entrance (i. 44). In order to do this it was necessary—for even miraculous histories prefer, in the secondary features, clinging to the natural course of things—that he should have entered upon the period at which embryos begin to move: hence the assertion that Elizabeth had been already pregnant for six months when Mary's visit to her was occasioned by the angelic message.

The hymn of praise which the mother of Samuel sings when she delivers up her infant, after being weaned, to his lofty calling, has been already spoken of as a model not likely to be left unused. It was obvious to put a similar hymn into the mouth of the father of the Baptist; but before the birth and circumcision of the latter gave a fitting opportunity for such an outburst, Mary comes in with her visit, and now she anticipates Zachariah in plagiarizing the hymn of praise of Samuel's mother (comp. Luke i. 47 with 1 Sam. ii. 1; Luke, ver. 49 with 1 Sam. ver. 2; Luke, ver. 51 with 1 Sam. ver. 3 ff.; Luke, ver. 52 with 1 Sam. ver. 8; Luke, ver. 53 with 1 Sam. ver. 5; moreover, Luke, ver. 48 with 1 Sam. i. 11), and leaves to Zachariah, for his hymn of praise on the occasion of the circumcision of his son, only an anthology from different passages in the Psalms and Prophets.

59. Birth of Jesus.

Annunciation of the birth of the Baptist; annunciation of the birth of Jesus; meeting of their mothers; birth and circumcision of the Baptist; birth and circumcision of Jesus;— thus, in Luke, the narratives are interwoven with one another. In Matthew, on the other hand, not only is nothing here said of the Baptist, but even the birth of Jesus is only alluded to once before it and once after it; while the birth itself and its attendant circumstances are not made the subject of a narrative.

In Luke, such a narrative is found (ii. 1—20). The basis of it, the taxation of Quirinus, as the occasion of the journey of the parents of Jesus, we have already examined, and found it to be an historical error, occasioned by a dogmatical necessity. The further features of the narrative are referred to this basis. As strangers, only brought to Bethlehem by the taxing, the parents of Jesus have there no dwelling-place, and the same occasion having brought many strangers to the same locality, the parents cannot find room even in the inn, but are obliged to find shelter in a stable—or, according to the apocryphal Gospels of the Infancy and several Fathers of the Church, in a cave not far from the place*—and to lay the new-born infant in a manger. Hence ensues the transition into the pastoral world, to which, however, the author of our narrative is led, not merely by the stall and manger, but is also concerned with it on its own account. The patriarchs of the Hebrew nation had been shepherds, and had received the revelations made to them in the midst of their flocks: the angel of the Lord had appeared to Moses, the first Saviour of the people, when he was keeping the flocks of his father-in-law, Jethro (2 Mos. iii. 1 ff.), and the ancestor of the Messiah, David, had been taken by God away from the flocks at Bethlehem, in order to feed his people (Ps. lxxviii. 79 ff.; 1 Sam. xvi. 11). In the same way, the Greco-Roman legends choose to represent their heroes, a Cyrus or Romulus, as being brought up among shepherds.† So also in this case they are poor simple shepherds in the field, not the Pharisees and Scribes, or the cruel King in the capital, who are thought worthy of the first intelligence of the birth of the Messianic infant.

It is night when the angel appears to the shepherds, and the glory of the Lord shines around them. This, again, is connected with another idea. According to Isaiah (ix. 2), the people that walks in darkness is to see a great light, and a light is to shine upon those that dwell in the land of the shadow of death. This prophecy is applied not only by Matthew (iv. 16) to the Messiah, Jesus, but also in the course

* Justin, Dial. c. Tryph. 78; Orig. c. Cels. i. 51; Protev. Jacobi, c. 18; Evang. de Nativ.; Mar. c. 13. Justin also refers to Isaiah xxxiii. 16.
† Herodot. i. 110 ff.; Liv. i. 4.

of the history of the Infancy in Luke (i. 79); it is the day-star from on high, the light that shineth in darkness (comp. John i. 5); and as soon as the symbol had got the privilege of being understood literally even once, the night-scene which we have in Luke was the natural result.

The angel that appears to the shepherds in the heavenly light, proclaims to them the birth of the Messianic Saviour in the city of David, and as a sign of the truth of his announcement refers them to the fact that on their return to the city they will find a new-born infant lying in a manger. So Isaiah (vii. 14) had given to Ahaz as a sign a child still unborn, but to be called on his birth by a name of joyful import. And it was altogether in the spirit of the Hebrew legend to represent sometimes the truth of a prophecy, sometimes the divine character of an event, sometimes the dignity of a man of God, as being guaranteed by the coincidence of an occurrence foretold as being about to happen immediately. (Comp. *e.g.* 1 Sam. ii. 34, x. 7 ff.; Matt. xxi. 2 ff.; Acts x. 5 ff., 17 ff.). As soon as this one angel has delivered his message, the heavenly hosts join in chorus, the shepherds return to the city, find the child, and tell the announcement that has been made to them in reference to it. At this the common hearers are surprised; but his mother keeps all these sayings in her heart, and ponders on them, as formerly Jacob had thoughtfully preserved in *his* heart what Joseph, his miraculous son, told him of his dreams.

The birth of Jesus having been thus glorified by angelic scenes, it seemed superfluous to embellish the scene of the circumcision, as had been done on the occasion of that of the Baptist. Only it could not be passed over (Luke ii. 21), in order, in accordance with the tendency of this history of the Infancy in Luke, to bring into relief the exact observance of the law on the part of the family of Jesus.

II. Jesus, the Creative Word of God, Incarnate.

60.

The view that Jesus was begotten by the Holy Ghost in the womb of a virgin, might indeed, as above explained, be reconciled with the Jewish idea of God, by the exclusion of every sensuous element from the conception. Still, as the consideration of this element could not be prevented from continually intruding, the theory retained something offensive, not only to the Jewish Christians, but also to those converted from the heathen, who had elevated their minds to a spiritual conception of the nature of the Deity. Christians, accordingly, of this description, and these in particular, were under the necessity of making their new form of religion independent of that of the ancient Jews, of attempting to raise their Christ above the nature of common humanity, and at the same time above the greatest of the prophets of the Old Testament. A method of doing so, and of keeping clear at the same time of that objectionable theory, appeared to present itself to them —a method by which the same object might be attained, and at last a point even higher might be reached.*

When it became impossible for the adherents of the murdered Messiah to consider him as dead, as a disembodied shade, *i.e.* when their faith in his resurrection and ascension to God arose, they attained to a conception of Jesus which, at least from the moment of his resurrection and ascension to heaven, placed him in the same rank with the rest of the

---

* Compare, on what follows, Zeller, on the Christology of the New Testament, Theological Annual, 1842, p. 51 ff.; Philosophy of the Greeks, iii. 2, p. 621 ff.; Schwegler, The Post-Apostolic Age, ii. 286 ff.; Hellwag, Theory of the Pre-existence of Christ in the Ancient Christian Church, Theological Annual, 1848, p. 144 ff., 227 ff.; Lücke, Commentary on the Gospel of John (third edition), i. 283 ff.; Baur, Christianity of the Three First Centuries, p. 308 ff.; Volkmar, Commentary on the Revelation of John, p. 72 ff., 113; Holsten, Paul's Vision of Christ, Journal of Scientific Theology, 1861, p. 231 ff.

court of God, the angels, nay, even above them, as a being to whom all power in heaven and earth was given by God (Matt. xxviii. 18). But if his existence had not begun until the time of his human birth, he could not be even in the rank of the angels, seeing that they were as old as the creation of the world. If he was to be made equal to them, he must have existed before his human birth; this must have been, not the origination of his person, but only a descent of it from his earlier supersensual existence.

The formation of such a view of Jesus as the Messiah was assisted by several Jewish notions. The Son of Man in Daniel, who comes in the clouds of heaven before the throne of God, and is endowed by him with dominion of the universe, might have been originally intended merely as a symbol to mean the people of Israel. But when, as is obviously the case in our Gospels, the term was considered to apply to the Messiah, the latter was naturally looked upon as a supernatural being. The name of Messiah, as well as the nation and their law, was considered by the Jews as among those things which had existed in the mind of God even before the creation of the world—that is, as God, as they were taught by their own selfishness to believe, made the world for the sake of the Jewish people, and for their sake also would send the Messiah into the world, he must, at the same time that he sketched the plan of the universe, have also had in his mind the Messiah and his mission to it. Now the course of ideas of this kind is well known. What was previously intended, is converted into a fact already executed: the ideal becomes the real pre-existence. From the description of God, as the God of Abraham, of Isaac, and of Jacob, Jesus inferred the continued existence of these patriarchs (Matt. xxii. 31 ff.). Just as easily might another person, on the supposition that the appearance of this Messiah was included in the eternal scheme of God in the creation, infer that he had been God at the time of the creation of the world. The description of Jesus as "the beginning of the creation of God," in the Revelation (iii. 3), stands on the dividing-line between the ideal and real apprehension of the notion.

Something similar might be suggested by a peculiarity in the Mosaic history of the creation. It is well known that in the first book of Moses the creation of man is told in two ways. First, i. 27, in the words, "And God made man in his own image, in the image of God made he him, man and woman made he them;" again, ii. 7, it is stated that God formed man of the dust of the ground, and breathed into his nostrils the breath of life, and then, subsequently, made the woman of one of his ribs. This double narrative, which has persuaded modern criticism that two distinct portions are combined in the first book of Moses, suggested to Jewish thinkers discoveries of quite a different sort. As it was said of man, in the first instance, that he was made in the image of God, and, in the second, that he was formed of the dust of the earth, it was supposed that the same man could not be meant, but that the first must have been the supersensual heavenly man, the second the sensual and earthly. We find this distinction in the Alexandrian Jew, Philo; we find it also in the Apostle Paul, and indeed applied to Jesus as the Messiah. According to Paul, Jesus is, in his nature, the other man, the second Adam, the image of God; who, as heavenly, is contrasted with the first earthly man (1 Cor. xv. 45; 2 Cor. iv. 4). He is called the second or the last, though created before the other, without doubt because he did not appear until after the first. God waited for the posterity of the earthly Adam to develop itself up to a certain point, and then, and not till then, in order to close the present period of the world, sent upon earth in human form the heavenly Adam, who since his creation had been with him, as the Son of God, in a glorified form of light. If the Messiah, as the heavenly Adam, had thus existed since the creation, he might still, even though he had not appeared among mortal men until the coming of Jesus, have influenced mankind, and especially the chosen people; and when Paul on one occasion (1 Cor. x. 4—9) calls Christ that spiritual rock which followed the Israelites through the wilderness, and warns the Corinthian Christians not to tempt Christ as some of them had done, we are at all events not compelled to see in the first case a mere allegory, or in the second by a forced construction to evade the inference that Paul conceived his Adam-Christ, even at the time of the march through the wilderness, to have stood in a peculiar relation to the people of Israel.

It is, as is well known, a disputed point whether he attributed to him a part in the creation of the world. When, indeed, we read in 1 Cor. viii. 6, " But to us there is but one God, the Father, of whom are all things, and we in him; and one Lord Jesus Christ, by whom are all things, and we by him;" we might at first sight suppose that these words can mean only that Christ was the Creator of the world, though in a secondary, more instrumental position. And if Paul is also the author of the Epistle to the Colossians, in which (i. 15 ff.) Christ is called the image of the invisible God, the first-born of every creature, for by him were all things created that are in heaven and that are in earth, visible and invisible; and if, therefore, the first passage is to be explained by the last, it would not be possible to doubt the creation of the world by Christ to be the doctrine of Paul. It is true, indeed, that according to the original Mosaic record, man, even the being created in the image of God, was not created until the sixth day, after everything else. And thus it is not exactly clear how he can be supposed to have taken part in the creation. But that his having been created would not exclude the possibility of his own creative efficacy, we see from this very passage of the Epistle to the Colossians: after he had been created by God, all else, it is said, was then created by him. But if the Epistle to the Colossians, together with those to the Philippians and Ephesians, belongs to a somewhat later period, and the passage in that to the Corinthians, taken by itself, admits of another explanation, still we see from them, as well as in the Epistle to the Hebrews, what the tendency was of the course of the development of these conceptions. The Epistle to the Hebrews, like that of the Colossians, while passing over the Pauline idea of the primeval man, connects the creation of the world immediately with the attribute of the Messiah, Son of God, taking it not in the Jewish theocratic, but in the metaphysical sense. The Son is the express image of the essence, the brightness of the glory of God, the First-born through whom God created the æons, *i. e.* the present and future, the visible and invisible world (i. 1—6), whom afterwards, out of consideration for men, he made to become like unto men, and to take upon him human flesh and blood (ii. 14 ff.). In fact, we have here already the same nature which the fourth Evangelist calls the Logos, only that the author of the Epistle to the Hebrews does not use this term. And this is the more remarkable as he is acquainted with it (iv. 12 ff.), and must have been acquainted with it through his education in the school of Alexandria and Philo.

Like the whole of the Alexandrine philosophy, the idea of the Logos in Philo has a double root, Jewish and Grecian. But it is not the speech of God for the purposes of creation (1 Mos. i.), for even in the application of it (Ps. xxxiii. 6), "By the word of the Lord were the heavens made, and all the host of them by the breath of his mouth," we have not yet even a poetical personification; and the Memra of the Chaldee Paraphrase of the Old Testament is to be considered rather as a retrospective effect of the Alexandrian idea of the Logos. On the other hand, through the whole Hebrew literature of Reflection and Proverbs, from the Book of Job and of Proverbs up to that of Sirach and the Wisdom of

Solomon, there runs the idea of the divine Wisdom, which in Job (xxviii. 12 ff.) is plainly only a poetical personification, but in the Proverbs (especially chaps. viii. and ix.) is described in such a manner that, even if the author did not intend it, might easily suggest a real personality. Wisdom here appears speaking in her own person. She boasts of having been made by God—as the beginning of his way before his other works. When he laid the foundation of the earth, she was by him, and was his delight, as she, on the other hand, has her delight in the sons of men. According to Sirach, also (chap. xxiv.), Wisdom was created by God before all time, proceeded at the beginning from the mouth of the Highest; she sought for herself a firm habitation among the nations, until she was told of God to tabernacle in Jacob,* and to have her possession in Israel (comp. Baruch iii. 36 ff.). In the Book of the Wisdom of Solomon (vii. 25 ff., x. 1 ff.), Wisdom is the effluence of the glory of God, and the brightness of the eternal light; the Spirit of God, that orders the world, and is the friend of men; that preserves goodness in the world; takes his dwelling in the souls of pious men; and in particular led the people of Israel on the march through the wilderness in the shape of the pillar of cloud and the pillar of fire. From this Wisdom of God, which forms and preserves the world, the last quoted apocryphal book distinguishes the Word of God, not only as the Word that creates, but also judges, and likewise represents it as such in a personal character. When the Egyptians continued in their unbelief in the presence of the miracles of Moses, then, in the midst of the silence of the night (Wisd. xviii. 14 ff.), the Almighty Word came down as a mighty champion, carrying his solemn command like a sharp sword, and placed himself (like the angel of the pestilence, 1 Chron. xxii. 16) between heaven and earth, filling all with death.

* Ver. 8, ἐν Ιακωβ κατασκήνωσον. John i. 14 (of the λόγος), καὶ ἐσκήνωσεν ἐν ἡμῖν.

Now the system of Greek philosophy that next to the Platonic obtained the greatest influence over the Jews in Alexandria was the Stoic. In this system, the term used to describe the divine Reason penetrating and artificially moulding the world was not Wisdom, but that by which the Alexandrian translation of the Old Testament and the Jews who spoke Greek universally designated the creative Word of God, the term Logos. This term, from a peculiarity of the Greek language, meant at the same time Reason and Word. The consequence was, that philosophising Jews in Alexandria soon accustomed themselves to ascribe to the divine Logos what had been before attributed to the divine Wisdom. Thus, in Philo especially, the contemporary of Jesus who survived him, the Logos on the one hand corresponds to that which in the proverbial literature of the Jews is the divine Wisdom, and on the other to that which in the Stoics is the Reason of the World, in Plato and the Neopythagoreans the Soul of the World and the World of Ideas. The Logos of Philo is the Mediator between God and the world; it stands on the boundary-line between the two, and makes their intercourse possible, inasmuch as, in a downward direction, and being the essence of the Divine Ideas, it informs the world with these, while, acting upwards, it represents the world, and especially men, with God. It is neither uncreate, or created as we are, but came into existence, being, however, the most ancient and most original of all that did come into existence; it is therefore a God to us, as beings who stand far below it, not God absolutely, but a second or subordinate God. This Logos, as an invisible angel, led the Exodus of the people of Israel out of Egypt, in the pillar of cloud and fire, and is probably to be understood by the superhuman appearance which, according to Philo, in the Messianic period, being cognisable only to the saved, but invisible to all besides, is to lead back the scattered Jews into the land of promise. Still, Philo conceived of the Messianic Prince, who was to place himself at the head of the returning people, as something distinct from this superhuman Reason. For he looked upon the Logos as supersensual, not capable of entering into matter, scarcely indeed as a definite personal Being.

But the combination of these two ideas, that of the Logos and of the Messiah or Christ, could not be long delayed. The Mediatorial character which the one had to sustain between God and the chosen people, the other between God and the world in general, could not fail to unite them. In the New Testament indeed they are not found in combination, except in the Gospel of John, or before it (i. 1—18). The Apostle Paul, though assuming an existence of the Messiah anterior to man, knows nothing of a Logos in Philo's sense. The term is found in the Epistle to the Hebrews; but in the same way as in the Book of Wisdom it is placed by the side of Wisdom, so the Logos is placed, as a sharp, all-penetrating and judging spirit (iv. 12 ff.), by the side of the Son who creates and redeems the world, the brightness of the glory, and the express image of God (i. 1—3). In the Revelation of John (xix. 13), "the Word of God" is written as his mysterious name on the head of Christ approaching as a conqueror. But by this Jesus is only intended to be described as the herald and executioner of the Divine sentence upon the world. This is shewn by the context, and especially by the sharp sword which (ver. 15) goeth out of his mouth, and which is this powerful Word of God. Besides, it is clear that the later author of the Gospel, who is likewise supposed to have borne the name of John, might take to this description of the Apocalyptic John and understand it in its metaphysical sense. It can however hardly be the case that the author of this Gospel was the first who completed the union of the two ideas. For it is found, if not earlier, at all events independent of him, in other writings of the same period, especially in those of Justin Martyr, who wrote in the interval between 147 and 160 A.D., and, as has been already remarked, it is found in him in a form differing in so many ways from the type of John, that we see clearly that he, like the author of the fourth Gospel, adopted the doctrine of the Logos as a current idea of the time, and used it in his own way for his theory of Christianity.

The entrance of the higher nature that appeared in Christ into the world of man is described by Paul (Rom. viii. 3) in the following words: "God sent his own Son in the likeness of sinful flesh," *i.e.* in a body which was like the sinful human body (only *like*, because he was himself without sin). When the Apostle expresses this idea in the following terms (Galat. iv. 4), "God sent forth his Son made of a woman, made under the law;" this has as little to do with the exclusion of male agency in the histories of the Infancy as given in Matthew and Luke, as when on any other occasion (Rom. i. 3 ff.) it is said of him that he was made of the seed of David according to the flesh, but declared to be the Son of God according to the spirit of holiness, by the resurrection from the dead. On the contrary, there is no doubt that Paul conceived of his Christ as a naturally-begotten man, with whom the Son of God, the heavenly Adam, perhaps before his birth, united himself.

Nor, in the Gospel of John, which describes the higher Spirit as the divine Logos, the only-begotten Son, who from the beginning was with God, and by whom all things were made, is anything more accurate stated with regard to the mode of his entrance into mortal life. It is only said (i. 14) that the Word became flesh, *i.e.* took a human body; but at what moment or how, we do not learn. We have, in this Gospel, quite as little reason as in Paul, for supposing the exclusion of male participation from his procreation. Not only by the Jews (vi. 42), but also by the Apostle Philip, after he had already recognised in Jesus the Messiah prophesied by the Law and the Prophets, is Jesus, without the hint of correction, described as the son of Joseph (i. 46). As faithful Christians, natural human beings in their origin, "are born, not of flesh and blood, nor of the will of man, but of God" (i. 13), so also, according to the view of John, might Christ himself, notwithstanding his perfectly human procreation, be the only-begotten Son of God. But the Evangelist does not give a hint as to when this union took place. When, indeed, it is said of the Logos, as the true light (apparently in reference to the period of the Baptist's ministry), that it lighteth every man that cometh into the world (i. 9), and immediately after, on the occasion of the baptism, the Holy Spirit is represented (i. 32 ff.) as abiding upon Jesus, the inference has been drawn that the fourth Evangelist conceived the baptism of Jesus to have been the moment of the union of the Logos with man.* But the Spirit in the form of a dove, which he represents as descending upon Jesus on this occasion, cannot be immediately compared with the Logos, but is a remnant of the most ancient view of the higher nature in Christ, which the Evangelist follows as traditional, though it did not fit in with his doctrine of the Logos; as the descent of the Spirit upon Jesus on the occasion of the baptism would not have fitted in with the synoptic notion of the procreation of Jesus by him. The most probable supposition is that the fourth Evangelist connected that union with the first beginning of the life of Jesus, after the manner of the Platonic incorporating of pre-existent souls, but passed over the history of the Infancy, partly because it was much more difficult to conceive the subordinate God incarnate in the age of infancy than the human being who had been begotten of God, partly because a Gospel of the Infancy was too humble for the lofty style and higher flight of his description.

But if the views of the Prologue of John, and those of the synoptic histories of the birth with regard to the origin of

* Hilgenfeld, The Gospels, p. 241. The Question of the Gospels, Theological Annual, 1857, p. 522. Comp. also Bretschneider, Probabil. p. 6, 128.

the person of Jesus, are equally unlike the more ancient view given in the history of the baptism of the Messianic preparation of that person, still they cannot therefore be reconciled with each other.

The solution of Justin,* that by the Holy Ghost or power of the Highest, which Matthew and Luke describe as the efficient cause of the pregnancy of Mary, only the Logos is to be understood, does not hold good. Whether Spirit or Word, there must always be a difference between, on the one hand, a divine nature that has become flesh in Jesus and abided immanently in him, and, on the other, merely a divine operation occasioning his procreation. In the latter case, the subject of the evangelical history is produced by this operation; in the other case it already exists, and only enters, in virtue of its incarnation, into another form of existence. In the one case, the personality of Jesus is a mixed product of fructifying divine operation and receptive human, *i.e.* female, co-operation; in the other, it is the pure, divine personality of the Logos, to which the human element in him stands in the relation only of a transitory appurtenance.

61.

But it was not merely when a loftier, superhuman subject for the personality of Jesus, the Messiah, was sought for that the divine Wisdom of the Proverbs and of Sirach presented itself, but Jesus, the Teacher, pointed in this direction. Wisdom frequently appeared in those writings as the Instructress of men: as soon as Jesus was looked upon as the ideal of a Teacher, it was obvious to put him in the place of Wisdom, the Instructress of men. When, in Proverbs (ix. 1 ff.), it is said of Wisdom that she hath built her house, she hath slain her beasts, she hath mingled her wine, she hath furnished her

* Apol. i. 31, 35.

table, she hath sent forth her maidens, she crieth upon the highest places of the city, "Come, eat of my bread and drink of the wine which I have mingled!" we are reminded of the evangelical parable of the Feasts (Matt. xxii. 1 ff.; Luke xiv. 16 ff.), where, likewise, the Master sends his servants into the streets of the city, with the invitation that his feast is prepared, his oxen and his fatlings are slain, and all is ready, only the guests are wanting. In this parable it is God himself who takes the place of Wisdom in the Proverbs, but we have already above seen a case in which, in the evangelical tradition, Jesus has been substituted for her. The speech about the prophets and apostles which were sent to the Jews and ill-treated and murdered by them, which Jesus in Luke (xi. 49 ff.) brings forward as words of the "Wisdom of God," are attributed to him in Matthew (xxiii. 34 ff.) as spoken directly by him and uttered in his own name; as the ancient Jewish-Christian writer Hegesippus describes the companions of Jesus as those who had been thought worthy to hear with their own ears "God-inspired Wisdom."*

The conclusion of the Book of Sirach (chap. li.) is a thanksgiving, in which the author, as a pupil and distributor of Wisdom, uses in part exactly the same words which in a wellknown passage in the first and third Gospels we find put into the mouth of Jesus. "I will praise thee, O Lord and King," he says (ver. 1 ff.) both for protection and preservation, and also for the gift of Wisdom which he has vouchsafed to him. And now he cries (ver. 23), "*Draw near unto me,* ye unlearned, seeing your *souls* are very thirsty (ver. 26); put your neck under the yoke, and let *your soul* receive instruction; I have had but little *labour,* and have gotten unto me *much rest.*" Here the words of Jesus in Matthew (xi. 25 ff.) cannot fail to occur to us: "I *praise* thee, Father, *Lord* of heaven and earth," after which follows the thanksgiving, peculiar indeed to him, for that God has hid these things from the wise and

* Quoted in Eusebius, Ecclesiastical History, iii. 32, 8.

prudent, and has revealed them unto babes. Then follows, exactly as in Sirach, the invitation, "*Come to me,* all ye that *labour* and are heavy laden, and I will *give you rest;* take my *yoke* upon you . . . . . and ye shall *find rest to your souls.*" Such a coincidence can hardly be accidental; but it may be supposed that possibly Jesus may have had in his mind the passage of the Book of Sirach, which was originally written in Hebrew.

But in the Proverbs (viii. 1—22 ff.) we hear Wisdom call, "The Lord possessed me in the beginning of his way, before his works of old. . . . . Before the mountains were settled was I brought forth. . . . . When he appointed the foundations of the earth, then was I by him as one brought up with him, and I was daily his delight. . . . . Now, therefore, hearken unto me, all ye children: for blessed are they that keep my ways, for whoso findeth me findeth life, and shall obtain favour of the Lord; but he that sinneth against me wrongeth his own soul: all they that hate me love death." Again, we read in Sirach (xxiv. 1 ff.), "Wisdom shall praise herself, and shall glory in the midst of her people. . . . . I came out of the mouth of the Most High . . . . (ver. 19 ff.). Come unto me, all ye that be desirous of me! . . . . they that eat me shall yet be hungry, and they that drink me shall yet be thirsty," &c. &c. When we are reading these speeches, we are looking into the very cradle of the speeches of Christ as given in John. The historical Jesus was combined with the Wisdom of the Apocrypha and the Old Testament, the office of Wisdom as the Instructress of mankind assigned to him, and also as helpmate of the Divinity at the creation. The asseveration of Wisdom, that whoso findeth her findeth life, that he that sinneth against her wrongeth his own soul, all they that hate her love death, is re-echoed again in many ways in the speeches of Christ in John (*e.g.* iii. 20 ff., 36, v. 24); the invitation of Wisdom to eat of her bread and to drink of her drink, nay, to eat and drink her herself, is also found in the mouth of the Christ of John (iv. 10 ff., vi. 51 ff., vii. 37), only that what Wisdom adds in Sirach, that whoso has eaten and drank her once will always hunger and thirst for her, is changed, in John, by Jesus into a higher sense, to the effect, that whoever comes to him and believes in him will never thirst, as the water which he gives becomes in man himself a well springing to eternal life (vi. 27, 35, iv. 14). The Vine, also, and its branches, to which Christ, in John, compares himself and his disciples (xv. 1 ff.), is taken from the speeches of Wisdom in Sirach (xxiv. 16 ff.). And, generally, the expression in the Book of Sirach, "Wisdom shall praise herself, and shall glory in the midst of her people," imparts its character to all the speeches of Christ in the fourth Gospel. Such a continuous glorifying and praising of itself is not the least offensive on the part of a divine idea or attribute personified, but becomes so immediately it is transferred to a real human person, even though compounded of God and man.

Thus, in his speeches, Jesus was identified with that Wisdom which speaks in the Old Testament and its Apocryphal books. And this Wisdom, in consequence of the familiarity of educated Jews with the Platonic and Stoic philosophy, was at a later period transformed in Alexandria into the idea of the divine Logos, and in the course of the second century Christianity forced its way into a circle thus cultivated. The natural result was, what we have in the Gospel of John, that Jesus in his speeches glorifies himself as the principle of Salvation and of Life, like the Wisdom of the Proverbs and of Sirach, and finally in the prologue is, in exact accordance with the doctrine of Philo, introduced as the Divine Logos, the Creator of the world.

THIRD GROUP OF MYTHS.

JESUS, THE SECOND MOSES.

62. HIS LIFE ENDANGERED AND PRESERVED BY THE STAR OF THE MESSIAH.

It may be said that whoever reads Suetonius intelligently cannot fail to be enlightened as to the mode in which the miracles of the evangelical history are to be viewed. For from the supernatural procreation till the ascension, the two lines of miracles run parallel; and though the Old Testament narratives of miracles may offer more decisive points for comparison, still on the side of Suetonius there comes under consideration the useful fact that his prodigies and miracles, when they cannot be explained on natural principles, are recognised by every one as fables, and now, considering the speaking similarity of the almost contemporaneous imperial miracles to the Christian, it begins to be too difficult at the present day to see in the one set fables, in the other true histories.

The theme of the group of narratives immediately before us—the life of a child destined for great objects endangered and miraculously preserved—is one of the fundamental themes of all heroic legends; which, not to go in this place beyond the point at which a real connection between the people and legends is probable or possible, we find recurring in the Hebrew, the Persian, the Greek, and Roman legend. To say nothing of the dangers which threatened the infant life of Zeus or of Hercules, and the mode in which they were averted, we find the theme in the histories of the infancy of Moses in the Pentateuch, of Abraham in the later Jewish legend, of Cyrus in Herodotus, of Romulus in Livy, and then in the same century in the history of the childhood of the first Roman Emperor in Suetonius, and of the Christian Messiah in the Gospel of Matthew (chap. ii.). The theme is carried out in all of these with features so similar, that it is impossible to overlook either the influence of one legend upon the other, or the common psychological source of all. This source is that law of the imagination which leads men to endeavour to make the value of a good, and therefore also of a great, man the more sensibly felt by the near approach of the possibility of his loss on the one side, and by the care of Providence for his preservation on the other. And as regards the influence of one legend upon the other, such influence on the part of the Mosaic legend upon the Christian is unmistakeable, on that of Persian on the Greek probable, on that of the Romans at least possible.

In the history of the Infancy of Jesus, the mode in which the danger is brought about is peculiar. The cause of it is a Star, which about the time of his birth appears in heaven, and guides Eastern Magi to Jerusalem, where their inquiries after the new-born King of the Jews attract the attention of Herod the Great to the latter. Thus the Star appears as the means which gives occasion to the danger to his life. Still the legend with regard to it had an object of its own. There is a belief coming from hoar antiquity even to our own times, that new appearances of stars, particularly comets, coming unexpectedly and vanishing again, prognosticate revolutions in human affairs, birth and death of great men, or, in better cases, good wine. Men start from the supposition that so striking a phenomenon in the heavens must have, corresponding to it, a similar one on earth, in the circumstances of mankind. Then, when among a hundred cases such a coincidence happens, this is looked upon as a proof of the hypothesis. The ninety-nine, meanwhile, are overlooked, in which the natural phenomenon passes without any historical parallel; and then, conversely, when an historical event happens which it is wished particularly to distinguish, some extraordinary natural phenomenon which never took place is invented to correspond to it. Whether in the case of a traditionary narrative of this kind we are to assume that the natural phenomenon really occurred, and was only brought by the narrator into close connection with an historical event with which it had in reality nothing to do, or that the alleged phenomenon rests entirely upon fiction, will have to be decided by the presence or absence of other unsuspicious statements with regard to that phenomenon, also by the character of the narrative and its sources. When Suetonius* relates that on the occasion of the first set of games which Octavian gave in honour of his great uncle, after his murder, a comet was seen for seven days, and was considered by the people to be the soul of the deified Cæsar, it is possible, independently of this superstitious application, that the notice of the appearance of a comet at that time may be perfectly correct, because the narrative contains nothing contradictory to the nature of such a meteor, and because the historian lived near enough to the time and the place of the occurrence to get credible information with regard to it. And we do, in fact, learn from Pliny† that in Augustus' own memoranda the phenomenon was mentioned. But when we read in a rabbinical author‡ that at the moment of Abraham's birth a star stood in the East which swallowed up four other stars, each of which stood in one of four quarters of the heavens, what is said to have happened is so extravagant, the date of the origin of the account is so far removed from that of the alleged occurrence, that in both respects it may be looked upon as a mere romance. Lastly, Justin§ tells a story about Mithridates, to the effect that in the year in which he was born, and in that of his accession, a comet appeared, each time for seventy days, every day for four hours, of so large a size and so bright that it occupied a quarter of the sky and outshone

---

* Julius, 88. Comp. Plutarch, Cæs. 69.   † Hist. Nat. ii. 23.
‡ Jalkut. Rubeni, f. 32, 3.   § Hist. Philipp. 37, 2.

the brightness of the sun. In this case, also, the description of the phenomenon is at least highly fabulous; and whether we are to believe or not the general statement, that in one, at all events, of those two periods (for the duplication is more than suspicious) a comet did appear, will depend upon an examination of the sources which Justin, or rather Trogus, from whom he extracts, made use of in the composition of his history.

Now, in the first place, the composition of the narrative in the Gospel of Matthew of the star that appeared on the occasion of the birth of Jesus, was not so far removed from the occurrence in question as to be doubted on this ground alone. A report of an extraordinary phenomenon having appeared in Palestine might just as easily have been prevalent in the country eighty, or even a hundred and more, years after the event, as that about the comet of Cæsar in the time of Suetonius, *i.e.* of Trajan. But here a distinction appears to the disadvantage of the evangelical narrative. The comet in Suetonius coincided with the games in honour of Cæsar, consequently with an event to which general attention was directed, and in connection with which the celestial phenomenon that coincided with it must have impressed itself upon the memory of the people, and have also been entered in contemporary memoranda. The birth-year of Jesus, on the contrary, apart from the evangelical narratives, the truth of which has still to be proved, was marked by no particular event as regards those who were living at the time. So that a hundred years after, it could scarcely have been known with certainty whether a phenomenon, supposing such a thing to have been surviving in the memory of men, was seen in that year or in another.

As regards, in the second place, the description of the star in Matthew, we learn that the Magi saw it in the East, and that when they had recognised it, we know not how, as the star of the new-born King of the Jews, *i.e.* the Messiah, they commenced their journey to Jerusalem. It is not said that the star continued visible during this journey. On the contrary, when, on the command of Herod, they had set forth on the road to Bethlehem, it comes into sight again all at once, and not only precedes them as a guide, but also continues stationary, in so marked a manner, over the house of Jesus' parents, that the Magi likewise stop, and, with their presents, enter the house. What sort of a star it was, we are not told; but whatever it may have been, it is impossible, if it was a natural star, that it should have done what Matthew says it did; and if it was a supernatural one, *i.e.* a star immediately sent from and guided by God, it should have done more, that is, it should have avoided Jerusalem and taken the Magi straight to Bethlehem, so as not to have aroused the old tyrant in the capital, and hand over the poor infants in Bethlehem unnecessarily to the sword. We must, therefore, in any case set aside everything supernatural in the star, such as its going before the Magi, and its stopping, and the only question is, whether we have reason also to give up the appearance of the star altogether, or to maintain it as historical.

Now no other historical document of that time, as far as we know at present, does accredit it; but Kepler—a great name—in order to get a datum for determining the true year of the birth of Christ, has calculated that in the year 748 of the city of Rome, two years before the death of Herod, a conjunction of the planets Jupiter, Saturn, and Mars, took place, and in this conjunction, Kepler, and after him a series of modern astronomers and theologians,* have found, as they suppose, the historical nucleus of the Star of the Wise Men in Matthew. But, independent of the fact that Matthew speaks not of a group of stars but of one star, a conjunction of two

---

* Comp. as a specimen of all the rest, Wieseler, Chronological Synopsis of the Four Gospels.

or even of three planets is not of such rare occurrence (between Jupiter and Saturn every twenty years) as to appear to Orientals, acquainted with the stars, so very extraordinary a thing as is represented in the narrative of Matthew. Hence even Kepler himself did not consider the mere conjunction of the planets by itself as sufficient, but surmised that a new and extraordinary star may have been combined with it, as was the case in his own time in the year 1604. Then these three planets were in conjunction, and on a sudden such a star did appear, and having shone for some time with the brightness of a star of the first magnitude, it gradually waned, and at last disappeared. As, however, there is absolutely no internal connection between the appearance of such a star and the conjunction of those planets, the truth or otherwise of the supposition, that as in the year 1604 after Christ, so also at the time of his birth, the appearance of an extraordinary star may have coincided with an ordinary conjunction of planets, remained undecided, until Professor Wieseler at Göttingen discovered, in Chinese registers, that in fact in the fourth year before the beginning of our epoch (and this epoch places the birth of Jesus just this much too late), a bright star did appear, and was visible for some time.

All honour to the accuracy of the registers of the celestial kingdom; all honour, too, to a theology whose zeal to rake together proofs of the truth of Christianity drives it to the wall of China! We, on our part, must confess that the journey is too far, nay, that it appears to us to be a circuitous route, as we think we have the object of the search in a better and more satisfactory form close at hand. For let us even suppose that we had for the birth-year of Jesus a comet, or an extraordinary, but still natural, star, still we have not such an one as Matthew describes his to have been. For that not only appears to the travellers, but actually goes before them. And it does not, like other stars, stop when the persons in motion stop, but stops first *where* they are to stop. Now a star is a heavenly body, existing for itself and for objects entirely distinct from our earthly affairs. On the other hand, we find exactly such a star as we require, a star from which all the services performed for the Messianic pilgrims might be expected which Matthew boasts that his star performed, in the fourth book of Moses (xxiv. 17). The Star out of Jacob, announced by Balaam, is not a real star, but the Star of the Messiah, and therefore could not refuse any service which it might be the pleasure of the Jewish-Christian faith to impose upon it in honour of the Messiah.

The episode of Balaam and his prophecy is, as is well known, one of the most beautiful poetical pieces in the Old Testament, composed at a happy period, when the spirits of the people had just been raised afresh by victories over hostile neighbouring tribes, especially Moab and Edom. The composer of the piece clothes this feeling in a narrative, according to which Balak, the terrified Moabitish king, makes Balaam the Seer come from the Euphrates against Moses, advancing victoriously out of the Desert, in order to curse Israel, but who, instead of cursing, is inspired by Jehovah with blessing and lofty prophecies in favour of his people. Among these prophecies is found also the following (ver. 17): "I shall see him, but not now; I shall behold him, but not nigh: there shall come a star out of Jacob, and a sceptre shall rise out of Israel, and shall smite the corners of Moab, and destroy all the children of Seth." It is manifest here that the expression, "a star out of Jacob," answers to that of "a sceptre out of Israel," to express the same object. The addition, therefore, in ver. 18, "Out of Jacob shall come he that shall have dominion," is not necessary in order to convince us that by the former ones a glorious Ruler is symbolically meant. It is equally clear, in the next place, that by this Ruler is meant, not the Messiah, but an historical King of Israel, perhaps the very one under whom the poet was living, and whose achievements, in order to exalt them the more, he represents as being foretold by a Seer as early as the time of Moses, though there may be a question as to what king is intended, whether David or a later one.

Now the Chaldee paraphrase of the Pentateuch, which is considered older than our Gospels, has, instead of the star, a king, and instead of the sceptre, the expression, an anointed one. And thus, if the allusion to the Messiah was not exactly established, still the way to it was prepared, as every king might be called an anointed one, or Messiah. It is certain that many of the later Rabbis understood the passage of the Messiah; and it is also probable that such an interpretation had already become traditionary in much earlier times, from the fact that the pseudo-Messiah, who kindled the Jewish insurrection under Hadrian, openly called himself, in accordance with this passage, Bar Cochba, *i.e.* Son of the Star. He might, indeed, style himself so, if he only understood the star as a symbolical description of the Messiah, but the spirit of literalism and astrological superstition of the time co-operated so far, that by the Star out of Jacob a real star came to be understood, which was to appear at the time of the Messiah and announce his coming. In the Apocryphal Testament of the Twelve Patriarchs, dating from the end of the first Christian century, it is said of the Messiah,[*] "And his star shall rise in heaven as a king's, beaming forth with the light of knowledge:" nay, as the birth of the Messiah was announced by a star, that of Abraham, on the part of the Jews, was represented as being so likewise. But if the expectation was once established that a star would appear about the time of the birth of the Messiah, it will be admitted that a Christian who cherished it must have been convinced; and as the author of an evangelical prefatory history would

---

[*] Test. Levi, 18; in Fabric. Cod. Pseudepigr. V. T. 584 ff.

naturally say, that the appearance of it coincided with the birth of Jesus, whether he knew anything of a particular celestial phenomenon or not—also that in the description which he gave of the Star of the Messiah, he would be guided not by historical inquiry, but solely by his own conception of the Star of the Messiah.

Consequently, the author of our narrative took the Star from the fourth book of Moses, and he took the Magi from the Star. For who could have observed it first and recognised in it the Star of the Messiah but men initiated into the secrets of natural, and especially astronomical, philosophy, and those too coming from the East, the ancient home of mysterious knowledge, probably from Babylonia, from the Euphrates, whence also Balaam came, who had beheld that Star from far off in the distant future, as now his successors saw it in the nearness of the present?

But the Magi bring presents for the Messianic child whose Star they had seen. Balaam had brought nothing of this kind; on the other hand, Balak had been compelled to persuade him to undertake the journey out by presents which he sent to him at the Euphrates (4 Mos. xxii. 7). Balaam came, persuaded by the gifts, and the result was that he saw immediately the Star out of Jacob; the Magi came guided by the Star in order to bring presents. Here there is in the copy a perturbation, only to be explained by the influence of another type, which, however, we have not to go far to seek. The Messiah was not merely the Star out of Jacob, he was also the Dayspring from on high (Luke i. 78; comp. Matt. iv. 16), the Light that, according to the prophecy of Isaiah (lx. 1 ff.), was to rise up over Jerusalem, and to which peoples and kings were to draw nigh with rich offerings. By this Light, indeed, the Prophet, as he expressly says, understood the glory of Jehovah, *i.e.* Jehovah himself, who being reconciled to Israel at the end of the Captivity, was to return to Jerusalem, which had been deserted by him in consequence of their sins (comp. lii. 7 ff.), in order to restore and to reign over them, now that they had been purified and received into grace. When, however, the return out of captivity and the restoration of the worship of Jehovah had taken place, and the further promise of glory had been in no respect fulfilled, the natural consequence was, that the promise was referred to a more distant future, which could be none other than the time of the Messiah. For him also the presents of gold and frankincense must be intended (ver. 6), which the Gentiles were to bring, as, indeed, it was said in the seventy-second Psalm (ver. 10), of a King who was to judge the people of Israel with righteousness, break in pieces his oppressors, help the poor and needy, and who shall be feared so long as the sun and moon endure,—thus of a ruler under whom at a later period it was impossible to avoid understanding the Messiah that the kings of Arabia and Saba shall bring him presents, and among them in particular gold. And it is, as it were, a sort of obscure reference to the real origin of this feature in the evangelical narrative that in ecclesiastical tradition the Wise Men from the East were, at an early period, supposed to have been Kings.

The narrative therefore in the first Gospel about the Magi and their Star is the result of a combination of the two prophecies of Balaam and the second Isaiah, understood in a Messianic sense. From the first comes the Star and the feature that those who see it are astronomers; from the other, the feature that they follow the celestial light, *i.e.* according to the combination of both prophecies, are led by the Star, and that they bring presents to the new-born Messiah, to which the Star leads them; to which the evangelical narrative, perhaps from Psalm xlv. (ver. 9), which is also interpreted in Heb. i. 9, in a Messianic sense, added the myrrh. Moreover, they who bring the offerings are represented in Isaiah as belonging to the foreign nations among whom the Jews had sojourned during the Captivity. So, also, in Matthew, the Magi are to be considered, not as foreign Jews, but as heathen, and the ecclesiastical legend, in taking the Wise Men from the East to be the first representatives of the conversion of the Gentile world to Christianity, has in this also shewn a more correct appreciation of the fact than many modern theologians, who, in order to make the inquiry of the Magi more intelligible, saw in them foreign Jews.

63.

In the evangelical narrative, the Magi, in order to find the new-born King of the Jews, turn immediately to Jerusalem. The reason of this representation might appear to be contained in the passage of Isaiah, according to which the bearers of the presents travel to this place. But the main reason is, that the tyrant Herod lived there. For the history of the Star and the Magi, although, as we have seen, of independent Messianic import, also serves the purpose, in the connected narrative, of exposing the life of the new-born Messiah to danger, and of bringing about a miraculous preservation from it, thus placing in so much clearer light the great value of his life, and the divine protection extended over it.

It has already been remarked that the history of the Infancy of the first Saviour of the nation served as a type for that of the second. Herod is the second Pharaoh, and he, like the latter, would have effected the murder of the one he wished to kill, together with that of the others, if that one had not been preserved by a higher Providence. Pharaoh, however, as we are told in 2 Moses i., was concerned with many children, not with the one alone, of whose birth and destination he knew nothing. His object in issuing the command to put to death all the infants of the Israelites, was only to prevent the dangerous increase of the people.

Herod, on the contrary, was concerned only with the one Messianic infant, of whose birth he had been told by the Magi; and it was only because he could not effect his object in any other way, that he gave orders to despatch all the male children of a certain age who might be found in Bethlehem, the supposed city of the birth. Meanwhile, like so many other Old Testament narratives, that of Pharaoh's murderous command has been further embellished in the sequel, and in a manner which made it still better adapted to serve as a type for our evangelical account. That Pharaoh, in issuing his command, should have made no particular reference to an infant of a destiny so exalted, and so dangerous to himself, as Moses, appeared but little in accordance with the importance of this child. So in Josephus,* who in all probability followed in this an old tradition, it is represented that Pharaoh was induced to give the order for a general massacre by a declaration of his scribes (as Herod, by the inquiries of the stranger astronomers), as to the approaching birth of an infant who should some time bring help to the Israelites and humble the Egyptians.

So far, the account of Moses follows the track of that of Cyrus, Romulus, and Augustus, and upon this track that of Jesus ran parallel to it. Pharaoh or Herod is, in the case of Cyrus, his grandfather Astyages, in that of Romulus and Remus, their great-uncle Amulius, in that of Augustus, the Roman Senate. Astyages had a dream, which the Magi interpret for him, that his daughter should bear a son, who would be king instead of him.† Amulius naturally feared the vengeance of the twins for the deposition of their grandfather.‡ Before the birth of Augustus, it was said to have been prognosticated at Rome by a prodigy that Nature was pregnant of a king for the Roman people.§ How prone the popular imagination of the Hebrews especially was to fictions

* Antiq. ii. 9, 2. † Herod. i. 108.
‡ Liv. i. 3. § Sueton. Octav. 94.

of this kind, is clear from the fact, that in later Jewish writings the account of the peril which threatened the life of the Lawgiver was copied also in the history of the Patriarch of the nation. In this case Pharaoh is Nimrod: in one account Nimrod sees a star in a dream; this star, according to the other account, actually appears in the sky, and his sages explain it to him to mean that a son is at that moment born to Tharah, from whom shall come a mighty nation, destined to inherit the present and the future world.* And when the same feature had been introduced into the history of the infancy of Jesus, it was at last, like the secondary rainbow, also introduced into the history of the infancy of the Baptist, who, having been endangered by the massacre at Bethlehem, was said to have been preserved by a miracle.†

Now in the legend of Cyrus, Romulus, and Abraham, the tyrants give special orders for murdering only the children who are pointed out as dangerous to them; the narratives of Moses, Augustus, and Christ, resemble each other in this, that the potentates seek to catch the destined infant, who is unknown to them personally, in a wide net together with others. In the original narrative of Moses, Pharaoh, as has been already remarked, does not even know generally that the birth of such a child is impending; in the later form of the legend in Josephus, like Herod in Matthew and the Roman Senate in Suetonius, he does know thus much, but, like them, he does not know which of the children that are to be born, or which have just been born, is the dangerous one. So Pharaoh gives orders to drown all the male children of the Israelites; the Senate, not to allow any male born in that year to be brought up; Herod, to despatch all male infants found in Bethlehem and the surrounding districts of two years old and under. At first, indeed, Herod wished to put

---

* Jalkut Rubeni, f. 32, 3, and the passage out of an Arabian writing in Fabric. Cod. Pseudepigr. V. T. i. 345.
† Protevang. Jac. c. 22 ff.

himself in a position, like the tyrants in the legends of Cyrus, Romulus, and Abraham, to attack the dangerous infant immediately, hoping to get information of it through the Magi on their return from Bethlehem; and it was not until they, in consequence of a warning from above, had avoided Jerusalem on their return, that he took other measures; and we now also understand for the first time why, just at the beginning, when, with his original purpose it could be of but little importance to him, he still had felt it necessary to make such careful inquiries of the Magi as to the time when the star had first appeared to them, in order thereby to get a datum for the probable age of the child. Now such an order for a general massacre, though not quite in accordance with the sagacity, is quite so, nevertheless, with the cruelty of the old Herod. Still it is rendered more than doubtful by the historical consideration that neither Josephus, who is otherwise so explicit about Herod, nor any older author, makes mention of it, excepting one of the fourth century after Christ, who manifestly confounded the execution of one of Herod's sons, ordered by him, with the notorious massacre of the infants told in Matthew.*

There is a discrepancy between our narratives in the mode in which they represent their miraculous child as being preserved from mortal danger. In the Mosaic and ancient Roman legend, in which, in accordance with the geographical character which the Nile plays in Egypt, the Tiber in Latium, the children were threatened with a watery grave, a basket laid upon the shore and the compassion of those concerned, are the means by which the infants are saved; in that about Cyrus, the sagacity and kindness of those who are charged with the commission of the murder; in the legend about Augustus, the interest of the Senators themselves who have had sons born to them in that year deprives the resolution of the Senate (of which, besides, quite as little

* 1 Macrob. Saturn. ii. 4.

is known from other sources as of Herod's massacre) of all effect; the narrator in the first Gospel here introduces a motive, much used, indeed, generally throughout the legendary history both of Jews and early Christians, but an especial favourite of his—a suggestion in a dream. An angel, appearing to Joseph in a dream, had already warned him not to be offended at the pregnancy of his bride (i. 20); then, in a dream (whether or not by an angel is not expressly said, but at all events by God), the Magi are cautioned, on leaving Bethlehem, not to return to Herod (ii. 12). Now while the latter is occupied with threatening the infants at Bethlehem with the massacre, the angel of the dream advises Joseph to fly to Egypt (ii. 13); immediately after the death of the tyrant, he tells him to return into the land of Israel (ii. 20); and then comes, by way of supplement, the recommendation of the dream not to go to Bethlehem, into the province of the no less cruel Archelaus, but rather to turn towards Galilee (ii. 22).

A miraculous star, and five miraculous dreams within a few years, of which four are imparted to the same person, however, is almost too much, especially if it can be shewn that several of these might have been combined, not only without disadvantage, but with manifest advantage. It is clear at once that the last warning by a dream might have been dispensed with, if by the one before the last Joseph had been recommended to go to Galilee, instead of indefinitely into the land of Israel. Still the separation into different dreams at least did no harm. On the other hand, as has been already pointed out, it was productive of very important harm that either the star, which was so conversant with pointing out the road, did not, instead of leading the Magi to Jerusalem, lead them straight to Bethlehem, and from thence home, or that the warning of the dream was not given on the way to Jerusalem before the visit there. For thus the interference of Herod and the massacre at Bethlehem might have been avoided. It is intelligible that God should permit cruelties of this kind in the regular course of nature and history; but it is incredible that he should himself produce them by his own extraordinary interference. In this case, the children at Bethlehem would have remained unhurt, had not the Magi given the alarm at Jerusalem, after having been guided to that city by the star.

We have, therefore, here, not only no natural or historical occurrence, but not even such an one as we might imagine to have happened on the supposition of a miraculous interference by Providence. We are therefore entitled all the more to consider it as one which a pious Christian from among the Jews would have imagined towards the end of the first century. Such a Christian would feel it necessary to have a massacre of innocents ordered by a tyrant, from which, by a miracle, the second great Saviour of the nation escaped, because the first Saviour also escaped, by a higher Providence, a massacre ordered by a tyrant, and because, over and above all that, the passage in Jeremiah about Rachel weeping for her children (xxxi. 15; Matt. ii. 17 ff.), a passage which did, indeed, in the mind of the prophet, refer to the carrying away of the people into captivity, might be applied to this massacre. And then of miraculous dreams, the more the better. Not only had the men of God of the old covenant had such, but it was especially considered as a mark of the last, *i.e.* of the Messianic times, that in consequence of the imparting of the Holy Spirit, men and women should prophesy, old and young see visions and dreams (Joel iii. 1; Acts ii. 17).

The method of preserving the Messianic child from the murderer Herod, pointed out to his guardian by the angel in the dream, is flight out of the country. In the Revelation of John (xii. 5 ff.), the child which the woman clothed with the sun and crowned with stars, standing upon the moon, is to bring forth, is caught up to heaven from before the Dragon that lies in wait for it to swallow it, while the mother flies into the wilderness. Cyrus, Romulus, are brought up among shepherds, Moses by the king's daughter, until a subsequent occurrence, that of killing an Egyptian, after he has grown up to manhood, occasions his flight out of the country (2 Mos. ii. 15). It is clear that it is this later flight of the first Saviour which the evangelical narrator has in his mind in describing the earlier occurrence in the life of the second Saviour, from the fact, that in assigning the motive for the return of the latter after the death of Herod, he uses the same words as the Old Testament writer uses in speaking of the return of Moses after the death of Herod: "Go," says Jehovah, in the latter case, "return into Egypt, for all the men are dead which sought thy life;" after which it says, "And Moses took his wife and his sons, and set them upon an ass, and he returned to the land of Egypt" (2 Mos. iv. 19 ff.). "Arise," says the angel, in the dream to Joseph (who lay asleep, Jehovah having appeared to Moses while awake, and having therefore made use of a different introductory expression), "and take the young child and his mother, and go into the land of Israel, for they are dead which sought the young child's life;" whereupon, we are also told, he arose, took the child and his mother, and came into the land of Israel (Matt. ii. 20 ff.). We see here how Joseph steps into the place of Moses, Mary into that of his wife, and the child Jesus into that of his children, and the ecclesiastical legend, with a true feeling as to the origin of the legend, has also, out of that of Moses, introduced the ass.

The first Saviour, having grown up in Egypt, *fled out* of Egypt to Midian; the last, born in Palestine, flies to Egypt, and subsequently returns from it again. In this, the narrator sees the fulfilment of the prophecy of Hosea (xi. 1): "Out of Egypt have I called my Son." By the term "Son," the prophet was, indeed, far from meaning the Messiah. Jehovah begins, "When Israel was a child, then I loved him;" then continues, "and out of Egypt I called my Son;" says further on, "he taught Ephraim to go, taking them by their arms, but notwithstanding they have offered to idols." Now in all this it is palpable that by the Son, as elsewhere by the Servant of God, no one is meant but the people of Israel. It is true, indeed, that the passage spoke of the Son of God; but the Son of God was, according to the Jewish-Christian interpretation, the Messiah, Jesus: if, therefore, God had called his Son out of Egypt, Jesus (and as a child, for in Hosea "teaching to go" is spoken of) must once have been in Egypt. That, according to primeval Christian logic, was a perfectly conclusive argument, of which the Jews, at all events, had no right to complain, as it was from them that the Christians had learnt this logic. Moreover, events of great antiquity rendered Egypt an obvious place for the infant Messiah to fly to. Even if the Lawgiver had fled not to, but out of, Egypt, it had repeatedly been the place of refuge for the Patriarchs from scarcity and famine. If, as Hosea had done, the people of Israel were considered as a whole, it might be said to have passed its earliest childhood (the Patriarchal age) in Palestine, and the later in Egypt, and had subsequently been called thence by God into the land of its destiny, and now it was obvious to copy this course of life of the collective Son of God, in the individual life of the personal one.

Finally, we have our first Evangelist's assurance that by Joseph's journey to Nazareth, the prediction of the prophet that "he should be called a Nazarene" (ii. 23) was fulfilled. From this we may see the lengths to which he was carried by his zealous endeavour to seek up supposed prophecies in the Old Testament, and the arbitrary manner in which he pressed such passages into the service, in defiance of all rules of correct interpretation. By this prophecy, nothing, certainly, is meant, but that in the prophets the Messiah is frequently designated as a Shoot of Jesse, for which Isaiah, in the passage best known, xi. 1, uses the Hebrew word *Nezer* (other prophets, as Jeremiah xxiii. 5, xxxiii. 15; Zech. iii. 8, vi. 12, the synonymous *Zemach*), in which, together with the literal meaning of the word, a mysterious allusion to Nazareth as the future home of the scion of David is supposed to be implied.

64. PARALLEL SECTION: PRESENTATION OF JESUS IN THE TEMPLE.

Turning now from this narrative in the Gospel of Matthew, we throw a glance of comparison on the one other Gospel which gives us a history of the Infancy—that of Luke. And we find in the same place an account totally different, differing from the other in substance and fundamental ideas (ii. 22—40). In Matthew, the glorification of the birth of the Messianic child by the star and the homage of the Magi, exposes his life to a danger from which he only escapes by flying into a foreign country in consequence of a divine warning, where he is compelled to remain until the death of the persecutor. Meantime, in Luke, he is brought to Jerusalem at the time appointed by law, *i.e.* forty days after his birth, in order to be presented to Jehovah as a first-born male. And on this occasion his mother, as having been lately delivered, presents her offerings of purification, and the homage which in Matthew the child receives from the Eastern Magi is performed by Israelites of strict piety. Not a word is said of danger, but the parents, after having satisfied the exigencies of their pious duty, return in peace to their home, taking the child with them (ii. 22—40). In Luke, therefore, the glorifying of Jesus is kept within a narrower circle than in Matthew, does not, as in the account of the latter, produce a tragical complication, but all goes off peacefully, and the complications that threaten the future are only alluded to preliminarily in the speech of the aged Simeon about the resistance which

Jesus is to meet with, and the sword which shall pierce his mother's soul.

Moreover, in the narrative of Luke no reference is observable to the antitype in the life of Moses. We find, indeed, in the introduction, the law of Moses quoted three times, once as to the days of the purification, then as to the redemption of the first-born and the offering of the mother, and at the conclusion we read, that after his parents had fulfilled everything required by the law of Moses, they returned to their home. And we see from this that the narrator, who, as we remember, also made express mention of the circumcision of Jesus, was much more concerned to shew that from the time of the earliest infancy of the Christian Messiah nothing had been neglected which the Mosaic law required in the case of a child. The Jewish zealot hated in Jesus the person who was to destroy Law and Temple (Matt. xxvi. 61; Acts vi. 14). Naturally they indulged in hostile fictions, specimens of which may be found in later Jewish libels,* to the effect that he was unlawfully begotten and unlawfully brought up. In opposition to this, it was important to shew that, on the contrary, Jesus had been the offspring of a strictly pious family, that the alleged Destroyer of the Temple had been early presented to God in the Temple, and received as the long-expected Saviour by devout and inspired attendants at the Temple. In this respect, the salutation of the infant Jesus by Simeon and Hannah, after being saluted at his birth by angels (also in Luke), and therefore in a still more glorious manner, was by no means superfluous from the Jewish point of view. It was not enough for the Jew to know what the relation had been between Jesus and the religion generally; he wished also to be accurately informed what the relation had been between him and Judaism, the Law and the Temple.

---

* Such as the book Tholedoth Jöschu; comp. Eisenmenger, Judaism Unveiled.

At the same time the salutation of the Messianic child by pious Israelites admitted of being used for another purpose. The chief offence which the Jews took at the Christian Messiah was the ignominious end, in a worldly sense, to which he came: the crucifixion of Christ was to them a stumbling-block which they could not get over (1 Cor. i. 23). When, then, a just and pious man like Simeon, waiting for the consolation of Israel, and inspired by the Holy Spirit, on first seeing the Messianic infant, predicted to that infant its future struggles, and to the child's mother her future agony, alluding, in a manner not to be mistaken, to the violent death of the former —in all this the lesson was involved that, correctly and spiritually understood, the Messianic idea did not exclude, but include, the mark of suffering and of death. When Simeon expresses himself to the effect that the child is set for the fall and rising again of many in Israel, and for a sign which shall be spoken against, in this an allusion was contained to the fact, that the resistance of the Jews to Jesus was already counted upon in the scheme of Providence, and that it was then for every single Jew to see that the Messiah set by God be not, to himself, a fall, but a rising again.

There is something in the arrangement of the presentation scene in Luke which may remind us of the Magi in Matthew. Simeon comes into the Temple impelled by the Spirit, from whom he has received a promise that before his death he shall yet behold the Messiah. In like manner the Magi came to Jerusalem, led by the star, which was to them a sign of the birth of the Messiah. As the Magi, when the star had made known to them the house in which the infant Jesus lay, did homage to him and offered him their gifts, so Simeon takes into his arms the child—which, as we must suppose, the Spirit pointed out to him at first sight as the one promised to him— and in inspired words offered him his homage. And as in the first case the arrival and inquiries of the Magi caused an excitement in the capital, so in this Hannah, the prophetess, takes care, by the reports which she spreads, that the circumstance shall not remain concealed from any one in Jerusalem who has faith in the Messiah. The resemblance may be accidental, and arise from the circumstance that at corresponding points of the history of the Messianic infancy similar features naturally appeared; still it is not impossible that the author of the narrative in the third Gospel knew that of the first, and purposely contrasted another with it. We know from Justin Martyr* that one of the accusations of the earliest opponents of Christianity was that the miracles of Jesus were only magical illusions; that he himself was a magician and impostor of the same description as several others who at that time travelled through the country with pretensions to higher powers. How an accusation of this kind might be supported by the narrative in the first Gospel of the flight to Egypt, the ancient home of sorcery, we see from the work of Celsus against the Christians, in which this heathen philosopher puts into the mouth of a Jew the assertion that Jesus did, in his youth, enter service in Egypt from poverty, and there learnt mystical arts which he practised after his return home.† This suspicion having been once excited, not merely the flight to Egypt, but also the contact with Eastern Magi, might be demurred to, and thus it might seem advisable to introduce Israelites of unimpeachable character, who, instead of stars and astronomy, were concerned with the Temple and the Holy Spirit. Thus, again, the concluding formula as to the child's increasing in wisdom and stature is of an ancient Hebrew character, being in fact copied, almost word for word, from a similar formula in the history of Samson (Judges xiii. 24 ff.).

Independently, however, of the inconceivable character of the accounts of the infancy in Matthew and Luke, or of the fact that in their individual features they are manifestly framed with a purpose in view, it is clear, lastly, that we

---

* Dial. c. Tryph. 69. † Orig. c. Cels. i. 28.

have in them not true histories but fictions, from the consideration that while each harmonises perfectly with itself, it is absolutely impossible to reconcile one with the other. We have already seen above that each of the two Evangelists starts from a different hypothesis with regard to the original dwelling-place of the parents of Jesus, inasmuch as in Matthew Bethlehem appears in that character, in Luke Nazareth. In accordance with this hypothesis, the parents of Jesus, in Matthew, continue after the birth of the child to live quietly in Bethlehem, receive here the visit of the Magi, and would never have thought of removal had they not, on account of the impending massacre of the infants at Bethlehem, been warned to go into Egypt by the angel in the dream. But having been informed here of the decease of the murderous tyrant, they would immediately have returned home to their Bethlehem if they had not been told in a dream that in Archelaus, now reigning over Judea, the case was one of like sire like son, and that they would therefore do well to avoid his district and to settle in Galilee. While, therefore, in Matthew the existence of the parents of Jesus gravitates throughout towards Bethlehem, from which they are removed only by a power from without, in Luke, on the contrary, Nazareth is this point, and in it, accordingly, the pendulum that has been set in motion comes as soon as possible to rest. Brought to Bethlehem, as strangers, by the taxing, they stay there only the forty days during which the condition of the mother on the one hand, the necessity of undertaking the journey to Jerusalem at the end of that period on the other, made their sojourn in the place near to the capital advisable; as soon as their business in Jerusalem is done, there is nothing to prevent them from returning to their distant Nazareth.

If both accounts were historical, they must admit of being incorporated into one another. The Magi must have come either before or after the presentation in the Temple, the presentation in the Temple must have taken place either before their visit, or, if not, after it, but still before the flight to Egypt, or, lastly, not until parents and child had returned again from Egypt. But whichever of these positions we attempt to adopt, the narratives will fit into none of them. If we make the presentation in the Temple precede, then immediately after this the family went back to Nazareth, and the Magi, coming afterwards, would find them no longer in Bethlehem, which Matthew expressly says was the case. Besides, if on the occasion of the presentation in the Temple, Hannah the prophetess had communicated to all who were hoping for it in Jerusalem the news of the birth of a Messiah, then on the subsequent arrival of the Magi the event could no longer have been, as Matthew represents it, a novelty in the capital. If then, by way of trial, we place the coming of the Magi, together with the flight to Egypt in connection with it, *before* the presentation in the Temple, we fall into a difficulty with the forty days which Luke introduces as the interval between the birth of Jesus and his presentation in the Temple. For when Herod inquired of the Magi how long it was since the star was first visible to them, he seems to have supposed that the Messianic infant had been born simultaneously with the appearance of the star; and when, in consequence of the information which the Magi gave him upon this point, he commanded the Bethlehemitish children up to two years old to be slain, he must have supposed the infant Messiah to be at least approximating to that age. Consequently from the birth of Jesus until the arrival of the Magi we should have, according to Matthew, to suppose more than forty days to have elapsed; and beside this, in the space of time above mentioned the Magi must be supposed to have withdrawn again, the parents to have travelled to Egypt in company with the child, to have stayed there till the death of Herod, and after it to have again travelled out of Egypt to Palestine. That is manifestly too much for six weeks; and hence the necessity of an attempt, however difficult it may be to succeed in it, one thing in the narrative of Matthew being so closely connected with another, to separate the Egyptian journey from the visit of the Magi, and to drive in, like a wedge between the two, the presentation in the Temple. So then, after the retirement of the Magi, the parents of Jesus would have travelled with the child to Jerusalem, and this must have taken place before the angel had advised the flight to Egypt on account of the danger threatened by Herod. But how is it conceivable that this angel should not, above everything, have prevented the journey, dangerous as it was, to the residence of the tyrant, or that, when the journey had been taken, and the news had been spread in the street, by the loquacious Hannah, of the infant Messiah having arrived in the capital, Herod did not seize him, and spare himself the expedient, as uncertain as it was odious, of the massacre at Bethlehem? On the contrary, the account of the presentation in the Temple in Luke does in no way presuppose such an occurrence as the arrival and inquiry of the Magi, but runs as if nothing had ever been heard of the thing before, and there had been no danger to the child heard of far and wide.

The unhistorical character, accordingly, of the two evangelical descriptions, which the character of each separately had indicated, is confirmed by their incompatibility, and we must therefore consider them as fictions, which the authors of the first and third Gospels either worked out themselves or adopted into their works. There is, however, still one thing which may surprise us. For observing as we do the Judaising element to prevail in the first Gospel and the principles of Paul in the third, if we keep together on the one hand the narrative of the star and the Magi, and on the other that of the circumcision and the presentation in the Temple, we might feel some surprise at not finding the latter in Matthew and the former in Luke, instead of the converse. For in the star and the Magi there is as manifestly implied a reference to the Heathen world and their admission into the kingdom of Christ, as in the prominence given to the circumcision and presentation in the Temple to the sanctity of the Jewish juridical system. But we have already found in the Gospel of Matthew, together with portions of an undeniably Judaising tendency, at the same time others in which the calling in of the Heathen was brought into view; and in the narrative of the Magi nothing is said decidedly as to the mode in which or the conditions under which they are to be admitted. On the other hand, it is the Apostle of the Heathen himself who declares that Christ, when he appeared on earth, was put under the law (Gal. vi. 4 ff.), so that the description in Luke might be considered only as an illustration of the expression of Paul in reference to the infancy of Jesus. Meanwhile, Paul immediately adds that the object of that ordinance in reference to Christ was, that he might redeem those who were subject to the law (ver. 5), and thus put an end to the law (Rom. x. 4), an idea which is not alluded to in the history of the Infancy in Luke. On the contrary, if we consider this preliminary history in connection with what is said with regard to John the Baptist, we cannot mistake the presence of a Judaising element both in form and substance. But we found in other instances Judaising portions of this kind incorporated into his Gospel by Luke, only balanced, at the same time, in some cases by portions of an opposite tendency, in others characterised in themselves by a catholic spirit. Characteristics of this kind, rendering Judaism unprejudicial to the general scheme of the Gospel, are found also in this case, either having existed originally in the narrative, in which case they might be adopted by the author of the Gospel with the less demur, or been introduced for the first time by himself. When Simeon calls the infant Messiah a Light to lighten the Gentiles (ii. 31; comp. Isaiah xlii. 6), the whole meaning contained in the narrative is comprised in this expression; as, on the other hand, in what Simeon says further on of the fall and rising again of many in Israel, and the opening of the thoughts of many hearts (ii. 34 ff.), the Jews are confronted as sharply as possible with the prospect of the sifting that is to come upon them, in which many will not stand.

II. Jesus, like Moses and Samuel, dedicated early to his high calling.

65.

Suetonius tells of Augustus,* that having been, as a little child, laid on the ground in the cradle in a room, he had vanished on the following morning, and, after a long search, was found at last in the highest part of the house lying towards the East.

Now it will be asked what resemblance this story is supposed to have to that of Jesus at twelve years old in the Temple (Luke ii. 41—52). Certainly the age, and what depends upon it, is in both cases different; but in both we have still the common feature that a child, destined to higher objects, is missed where he is ordinarily to be found, and discovered in a place dedicated to God. This, indeed, in the narrative about Augustus, is not a temple; but the East is the sacred quarter of the heavens, and the high tower, as Suetonius expresses himself, alludes to the neighbourhood of the gods, whither, as we must suppose, the child Augustus was removed out of his cradle in a supernatural manner. As in the case of Christ, so also in that of Augustus, lofty destination was identical with lofty extraction; for it is hardly possible that the anecdote above quoted should have arisen without reference to the legend of Apollo having been the

* Octav. 94.

father, whose property, as the Sun-god, the East especially was, as in our evangelical narrative the answer of Jesus as to his Father's house manifestly contains an allusion to the history of his supernatural conception.

As Jesus was a Son of God in human form, so also was Cyrus, who was brought up as a shepherd's son, a king's grandson in the form of a slave, and also in his case his royal nature and destiny broke through the disguise at an early age, namely, in his tenth year.

Having been elected king by his playfellows when he was about this age, he exercised the duties of his office in so dignified a manner, that the discovery of his real extraction immediately followed.*

In the case of Moses, it was somewhat late before his destination as the Saviour of his people declared itself in a similarly pre-eminent manner. For the purposes of the powerful assistance rendered to a fellow-countryman, which is said to have been the means of this declaration, it was necessary that he should be "grown," as the narrative in Moses (ii. 11) says, though not perhaps exactly forty years old, as the Acts of the Apostles (vii. 23), resting upon later Jewish tradition, more accurately defines his age. But we know that a statement differing from this, and of Rabbinic origin, made him twenty years of age on that occasion, and even if great physical power could not have developed itself before that period of manhood or youth, still the distinguished intelligence of the Lawgiver was represented to have come out in his earlier years. According to Josephus,† his intelligence was out of all proportion to his age; according to Philo,‡ Moses, as a boy, was attracted, not by child's play and trifles, but by serious occupation, and at an early period teachers had to be engaged for him, to whom, in a short time, he shewed himself superior by natural genius.

Samuel was still an infant when his mother brought him

---

* Herod. chap. i. 114 ff. † Antiq. ii. 9, 6.
‡ De Vita Mosis, Opp. ed. Mang. ii. 83 ff.

to Shiloh for the constant service of Jehovah in the Tabernacle (1 Sam. i. 25), and still a boy when the call and address of Jehovah came to him for the first time in the night (iii. 1 ff.). In the Old Testament his age is not given more accurately; but as the Acts of the Apostles says with reference to Moses, so also Josephus* says of Samuel, on the authority, no doubt, of a later tradition, that he began to prophesy at his twelfth year. For it was from the twelfth year that, according to the Talmud, a boy was considered among the Israelites to be of the age of discretion; this age, as the fourteenth year with us, was looked upon as the transition from the period of boyhood to that of youth: hence in a record of Christian origin indeed, but probably in accordance with Jewish tradition, the wise judgments of Solomon and Daniel (1 Kings iii. 23 ff.; Susanna 45 ff.) were placed in their twelfth year.† It is clear, however, from other features that the history of Samuel's youth served as a copy to our evangelical historian, not only in this instance, but in those also of an earlier period. In the first place, he introduces his narrative with the remark (ver. 41), that the parents of Jesus travelled every year to the Passover at Jerusalem. Similarly it is remarked of the parents of Samuel, not merely introductorily but repeatedly (i. 21, ii. 19), that they went every year to Shiloh in order to make an offering to Jehovah. Secondly, the remark at the end of the evangelical narrative that the boy Jesus increased in wisdom and stature, and in favour with God and man (ii. 52), is manifestly copied from the concluding remarks as to the child Samuel, that he grew and was in favour both with the Lord and also with men (ii. 26).

If we pass from these grounds for the origination of a narrative of this description, grounds existing in the very nature of the heroic legend, and from those, more special, existing in

---

* Antiq. v. 10, 4. † Ignat. Epist. ad Magnes. 3.

the lore of the Hebrew prophets, to the peculiar form of the Messianic legend, we must remember that the operation of furnishing the man Jesus with the powers required for his Messianic calling was at first connected with his baptism by John, consequently transposed to a mature age, and that it was not until a later period that those powers were considered to have been produced by a supernatural principle, and his higher Messianic powers to have been peculiar to him from the beginning of his life. Now, if the transition were made, as our first Evangelist makes it, immediately from the birth and earliest infancy of Jesus to his baptism, there was between the two events far too large a gap, and the question might be put: Well, but if your Jesus was full of the Holy Spirit from his mother's womb, how happens it that the Spirit was so long idle with him, and that it was not until the years of manhood that he gave proofs of his power and wisdom? This question, through which there was always danger of the Ebionitic doubts as to the supernatural conception of Jesus insinuating themselves again, was barred by apocryphal Gospels of the Infancy by means of narratives, according to which Jesus, while still a child, performed miracles, spoke when in the cradle and declared himself to be the Son of God, disclosed to his tutor in the alphabet its mystical meaning, and, in general, embarrassed all his teachers by his questions before his twelfth year.*

The narrative of Luke, as a comparatively healthy product of primeval Christian invention, stands in favourable contrast with these late results of the operation of a wild imagination. In the first place, it altogether avoids the performance of the miracles. But as to the wisdom, it does indeed transgress the limits of the human and the probable. For it represents Jesus at twelve years old, instead of sitting at the

* Comp. the Protevang. Jacobi, the Evang. Thomæ; also the Arabian Gospel of the Infancy in Thilo's Codex Apocr. i.

feet of his teachers, as would have become his age, and as propriety required (comp. Acts xxii. 3), as sitting in the midst of them and on a par with them; and, moreover, as calling God his Father in a sense which assumes either the truth of the history of his supernatural procreation, or a maturity of religious development which, naturally, a boy could not have. Still it does not offend so glaringly against nature as those apocryphal stories do; but, apart from that designation of God as his Father, does not go further than the vain Josephus does in reference to himself, when he speaks of the notice which he excited in his fourteenth year by his premature genius and knowledge.* And even in this our narrative gives a very appropriate representation when it places the stepping-stone between the birth and early infancy of Jesus on the one hand, and his mature age on the other, exactly on the intermediate point between the age of boyhood and that of youth.

The narrative begins with an illustration of that which is the fundamental theme of the whole of the history of the Infancy in the third Gospel, the account, that is, of the mode in which the strict piety of the parents of Jesus shewed itself in their annual journeys to the feast of the Passover at Jerusalem. Immediately on the occasion of the departure of the parents from Jerusalem, the child remains behind, and they seek for him in vain. Thus it appears at once that his ways are not the ways of ordinary men, that he follows a higher law of his own: in his question on the occasion of their finding him again—why had they sought him, did they not know that he must be about his Father's business—he makes them feel this, not without a degree of harshness, which is palliated however by the concluding remark as to his continuous obedience (ver. 51), and is certainly exceeded by John in a speech uttered on another occasion: "Woman, what have I

---

* Vita, 2.

to do with thee?" The inferiority in intelligence on the part of the human parents to the Son of God is further illustrated by the author in the addition of the words, that they did not understand his questions (ver. 50), as in the former section he had remarked their surprise at the speech of the old Simeon (ii. 33). But if it had been true that even before the birth of Jesus the angel had foretold both to Mary and to Joseph that the child, as a being begotten by the Holy Spirit, would be called the Son of God, they must necessarily have understood what he meant by his Father's house; and when the evangelical narrator represents them as not understanding, he betrays himself to be not an historian but a narrator of miracles, whose style is appropriately characterised by accounts of the continuous astonishment and perplexity on the part of the human beings who are placed in contrast with the performer of miracles. The remark, lastly, which had already been made when the shepherds told their stories (ii. 19), that Mary kept all these sayings in her heart, shews that the author had in his mind Joseph, the miraculous child of the Old Testament, in whose history it is likewise said, in reference to the important dreams which he told as a boy, that his father kept the saying (or the circumstance) in his mind.

III. THE MESSIAH, JESUS, WITHSTANDS THE TEMPTATION TO WHICH THE PEOPLE IN THE WILDERNESS, LED BY MOSES, YIELDED.

66.

At the age when young men become their own masters, and shew whether they are to pursue the paths of virtue or of vice, the Hercules of Prodicus underwent his temptation, or (according to the expression of Xenophon[*]) had the choice

[*] Memorab. ii. 1, 21.

given him. Abraham must have been advanced in years when, being commanded to sacrifice his only and late-born son, he was subjected to his temptation—the hard trial of his faith and obedience (1 Mos. xxii.). On the other hand, the people of Israel was, as the prophet says, still young when Jehovah called it, as his Son, out of Egypt (Hos. xi. 1), and during the period of forty years tried him in the wilderness with all sorts of hardships in order to search his heart, and to discover whether he would keep the commands of God or not (5 Mos. viii. 2). David also, immediately at the outset of his public career, after having been first (according to the combined accounts of the compiler of the Books of the Kings) anointed by Samuel and filled with the Holy Spirit, had to submit to a dangerous trial, the battle with the gigantic Philistine Goliath (1 Sam. xvii.). These trials had been successfully withstood by Abraham and David, as also by Hercules; but the people of Israel yielded to the temptation, and had been so carried away as to murmur at Jehovah, to practise licentiousness and idolatry. In this they had acted in the same way as the first pair of human beings, who had also given ear to the seducing voice of the serpent and sinned against the command of God, thus drawing upon themselves banishment from Paradise and from the tree of life.

As the Mosaic history generally survived in the memory of the Israelites, so, in particular, as warning examples, did these trials in the wilderness, so ill withstood, together with the divine punishments which they brought with them. "Now all these things," writes the Apostle Paul, after giving short accounts of these occurrences, "happened unto them for ensamples, and they are written for our admonition, upon whom the ends of the world are come" (1 Cor. x. 6—11); and so, on another occasion, fearing lest his Corinthian Christians might, in their simplicity, allow themselves to be deceived by false preachers, he reminds them of Eve who was beguiled by the subtle serpent (2 Cor. xi. 3).

It was the calling of the Messiah to restore that which was corrupt, to do well what others had done ill. It was necessary, therefore, that he should withstand temptation better, and that Jesus, as the Messiah, should have withstood it better than the people in the wilderness, or the first parents in Paradise. Now the whole life indeed of Jesus, and especially his suffering, had been a series of such trials (Luke xxii. 28; Heb. iv. 15); but we see at once how strong the inducement must have been to separate off one single solemn act of temptation, and, as in the case of Abraham's trial, the temptation of the first parents, to delineate it with dramatic picturesqueness (Matt. iv. 1—11; Mark i. 12 ff.; Luke iv. 1—13).

There was another circumstance that co-operated to this end. Abraham, the people in the wilderness, had been exposed to temptation by God himself, and, indeed, with a good intention, for the people had only to withstand it as their ancestor had withstood it. But as time went on, it appeared objectionable to refer temptation immediately to God. Many thus fell, who would otherwise have continued upright; many were thus brought into trouble which they had not deserved; did not God, if he had exposed them to it, appear in the light of a jealous Being, rejoicing in mischief? God must himself participate in evil, it appeared, if he could tempt any one to evil (James i. 13). Hence the inclination arose, at an early period, to assign to Temptation another author. In Genesis, the being which excites in Eve the desire to act in opposition to the divine command, is the serpent, as being the subtlest of the beasts of the field; a fabulous representation, which could not long hold its ground. Now the Israelites in captivity became acquainted with the Zend religion, which assumed the existence of a good and evil principle, and looked upon the development of the whole system of the world as a battle between the two opposing principles. This theory suited the Jewish people in the crisis through which it was passing at that time, and thus especially the conception of the Persian Ahriman adapted itself to the limitation that he did indeed counteract the operations of the God of goodness, but remained nevertheless strictly subordinate. He was the Enemy (Satan), the Accuser and Slanderer of men to God, who by his doubts of the constancy of Job's piety caused God to tempt him by heavy sorrows: he it was also who, disguised in the form of a serpent, tempted the first parents in Paradise, and thus brought death and destruction into the world (Wisd. ii. 24; 2 Cor. xi. 13; Revel. xii. 9 ff.).

With regard to the change in the Jewish views of the world, nothing is more instructive than a comparison of the motives assigned in the older Book of Kings and the later Book of the Chronicles for the numbering of the people undertaken by David, and so severely punished by Jehovah. "And again the anger of the Lord was kindled against Israel," we read in the first account (2 Sam. xxiv. 1), "and he moved David against them to say, Go number Israel and Judah." In the second, on the contrary (1 Chron. xxi. 1), "And Satan stood up against Israel and provoked David to number Israel." Now, if the history of the patriarchs and of the journey through the wilderness had been also written in the later period after the Captivity, we should probably find Satan in like manner represented as being implicated in the temptations to which Abraham and the people of Israel were exposed. In the Talmud, at all events, this is actually the case. In the Babylonian Gemara, God is represented as being stirred up by Satan to try Abraham, as in the prologue of the Book of Job to try Job. Satan, accordingly, meets Abraham as he goes out to sacrifice his son, and personally tempts him. In like manner in the march through the wilderness it is Satan, according to the later Jewish statement, who, while Moses lingers on the mountain, persuades the people of his death, and thus seduces them to the worship of the calf.*

All that was bad and evil in the world, especially in so far as it concerned the people of Israel, being thus referred to Satan as its first cause, it was a natural result that the Messiah, who was to purify the people from their sins and to deliver them from the evils which oppressed them, should be opposed to Satan as his antagonist and conqueror. Christ is come to destroy the works of the devil (John iii. 8), to destroy bad spirits (Mark i. 24; Luke iv. 34); he sees Satan fall like lightning from heaven (Luke x. 18), the Prince of this world, who is no other than the devil, cast out (John xii. 31). But for this end it was necessary first to conquer him. If he attacks Christ, he must find nothing in Christ on which he can lay hold (John xiv. 30). But attack him he will, as surely as he attacked so many Old Testament saints, and also as certainly as he still in the Christian world goes about seeking whom he may devour (1 Peter v. 8). In ordinary cases, this sifting by Satan consists only in the entrance of evil, in tempting thoughts (Luke xxii. 31; John xiii. 2). But against the Messiah, since a decisive battle was to come off, a personal appearance of Satan was required, for, as it were, a duel with the Son of God. As David confronted the proud giant of the Philistines, so must the Messiah confront Satan, the Prince of the world; as David overthrows the former by the stone out of his sling, so does the Messiah put Satan to flight by the weapon of the Word of God; the Holy Spirit approves itself in both, they having received it immediately before, the one through the anointing by Samuel, the other through the baptism of John.

The period at which the history of the temptation is placed, being thus fixed by this type of David, or, generally,

---

* Gemara Sanhedr. in Fabric. Cod. pseudepigr. V. T. p. 335. Schabbat bab., quoted in Gfrörer, The Century of Salvation, ii. 381.

by the consideration that the communication of the Spirit just received is to approve itself under the strongest trial, so also the locality of the scene, the duration of Jesus' continuance upon it, the substance moreover and form of the temptation, as well as the resistance offered to it, are all copied from the Mosaic history. The theatre is the wilderness, not merely because it was always considered among the Jews as the dwelling-place of evil spirits (3 Mos. xvi. 8—10; Job viii. 3; Matt. xii. 43), but, above all, because the people of Israel also were tempted in the wilderness. The time of trial for the people in the wilderness had lasted forty years; in the case of the Messiah, the substance of these forty years was compressed into as many days; which at the same time was connected with the character of the first temptation prepared for him by Satan.

For the first temptation encountered by the people in the wilderness had been hunger, and they had yielded immediately to this first so far as to murmur against Moses and Aaron, *i.e.* in the last resort, against Jehovah himself (2 Mos. xvi.); nay, soon after, being dissatisfied with the manna given them, they desired meat (4 Mos. xi.). Therefore it was by hunger first that the Messiah was to be tempted: in order to feel hunger he must have fasted: now Moses had fasted during the march through the wilderness, on Sinai (as Elijah had done subsequently and similarly, 1 Kings xix. 8), forty days (2 Mos. xxxiv. 38; 5 Mos. ix. 9). So also Christ fasted in the wilderness forty days, and after the lapse of these he felt hunger, whereby Satan hoped to be able to get him into his power. It would be to no purpose to tempt the Messiah to murmur, as in his case the fasting was voluntary; consequently the Tempter fixes upon his character as the Son of God, and endeavours to seduce him to aid himself by his own power. The form in which he does this, the demand made to him to change at a word the stones that lie around him into bread, is determined partly by the stony ground of the desert, partly by proverbial language met with elsewhere also in the New Testament. God, said John the Baptist, likewise in the desert, could, in case of necessity, raise up children to Abraham from these stones (Matt. viii. 9); and coinciding still more closely with this feature of the history of the temptation, Jesus had asked whether any one would give his son a stone when he asked for bread (Matt. vii. 9). So much the more suitable it must have seemed to Satan's mischievous nature to refer a hungry person to stones instead of bread, with the additional demand to forestall God by a miraculous word, and change them into bread. But, notwithstanding the fact that a particular feature is taken from elsewhere, the temptation of the people of God in the wilderness is throughout the real antitype of the history of the temptation. This appears immediately from the answer by which Jesus repels this first attack of the Tempter. At the close of the march through the desert, Moses, according to the representation in Deuteronomy, calls upon the people to remember all the way which Jehovah led them all the time in the wilderness and proved them, and says, among other things (5 Mos. viii. 3): "He humbled thee and suffered thee to hunger, and fed thee with manna (which thou knewest not, neither did thy fathers know), that he might make thee know that man doth not live by bread only, but by every word that proceedeth out of the mouth of the Lord doth man live." These last words are the very words with which Jesus replies to the Tempter (Matt. iv. 4), appealing at the same time to what "is written," and thus the latter, baffled at the first onset, applies himself to a second.

In order to understand this second temptation, we must start from the words at the end of it, the answer of Jesus: "Again it is written, Thou shalt not tempt the Lord thy God." In the passage of the fifth book of Moses, from which also this text is taken (vi. 16), it is said more accurately: "Ye, that is, the people, shall not" (when ye come into the land of Canaan, "tempt the Lord your God, as ye tempted him at Massa." That is at the time when from want of water in the wilderness they murmured against Moses and Aaron (2 Mos. xvii.); for this was considered a "tempting" of God, implying as it did a doubt of his miraculous support (ver. 7). This tempting of God, or, as he seems to understand it, of Christ, is also numbered by the Apostle Paul among the things in which the Christians are to make the precedents of the Israelites in the wilderness a warning example to themselves, so as to escape similar punishments (1 Cor. x. 9, where 2 Mos. xvii. 1 ff. is combined with 4 Mos. xxi. 4 ff.). Also, in that portion of the prophet Isaiah, so much read among the first Christians on account of its supposed Messianic importance, chap. vii., where king Ahaz, encouraged by the prophet to demand an accrediting sign, answers (ver. 12), "I will not ask, neither will I tempt the Lord," the expression has without doubt the same meaning, but might possibly be also explained to mean that the king would not make of God any improper demand, as in Ps. lxxviii. 18, it is said in reference to this murmuring of the Israelites for meat (4 Mos. xi.), "And they tempted God in their heart by asking meat for their lust." Now what improper demand was there that could be suggested by Satan to the Messiah to make of God? Ps. xci. 11 ff., it is said of him who stands under the protection of the Most High, as in the most distinguished sense was the case with the Messiah, that God shall give his angels charge over him to keep him in all his ways, that they shall bear him in their hands, that he strike not his foot against a stone. This, literally understood, might be taken to mean that the Protected of God might throw himself without danger from a height, as God's angels would support him and bring him without hurt to the ground. Satan, therefore, calls upon Jesus to do this; and as in another Psalm it is said of a man of clean hands and a pure heart, again therefore pre-eminently of the

Messiah (Ps. xxiv. 3, comp. xv. 1), that he shall ascend into the hill of the Lord and stand in his holy place, the Messiah also is now to ascend the pinnacle of the Temple and throw himself down from thence—to which proposal the answer came in quite suitably in the text, "Thou shalt not tempt the Lord thy God."

One of the most prominent warnings drawn by the Apostle Paul in the often-quoted passage of the first Epistle to the Corinthians, from the history of the march through the wilderness, is that in chap. x. 7, not to be idolaters, as some of them (2 Mos. xxxii. 6) were. In the same section, idolatry (in accordance with the view prevailing among the Jews), is explained to be a worship of devils (x. 20 ff.); and the Prince of the devils is, according to this mode of conception, Beelzebub (Matt. xxii. 24), *i.e.* Satan. For a considerable time the Jews must have seen the sovereignty of the world in the hands of idolatrous people; consequently, according to their ideas, the supreme idol, Satan, was Prince or God of the present world (2 Cor. iv. 4; John xxii. 12, 31, xiv. 30, xvi. 11). So the temptation to idolatry, which as the antitype of the nation the Messiah had to undergo, took the form, according to the ideas of this later period, of a demand to worship the devil; and to this demand the devil might add as an inducement the promise to surrender to the Messiah the whole of this world, the disposal of which belonged to him as the Lord of it. In order to invest this inducement with the greatest possible strength, it was necessary to shew to Jesus this world in all its glory, and with this view he takes him to the top of a high mountain, as Jehovah had taken Moses before his death to Mount Nebo, and made him survey the whole country which he would give to the people of Israel (5 Mos. xxxiv. 1 ff.). It is clear that the Messiah would yield to this temptation as little as to any of the others, and in this case the weapon with which he repels the tempter is an expression from the speech of Moses at the end of the wanderings in the desert, *i.e.* the command to the people to worship Jehovah, to the exclusion of all other Gods.

Beaten thus in three onsets, Satan is compelled to give in, and retires, but, as Luke adds, only to renew his attack at a more convenient season. There is no doubt that by this later attack Luke meant the suffering of Jesus. And this, not indeed in Luke, but in Matthew, is opened by three courses, as, in the Garden of Gethsemane, Jesus thrice separates from his sleeping disciples, in order to pray to his Father for the putting away of the cup of suffering (Matt. xxvi. 36—45). In like manner, Peter thrice denies his Master (Matt. xxvi. 69—75), and so it followed that his love for him must thrice be called in question (John xxi. 15—17): all instances in which the triple repetition has the same ground, the natural preference, not merely of the Jews, but of others, also, for the number three, which must also have appeared especially appropriate for the arrangement of dramatic scenes, like that of our history of the Temptation. Hence, also, the narrative of the Gemara above mentioned represented Satan as having three courses with Abraham; while other rabbinical accounts, perhaps in accordance with the number of Egyptian plagues, speak of ten temptations of Abraham.

In the summary accounts in Mark, the *number three* of the temptations has disappeared, and it is only said, "And immediately (after the baptism of Jesus) the Spirit driveth him into the wilderness, and he was there in the wilderness forty days, tempted of Satan, and was with the wild beasts, and the angels ministered unto him." Whether the wild beasts are intended to colour more highly the picture of "the wilderness" (comp. also 2 Macc. v. 27), or to represent Jesus as the second Adam, still it is an extravagant feature, and when taken in combination with the rest of the description, which is so abbreviated as to be almost unintelligible, does not say much in favour of the originality of this account, and of the second Gospel generally. Even the account in Luke, in comparison with that of Mark, looks like one at secondhand, partly from the fact that, at all events according to the common reading, he is the first to speak of the Temptation as continuing for the forty days, and then represents the three separate acts of the Temptation as following upon the close of them, partly from the artificial touching up of the narrative of the latter as given in Matthew. For an artificial touch it is when Luke puts the temptation to worship the devil second, and that to throw himself down from the pinnacle of the Temple third. For in point of substance the call to worship him is the strongest that the devil could make upon Jesus, and forms, therefore, a suitable conclusion; what induced Luke to modify this order was undoubtedly the reflection, that it was more improbable that Satan should have gone with Jesus out of the wilderness to the mountain, and then into the city, than out of the wilderness into the city, and then out again to the mountain—a reflection little suitable in the case of a narrative like ours, where a probability more or less was of little consequence. A second hand also is betrayed by additions such as the following: that the devil shewed Jesus all the kingdoms of the world "in a moment;" that he makes his own dominion over the world the ground of his offering it to Jesus; and that, in conclusion, he is said to have departed from him only "for a season," seeing that he never appeared to Jesus again, at least in this manner, *i.e.* personally and visibly. Meantime, Luke loses the conclusion of the narrative in Matthew, which Mark, in spite of all his abbreviations, preserves, that after the departure of the devil, angels came and worshipped Jesus. They refreshed him subsequently, as an angel did Elijah preliminarily (1 Kings xix. 5 ff.), though not with earthly, but, undoubtedly, with heavenly food; with the bread of angels, as the manna was called, according to later Jewish notions (Ps. lxxviii. 25, in the Greek translation; Wisd. xvi. 20); and thus proof was given of the confident assertion made by Jesus at the beginning, that for the support of the pious God is not confined to common material bread.

The fourth Gospel has no history of the Temptation—nay, as if it were intended to be pointedly excluded, the particular events, from the time of the baptism of John to the first performing of miracles by Jesus, are connected by the strictest dates (as, on the next, on the third day) so closely together, that the Temptation, with its forty days, can find no place between them. Here, accordingly, John has certainly one incredible history less than the Synoptics, but he passes it over, not because he found it insufficiently accredited from an historical point of view, but because, dogmatically, it was not to his taste. In his dogmatic theory, indeed, the devil, as the author of sin among men and as the antagonist of Christ, had a prominent place; but the idea of his appearance in a sensible form was opposed to his Hellenistic education, and that Jesus should have condescended to enter into a formal conflict with him as a being of equal rank, appeared to John to be unsuitable to the dignity of the Son of God in *his* sense. So on this, as on many other occasions, the author of the fourth Gospel endeavoured, while sacrificing the form, to retain the substance and the result, of the history of the Temptation, and in doing so adhered to the reference made by the third Evangelist to the suffering of Jesus as a renewed attack of Satan upon him. In this sense he refers especially (xiii. 2) the treason of Judas to the inspiration of Satan, thus following Luke (xxii. 3), but avoiding his language, which reminds us of a formal possession by a devil, though he retains that language (vii. 70) when it suits the purposes of his own representation. Further on, too, and before the opening of the regular history of the passion, he comprises all that can be looked upon as the real dogmatic meaning of the history of the Temptation in the words which he puts into the mouth of his Christ (xiv. 30) —"The prince of this world cometh, and hath nothing in me."

Thus, looking upon the history of the Temptation as a Messianic myth, we escape, in the first place, the necessity of having recourse to any of those traditional quibbles by which attempts are made to make that history and its forty days fit into the tissue of the Johannine narrative which is here so closely woven. With this view, apologistic theology has scarcely left a place unattempted between the beginning of the historical narrative of the fourth Gospel, chap. i. 19, and iv. 54. In every case, however, with equally bad success, as the object of the narrative of John is not to leave a place where that of the Temptation may possibly be inserted, but conversely, in all probability, absolutely to exclude it. But even independently of this incongruity between the fourth Gospel and the Synoptics, which, with our view of the former, proves nothing against the narrative of the latter, this narrative in itself presents difficulties so numerous and so important, that a mode of looking at it which cuts these absolutely away must be considered a welcome discovery. For few persons at the present day will be bold enough, with Ebrard, to assert that the dignity of Jesus as the second Adam required that Satan should appear to him, as to the first, personally and visibly, not as to the latter under the disguise of an animal, but undisguised in his own figure. And it is only necessary to allude to the evasions of a vision, a dream, a parable, &c., in order to shew that in view of the text, which manifestly speaks of a real objective occurrence, they are as inadmissible, as the assumption of a myth, provided only the right point of view is taken, is natural and probable.

By introducing the history of the Baptism and that of the Temptation, we have already overstepped the line which is generally considered to bound the preliminary history of the Gospels, and lately, also, as that within which the admission of mythical elements is no longer contested. The whole school of theologians which received its stamp from Schleiermacher, and as the representatives of which we would here name only De Wette and Hase, agree with their master in giving up as untenable, and to even a greater extent and more fully than he does, the historical character of the accounts of the birth and infancy, and consider these as a tissue of primeval Christian legends and fictions, out of which no historical nucleus, even supposing such a nucleus to be contained in them, can be now extracted.* In making these admissions, they follow the example of wise and decisive generals, who, in order to be the better able to maintain a fortress, surrender untenable outworks, and do not even hesitate to burn them down themselves. In modern times, indeed, there has been ample opportunity for discovering that the preliminary history of the Gospels may, as against the siege artillery of criticism, be compared to such untenable outworks. And nothing but the stiff-necked stupidity of the old Tubingen school, or the pettifogging obstinacy of the modern Church tendency, can blind themselves, like Smith or Ebrard, to this daylight so far as to think of maintaining this portion of the evangelical history to be perfectly historical.

Still there is something in the conduct of theologians of the latter description, in which we are bound to do them justice, as compared with the former. The burning of a suburb is only advisable when it is cut off from those parts of the city which are intended to be preserved, or when the latter are made of materials so incombustible that there is no fear of the fire spreading from the one to the other. On the other hand, if this is possible or even probable, it is generally considered better to let the suburb stand, and to see how long it can be held, than to set it on fire and so precipitate the destruction of the whole place. Indeed, if we were to

* Hase, Leben Jesu, § 26.

listen to theologians of the first description, we should have to believe that the evangelical account of the public life of Jesus was in every way fortified against such danger. The testimony of the Apostle is supposed to answer the purpose of a trench and wall; this (according to Acts i. 21 ff., x. 36 ff., comp. with Mark i. 1) begins first with the baptism of John.* But these theologians do not recognise apostolical testimony in the synoptic Gospels at all; and as to that of John, whom they cannot give up as an eye-witness, they have lately made it illusory by those well-known alibis which they bring in whenever he tells anything which they cannot believe. But as regards the more durable material of which the narratives of the public life of Jesus are supposed to consist, they put just within the wall of defence, first the history of the Baptism with the dove and the voice from heaven, the first of these being also found in the account of the eye-witness John, as well as the history of the temptation with the personal appearance of the devil—material as combustible certainly as any in the history of the Infancy, and, consequently, not merely endangered by the fire kindled in the suburb, but with no hope of escape from its ravages. Or if we begin with the conclusion of the evangelical history, then the narrative of the ascension of Jesus is the exact parallel to that of his supernatural conception, the history of the transfiguration to that of the baptism, and then there run through the whole of the department of the life of Jesus the narratives of his miracles, which likewise consist of similarly combustible material. If this is the case in the interior of the fortress, it is well indeed to think twice before firing the outworks; and if I had the misfortune to be inside, I should be on the side of those who preferred defending the whole, outworks included, though with uncertain success, rather than set the latter on fire, and so sacrifice everything to

* Hase, Leben Jesu, as quoted above.

certain destruction. The real difference between the history of the Infancy of Jesus and that of his public life, as it lies before us in the Gospels, is only this, that in the former there is, independently of a few quite general notices, nothing whatever historical; in the latter, in the midst of what is unhistorical, there is still much that is historical on which the torch of criticism cannot lay hold. This historical element, however, is at the same time the natural element: the supernatural in the history of the public life of Jesus is so similar to that in the history of the Infancy, that whoever recognises the necessity of maintaining the historical character of the one will also find it the best course to admit no doubt to arise in his mind as to the historical character of the other.

SECOND CHAPTER.

MYTHICAL HISTORY OF THE PUBLIC LIFE OF JESUS.

67.

THUS we see that the history of the birth and infancy of Jesus, a few meagre historical notices excepted, is throughout a tissue spun from dogmatic conceptions, and was, therefore, necessarily drawn within the circle of our present exposition, the object of which is to point out the progressive formation of the mythical history of Christ. In the former Book, in which we were concerned with the real history of Jesus, we had nothing to do with that earlier account. But in the history of his public life, there is, as the analysis contained in the former Book has shewn, much that must be recognised as historical both in the facts, and especially in the speeches of Jesus, and we shall now therefore be concerned with all that remains, and which did not come under our notice in the historical synthesis of the former Book.

The miraculous element will obviously come first under this investigation, comprising not only the miracles which Jesus performed, but also those which were performed in his company, or in reference to him; much also that does not indeed, like the miracles, contradict the laws of Nature, but those of historical probability—events, that is, with regard to which it is easier to understand how they may have arisen as reflexes of sacred or poetical fiction, than that they really happened. It is clear, of course, that such an investigation will contain points open to dispute; we shall therefore content ourselves with bringing forward at present only those portions of the history of the public life of Jesus in which the mythical formation may be pointed out with some degree of certainty. Portions of this description are the accounts, throughout, of the relation of Jesus to his precursor and his own disciples; towards the conclusion, those of the transfiguration of Jesus and his entrance into Jerusalem. Meanwhile the accounts of miracles performed during this period are numerous, and continue from the beginning to the end of the period.

FIRST GROUP OF MYTHS.

JESUS AND HIS PRECURSOR.

68.

It was recorded, historically, John baptized Jesus. It was attempted to be established dogmatically, by his baptism, as by an anointing, John dedicated Jesus to his Messianic office. Hence the history of the Baptism already considered.

It was recorded further, historically, that the Baptist, after having baptized Jesus, did not attach himself to him, but continued the exercise of his baptismal function as before. This, naturally, did not suit the dogmatic interests of Christendom: it was supposed that the Baptist himself must have acknowledged Jesus as the Messiah. We have seen how the synoptic tradition endeavoured to shew this by its mode of representing the history of the Baptism. It made John an eye and ear witness of the miracle which was supposed to take place on that occasion, and thus it followed as a matter of course that he represented what was said as being said to himself, and recognised Jesus as the person which the voice from heaven declared him to be. He had already referred to a Mightier than himself who was to come after him, and to baptize with the Holy Spirit; it is not expressly said that in doing so he had in view the person of Jesus of Nazareth, but, according to the history of the Infancy in Luke, it is to be presumed he had; and when, according to Matthew, he attempted to deter Jesus from coming to his baptism with the declaration that he, the Baptist, had more need to be baptized by Jesus, he must have recognised the latter, even before the miracle of the baptism, as that Mightier of whom he had spoken. The Hebrew Gospel gave to this recognition of Jesus on the part of the Baptist a palpable expression, making the latter fall at the feet of Jesus and pray to be baptized by him.*

The question, however, still remained, why the Baptist, when that Greater One, for whose coming he was only to prepare, had been pointed out, and, as it were, placed before him by God himself, did not immediately desist from his own function and attach himself to him? To this question the synoptic tradition replied by pointing to the forty days' sojourn of Jesus in the wilderness, where it was necessary that the Messiah should be alone. Further on, Matthew and Mark represent, as we are almost compelled to suppose, the imprisonment of the Baptist as taking place during, or at the conclusion of, this sojourn, when of course there would be an end to the possibility of John's attaching himself to the Messiah.

Now it was known, or believed to be known, that John had not been immediately put to death, but kept for some time in prison, and as during this time Jesus was supposed to have begun his public ministry, it was considered inconceivable that the Baptist should not have had intelligence of this (Matt. xi. 1 ff.; Luke vii. 18 ff.). The far-spread rumour of the miraculous deeds of Jesus must, it was thought, have come to his ears in spite of the prison walls; and as he had from the first proclaimed one who should come after him, the question forced itself upon him whether the man who performed such deeds was not he that should come, and to proclaim whom he had been sent. If he had indeed

* Epiphan. Hæres. xxx. 13.

already on the occasion of his baptism seen the Holy Spirit hover over Jesus in the shape of a dove, and heard the heavenly declaration of his being the Son of God, he must have known, without further questioning, that Jesus, and no other, was he that should come; and if he had, moreover, heard meanwhile of his miraculous deeds, this could only strengthen him in his conviction. The synoptic Gospels represent him as not only asking the question, but as adding to it the expression of still further doubt as to whether another is to be looked for. Now he could only do this in case he had either become doubtful as to the meaning of the baptismal miracle, or this miracle had not taken place at all. Our narrator, however, does not give the slightest hint of his having been guilty of the grievous sin of falling away while in prison from his belief in the miraculous sign of which he had been thought worthy to be the witness. We must, therefore, suppose that this account does not assume the existence of that of the baptism as we now have it, *i.e.* that the account of the message of the Baptist out of the prison comes originally from an author who knew nothing of the miraculous occurrence at the baptism. So the question which John is represented as asking, is one which might have been asked by any other person, namely, as miracles might be ascribed to any one else, whether those which Jesus was said to be performing do really indicate the expected Messiah, or whether, as had already been the case so often before, the hope of that Messiah's coming was to be still further delayed. Jesus is said to have replied to this question in words which, if they were ever uttered by him, might, according to an explanation given above, apply only to the moral miracles of his ministry, but are understood by the Evangelists as referring to the real material miracles which Jesus performed.*

It is not said what the effect of this answer upon the Bap-

* See above, First Book, Vol. i. p. 364.

tist was—whether or not it led him to recognise Jesus as him who should come. Instead of this, a speech about John is put into the mouth of Jesus, which he might, indeed, have spoken without this message having been sent at all, but which was brought in here because it appeared adapted to remove much of the difficulty involved in the fact that the Baptist did not attach himself to Jesus. For in this speech (Matt. xi. 7 ff.; Luke vii. 24 ff.) John is recognised, on the one hand, as the promised Messianic forerunner, as the most exalted personage of the ancient time. On the other hand, he is made to draw a strong distinction between himself and the children of the more modern period, that of the Messianic kingdom of heaven; nay, even to subordinate himself to the least of them. And thus it might be less surprising that he failed fully to understand him who had introduced this modern period.

Luke also states summarily that John had been imprisoned by Herod (iii. 20); but the statement in Matthew as to when this was done, and that he sent the message to Jesus straight out of the prison, is not given in Luke. Thus the result of the account of this message—which is not said, indeed, to have had any result at all—becomes unsatisfactory in another point of view. If John, when the Greater One whom he had announced had begun his public ministry, and who had, moreover, now so expressly answered his doubts, was still at liberty, and not prevented from shewing his subjection to him, why did he not do so? He must, it was supposed, have done so, not, indeed, to the extent of giving up his own baptism and attaching himself to him—for that he did not do so, the continuance of his own school, which was kept so decidedly distinct from that of the followers of Jesus, was too significant a proof—but in such a manner, that instead of putting the question as to whether Jesus was he that should come in a doubting spirit, he answered himself and others in a spirit of the firmest faith, and made declarations of his relation to him, which must have removed all difficulty. The fourth Evangelist gave this turn to the narrative (i. 19—28), and in doing so not only followed Luke, as he does on many other occasions, but also continued and completed what Luke had left unfinished.

In Luke, the Baptist refers to a Mightier who was to come after him, and the motive for making this reference is stated to be the surmise, on the part of the people who flocked to him, that he might be the Messiah. Luke had also given it the more decisive meaning of a disavowal of the dignity, and a transference of it to the One who should come after him (iii. 15; comp. Acts xiii. 25). For the fourth Evangelist this was not quite official enough. It was not enough that the people should only have entertained that surmise quietly in their hearts; they must have expressed it in the form of a question put to the Baptist; and the people who so put it could not have been mere common crowds, but must have been emissaries of the Jewish government in Jerusalem, Priests and Levites, in order that Jesus might appeal to the declaration of the Baptist made to them as convincing human testimony. But here arose the difficulty, that a proceeding which was intelligible enough on the part of an unprejudiced and excitable mob, is, in the case of the Jewish hierarchs and their Pharisaic messengers, inconceivable. It is inconceivable that they should have offered to the Baptist, whose preaching of repentance could not possibly have been agreeable to them, and who had, moreover, expressly attacked the sect of the Pharisees, the titles in succession of the Messiah, of Elijah of that Prophet, in order, after all, to meet with a refusal. Not a hint is given by the Evangelist that they did this with a malicious intent—with the intent, that is, of seizing John in case he assumed the title, as they subsequently seized Jesus, of bringing him into suspicion with the Romans and dragging him to punishment. On the contrary, the object of the Evangelist seems simply to have been to represent John as refusing those titles; but he could only refuse them in case they were offered to him. In Luke he had only disclaimed the title of Messiah in favour of Jesus, while in all the Synoptics he is declared by Jesus himself to be in a certain sense Elijah, and a prophet in the highest sense (Matt. xvii. 12 ff.; comp. xi. 9, 14). In the fourth Gospel it was necessary that he should be represented as refusing the two last titles, partly in order to place himself still further below Jesus, partly because the view of the Baptist as another Elijah was too Jewish for the author.

But the fourth Evangelist has also managed to preserve the mission of the two disciples of John to Jesus, only in a form modified after his own fashion. In his Gospel, John sends two of his disciples to Jesus as he is passing by. He does this, not at a later period out of the prison, but soon after the baptism, and not with the doubting question as to whether he is the coming One, but with the decisive assertion that he is the Lamb of God who takes away sins. In the Synoptics, Jesus bids the messengers tell their master what they hear and see; here, in answer to the question of the two disciples as to where he dwells, he says, "Come and see." Upon this the two, instead of turning back to John, as the synoptic emissaries do, remain in the train of Jesus and bring to him other disciples (i. 35 ff.).

The question of the Baptist, as put by the two disciples in Matthew and Luke, standing as it does now in the account of those two Evangelists after the history of the Baptism, could only be understood as arising from doubt and difficulty. But the fourth Evangelist preferred modifying this feature and making it harmless, to leaving it uncorrected. The offence, therefore, was transferred to the disciples of the Baptist; they, and not their master, are said to have been offended at the fact, that he, who had formerly been on the Jordan following their master, is now attended by more people than John himself; and it is not Jesus who sends to John, but John himself gives to his disciples the explanation that solves the difficulty (iii. 22 ff.). The connection between the complaint of the disciples of John to their master and the dispute with a Jew about the purification, *i.e.* the purifying virtue of baptism (ii. 25), and John's comparison in his answer of Jesus with the bridegroom, and of himself to the bridegroom's friend (ver. 29), reminds us of another synoptic passage (Matt. ix. 14 ff.), where the disciples of John put to Jesus the question, why they and the Pharisees fast so much, and his disciples do not fast. Jesus answers them, that it is not fitting that the children of the bride-chamber mourn and fast, so long as the bridegroom is with them. This passage also has been touched up by the fourth, and a turn given to the comparison of Jesus to the bridegroom, such that the time of the bridegroom's presence is not, as in the Synoptics, contrasted with that when he will be taken away from his followers, *i.e.* the lifetime of Jesus with the time after his death, but the Bridegroom, *i.e.* the Son of God who came from heaven, with his forerunner, who is only of earthly extraction. When on the same occasion the Baptist declares himself to be he who must decrease as compared with Jesus who must increase, he says of himself the same, in reference to Jesus, as the author of the Books of Samuel says of Saul in reference to David (2 Sam. iii. 1); and that this declaration may have its full value as a voluntary self-subordination, it is expressly said that he had not yet been thrown into prison (ver. 24), so that he may appear to have laid down his arms at the feet of Jesus, while still at liberty and without compulsion.

The contradiction to Matthew, who does not represent this public ministry of Jesus as beginning until after the imprisonment of the Baptist, is here obvious; but beside this, the fourth Evangelist gives us a representation of the Baptist which corresponds neither with the description of him in the three first Gospels nor with historical probability, and can only be explained from the peculiar character of this Evangelist. It is true, indeed, that he gives us no description of the coarse exterior, the clothing and mode of life, of the Baptist. But this may be thought of the less importance, as he does apply to him the passage in the Prophet of the Voice in the wilderness, in the same way as the Synoptics do (i. 23). In the Synoptics his preaching consists of two parts: Repent, for the kingdom of heaven is at hand. John entirely omits the first part, in order to bring out the other at so much greater length, and in more free and lofty language. Like the Synoptics, he represents the Baptist as referring to a Mightier and Higher than he who should come after him; but the higher dignity of this personage is characterised with features which are foreign not only to the synoptic Baptist, but also to the range of thought of the Synoptics themselves. The statement that he is the Lamb who taketh away the sins of the world (John i. 29, 36), involves an application of the prophecy in Isaiah (liii. 4 ff.) to Jesus, which is not indeed unknown to the three first Evangelists, seeing as they do in the dying Jesus a sacrifice for many (Matt. xx. 28; Mark x. 25; comp. Matt. xxvi. 28): but it does not occur to them to ascribe to the Baptist a view which did not begin to dawn upon the disciples of Jesus until after his death. But the Baptist also declares in the fourth Gospel that Jesus who comes after him is only preferred before him because he had been before him (i. 15, 30), only stands above all because he comes from heaven and testifies upon earth what he had seen and heard there (iii. 31 ff.). Now this view of a heavenly pre-existence of Jesus before becoming man is foreign not only to the synoptic Baptist, but to the Synoptics themselves, and peculiar to the fourth Evangelist alone, who, in his subjective way, attributes it to his own Baptist, and, to leave no doubt as to its interpolation, puts into his mouth exactly the same expressions and turns of language as he had just before represented Jesus as using in his conversation with Nicodemus. Jesus had said to Nicodemus, "That which is born of the flesh is flesh; and that which is born of the spirit is spirit: we speak that we do know, and testify that we have seen, and ye receive not our witness" (iii. 6, 11). The Baptist says of Jesus, "He that is of the earth is earthly, and speaketh of the earth; he that cometh from heaven is above all, and what he hath seen and heard he testifieth, and no man receiveth his testimony" (iii. 31 ff.). Now, as in the fourth Gospel the Baptist, Jesus, and the Evangelist, where he introduces his own reflections, all move within the same round of thoughts and phrases, only three cases are here conceivable. Either Jesus as well as the Evangelist learnt this mode of thinking and speaking from the Baptist; or the Baptist as well as the Evangelist took it from Jesus; or, finally, the Evangelist lent his mode of thought and expression to Jesus as well as to the Baptist. The first supposition is opposed to that religious respect which is thought due to Jesus, and it is also opposed to historical probability, as the synoptic Gospels know nothing of such thoughts and expressions in the mouth of the Baptist, and speculations of this kind are not at all suited to his standpoint. The second, adopted, e.g. by Hengstenberg,* that the Apostle John not only copied his own mode of expression from that of Jesus, but also told his earlier teacher, John the Baptist, while he stayed with Jesus in his neighbourhood (John iii. 22 ff.), of the dialogue which the latter had just held with Nicodemus, and that the Baptist immediately appropriated the watchwords out of it—this, certainly, is far less natural and probable than the third, that the Evangelist represents both the Baptist and Jesus as speaking in the style in which he himself was accustomed to speak when he wished to utter his own deepest religious convictions, and that here in particular he puts the same thoughts and turns into the mouth of the Baptist as were still floating in his mind and

* In his Commentary on John.

ready to issue from his pen, after writing down immediately before the dialogue of Jesus with Nicodemus.

In the three first Gospels, also, the Baptist, in the spirit of the tendency of these writings, is engaged as the forerunner of the Messiah Jesus, but still in his austere preaching of repentance something of his own is left him. In the fourth Gospel, all independent existence is taken from him; he exists only as a witness to him who is to come after him, and, as it were, as a wooden sign-post: he is like the heroes of the most modern dramas with a purpose, which are deprived of every rationally human characteristic, stuffed out and crammed with the straw and chips of the subjective pathos of the composer.

SECOND GROUP OF MYTHS.

JESUS AND HIS DISCIPLES.

69.

Historically, it was known that there had been, among the most eminent disciples of Jesus, several fishermen and at least one publican. In reference to the first, also, the saying of Jesus had been preserved, that, instead of fishermen in the ordinary sense, he would make them fishers of men.

Now it was known, further, from the legends of the prophets in the Old Testament, how, *e.g.* Elijah was supposed to have called his servant and successor Elisha. The latter was ploughing and driving twelve oxen before him when the prophet threw his mantle over him; then Elisha left the oxen and followed Elijah (1 Kings xix. 19 ff.).

It is impossible, in considering this narrative, not to remember the well-known story in Roman history, relating how, when the perils of war became threatening, the emissaries of the Senate summoned L. Quinctius Cincinnatus from his little farm on the other side of the Tiber, where he had laid aside his toga, and was engaged in ploughing or making a ditch.* This may really have occurred, for it is agreeable to the simplicity of the ancient Roman habits that so eminent a man should have been cultivating his own ground, and that the Senate should have summoned him from this occupation to the dictatorship may be naturally explained from the fact, that he had already approved himself to his fellow-citizens in the discharge of several high offices. Still, even in this case a legendary origin of the story is possible, as the imagination is not merely attracted by the contrast between an humble material occupation and a call to an exalted position where such contrast really exists, but has a pleasure in inventing it even where it does not exist.

So also as regards the two biblical narratives, the supposition that an Elisha may have been previously a husbandman, a Peter and a John fishermen, involves no difficulty; and, so far, the history of their calls, in the form in which we read it, would not lie out of the range of historical probability. Only in this case there is one difference. These men were not summoned, like Cincinnatus, in consequence of the proofs of their competency which they had given to those who summoned them, but Elisha by an immediate divine command (ver. 16), the apostolic fishermen in virtue of the penetrating eye of the Messiah, by means of which he saw what was in men at the very first interview. The summoning of Cincinnatus, though at first sight surprising, is still a well-grounded, naturally-connected event; this natural ground is wanting to the call of the disciple of the prophet as well as to that of the Apostles; and thus, while in the case of the Roman narrative we only found it possible that it might be a legendary fiction, we recognise that character as really present in the other.

Several of the most distinguished disciples of Jesus may have been previously fishermen, and Jesus may have named

* Liv. iii. 26.

them, when he called them, fishers of men, in allusion to their earlier occupation; just as he compared the kingdom of heaven to a net in which fishes of every kind are caught (Matt. xiii. 47 ff.).. But he may also have so entitled them after they had long quitted their earlier trade; nay, he may even have used the expression that he would make them fishers of men when, after a longer acquaintance with them, he recognised their competency for the apostolical office, without such a scene having actually occurred as Matthew describes (iv. 18—22), and Mark (i. 16—20).

That, however, we have in this scene a product of legend, is clear, not merely from its similarity to the calling of the prophet in the Old Testament, but also from a remarkable difference between the two. Elisha had begged permission from Elijah, when he summoned him first, to say farewell to his parents, had received this permission at once, and did not follow Elijah until he had taken leave. In the evangelical narrative we find this feature withdrawn. The elevation of the Messiah above the mere prophets must, it was thought, be proved by the fact that, on the occasion of his summoning a follower to attend him, no such delay could be thought of. The fishermen called by Jesus follow him instantly and unconditionally; they quit not merely the occupation in which they are engaged at the moment, but the sons of Zebedee abandon their father, and Mark alone, in order not to leave him quite helpless, and so represent his sons as too neglectful, associates with him permanent hired servants. And this request for delay was not only omitted from this calling of Apostles, but, with a call that had succeeded, having been accepted at once by the persons called, these cases were contrasted which failed in consequence of a request for delay, or in which, at all events, this request must have been rejected. The significant words of Jesus, "Leave the dead to bury their dead," and, "No man, having put his hand to the plough, and looking back, is fit for the kingdom of God," must be supposed to have been uttered on occasion of such requests, when in the one case a person called had wished to bury his father, and another had expressed a wish to take leave of his friends (Matt. viii. 21 ff.; Luke ix. 59—62).

But a simple unmiraculous history, like that of the calling of the Apostles, as given in Matthew and Mark, who follow him, was far from satisfying the imagination of the primeval Christian circle. For us, indeed, it is miraculous enough that Jesus should, without hesitation, have called men to follow him whom, if we are to believe the narrative, he saw for the first time, or knew no more of than if he had, and that these men should also, without hesitation, have obeyed the call; but the devout listeners to evangelical preaching required more than this. The declaration of Jesus that he wished to make those who had been called fishers of men, was a mere verbal expression: at this turning-point of the evangelical history, on so eventful an occurrence as the calling of the first Apostles, a corresponding fact was wanted, a miracle that should at once strengthen and realise that expression. As already remarked, Jesus had compared the men whom he gained over to the kingdom of heaven to fishes that had been caught, the kingdom of heaven itself to a net thrown into the sea; if, therefore, caught fishes meant converted men, a miraculously rich draught of fishes which Jesus now gave to his disciples, was the symbol of the numerous conversions to faith in him which those disciples were subsequently to succeed in making. The narrative appears in this modified form in Luke (v. 1—11), who accordingly omits the simple narrative of the calling in the two first Evangelists. He places it a little later, and introduces it in a different manner. In Matthew and Mark, Jesus, walking about on the shore of the Sea of Galilee, sees first the brothers Simon and Andrew throwing their nets, calls upon them, as he stands upon the shore, to follow him as fishers of men, whereupon they leave their nets and join him;

then he sees likewise James and John, with their father Zebedee, in the ship, occupied with mending their nets, and calls them to him with the same result. In the corresponding passage in Luke, he sees, while teaching on the seashore, and thronged by the number of his listeners, two ships, one of which belonged to Peter, the other to the two sons of Zebedee, who were occupied together on the land with washing their nets; he embarks on board one of these, orders Simon (Andrew is not mentioned in the narrative of Luke) to put off a little from the shore, and thus, sitting in the ship, instructs the multitude; after finishing his lecture, he calls upon Peter to go out into a deeper place, and to throw out his net for fish. Peter, though demurring on the ground of their unsuccessful labour during the past night, consents, on the command of Jesus, to make the attempt, and now, in conjunction with his sailors, he catches such a quantity of fish, that not only does the net break, but, while they are emptying a portion of their booty into the ship of the sons of Zebedee, both craft threaten to sink. Upon this, the surprise of the people, and especially of Peter, at such a miracle, almost borders upon terror; but Jesus pacifies the latter by telling him that from henceforth he shall catch men, and in consequence of this, the men leave all and follow him. On reading this, we see on the one hand that we have, only in a miraculous form, the same narrative as in Matthew and Mark; and, on the other, there can be no doubt that the miracle is symbolical, and, in accordance with the parable of Jesus already quoted, realises, under the image of a great draught of fishes, that ministry of the Apostles which followed, and which was so richly blessed.

And then it becomes a question whether we ought not to go further, and look for symbolical allusions even in separate features of the narrative. When Peter meets the command of Jesus to move out into deeper water, and then to throw out the nets, with the mention of the ill success of their work during the past night, and then, following that command, gets so large a draught, we may at first sight find nothing in this but the contrast between the poor material produce of their ordinary trade and the rich spiritual fruit of the higher calling imposed upon them by Jesus; and so likewise the tearing of the net, and the necessary partition of the booty between two ships, may be taken only as a picturesque indication of the magnitude of the draught. But is it not possible that the author of the third Gospel, who is also the author of the Acts of the Apostles, when he speaks of the toil of the apostolical fishers of men, which was at first fruitless, and then, when they repeat it at the command of Jesus, was so richly blessed, may have had in his mind the slight success of evangelical preaching among the Jews, and the result of it, favourable beyond expectation, among the heathen;* when he speaks of the tearing of Peter's net in consequence of the enormous draught, he may have referred to the threatening schism in the Church in consequence of the ministry of Paul; and in the partition of the draught into two boats, may have alluded to the rise of the heathen Christian Churches by the side of the Jewish Christian? This is a question deserving of all consideration, and which may perhaps, by comparison with a further narrative, obtain still further light.

The fourth Gospel, in its supplementary chapter (xxi. 1—14), has also a miraculous draught of fishes, and the fact that it places this, not, as the third does, at the beginning of the public life of Jesus, but at the extreme end of his walk on earth, in the days of his resurrection, will not prevent us, any more than many other such discrepancies, from seeing in it nothing but a modification of the draught of fishes in Luke. With this narrative the author has interwoven traits from two other miraculous accounts, the Walking on the Sea and the Feeding; but in this place these features, the basis of

---

* Comp. Volkmar, Religion of Jesus, p. 316.

the whole, namely, the moving about of the risen Jesus, being miraculous, appear as in themselves divested of their miraculous character: Jesus does not walk upon the sea, which would not have been anything remarkable in the case of a person who had risen from the grave, but stands upon the shore, and Peter does not attempt to go upon the waters, but swims over in an ordinary manner, and subsequently the bread and the fish are there, how we know not, but without anything being said of miraculous production or increase. But even apart from these admixtures, the history of the draught of fishes appears changed in many ways. Besides Peter and the sons of Zebedee, Thomas and Nathanael are also here, and two disciples, not named, also; the narrative, moreover, does not, like that of Luke, begin on the day following the night of the unsuccessful toil, but accompanies Peter and his companions to their fruitless work during the night, and represents Jesus as appearing first, not during the course of the next day, but at the very first dawn of the morning. But where it is said of those who had gone forth to fish, "That night they caught nothing" (ver. 3), exactly as in Luke, Peter answered the Lord, "We have toiled all night and taken nothing" (ver. 5); and when, in the morning, Jesus, on the disciples answering in the negative his question as to whether they had anything to eat, calls upon them to throw out the net on the right side of the ship, and they shall find (ver. 6), as in Luke he orders Simon to push out into deeper water and to let down the net into the water for the draught (ver. 4); and where, according to both accounts, they get so rich a one that the blessing becomes a burthen to them—it is impossible to mistake, in the two accounts, a variation upon the same theme.

The discrepancies which appear in the description of the successful result confirm this conclusion instead of weakening it. Luke only speaks of a great multitude of fishes, but the author of John xxi. gives their number definitely at 153, and large fishes too; according to Luke, their multitude and weight tears the net; in John, it is only said they were not able to draw it up, not that it was torn, notwithstanding the multitude of the fishes; lastly, in Luke, the fishes are divided between the two boats, which threaten to sink in consequence, while in John they are drawn in the net to the shore. In reference to the number 153, there is a remarkable observation of the learned father of the Church, Hieronymus. "The "writers," he observes,* "upon the nature and characteristics "of animals, and among them the excellent Cilician poet, "Oppian, say that there are 153 species of fishes; all these "were caught by the Apostles, and none were uncaught, just "as great and small, rich and poor, all sorts of men, were "drawn to happiness out of the sea of this world." Hieronymus, therefore, considers the number 153 as that of all species of fishes adopted by the writers on natural history of that time, especially by Oppian. And in the fact that exactly this number of fishes were caught by the Apostles at that time, he sees a prophetic symbol of men of all kinds being incorporated by the preaching of the Apostles into the kingdom of God. Now as regards Oppian, in his poem upon fishing—written, however, according to the most probable supposition, in the last year of Marcus Aurelius, and therefore later than the fourth Gospel—we do not find any exact number of the species of fish given; and if we count their numbers, we may, according as we take in or not the subdivisions into which many of the same species may be distributed, and count similar names twice or not, possibly make out 153, but also quite as easily more or less. Hieronymus, however, only refers to Oppian among others, and therefore there is still a probability that in some writer on natural history, now lost, that number may have been more definitely given.

Be this, however, as it may, it is clear from another feature

---

* Comment. upon Ezekiel, 47.

in which the narrative of John differs from that of Luke, that the fishes thus caught have a symbolical reference to the men to be incorporated in the kingdom of God. In Luke, the net splits; in John, it is expressly stated that, in spite of the multitude of fishes, it did not split. At first sight, indeed, this only looks like an exaggeration or completion of the miracle, as we must suppose that he who gave the fishes could also give the net the supernatural strength required to hold them. Meanwhile, we observe that this non-tearing of the net is peculiar to the supplement of the same Gospel, which (with the same Greek word, and that too the word from which Schism, *i.e.* division of the Church, is derived) says also of the coat of Jesus that it was not rent (xix. 24), and which attaches so much importance to the combination into one flock of the sheep out of two folds, that is, of the Christians from among the Jews and the Heathen (x. 16); and observing this, we can scarcely avoid seeing in the non-tearing of the net on occasion of the great draught, the symbol of the assumption that the entrance of the Heathen into the kingdom of Christ is to produce no schism; that, as the author of the Epistle to the Colossians expresses himself (iii. 11), there is no longer here either Greek or Jew, circumcision or uncircumcision, no longer barbarian or Scythian, slave or free, but Christ is all in all. There is also a suitable connection between this supposition and the fact that, in the narrative of John, one ship only, from first to last, is spoken of; consequently no distribution of the first into two, as in Luke, but the whole draught is dragged to the neighbouring shore, in order to be laid at the feet of Jesus. Between the date of the composition of the third Gospel, together with the Acts, and that of the fourth and its supplementary chapter, the development of the relations between different parties had made such progress, that the peaceful juxtaposition of a Jewish and Gentile Christendom was no longer considered sufficient, but it was the wish of the Church to present itself to Christ on his second advent as one and undivided.

But it was known, moreover, that besides the fishermen, among the more confidential disciples of Jesus, there had been also among them one or two publicans; and it was also known that, on the part of Pharisaically disposed Jews, much offence had been taken at the harmless intercourse of Jesus with people of this class.

Now the transition of a fisherman from his former trade to the discipleship of Jesus may have taken place in many ways, without the necessity of Jesus summoning him away from the act of casting or mending his net. But the legend chose only the latter form, as being the most picturesque. Thus, also, the same thing may have happened in one way or another, quite gradually and naturally, in the case of a publican. But the course of the legend was exactly the same in the one case and in the other. As Jesus had seen the fishermen in the boat with their nets, so must he have seen the publican sitting at the seat of custom; as he called the former, so must he have called the latter, to follow him, whereupon, as the fisherman had done in the former case, so in this the publican left all and followed Jesus (Matt. ix. 9 ff.; Mark ii. 13 ff.; Luke v. 27 ff.). In this case there is no such expression recorded corresponding to that descriptive of the relation which the fisherman's future occupation is to bear to their past one, namely, that of "fishers of men," but the other circumstance, historically well known, that much offence had been taken at the friendly intercourse of Jesus with publicans, was brought in here, and thus a phrase, though of a different kind, was gained for the embellishment of the scene. Jesus certainly may have dined with the publicans whom he found susceptible of his influence, without having previously summoned them directly from the seat of custom. But still, when once such a history of the calling had gained ground, the publican's dinner, with the expression of Jesus, "I am not come to call the righteous, but sinners to repentance," and "the whole need not a physician, but the sick," were admirably adapted to be connected with it.

The publican thus called by Jesus is named in the first Gospel Matthew. Referring to the history of his call, the catalogue of the Apostles describes him as the publican (x. 3). Mark and Luke give him the name of Levi. They have no person of this name in their catalogue of the Apostles, but the name of Matthew is found there as well as in the others, without, however, being described as the publican—a proof that they did not refer this history of the call to him, as they would have done if their Levi had had the surname of Matthew. As, however, histories of "calls" were narrated without names (Luke ix. 59 ff.), because the words of them were considered as of principal importance, there might also in another case be a variation in the name, and the more readily in one like that before us, where the history of the "call" comes in only as an introduction to the scene and speeches on the occasion of the publican's dinner.

Another entertainment at the house of a publican is peculiar to the third Gospel. It is placed in the last period of the life of Jesus, when he was passing through Jericho on the road to Jerusalem (Luke xix. 1—10), where, moreover, all the Synoptics represent the healing of a blind man to have occurred. The publican, of the name of Zaccheus, is not an ordinary personage, but a chief among the publicans and rich: he is not sitting at the receipt of custom till Jesus calls him; but when he hears of his approach he rises up to see the great performer of miracles, which he cannot do, because of the press and being little of stature, without climbing a mulberry-tree on the road. There Jesus sees him, bids him come down in haste, because he must on that day abide in his house; and Zaccheus obeys his call, not only overjoyed at it, but also declaring himself ready to give liberally to the poor, and to restore in full measure anything that he has wronged any man of. Upon this Jesus, in answer to the Jews who murmur, palliates his assertion that salvation had that day come to that house, by referring to the fact that the publican also was a son of Abraham, and ends with the words, that the Son of Man was come to seek and to save that which was lost. That reference to Abraham has been considered as an indication of a Jewish-Christian source, from which Luke may have drawn.* It would, however, be quite in accordance with his manner if he understood the words, "Son of Abraham," in a Pauline sense (as in Galat. iii. 7 ff.), according to which faith in Christ stamped even a Heathen (whom the publican resembled) with the character of a Son of Abraham.

70.

The fourth Evangelist also speaks of a fig-tree, and of Jesus having observed one, who subsequently became a disciple, not indeed upon, but under it; and as in Luke Zaccheus, after having come down from the tree and disclaimed all unrighteous gain, is declared by Jesus to be a Son of Abraham who is saved, so in John, Jesus calls Nathanael, after having seen him under the fig-tree, a true Israelite in whom there is no guile. The mode, however, in which Jesus sees Nathanael is not, as in the case of Zaccheus, a natural, but a supernatural sight, and is recognised by the person so seen as a complete proof of the Sonship of God in Jesus.

This, however, apart from the fact that in the case of Zaccheus no "call" to discipleship in the narrower sense is in question, is the only resemblance between the histories of calls in the three first Evangelists and those in the fourth. The fourth Evangelist also describes the beginning of the acquaintanceship between Jesus on the one hand, and Peter

* Köstlin, Synoptic Gospels, p. 223.

and Andrew on the other, and probably, though without naming him, of Jesus with John. On the other hand, the name of James is not found either here or throughout the Gospel, except in the supplementary chapter. Instead of him, Philip is mentioned, whom we also find in the catalogues of the Apostles in the Synoptics, and Nathanael, who had been already named, and who is known only to the fourth Gospel. Mention is also made of the manner in which they came into connection with Jesus. All the more immediate circumstances are different in John from the other Gospels.

In the first place, if we had merely the fourth Gospel, we should have no inkling whatever of any of the disciples of Jesus having been previously fishers or publicans (apart, again, from the supplementary chap. xxi.). On the contrary, it informs us that one of them, and he the one who is of the greatest importance in the author's view, had been an acquaintance of the High-priest (xviii. 15)—a fact of which the three first have not the slightest knowledge. Quite as little as of the secret discipleship of Nicodemus, the ruler of the Jews (iii. 1 ff.), and of the fact that, generally, as the fourth Gospel states, many of the chief rulers believed Jesus, though secretly only, from fear of the Pharisees (xii. 42).

The fact that the preaching of Christianity found at first a response mostly among the lower orders of the people, that not many rich in worldly goods, not many of the powerful and great, were to be found among the first believers, might be accounted for by the consideration that Christianity, when opposed to the wisdom of the world, appeared only all the more as a divine revelation (Matt. xi. 25 ff.; 1 Cor. i. 25 ff.). On the other hand, however, the reproach of the opponents of Christianity, as we find it in Celsus,* about the middle of the second century, that Jesus had as his disciples only abandoned men, publicans, and sailors of the lowest kind, contained a story which became the more painful in propor-

* Orig. c. Cels.

tion as Christianity gradually penetrated into the higher circles of society. It may, therefore, only appear natural that a Gospel, the product of a highly-educated mind, intended also to satisfy Christians of superior rank and cultivation, should have taken up a different position with reference to that fact. The allegation that none of the Rulers or Pharisees, but only the lowest of the people, believed in Jesus, is indeed put into the mouth of the Pharisees as an unrefuted reproach (vii. 48 ff.), and thus the objective fact is necessarily recognised: but we are also assured that many of the Elders of the people (provided they were not Pharisees) believed in Jesus inwardly and in their hearts, but kept their belief secret for fear of the condemnation of the Pharisees, and, like Nicodemus, chose the night time for their interviews with Jesus (xii. 42, xix. 38 ff.). It agrees with this that of the Apostles it is the favourite disciple who is raised to a higher sphere by his acquaintance with the High-priest, and in the case of the others no mention at least is ever made of their earlier career as fishermen or publicans.

When the obvious motives for representing the call of the disciples as having summoned them from fishing and the seat of custom disappeared, so much the more did the Baptist present himself to the fourth Evangelist as the agent who must have brought about the connection between Jesus and his first disciples. The disciples were exalted if, instead of coming from a low industrious occupation, they came out of the preparatory school of the Baptist. And the more the fourth Evangelist represented him only as the forerunner of Christ, so much the more natural was it that beside the people, some of whom continued in unbelief, some came only to a half imperfect faith, he should have introduced to Christ the first of the true and entire believers, the Apostles. So when he had described to the multitude gathered round him that Jesus, who was approaching him, as the Lamb of God that taketh away the sins of the world, he then, the next day, when Jesus is passing by, a second time repeats the same description in the presence of two of his own disciples, with the result that both follow Jesus, ask him where he dwells, are invited by him to come and see for themselves, continue the remainder of the day with him, and also, we must suppose, remain always after in his company (i. 35 ff.). From this first stem, so far as the Evangelist informs us of the manner in which the disciples come together, grows, branch by branch, the company of Jesus' disciples. Andrew, one of the two to whom John points out Jesus, brings his brother Simon to Jesus; Philip, whom, as it would appear, the fact of his being the countryman of the two brothers just named puts in the way of Jesus, is called by him himself; and Philip, again, brings Nathanael to him.

As the fishing had disappeared, so also does the expression about fishers of men. Instead of this expression, which in Matthew and Mark is referred to the two sons of Jonas, and which, moreover, Luke had represented as having been applied only to Simon, the Evangelist introduces here one that applies only to Simon, in the addition of the name of Peter. This the two older Evangelists represent as coming considerably later, after long acquaintance of Jesus with the disciple. John, with great improbability, represents the name as having been given on the first meeting of the two, and in such a manner that Jesus would appear to have taken a supernatural view not merely of his character as Peter, or the Rock, but also of the name he bore as a citizen and son of his father (ver. 42). Quite as supernaturally he discovers at a distance the guilelessness of Nathanael when approaching him, and as a proof of his ability to do this he appeals to the fact that before Nathanael came within his natural range of sight he saw him under the fig-tree. The attempt to explain the former from physiognomical knowledge of the human countenance, the latter as casual and transient observation, is absurd in the presence of a Gospel which expressly says of the Jesus who is described in it that he did not consider it necessary that any one should testify to him about men, as he himself knew what was in man (ii. 25); it was but a slight thing for a Jesus who had seen God before the world began, to have seen Nathanael under the fig-tree before Philip called him.

It is well to pay especial attention to the changes which the fourth Evangelist has made in the order in which the first disciples attached themselves to Jesus. In Matthew and Mark, Jesus first calls the two sons of Jonas, of whom Simon has the precedence, then the two sons of Zebedee, James having the precedence. In Luke, from first to last, Simon only does anything, Andrew is not named at all, James and John only supplementarily as Simon's helpers. In the fourth Gospel, only two nameless disciples are first spoken of, who, on the Baptist pointing out Jesus, follow him (i. 35—37); we then discover (i. 41) one of these to have been Andrew, the other continues in the obscurity of his incognito, which in the course of the Gospel gradually clears, so far that John comes out more and more plainly. Peter, therefore, who stands foremost in all the other accounts, is not in this Gospel even one of the pair first called, but it is composed of Andrew and the supposed John. And it is only by the agency of his brother Andrew, who everywhere else is second to him, and is altogether passed over by Luke in the history of the call, that Peter is brought into connection with Jesus; while James, John's brother, who is everywhere else, when they are named together, named before him, is not mentioned either here or all through the Gospel. The prince of the Apostles does indeed receive his traditional honour in the addition of the name of Peter; but his claim to be the first-born of the Apostles is altogether disallowed, in favour indeed, to some extent, of his brother, but at the same time of the unnamed party who throughout the whole Gospel is at his side and pushes himself before him before he is aware. We have here the first intimation of a cleverly-laid plan, of the greatest importance, indeed, for the understanding of the fourth Gospel, but only to be explained without compromising the character of its author, if that author is *not* John. If not, then what tells in favour of this Apostle is not said by himself for himself, but for a principle represented by the author, of which principle the chief support is John.* Let us examine this relation a little more accurately.

In the time of the Apostle Paul, we find the three men, James, Cephas, and John, spoken of as the three pillars of the primeval Church at Jerusalem (Galatians ii. 9). That powerful James cannot have been the son of Zebedee, for he had been already put to death (Acts xii. 2). If, therefore, he was one of the Twelve, he must have been the other James of our lists of the Apostles, the son of Alpheus. But the ambiguous phrase in Galatians (i. 19) leaves it uncertain whether he was an Apostle or not; but he is here called a brother of the Lord, by which term, if we look upon him as the Apostle James the son of Alpheus, only a cousin of Jesus might be meant. According to what was said above, it is more probable to me that he was a real brother of Jesus, and in that case not one of the Twelve. And thus also the following phenomenon may be explained. In the three first Evangelists, as well as in the Epistle to the Galatians, we find the same names at the head of the disciples, Peter, James, and John. But in the synoptic Gospels, James is not the brother of the Lord, but the brother of John, the son of Zebedee. It is conceivable, certainly, that Jesus considered these three men as the most faithful or the most competent of the Apostles, thought them deserving of his particular confidence, and treated them as it were a select committee of the college of Twelve. The instances, indeed, which the

* According to Renan, vexation at not having been brought forward with sufficient prominence was, in fact, one of John's principal motives for writing an additional Gospel himself.

Synoptics give of his having done so are, historically, more than doubtful. He is said to have taken them apart on the occasion of his Transfiguration on the mountain, on that of the Agony in Gethsemane, and on that of the raising of the daughter of Jairus,—mysterious occurrences, at which the narrators intend to imply that only persons of advanced religious culture, and more deeply initiated than others, were present. We are naturally here reminded of the old story in Clement of Alexandria, that it was to James, John, and Peter, that the Lord delivered, after his resurrection, the Gnosis, an esoteric doctrine.* The James of whom Clement here speaks is not indeed the son of Zebedee, but, according to his description, James the Just, *i.e.* the brother of the Lord; but how close these two came together in the tradition of the Church, how, to a certain extent, they changed places with each other, is clear from another expression of the same Clement, in which he praises the three Apostles, Peter, James (son of Zebedee), and John, for having, with a modesty that did them honour, refrained from electing one of themselves Bishop of Jerusalem, and appointed James the Just to that office.† The evangelical triumvirate, therefore, Peter, James, and John, appears to be a reflection of the later and historical one of the same names; and it was only the notorious fact that, in the lifetime of Jesus, James, the brother of the Lord, was not one of his disciples, that necessitated the introduction of another James instead of him, who was known as one of the Twelve.

It is well known that the distinguished historical triumvirate was disposed to strict Judaism; it was only with difficulty that Paul could get them to recognise him in his ministry as an Apostle of the Heathen (Galat. ii. 1—10), and even afterwards he was kept in continual conflict with the adherents of the triumvirate, especially those of James (Galat. ii. 12). It formed the rallying-point of Jewish Christianity; and again

* Eusebius, Church History, ii. 1—4. † Eusebius as quoted, iii.

one of the supports of the triumvirate itself was the distinguished position which the synonymous triumvirate was supposed to have held in the lifetime of Christ. However ironically Paul may have spoken of those three supposed pillars of the Church, they continued even after his death to be obstacles to progress, as long as two of them, the same personally, the third as a synonymous double, occupied in the evangelical tradition the position nearest to the person of Christ. In order to make a breach for progress, it was necessary that the triumvirate should be broken, and this the fourth Evangelist undertook to do.

By a bold stroke he seized hold of John above every one else, for the purposes of carrying out the opposing spiritual tendency. For a bold stroke it was, indeed madly so, in presence of the Apocalypse and historical record; so he proceeded with the greatest caution. Throughout the Gospel he never names John, he only lets him be guessed at. First he introduces in the most unobtrusive manner an unnamed party with Andrew (i. 35—41), who, however, can be neither Peter, nor Philip, nor Nathanael, as these are distinguished from him, as having come to Jesus subsequently. Then, when further on Peter, Andrew, Philip, Thomas, have been spoken of by name, some of them repeatedly, we meet at the last supper of Jesus an unnamed disciple, whom Jesus loved, who also at table lay on Jesus' bosom, and to whom Peter makes a sign to ask Jesus something (xiii. 23 ff.). After the arrest of Jesus, it is "another disciple" who, as an acquaintance of the High-priest, procures for Peter the entrance into the palace (xviii. 15). Then, beneath the Cross, we again meet with the disciple whom Jesus loved (xix. 26), who, as an eye-witness, accredits the wound in the side of Jesus (ver. 35), and immediately afterwards we are given to understand that this favourite disciple and that "other disciple," consequently and without doubt the nameless one who just at the beginning was introduced with

Andrew, are one and the same person (xx. 2). Lastly, in the supplement to the Gospel, among seven disciples, some named, some not named, the disciple whom Jesus loved, and who at the last Supper had lain upon his bosom, appears and is indicated as the author of the Gospel (xxi. 7, 20, 24). But no name is given even here, and it cannot be strictly proved out of the fourth Gospel in itself that by the disciple so mysteriously alluded to we are to understand John to have been meant at all. A comparison with the three first Gospels might help us a little if anything which in the fourth Gospel is ascribed to "the other," or to the favourite disciple, was told in them of John; but this is not the case. Still the tradition of the Church has undoubtedly apprehended aright the meaning of the author in having always looked upon this nameless disciple as John. For if the first readers of the Gospel were to understand who was meant, he must have been an Apostle very well known and much respected in the country in which it appeared; and in Asia Minor, and especially in Ephesus, to which both external and internal evidence point as the cradle of the fourth Gospel, this was pre-eminently John. The later supplement, indeed, alone says expressly that the nameless disciple was at the same time the author of the Gospel, but even the Gospel itself intends, most probably, to give its readers to understand the same thing (xix. 35). But this John of the fourth Gospel is no longer the Judaizing Pillar-Apostle, who gave Paul so much trouble; but as the bosom disciple of the Johannine Christ, as author, or at all events voucher-man, of the Johannine Gospel, he is made the propagator of a spiritual, universal Christianity, advanced beyond that even of Paul himself. And John, thus spiritualized, is taken out of the synoptic triumvirate, and, as the favourite disciple, is placed above all the rest, in a sense of which the three first Gospels are entirely ignorant.

Of the two other members of the triumvirate, James has absolutely disappeared. As regards the brother of the Lord, the James of the historical triumvirate, there is no Gospel in which it is said so expressly as in the fourth that the brothers of Jesus did not believe in him. Of their subsequent belief, either the author took no notice, or intended to intimate that their Judaizing faith was no better than no faith at all. In any case, as his Jesus, speaking from the Cross, presents the disciple whom he loved to his mother as her son, and the latter takes her under his protection at once (xix. 26), John, according to Baur's acute observation, is put in the place of the brothers of Jesus, especially of James, and the bosom disciple is at the same time declared to be the true spiritual brother of the Lord. Having thus set aside the Judaizing brother of the Lord, the fourth Evangelist had no further motive for bringing forward into prominence, as the Synoptics do, James the son of Zebedee, and would even have counteracted his own purpose if he had done so; thus we can understand his silence about him, a silence which, on the supposition that the author of the Gospel was really John, the brother of this James, is not intelligible by any turn of apologetic theology, however subtle.

The author of the fourth Gospel found no difficulty in avoiding the name of James, as the brother of the Lord had not, in the lifetime of Jesus, belonged to his nearest circle, and the son of Zebedee had been put to death at an early period, and had long since fallen into oblivion, at least in the tradition of the churches out of Palestine. But Peter could not be thus dealt with. He, in the lifetime of Jesus, had been famous as one of his most confidential disciples; now he was the head of Jewish Christianity, and, especially since his name had been brought into connection with Rome, the capital of the world, continued to labour in the Church, and therefore also lived in her traditions. A Gospel silent about Peter would have been no Gospel at all, and a Gospel attempting to deprive him of the distinguishing characteristics usually associated with his image could only have found a response in very limited and distant circles. This had been well considered by the fourth Evangelist. So he does not deprive the prince of the Apostles of any of his traditional honours; informs his readers both of the famous surname which Jesus assigns to him (i. 43), and of the strong confession of faith of which before all the Apostles he delivers himself (vi. 68 ff., comp. Matt. xvi. 16); represents him as coming forward in action quite as often as the other Evangelists do—nay, on some occasions even oftener; but still he is adroit enough almost always to append to these advantageous characteristics, and the more as the history approaches nearer to its conclusion, a slight "but" which disparages them, or he shares them between Peter and his own hero John in a way which gives an advantage to the latter. Thus there is indeed much beauty in the zeal with which Peter, on the occasion of the first supper, first of all will not hear of the washing of the disciples' feet by Jesus, and then desires to have both his hands and his head washed by him (xiii. 6—10); but there appears at the same time in this jump from one extreme to the other, a violence which passes over the deep meaning of the act of Jesus without any fine perception of its meaning. Likewise all the Evangelists do indeed tell of a disciple who, on the occasion of the arrest of Jesus, cut off the ear of a servant of the Highpriest, but the fourth is the only one who names Peter as the disciple who did it (xviii. 10). And in doing so he invests him with another characteristic of that carnal zeal which made it more difficult for him to penetrate into the spirit of his Master.

But the subtle calculation of the fourth Evangelist shews itself first in those cases in which he places his other or favourite disciple in juxtaposition with Peter. Above we have started from a case in which, like the Synoptics, he makes Peter come into connection with Jesus among the four first,—not, however, as the first of all, but the third, while the supposed John is among the first; Peter being called not immediately by Jesus, but by the agency of one of the two first. This agent is here his brother Andrew; in other cases it is the favourite disciple. The Hellenes, who at the last Passover wished to make the acquaintance of Jesus, apply, not to Peter, but to Philip, and he to Andrew, both then to Jesus (xii. 20 ff.). In like manner, Peter himself, in order to extract from Jesus which of his disciples he intends to indicate as his betrayer, is obliged to bespeak the mediation of the favourite disciple who is lying on Jesus' bosom. After the arrest of Jesus, Peter does indeed follow him, even in the fourth Gospel, into the palace of the High-priest; but not only does the other disciple also go in with him, a fact unknown to the other Gospels, but it is he to whom, by means of his acquaintance with the High-priest, Peter is obliged to apply before he can get leave to enter (xviii. 15). On the occasion of the crucifixion and death of Jesus, Matthew and Mark represent only the women who came with him from Galilee as being spectators. Luke, indeed, adds all his acquaintances, but only at a distance (Matt. xxvii. 55 ff.; Mark xv. 40 ff.; Luke xxiii. 49). The fourth Evangelist places the women with the mother of Jesus near the Cross, and associates with them here the favourite disciple, in order to bring him, by means of the mother of Jesus, into a very peculiar relation to the latter, of which we have spoken above. But the proceeding of our Evangelist is most remarkable in the history of the Resurrection, in which he places the favourite disciple in juxtaposition with Peter, who, according to Luke, runs to the grave, and in an underhand manner deprives the latter of his rank (xx. 2—9),—a proceeding which the author of the supplementary chapter has imitated in the account of the draught of fishes (xxi. 7).

Reviewing from this point the accounts of the "calls," we can no longer think of attempting to reconcile those of the Synoptics and John of the mode in which the first disciples became connected with Jesus, as, on the contrary, we recognise in the latter a remodelling of those of the Synoptics in the spirit of the peculiar position and tendency of the Gospel of John. We may, however, congratulate ourselves on being elevated by this knowledge above the apologetic tricks and artifices by which it is intended to be made intelligible how the same men, after having been introduced to Jesus by the Baptist, or like Peter through his brother, and having already attached themselves to him, are said to have been called upon by him to follow him, as if they had been altogether strangers. In Matthew and Mark, Jesus says to Simon and Andrew, "Follow me." By these words a continuous attachment is confessedly implied. Undoubtedly also nothing else can be intended, when in John he says to Philip, "Follow me." In like manner, the two first Evangelists, as well as the fourth, say of Andrew and John that they followed Jesus. And manifestly the one account as well as the other intends it to be understood that they immediately accompanied Jesus as disciples; and there could have been as little need of a further calling, as stated in Matthew and Mark, after the act of attachment recounted in John, as after the former call and the success that attended it those men can have been unacquainted with Jesus until introduced by the Baptist to him.

THIRD GROUP OF MYTHS.

JESUS AS A PERFORMER OF MIRACLES.

71. MIRACLES OF JESUS. CURES OF THE BLIND.

The miracles which our Gospels speak of Jesus having performed might be divided into two, or, if we will, into three classes, according as they are said to have been performed on human beings or on lifeless nature, and the first on the human organism either dead or diseased.

With regard to the first class, the cures of the sick, we have already in an earlier investigation* admitted that supposed miracles of this sort may sometimes have been really performed by Jesus, though only in a manner perfectly natural. As the Jewish people expected from a Prophet, and still more from the Messiah, miracles, especially miraculous cures, and Jesus was considered a Prophet, and subsequently the Messiah,—it would, we said, have been extraordinary if many sick persons when in his presence, on being accosted and touched by him, had not really felt themselves relieved, and either permanently or transiently better. We thought this more intelligible in proportion as the sufferings of these persons were open to physiological influence, consequently more so in the case of persons afflicted with mental, nervous, and even muscular diseases, than with diseases of the skin or deprivation of a sense; while in the case of those who were already dead, or those of extra-human natural objects, every explanation of that kind entirely failed. The explanation of miraculous narratives of this latter description must be looked for, not in psychology and physiology, but in the history of religion; it lies in the Jewish and original Christian expectations of the Messiah; and as even those cures of Jesus which we recognise as naturally possible would not have succeeded had not the power to perform them been attributed to him as a Prophet, the distinction between the two classes is only this, that in consequence of Jewish expectations Jesus considered to be the Messiah, or at all events a Prophet, was really instrumental in introducing one portion of those effects, while an incomparably larger portion was subsequently attributed to him in the legend.

We have already learnt the prophetic programme which lies at the bottom of the miracles told of Jesus; it is in the

* First Book, § 42.

words in Isaiah (xxxv. 5 ff.): "Then the eyes of the blind shall be opened, and the ears of the deaf shall be unstopped; then shall the lame man leap as an hart, and the tongue of the dumb sing." This passage, though it stands in the first section of the oracles of Isaiah, still, like the second, belongs to the period at the end of the captivity, and describes how, from joy at the permission to return, the poor exiles shall forget all their sorrows, shall feel themselves healed of all their maladies. But as all these prophecies, when with the return from captivity the expected period of bliss did not occur, were extended in their application to the Messianic age, the ideas of which were continually taking a form more and more supernatural, so the prophecies originally intended to be only symbolical, of the blind regaining their sight, of the leaping of the lame, and so on, were, in the sequel, understood actually and literally of the miracles of the future Messiah, and our evangelical narratives of the miracles are for the most part only illustrations of the passage of the Prophet so understood. This passage, moreover, as applied by Jesus to himself, underwent certain modifications upon which we must remark. Jesus (Matt. xi. 5) directs the emissaries of the Baptist to tell the latter what they see and hear as being performed by him. "The blind receive their sight and the lame walk, the lepers are cleansed and the deaf hear, and the dead are raised up." In the first place, therefore, the dumb who are mentioned in the passage of the Prophet are not mentioned in the speech of Jesus, though undoubtedly they are comprised among the deaf whom he names, because both maladies frequently appear in connection, and in the Gospels the deaf, cured by Jesus, are generally at the same time described as dumb (Matt. ix. 32; Mark vii. 32 ff.). On the other hand, there is nothing said in the passage of Isaiah of the cleansing of lepers and raising of the dead of which Jesus speaks; but miracles of both kinds are found in the legends of the Prophets in the Old Testament. Elisha cured a leper, and he, like his master

Elijah, raised a dead man. The expulsion of evil spirits, which plays so large a part in the evangelical accounts of miracles, is not mentioned either in the passage in Isaiah or in the legend of the Prophets, because in those early times "possession" was not yet the order of the day; it is wanting, also, in the speech of Jesus, which had only to enumerate as fulfilled by him those prophecies, or types of miracle, the fulfilment of which was to be expected from the Old Testament.

For the production, therefore, of the evangelical accounts of miracles, there have, from the first, been two factors at work, which may be distinguished as an ideal and a real factor. What is said in the passage in Isaiah of the cures of the blind, the deaf, and the lame, interpret it as we will, is in no way to be understood of a miraculous restoration, but non-literally and ideally; on the other hand, the acts of Elijah and Elisha are told as real actual miracles, and the later Jewish conceptions of the Messiah expected the same from him.* In like manner, in the speech of Jesus, Matt. xi. 5, the cures and raisings were, in their original sense, undoubtedly understood only morally and ideally, as effects of the preaching of the Gospel to the poor; the evangelical legend understood them literally, as real physical miracles, though here and there, in the final remodelling of this legend in a mystical and artistic spirit, such as we find in the first Gospel, the original ideal character of these miracles again appears.

If we first take the miraculous cures by classes, and in the order which the speech of Jesus which we have just quoted suggests, the Evangelists speak both generally of many blind, among other sick persons, whose sight Jesus restored (Matt. xv. 30; Luke vii. 21), and give us several particular accounts of cures more or less in detail. The three first Evangelists have in common a cure of a blind man, which Jesus is said

---

* See above, Introduction, § 25.

to have performed on the road to Jerusalem at the last principal station, Jericho (Matt. xx. 29—34; Mark x. 46—52; Luke xviii. 35—43). According to Matthew and Mark, this miracle was performed on going out of the city; according to Luke, on going into it; and we see at once from this discrepancy how little the Evangelists cared about details of this sort, which are of importance to the historical writer. For the only reason why in Luke it was necessary to represent Jesus as performing the miracle before entering the city, is this—that Luke had something to tell of his passage through the city, of which Matthew and Mark have nothing particular to say. What Luke had to tell of is the meeting with Zaccheus. Now if, as he continues to do from the middle of the eighteenth chapter, he had chosen to follow the arrangement of Matthew, and consequently (omitting the history of the mother of Zebedee's sons, for the substance of whose speech he reserved a place further on) had made the cure of the blind man follow immediately upon the announcement of his suffering, then Jesus, when he healed the blind man, ought not to be represented as having passed Jericho, because, had he done so, he could not have met with Zaccheus in Jericho, a circumstance which Luke wished to speak of at some length. Another discrepancy is, that in Matthew there are two blind men, in Mark and Luke only one, and that in Matthew Jesus touches their eyes, while the two other narrators say nothing of his having done so. Exactly in the same way, Matthew represents Jesus as proceeding with two blind men in an earlier cure, of which the other two know nothing (ix. 27—31); and thus he may have transferred the number two and the touching from one narrative into the other, as naturally such a history might be told, sometimes of one, sometimes of two blind men, sometimes assigned to one district, sometimes to another, and with different details: a miraculous cure of the blind must be had: the particular attendant circumstances were unimportant.

The trait in the narrative of the blind men persisting in appealing to Jesus as the Son of David, has lately suggested an interpretation of their blindness as symbolical of the blindness of Jewish Christianity, which in Jesus sees only the Son of David, until Jesus himself opens its eyes.* Now we have above attempted to shew that Jesus, in ascribing to himself the cure of the blind, only understood this symbolically, as when, in the appearance alleged to have been vouchsafed to Paul, he says that he sends him to the Heathen to open their eyes, that they may turn from darkness to light (Acts xxvi. 18). But that Matthew, or any one of the three first Evangelists, did, in their histories of the cures of the blind, ever think of such a thing—this is an hypothesis which on the very face of their narratives we must altogether deny. The idea of Christ as the opener of the eyes of the spiritually blind, had, when those Evangelists wrote, long disappeared under the sensuous conception of a material miracle; and the particular features of these narratives must always be explained upon this conception of the nature of a miracle, unless, as above, in the history of the draught of fishes, the spiritual reference is transparent; and this is not the case in these synoptic histories of the cures of the blind.

In the first place, the continued formation of these narratives proceeded in anything but an ideal direction. In the description of the cure of the blind man at Jericho, even Luke, and still more Mark, distinguishes himself by the addition of traits which only serve to increase the vividness and picturesqueness of the scene: among these are, in the case of Mark, the name and father's name of the blind man,† the address of the people, and the casting off of his coat by the subject of the cure. Mark also has, as if dissatisfied with the

---

* Volkmar, The Religion of Jesus, pp. 235—250.

† There have been all sorts of surmises as to the source from which Mark may have taken the names of Timæus and Bartimæus. What if this source were no other than the Greek tense of $\tau\iota\mu\acute{a}\omega$ ($\dot{\epsilon}\pi\epsilon\tau\acute{\iota}\mu\eta\sigma\epsilon$ and $\dot{\epsilon}\pi\epsilon\tau\acute{\iota}\mu\omega\nu$)?

narratives of his predecessors, a history of the cure of a blind man peculiar to himself. This he has introduced between the narratives of the leaven of the Pharisees and of the confession of Peter, and with the history of the cure of a man deaf and dumb, likewise peculiar to himself, has arranged it exactly according to his taste (viii. 22—26). The blind man who is brought to Jesus at Bethsaida is taken by him first out of the town; for the miracle is a mystery which the uninitiated must not witness; and therefore, when it is completed, the publication of it is forbidden, as is done on several occasions in Matthew and Luke, but most industriously in Mark. Then Jesus spits in the eyes of the blind man, just as the subservient Procurator of Egypt made Vespasian,* whom he had just saluted as Emperor, spit in the eyes of a man alleged to be blind, because in the case of magical cures, according to the superstition of the times, saliva was an important ingredient.

Again, the blind man does not see perfectly all at once, but on Jesus asking him, after having applied the saliva and laid his hands upon him once, whether he sees anything, and receiving the reply that he sees, only indistinctly, men walking as trees, he lays his hands once more upon the blind man's eyes, and then, and not before, his restoration to sight is perfect. At first sight this looks like a diminution of the miracle, inasmuch as the sanatory power of the performer appears not to be absolute, but has as it were to contend with the resistance of the complaint; and it is on this feature, therefore, that the natural explanation of the miracles mainly rests its assumptions. But this is not what is intended by Mark: on the contrary, his object is to bring the miracle, without prejudice to its value as such, more within the range of our conception by dividing it into its successive factors: certainly an unsuccessful effort, and one by which he loses more than he gains. Miracles, as instances of the inter-

* Vol. i. p. 369.

ference of absolute causality with the chain of finite causes, are essentially sudden events, and are only brought into contradiction with themselves by being divided into separate factors.

We find the author of the fourth Gospel following in the steps of Mark, and carrying still further the practice of which he sets the example in the way of giving picturesqueness to the miracles, and exaggerating their miraculous features. Instead of the two accounts of cures of the blind in Matthew and Mark, he has only one (ix. 1—41), but this, far otherwise than the single one in Luke, is of a character such as to make all others superfluous. For the blind man whom Jesus healed according to John, and not in Bethsaida or Jericho, but in the capital itself, was not an ordinary blind man, but blind from his birth, consequently a man blind, as it were, absolutely, whose cure was possible only by an absolute miracle; an idea which the author puts into the mouth of the man himself who had been cured, when he represents him as saying, in opposition to the unbelieving Jews, that since the world began (ver. 31) it has not been heard that any one has opened the eyes of one born blind. By way, moreover, of an external and visible instrument for the cure, Jesus avails himself not merely of the saliva; he spits, not immediately into the eyes of the blind man, but upon the ground, and, making clay, anoints his eyes; a feature which serves at the same time to constitute a work over and above the miraculous cure, *i.e.* a violation of the Sabbath. Then the clay has to be immediately washed off if the blind man is to enjoy his lately given power of sight: so Jesus sends him to wash, not indeed in the Jordan, as the Prophet Elisha sent the leprous Naaman (2 Kings v. 10), but to the neighbouring pool of Siloah, from which he returns with his sight restored. All these features are attributable partly to exaggeration, partly to an attempt to invest the miracle with picturesqueness and a magical character. There is this addition also, that the fact is laboriously ascertained, in a manner unknown to the older Evangelists in their miraculous histories, by a regular examination and hearing of witnesses. The speeches of the neighbours, when the well-known blind beggar comes back to them seeing, are in themselves mere surmises, as they may be deceived by a likeness to the real blind man (ver. 9); his own declaration in answer to these questions, especially as he has no accurate knowledge of his benefactor, and is therefore so far unprejudiced, is of more importance; but before the authorities, before whom he is represented by the Evangelist as being summoned in order to give official corroboration to the occurrence, even this declaration does not suffice: his parents are summoned, as they alone can give credible evidence that their son was blind from his birth. If any doubt remains, it is quashed by the remark that the Jewish authorities had laid the confession of Jesus being the Messiah under the ban of excommunication; if, nevertheless, the man not only adhered to his statement as to the reality of his cure, but also made no secret of his belief in the prophetic dignity of Jesus, he spoke to his own injury; and this, as the Evangelist intends to imply, he would not have done, if he had not been firmly convinced of the miracle that had been performed upon him.

But while the fourth Evangelist thus carries miracles to the extreme of external reality, and thus gives the finishing-stroke to the tendency originated by Mark, he endeavours at the same time, in a manner of which his predecessors afford no example, to bring into view the ideal meaning. Thus, in this instance, the miracle is introduced and carried on from first to last, not by any request for help on the part of the sufferer, but by a dogmatic question which the disciples connect with his condition, a question which is answered by Jesus in words to the effect that the man was purposely born blind, that by his being cured God's almighty power might be manifested in him. This manifestation or glorification of

God by the Son consists, in John, not merely in the performance by Jesus of something which surpasses human power, and which at the same time, by its beneficial, charitable character, is worthy of God, but it is in reality a phase in the operations of God and his creative word reflected as it were symbolically in the miraculous acts of Jesus. The divine Logos is, according to the Alexandrine doctrine, the principle of life and light for the world, the nourishment of souls; the Johannine Jesus exhibits himself in each of these capacities by one or more miracles. As regards that which we are considering, it is said of the Logos in the preface: "In him was life, and the life was the light of men. And the light shineth in darkness, and the darkness comprehended it not. . . . . But as many as received him, to them gave he power to become the sons of God, even to them that believe in his name" (i. 4 ff., 12). Now at the conclusion of our miraculous narrative, the Jewish rulers having shewn themselves incorrigible, the man who had been cured having declared his faith in Jesus as the Son of God, Jesus says: "For judgment am I come into this world, that they which see not might see; and that they which see might be made blind." Again, when the Pharisees ask him whether they also are blind, Jesus answers, that if they were so, *i.e.* knew themselves to be so, it would be well; but that as the knowledge is wanting, the capacity for improvement is wanting also (31—41). Now we see that the purport of all this is, that the man born blind who was made to see, first physically, then spiritually, represents those men who, though originally belonging to the world, *i.e.* to darkness, have nevertheless the power and the will to comprehend the light, and thus to become children of God: the Jews, on the other hand, represent those who shut out the light, and continue in darkness, *i.e.* in sin. For the completion of the allegory it would be an appropriate addition to say that, as he who is physically blind, and spiritually conscious of his blindness, comes to see not merely spiritually, but also physically, so those who see physically, and think they see spiritually, will at last be convinced, not merely of their spiritual blindness, but also be struck with physical. But this would contradict the declaration of the Johannine Christ, that he is not come to condemn the world, but to bless the world, and that the unbeliever is already condemned in himself (iii. 17 ff., xii. 47 ff.). From Jesus, as the divine creative Word, only what is affirmative can proceed—only Light, Life, and Salvation : he neither requires nor needs to perform a penal miracle; the creature who excludes him he need but leave in the condition of unhappiness in which it is already without the operation of Jesus, and thus it is punished sufficiently.

Thus the miracle in John is penetrated in all its features by the ideal spirit : it is throughout symbolical, and at the same time throughout real; it would be the greatest misunderstanding to suppose that the fourth Evangelist did not mean to say that what was so important really happened. We see even from one single feature in the narrative how little in his view the one excludes the other, and also how strangely such a view of the world was formed. The name of the pool in which Jesus bids his blind man wash, the Hebrew word Siloa, meaning without doubt a flow of water, is said by the Evangelist to be by interpretation Sent (ver. 7); he looked, therefore, upon the spring and the pool as being, by these names, prophetic of the God-sent Jesus, or of the sending of the blind man to it, a prophecy which at the same time existed as real water, that being already the literal meaning of the word.

72. Cures of Cripples.

In the answer to the Baptist, so often mentioned, Jesus speaks of cripples as second in the list of those who are cured by him. Cripples are also among the many kinds of sick who are brought to Jesus previously to the second feeding, for the purpose of being healed by him; and the people are surprised when, among the blind who have been made to see, &c., they observe the lame also walking (Matt. xv. 30 ff.). In other places they are more generally paralytics, translated by Luther the palsied, who are spoken of (Matt. iv. 24, viii. 6, ix. 2); these, according to the meaning of the word, were those sick persons whose muscles on one side were "slackened," *i.e.* crippled; while the description of the sick man, Matt. ix. 2 ff., applies to entire lameness, at least of the feet; that of the other, Matt. viii. 5 ff., to a painful palsy. The necessity of Jesus having cured sick of this description, was implied in the literal understanding of the prophecy of Isaiah, "then shall the lame man leap as an hart" (xxxv. 6); a prophecy preceded (ver. 3) by the command, "strengthen ye the feeble knees!" where the Greek translation has the same word as that by which Luke (v. 18, 24) describes the paralytic man. It is not so clear in the evangelical narratives that the passage in Isaiah is the root of these miraculous histories, as it is in one which we find in the Acts. It is well known that in that book the first miracle by which the Apostles prove their exalted mission is the cure of a lame man, who was begging before the Temple at Jerusalem, performed by Peter. Of this man it is said, that when Peter had commanded him in the name of the Lord to rise up and walk, immediately his feet and anclebones received strength, and he, leaping up, stood and walked, and entered with them into the Temple, walking and leaping

(Acts iii. 7 ff.). In the *leaping*, so repeatedly mentioned, on the part of the lame man, the leaping like a hart promised in Isaiah is not to be mistaken; while the strengthened legs and ancle bones remind us of the strengthening of the feeble knees in the same prophecy.

The history of the servant of the captain at Capernaum, whom moreover only Matthew describes as paralytic, will come into consideration further on under a different point of view: the classical history of the cure of a paralytic is that of the man who, likewise at Capernaum, is brought on a bed to Jesus, and to whom he first announces the forgiveness of his sins, and then, when the scribes take offence at his doing so, bids him take up his bed and walk (Matt. ix. 1—8; Mark ii. 1—12; Luke v. 17—26). We have here nothing more to do with the question as to whether the cure of a sick person of this description may have been possible, in virtue of the confidence which he may have had in Jesus as a Prophet; we have not, speaking generally, disputed the possibility in the former Book; but in any case these evangelical narratives are so modified according to the conception of Jesus as a performer of miracles, that the real facts, possibly lying at the foundation of them, can no longer be extracted. We see the liberty taken in the remodelling of these accounts, by the discrepancies of the several Evangelists from one another. Matthew only says simply that Jesus went across the sea into his city of Capernaum, that there they brought to him a lame man lying on a bed, and when he saw their faith he assured the sick man of the forgiveness of his sins. The faith of the people, of the bearers, and of the sick man himself, was, according to Matthew, known to Jesus merely from their having taken so much trouble to drag the sufferer there; to Luke, this proof of faith did not appear sufficiently special, and as he thought it necessary to introduce the interference of the scribes, to whom he adds the Pharisees, by representing them as being from the first collected round Jesus, he prefers making the press so great that the men with their pallet-bed cannot penetrate to Jesus, but find themselves compelled, carrying it as they are, to break a separate passage through the roof of the house, and to let down the sick man upon his bed from above into the middle of the room in front of Jesus. It is not out of Matthew, at all events, that Luke gets the notion of Jesus having been in a house, but he wanted this feature in order to bring out the peculiar proof of faith which he had imagined. In speaking of the passage through the roof, or through the tiles as he expresses himself, there is no doubt that Luke was thinking of the opening which, according to Eastern architecture, was left in the flat, tiled roofs of the houses, by means of which the roof could be reached from the interior, and the interior from the roof; it was through this that, according to the notion of the Evangelist, there being no regular staircase and a ladder could not be used for the purpose, the bed with the sick man on it was let down, as it appears, by ropes into the room where Jesus was teaching. Whether the author of the second Gospel was not acquainted with this peculiarity of the houses in Palestine, or whether he wished to place the faithful zeal of the people in a still clearer light, he takes no notice of the opening already existing in the roof, but represents the bearers, whose number he fixed at four, from the four corners of the bed, as first breaking a hole through, without remembering that by doing so he exposed the assemblage immediately under it to the danger of being crushed by the falling bricks. No one who remembers merely the history of the unfruitful fig-tree, will deny that such precipitancy is quite in the style of Mark, and he will also mark this narrative as one of those which negative the possibility of Mark being the original Evangelist.

There is a miraculous cure connected with this occurrence which the three first Evangelists represent as taking place on the Sabbath, so that in the former case the rock of offence for the scribes being that Jesus arrogated to himself the power of forgiving sins, in this his sanatory work is called in question as a violation of the Sabbath. Even the arrangement, according to which all the Synoptics place the healing of the withered hand immediately after the history of the plucking of the ears of corn on the Sabbath (Matt. xii. 9—14; Mark iii. 1—6; Luke xi. 6—11), shews us that they are less concerned with the miracle itself than with its having been performed on the Sabbath. The mode of keeping the holiday of the Sabbath and the extent of licence allowed on it was a disputed question between Jesus and Pharisaic Judaism, and we therefore find it returning upon us in the Gospels under different forms. The question might be connected with any act, however natural; with the plucking of the ears of corn by the disciples, which, in the Mosaic law, was not considered as injuring another man's property, and was so far generally permitted (5 Mos. xxiii. 25); and as it could not be called regular work, especially in case of want, it was considered by Jesus as allowable even on the Sabbath, and on the other hand, by the pedantry of later interpreters of the law, among the labours forbidden on the Sabbath. If, on an occasion of this kind, Jesus met the objection of the Pharisees by the example of David, who, when compelled by hunger, did not hesitate to appease it both in his own case and that of his followers with the shew-bread in the Temple, which was generally reserved for the priests alone, he might, in those cases in which, not his own necessity, but that of others whom he wished to help, made him commit an alleged violation of the Sabbath, avail himself of the example of the animal which the owner did not hesitate to try to rescue, even on the Sabbath, from a pressing danger. It is clear that a proof thus adduced by no means necessarily presupposes a miracle as the occasion of thus adducing it; on the contrary, it suited any perfectly natural act of charitable assistance. But it is also equally clear that when men were accustomed to expect miracles of Jesus, the performance of those miracles on the

Sabbath must have appeared a suitable occasion for illustrations such as this. It might seem so even when it was supposed to be effected by the mere word of Jesus; as a Rabbinical school of that time interdicted even the consolation of the sick on the Sabbath.

The illustration of the sheep which is dragged out of the pit on the Sabbath-day is only on this occasion found in Matthew; in Mark and Luke, Jesus only put to the Pharisees, who are lying in wait for him, the question as to what is lawful on the Sabbath-day, to do good or evil, to save souls or to destroy them? On the other hand, Luke has introduced the illustration of the domestic animal into two other miraculous accounts,—a further proof that in narratives of this kind less emphasis was laid upon the miracle than upon the words of Jesus referring to the proper mode of keeping the Sabbath. On one occasion (Luke xiv. 1—6), on the Sabbath-day, at the house of one of the chief Pharisees, Jesus meets with a man sick of the dropsy, and having healed him in spite of the suspicious silence of the Pharisees to his question as to whether it is lawful to heal on the Sabbath-day, he puts to the Pharisees the further question as to which of them, whose ass or ox has fallen into the pit on the Sabbath-day, will hesitate straightway to pull him out? On the other occasion (xiii. 10—17), there is in a synagogue a woman bowed by disease for eighteen years. He makes her straight by calling to her and laying hands upon her, meeting the objection of the ruler of the synagogue by asking him whether each one of them does not on the Sabbath loose his ox or his ass from the stall, and lead him away to watering?—where the discrepancy in the image is occasioned by the circumstance that the woman's malady is looked upon as a case of being bound by Satan, from which Jesus releases her.

Of these cures, the latter especially, supposing it to have been preserved for us in a strictly historical account, might be understood as a cure effected psychologically by the impression made by the word and touch of Jesus upon the faith of the sick woman. Dr. Paulus has proved, by reference to original authorities, the occurrence of an exactly similar case in modern times.* But the sudden cure of a dropsical man will not adapt itself to such a theory ; and the history of the withered hand has too manifest a precedent in the legend of the Hebrew prophet to leave us doubtful as to the origin of it. It is frequently the case, and is so here, that the miraculous account in the New Testament is distinguished from that in the Old by the circumstance that in the latter the malady is first miraculously inflicted as a punishment, and then miraculously removed, while in the former, in accordance with the spirit of the Gospel, the malady is *given* and only removed by the humane performer of the miracle. Thus in the Old Testament (1 Kings xiii. 4 ff.), it is a miraculous punishment inflicted by God that the idolatrous Jeroboam has his hand, blasphemously stretched out against a prophet of Jehovah, withered for a moment, *i.e.* so stiffened that he cannot draw it back to him ; and it is not until at the king's request the prophet intercedes for him with Jehovah, that by a second miracle, and that a miracle of grace, its restoration is effected. In the evangelical narrative, the hand of the sufferer is already stiff from disease, and this stiffness shews itself, not, as in the case of the king, in which it was a punishment for a blasphemous stretching out of the hand, in his inability to draw it to him, but conversely in his not being able to stretch it out ; and his cure by Jesus consists in his being enabled to stretch it out. But if we compare what is said in the first instance of Jeroboam (ver. 4), " And, behold, his hand which he stretched out withered," with what is said in this (Matt. ver. 10 ; Mark ver. 1), " And, behold, there was a man with a withered hand ;" and then

* See above, § 42.

the words at the conclusion of the first cure (ver. 6), "And the hand of the king was restored again and was as before," with those at the conclusion of the second (ver. 13), "And his hand was restored again and was as the other,"—the imitation can scarcely be overlooked. But that these were exactly the maladies, the cure of which was at that time expected of one "who enjoyed the favour of Heaven and the friendship of more exalted beings," is shewn by the often-mentioned narrative of Tacitus, according to which, in order to give Vespasian an opportunity of proving his power of performing miracles, a man with a maimed hand (according to Suetonius, with a lame leg) was, with a man perfectly blind, stationed in the way of that emperor.*

In the case of this class of miracles also, we find all the elements that in the earlier Gospels appear scattered and dispersed, collected in the fourth, exaggerated on the one hand and spiritualised on the other. We find, also, that the form in which they are presented in the fourth Evangelist is in immediate connection with that in which they are presented in the second. The history of the sick man at the pool of Bethesda at Jerusalem (John v.) refers to a lame man, in the same way as the history of the cure of the paralytic at Capernaum; it is at the same time the history of a cure on the Sabbath, like that of the man with the withered hand, the dropsical man, and the bent woman. In this it surpasses the former account partly in the brilliancy of the stage upon which the miracle is performed, partly in the account of the duration of the sickness, which is wanting in the case of the paralytic at Capernaum; this in the case of the bent woman goes to the extent of only eighteen years, while here, in John, it is represented as amounting to thirty-eight; and again it endeavours to excel the histories of the cures on the Sabbath-day by a more profound view of the question, in which at the

* Tacit. Histor. v. 81. Sueton. Vespas. 7.

same time is involved the spiritualisation and symbolising of the whole miraculous narrative.

The pool of Bethesda (about which, independent of the fourth Evangelist, we find no information either in Josephus or in the Rabbis), with its five halls full of the blind, the lame, and other sufferers, is, as it were, a great hospital theatre, upon which the great practitioner of miracles appears, and selects the patient who has been longest ill of the most obstinate disease, in order in the most brilliant manner to prove himself, by operating upon him, as the divine Creative Word that gives life to all. The fact that higher powers already had power over the pool itself, an angel descending from time to time in order to move the water, after which the patient who first entered was healed,* and that this angelic operation proves insufficient for the cure of the one who requires curing most, places Jesus, who heals him, so much the higher; while this feature, in connection with the whole description of miraculous cure, suggests the supposition that something symbolical may be concealed under it. The thirty-eight years of sickness have been looked upon as the type of the thirty-eight years which the people of Israel were compelled to pass in the wilderness before they reached the promised land (5 Mos. ii. 14);† and I am surprised that, in the case of the five halls, the five Books of Moses have not been thought of, for these are, at all events, principally to be understood as among the writings in which, as Jesus remarks on occasion of this miracle (v. 39, comp. 45 ff.), the Jews think they have eternal life, but in which they can as little find it without Christ as the sick man could find a remedy without him in the halls of the pool of Bethesda. According to believing

---

* The most convincing critical grounds are in favour of the genuineness of ver. 4, which contains the notice of the angel; comp. Hengstenberg, Commentary on the Gospel of John, i. 300.

† Krafft, Chronology and Synopsis, p. 98; Hengstenberg, Commentary on the Gospel of John, i. 300.

interpreters, the historical validity of the narrative is not supposed to be damaged by this symbolical explanation; on the contrary, that opinion is that, by an arrangement of Providence, Jesus had here to meet with a man who, in the number of years of his sickness, presented himself as a type of the people of God—as "the sick man Judah," as Hengstenberg expresses himself in the style of the most modern time. From our point of view, the story has already lost all historical value, and the indication of its supposed symbolical meaning has for us only the merit of suggesting more definite grounds of explanation of the particular features of the story, while the uncertainty of such explanations cannot in any way shake our conviction that narratives of this kind are in any case unhistorical.

That the Johannine narrative in particular is copied from the synoptic account of the man with the palsy at Capernaum, may be seen from the different features which are common to both. Thus even the reference to the forgiveness of sins is not wanting in John, only that he has changed the preliminary words, "Thy sins are forgiven!" into an expression added afterwards, "Sin no more, lest a worse thing happen to thee" (v. 14). But it is impossible to mistake the resemblance in the manner in which the miraculous command of Jesus to the sick man is expressed in the two narratives. The Synoptics give the words twice over, once conditionally, on the question of the Pharisees, whether is easier to say to a man in this state, Thy sins are forgiven thee, or, Arise (Mark, take up thy bed) and walk! Then follows, as an actual command given to the sick man, Arise, take up thy bed and go home! The fourth Evangelist, not having premised any announcement of the forgiveness of sins, has not the preliminary question, but only the actual command, compounded, however, of the two speeches in the Synoptics. He keeps to the first form, though adopting, like Mark, out of the second, the bed which was to be packed up; but that in doing so he has particularly followed Mark, appears from the fact that both, in describing the bed, coincide in the use of a remarkable word. Matthew twice speaks of it by the most ordinary word, bed; Luke also once, and twice by the diminutive meaning, little bed; at last periphrastically that upon which the sick man lay. On the other hand, Mark uses throughout, *i.e.* four times, and likewise John five times, a word which is not, indeed, elsewhere unknown in the New Testament, but is quite as strange as if in English we were to describe a bed by the term *pallet*, and which therefore, as it is not found elsewhere in John, but does appear again in Mark, makes it probable that the former copied from the latter.*

Here, too, as in the case of the history of the man born blind, it is an arrangement peculiar to the fourth Evangelist that the fact of the miracle is established by a formal hearing. The Jews, *i.e.* the Jewish authorities, seeing the man carrying his bed, remark to him that it is not permitted on the Sabbath-day. He replies, that he who had enabled him to walk, ordered him to do so. They desire to know who it was. He declares that he does not know himself, as Jesus, after giving the miraculous command, had gone away to avoid the multitude. Jesus then again meets the man whom he had healed in the Temple, where he gives him the caution mentioned above; and on this occasion the man must have learnt his name, for he now announces to the Jews for the first time that it was Jesus who had made him whole. While, however, in the history of the man born blind (who, moreover, was already acquainted with the name of Jesus, but knew nothing else about him), the inquirers press him and his connections still further, in order to learn the description of the malady and the mode of cure applied by Jesus, in the case under consideration, as soon as Jesus is discovered to have been the author of the violation of the Sabbath, they cease from their

* The word κράββατος, which appears in Mark vi. 55, Acts v. 15, ix. 33, appears in the same meaning of a portable sick bed. Comp. Catull. Carm. x. 22.

examination, in order to direct their attack upon him. Then the description becomes very far from clear. "Therefore," it is said, "did the Jews persecute Jesus, because he had done these things on the Sabbath-day. But Jesus answered them," &c. &c. Now an objection, a reproach, an accusation, may be answered; persecution, on the contrary, unless the word is to be understood in its absolutely literal meaning, is a long-continued act, which a man may avoid, which he may take precautions against, but which he cannot answer. After the first answer attributed to Jesus, it is then said further, "Therefore the Jews sought the more to kill him;" and thereupon Jesus "answers" a second time, and in a long speech too, which must have given the Jews, if they really did wish to kill him, plenty of time and opportunity for doing so. We see that as soon as the man who had been healed had pointed out Jesus to the Jews as the author of the desecration of the Sabbath, the narrator considers the scene as at an end; he is then only concerned with the speech of Jesus which he wished to connect with it, and which he therefore introduced so unsatisfactorily, alleging it to be an answer to a persecution.

It was this speech that the Evangelist had in view at the very first, when he placed the miraculous cure on the Sabbath-day. The activity attributed to Jesus on the Sabbath might give him an opportunity of exhibiting the never-resting character of the divine Logos. In order, therefore, to combat the objections of the Jews, he avails himself, not of the practical argument drawn from the ox and the ass, or from David and the shew-bread, as in the Synoptics (though arguments of this kind were not unknown to the author of the fourth Gospel, as we see from vii. 27), but of the metaphysical one, that as God, his Father, works and creates throughout the rest of the Sabbath without interruption, so also incessant work is proper for him as the Son who in all his doings rules himself after the example of the

Father. The doctrine of uninterrupted creation on the part of God was a fundamental doctrine of the Jewish Alexandrine philosophy; the same never-resting activity belonged to the Logos as the agent of the operation of God in the world; the dignity of Jesus, as the Logos incarnate, could not be more emphatically illustrated than on an occasion on which the Jewish opponents attempted to limit his divine and infinite energy by their national Sabbatarian law. It has, therefore, been rightly said that of the doctrine of the Johannine preface (i. 4), "In him, the Logos, was life, and the life was the light of men," the last half is illustrated* in the history of the man born blind, the first in the history we have been considering; only we must always remember this, that in the mind of the Evangelist these histories are to be taken as entirely literal as well as entirely symbolical occurrences.

Independently, however, of the connection between the fundamental idea of the speech and the system of Philo, it is clear that it was arbitrarily invented by the fourth Evangelist, from, among other things, the unhistorical feature which constantly recurs in the fourth Gospel. It is this, that when Jesus calls God his Father, the Jews see in his doing so a virtual equalization of himself with God (ver. 18). To do this did not occur to the actual Jews. They were accustomed to the description of the Messiah, nay even of ordinary kings, as Sons, *i.e.* protégés and vicegerents of God, as a title that assumed nothing at all. In the next place, it is seen from the fact that a series of the propositions of the speech appear, some in the Preface (comp. ver. 37 with i. 18), some elsewhere, as the Evangelist's own words (comp. ver. 32 with xix. 35; ver. 44 with xii. 43), or as those of the Baptist (comp. 20 with iii. 35); still more are repeated in the first Epistle of John (comp. ver. 24 with

---

* Baur, Critical Investigations into the Canonical Gospels, p. 176.

1 John iii. 14; ver. 34 and 36 ff. with 1 John v. 9; ver. 38 with 1 John i. 10; ver. 40 with 1 John v. 12; ver. 42 with 1 John ii. 15); the last of which is indeed only a proof resting upon probability for those who consider the first Epistle of John as earlier than the Gospel, while the first is sufficient to corroborate the conclusion which forces itself upon us in reference to all the speeches of Jesus in the fourth Gospel.

73. CURES OF LEPERS AND OF THE DEAF AND THE DUMB.

In the speech of Jesus (Matt. xi. 5), the mention of the maim is followed by that of the lepers, and in his address to the Twelve when he sends them forth (Matt. x. 8), they are empowered to perform especially cures of lepers, among those of other sick persons. Jesus could not have taken the lepers out of the passage in Isaiah, as he did the blind and lame, since the prophet, in that passage, makes no mention of them. For such mention would not have been suitable to the character of that refreshing joy of the people at the termination of their captivity, which the prophet wished to describe as causing them to forget all sorrows. But as a programme of the Messianic miracles, that prophetic utterance was, as has been noticed above, supplemented out of the prophetic type. In the prophetical legend, leprosy plays a considerable part, as it also does among the sicknesses traditional in Judea, and, accordingly, in the Law of Moses (3 Mos. xiii. 14). A complaint so malignant, so obstinate, and especially terrible from the exclusion which its infectious character rendered necessary, was especially adapted to be considered as a divine punishment or trial (look at the account in Job), and the cure of it as a divine blessing. So among the miracles which Jehovah qualifies Moses to perform in order to accredit him with the people, the production and removal of the leprosy takes nearly the first place (2 Mos. iv. 6 ff.). Jehovah commands him to put his hand into his bosom, and to pull it out again: it was as white as snow; and when he had put it in a second time, and taken it out again, it was again whole like the rest of his body. This is only as it were a miraculous trick on the part of the Deity; but on another occasion the infliction and removal of the leprosy is in bitter earnest. Miriam, Moses' sister, having had the audacity to rebel against her brother, the wrath of Jehovah was inflamed against her, and she became as white as snow from leprosy; it was not until Aaron had interceded with Moses for her, and the latter had again interceded with Jehovah, that after seven days exclusion she was again received as clean (4 Mos. xii. 1—15). Then there is the case particularly celebrated, and mentioned also by Jesus himself, in a passage of the third Gospel (Luke iv. 27). It is the cure of a leper by the prophet Elisha, from whose history so many other features have entered into that of Christ (2 Kings v. 1 ff.). The Syrian captain, Naaman, suffering from leprosy, addresses the prophet on the subject of his cure. The latter commands him to bathe seven times in the Jordan; but the warrior is offended, and considers himself only recommended to have recourse to an ordinary mode of cure by bathing, whereas he had expected that the prophet, calling upon Jehovah his God, would have come to him, passed his hand over the diseased part, and so have removed the eruption. But he allows himself to be persuaded to follow the prescription of the prophet, and after seven immersions in the Jordan finds himself perfectly cured; while the prophet immediately after feels it his duty to transfer the leprosy to his own avaricious servant Gehazi.

In this instance, also, the Messianic life, in the form at least in which it entered into Christianity, omitted the penal side of the Old Testament miracle, but the Messiah could not be deprived of that of healing and grace. Thus, among the very first sick persons who apply to Jesus to be healed, it is, according to all the synoptic Gospels (Matt. viii. 1—4; Mark i. 40—45; Luke v. 12—16), a leper, who falls down before him and declares his conviction that if he will he can make him clean. Jesus, touching him, declares his willingness, and in a moment the man is so clean, that Jesus can command him to shew himself with confidence to the High-priest, and to prepare his offering of purification. The attempt to explain this narrative on the supposition that the man was already as good as cured, that the leprosy was in its last stage, and that Jesus only pointed this out to him, consequently did not make him clean, but only declared that he was so—this rationalistic explanation is as violent when applied to the evangelical narrative, as it is, from our point of view, ridiculously superfluous. We have here a prophetico-Messianic myth of the clearest stamp; it wants no natural explanation, but simply an explanation, which we have given, founded upon the principle of gradual formation and development.

There is a second cure of leprosy in Luke, and in this instance there are ten lepers all at once who are benefited by the healing power of Jesus (xvii. 11—19). Engaged in the journey to Jerusalem, and while travelling on the boundary between Galilee and Samaria, he is met outside a village by ten lepers, who stand at the distance from him required by law, calling out to him with a loud voice to have mercy upon them. Without touching them, as he does the diseased person in the former case, or even calling them to him, he commanded them to go and shew themselves to the priests; and while they went they became clean. Now at this point the account, considered as a miraculous one, would have been properly at an end, and we should so far have considered it simply as a variation upon the former one, though the remarkable exaggeration in the number, increased as it is from one to ten, might to a certain extent surprise us. But the narrative of Luke does not end here. On the contrary, when the ten find themselves cured, nine of them go forward on their way, while one returns to fall at the feet of his benefactor with thanks, and this one is a Samaritan. In this man's presence Jesus proceeds to speak unfavourably of the nine Jews who have left the duty of returning thanks to one who was not a Jew. He then dismisses the Samaritan with the declaration that his faith has made him whole.

Now in this turn given to the conclusion we may recognise, on the one hand, an imitation of the conclusion of the history of Elisha and Naaman, which the former account of leprosy had left unnoticed. For Naaman, when he found himself cured, had likewise returned to give thanks to the prophet, and to acknowledge the God of Israel as the only true God, and Naaman was likewise a stranger, as the Samaritan in this case. And he is also described by Jesus in Luke as the only one among several, when the former says (iv. 27) that in the time of the prophet Elisha there were many lepers in Israel, and none of them was made clean, but only Naaman the Syrian, just as in this case ten were cleansed, but none of them, like Naaman, shewed themselves by gratitude to be deserving of cure, but only one Samaritan. Elisha dismisses Naaman, after declining his presents, with the parting words, "Go in peace." Instead of this, Jesus takes leave of the grateful Samaritan with the formula that occurs in other places on the performance of miracles, "Go thy way; thy faith hath made thee whole." Now it is easy to see that these last words, which were entirely in their place on the occasion of the healing of the woman with the issue of blood (Luke viii. 48), or the blind man at Jericho (Luke xviii. 42), are here unsuitable; for if the Samaritan had been healed on account of the faith he exhibited in his return to Jesus, why were the others healed who gave no such proof of their faith? Consequently, this concluding expression has been transferred by the Evangelist from other miraculous accounts into this; without them, the narrative has, in the question of Jesus, whether, of the ten, none have been found to give honour to God but only this stranger, as instructive a conclusion as the parable of the Good Samaritan, in the question (x. 36), which of the three was neighbour to him that fell among thieves—who is likewise a stranger.

The miraculous account of which we are speaking, and which likewise is peculiar to Luke, has, generally, the most striking similarity to this parable, which is also peculiar to him; both belong to his Samaritan stories, which are so closely connected with the tendency of his Gospel. In the miracle, the only one of the ten who is grateful is a Samaritan, and the same is the case in the parable, where a Samaritan is the only one of the three who is *good;* while in both the others all genuine and regular Jews shew themselves ungrateful and uncharitable. The number ten, like the number three, is a round number and suited to a parable, the first meeting us again in the parable, for instance, of the Ten Virgins (Matt. xxv. 1 ff.). We cannot say that the story, like that of the Good Samaritan, was originally given by Jesus as a parable, and at a later period taken historically. When we are told something about an indefinite subject, as a king, a traveller, a sower, or even a third person with a favourite name, like Lazarus, an instructive moral being subjoined, the parable character is easy to recognise; but when a man tells of something as having really occurred to himself, he has either improperly disguised the fact or imposed upon his hearers. We have as little right to impute to Jesus the one as the other, and can therefore, in the case of the miraculous story in question, only suppose that it is the work of a later hand, who gave to the old prophetico-Messianic theme of the healing of leprosy a turn favourable to the Gentiles, whether it were that in doing so he was thinking of the parable of the Good Samaritan, or that he himself was also the author of the latter.

In this class of miraculous accounts the fourth Gospel deserts us altogether; lepers are not mentioned. The reason is, indeed, that in the comparatively cleanly Grecian world of Asia Minor, in which the author lived, maladies of this kind were not so common as among the Jews in Palestine, also that they could not be so easily adapted to his symbolical system, which consists in the opposition between light and darkness, life and death.

This is also the case with the deaf, who occupy the next place in the answer of Jesus to the emissaries of the Baptist. In the passage of Isaiah from which they are taken, the dumb also are especially mentioned with them. In the Greek of the Gospels the same word means deaf and dumb; and hence it is that Matthew and Luke, who represent Jesus as saying nothing in his answer of dumb persons, but only speaking of deaf to whom he restores the power of hearing, say, in their accounts of miracles, nothing of deafness cured by him, but speak only of the dumb to whom he restored their powers of utterance. Mark, on the contrary, on two occasions, once in a history of a cure peculiar to himself, the second time in an account in which the two others only mention possession by devils, connects deafness and dumbness together.

Of these narratives, the two first, at least in Matthew, are repetitions of each other. On one occasion (ix. 32—34) there is brought to Jesus a man dumb from possession, who speaks after the devil is driven out, at which the people express their surprise at something the like of which has not been seen in Israel, while the Pharisees say that Jesus drives out devils by the prince of the devils. On the other (xii. 22—24; comp. Luke xi. 14), a man possessed is brought to Jesus. This man is blind and dumb; Jesus heals him so that he can speak and see; the people surmise that the performer of the miracle is the Son of David, but the Pharisees say that he only drives out devils by Beelzebub the prince of the devils. Here it is clear that the author of the first Gospel found in one of the sources of his history, the account of the cure of a man dumb from possession by a devil,—in another, of a man blind and dumb also from possession,—stories of this kind being current in different forms and combinations; and that he, believing them to be two different occurrences, incorporated in his Gospel two narratives, placing one at an earlier, the other at a later period; while Luke, though not perhaps acquainted with the true state of the case, considered the introduction into his Gospel of two accounts so exactly resembling each other as superfluous.

From the standpoint of belief in devils, it was natural to look upon the dumb as possessed, when we consider the uneasy gestures of persons so affected; it was less obvious in the case of the blind. When, however, we see how delusion had drawn within its circle even cases of diseases of the limbs and muscles, as that of the bent woman, the notion of possession by devils as a cause of blindness cannot surprise us very much. It is a different thing when a sick man, whom Matthew calls a lunatic, but describes, as Luke also does, as one possessed by a devil, is at the same time described by Mark alone as dumb and deaf (ix. 17, 25). As this is the case in which the power of the disciples is insufficient, and Jesus himself is obliged to interfere, we see that Mark, by aggravating the malady, perhaps with reference to the dumb man by possession in Matthew, wished to represent the case as a particularly difficult one.

It is manifest that in delineating both the circumstances of the sick man and the scene between his father and Jesus, Mark was performing a task in which he took particular pleasure. This is a point to which we shall return hereafter. So also the account of the man with an impediment in his speech (vii. 32—37), together with that which we have considered above, the healing of the blind man at Bethsaida, is the true model of a miraculous narrative in the taste of our second Evangelist. In addition to the mysterious taking apart of the sick man, and the alleged command at the conclusion not to publish the fact, we have here also the Aramaic word with which Jesus orders the closed ears of the deaf man to open. This word, which the author has to translate for his readers, he gives, as a sort of talisman, in its original foreign form. We do not find here the description of the gradual process of the cure, as in the history of the blind man. So, instead of this, the manipulation by Jesus, in connection with the fact that in this case a double defect was to be removed, is described all the more at length; here he touches the man's tongue with the spittle, which, in the other case, he spits immediately into his eyes, while he put his fingers into his ears. Then, in addition, we have a sigh and look upwards to heaven, giving an effect to the scene, which we only find repeated in the history of the raising of Lazarus in the fourth Gospel. At the conclusion, the people cry out in an excess of admiration, "He hath done all things well; he maketh both the deaf to hear and the dumb to speak." Now this means nothing else but that Jesus has performed what, according to the passage in the Prophet, was expected of the Messiah, and what, therefore, Jesus, as soon as he was recognised as the Messiah on better grounds, must, it was taken for granted, have done, whether he really did it or not.

74. Cures of Persons possessed by Devils.

According to the speech of Jesus, which we are following in the consideration of his miracles, we should come next to his raisings of the dead. But there are still several kinds of miraculous cures which, though not mentioned in that speech, must nevertheless be noticed.

Among these are the cures of driving out devils, of which

Jesus makes no mention in that speech, in which he only appeals to those miracles which were expected of the Messiah, in accordance, partly with the prophecy, partly with the precedent of the Prophets of the Old Testament, in whose times, even the latest of them, possession had not been heard of. Now it has been already explained above, that of all the cures performed by Jesus of which the Gospels speak, that of those maladies which were supposed to be caused by demoniacal possession, has most natural possibility and historical probability in its favour. If Jesus cured sick persons at all, supposed demoniacs were certainly among them.

It does not, however, follow from this that the accounts of those cures as we find them in the Gospels are historically accurate. On the contrary, we cannot conceive of any of these as having been naturally performed exactly as we are told they were. And it would also be a remarkable thing if the excitement which the idea of a personal presence of evil spirits, and an encounter between them and the Messiah, imparted to the imagination, had not resulted in a manifold embellishment of such stories. Apart from the summary statements that Jesus or his disciples drove out devils (the former we find in Matt. iv. 24, viii. 16; Mark i. 34, 39, iii. 11; Luke iv. 41, vi. 18; the latter, Matt. x. 1, 8; Mark iii. 15, vi. 7, 13; Luke ix. 1, x. 17, 20), and from those narratives in which the possession appears only in the second degree, as the cause of other maladies, as in the cases of the blind and dumb in the accounts just spoken of, or where the sick person, the case being one of a cure at a distance, remains in the background, as in the instance of the demoniac daughter of the Canaanitish woman; apart from these, we have in the synoptic Gospels three cases of this kind, of which the first is described as simple, the two others as complicated and difficult.

Even in those summary accounts in Luke and Mark, especial stress is laid upon the fact, that the devils in the persons possessed recognised Jesus as the Messiah. The unclean spirits, says Mark (iii. 11; comp. Luke iv. 41), when they saw him, worshipped him and cried out, Thou art the Son of God; whereupon Jesus, if he allowed them to speak to him at all (comp. Matt. i. 34), forbade them, under a heavy penalty, to publish abroad that he was so. The devils, it was supposed, must of course know the Messiah who was some time to deliver over to damnation themselves and their prince (Matt. viii. 29, xxv. 41; Mark i. 24; Luke iv. 34; Revel. xx. 1 ff., 10); and by force of the penetrating sight of their spiritual nature, they would have considered no one as such who was not so really. Consequently, if they recognised the Messiah in Jesus, this, from the standpoint of Jewish popular ideas, was a strong proof that he was the Messiah. At the same time, there resulted the practical contrast in the fact, that while Jesus was in vain labouring among his contemporaries to plant the faith in him as the Messiah, he, on the contrary, with the more sharp-sighted devils, had only to take care that they did not proclaim him to be the Messiah more than his modesty allowed. But inasmuch as in those possessed of devils we see nothing but cases of natural sickness, so neither can we ascribe to them any such penetration into the character of Jesus in its most profound depths, *i.e.* we cannot assume, what the Evangelists plainly state to have been the case, that as soon as a man in this condition got sight of Jesus, he recognised him as the Messiah without knowing anything further about him; but when such a recognition took place, we must suppose that something had happened beforehand, tending to impress the sick man in a natural manner with this conviction.

Such an explanatory circumstance is suggested by the evangelical narrative itself of the demoniac in the synagogue at Capernaum (Mark i. 21—28; Luke iv. 31—37), representing, as it does, Jesus as giving a lecture previously, and thus making a strong impression on the assemblage. The effect produced by this upon a person present suffering from demoniac symptoms, might easily be such a state of excitement that he would fall into a paroxyism, in which, in the character of the demon, he would beseech the mighty man of God to leave him alone. The Evangelists, indeed, do not put the two things originally in connection, but represent the demon as drawing his knowledge purely from himself, so that even if Jesus had not spoken he would have known him to be what he was. They also represent him as declaring Jesus to be not merely a Prophet, but the Holy One of God, *i.e.* the Messiah, which seems inconceivable at the first beginning of the ministry of Jesus, since, according to a very credible tradition, the view that Jesus was the Messiah did not spring up even in his own immediate circle until much later. Our narrative, therefore, either places the standard of the dignity attributed to Jesus by the subject of the possession too high, or the occurrence is placed much too early. But from the impression which Jesus made upon the sick man by his speaking, his personality, and all the rumours about him in the district, the sequel, as stated by the Evangelists, may be naturally explained. If the man recognised in Jesus only a prophet, he must still have attributed to him, according to Jewish ideas, a divine power given from above for combating the power of evil—consequently, the kingdom of devils; and as soon as Jesus, sharing or availing himself of this opinion, commanded the demon to depart out of the man, this might have the effect, as we are told, of producing a crisis, amid violent spasms, which put an end to the morbid condition—whether for ever or not, we know, in this case, as little as in that of any other of these evangelical narratives. Still, a permanent cure of such a malady by psychological impressions would not be unheard of.

The case is different with the narrative, which is common to all the Evangelists, of the possessed Gadarene, or Gadarenes (Matt. viii. 28—34; Mark v. 1—20; Luke viii. 26—39).

This, among the evangelical stories of possession, is the show-piece; richly embellished with every accessory, possible and impossible, the latter indeed being that which in certain circles always makes the greatest impression. With reference, moreover, to this embellishment, there is, between the different accounts, a discrepancy by no means unimportant, features which are found in Mark and Luke being wanting in the description of Matthew. Conversely, the latter has an advantage over the two former, in so far as he speaks of two persons possessed, while these speak only of one. These discrepancies have been interpreted to his disadvantage, and only a very faded tradition found in his account, in which, in particular, the plurality of demons in the one sick man had changed into a plurality of demoniacs; but it would be just as easy to suppose, conversely, that in order to bring out the plurality of demons the more decidedly in each individual affected, only one so affected was spoken of in the later repetition. In all other portions, at all events, the narrative of Matthew, in comparison with those of the two others, appears as the simpler. Even in his description of the state of the two men possessed, he says in his few words respecting their great fierceness, "so that no man could pass by the way on which they dwelt," as much as the others say, especially Mark, with their lengthened descriptions. The address of the possessed to Jesus is, according to all three, in all essential points the same as in the former history; the question, that is, as to what they have to do with him, and the prayer not to torment them before the time. It is, however, more natural that the man possessed should have made it when Jesus came into his neighbourhood, than that, as Mark especially says in contradiction to Matthew, he should have run from far off to meet the personage so dreaded. The narrator, finding this not quite conceivable, endeavours to suggest a motive for it in a previous command of Jesus that the devil should come out of him; a command as to which we are at a loss to see when Jesus was supposed to have given it if the man possessed had not been before in his neighbourhood. Indeed, Matthew's representation is more natural even from the miraculous point of view; for that a man thus diseased should have recognised Jesus as the Messiah at first sight is less conceivable on the further shore, where the events take place, and where Jesus was less known than on the Galilean side. How many devils there were in each of the possessed, and even that there were several in one, is not said in the first Gospel at all; the question of Jesus as to the name of the devil, and the answer that he was called Legion, because there were many of them, is an addition of the second and third Gospel. And it is obvious to surmise that the plurality was only an inference drawn from the feature which follows, which Matthew has in common with the others, the prayer, that is, of the devils to be allowed to pass into the swine. This might seem to assume an equality in number between the devils and the swine, on account of which the herd in the one case is balanced by a legion in the other.

The feature of the swine is one at which the faith of even the most credulous expositors is accustomed to falter. For even if the possession of human souls by evil spirits is conceivable, it is not easy to see how the souls of animals can be possessed in the same way; and even if this notion is admissible, there is a difficulty in the contradiction involved in the alleged behaviour of the evil spirits. First they are said, in order to avoid the necessity of going down the precipice or out of the country, to pray to be allowed to take up their quarters in the swine, and immediately after, when their prayer has been granted, to have given the creatures the impulse to rush into the sea, and so to have themselves destroyed the very quarters they had asked for. Real devils could not have acted so stupidly, but a legend or fiction might easily fall into such a contradiction, when in sketching its different features it was led by different views and objects.

As in this place not merely a simple history of an expulsion of devils was to be given, but one remarkable in every way, it was considered necessary not merely that the devils should go out of the man, but, as a proof that they had really left him, passed into another object. The object best suited for this was the unclean animal, the swine, and, if there was a herd of them, a plurality of devils might be inferred from this circumstance, and thus a still further exaggeration for the whole history be gained. The prayer of the devils might be alleged as a cause for their going into the swine, and the idea of this prayer resulted from that current at the period, that beings of this sort preferred a parasitical existence in bodies, even those of brutes, to a disembodied life in the desert or possibly in hell. But how was it to appear that they had really gone into the swine? It was impossible that they should speak out of swine as out of human beings: they might fall to the earth and exhibit contortions, but, considering the strange movements which these creatures often indulge in of themselves, this would be no certain sign. So nothing remained but, what the brutes would certainly not otherwise have done, to rush spontaneously to destruction, *i.e.* to be driven to it by the devils; a feature which, independently of the particular case and the prayers of the evil spirits that had preceded, was suited to their destructive nature. There were other stories current at the time of such proofs of expulsion of spirits. Josephus* tells of a Jewish exorcist who, by means of a magic ring and Solomonian talismans, drew devils out of the nose of persons possessed by them; that in order to convince the bystanders that the evil spirit had really gone out, he placed close by a bucket full of water, and ordered the devil to upset it, which the latter really did; and Josephus assures us that he himself had been a joint spectator of this proof of the incomparable wisdom of his countryman Solomon. In like manner

* Antiq. viii. 2, 5.

Philostratus* tells how Apollonius of Tyana ordered a devil who had possessed a youth to depart with a visible sign, upon which the devil entreated to be allowed to upset a statue that stood near, and this statue did really fall over just at the moment when the devil left the young man. Such an object however being, as these stories say, close at hand, there was, no doubt, room for deception; but how could this be supposed possible when, like the herd of swine, according to Matthew's express assurance, it was a considerable distance off?

In Matthew, the narrative concludes by saying that the inhabitants of the town, on hearing the account given of the transaction by the swineherds who had fled into it, came out and besought the performer of miracles, who thus threatened their material interests, to apply his energies elsewhere. This is also in the accounts of the two other narrators; but besides this they describe further the condition of the man who had been healed: how he who had been just before a wild and raving maniac, sat at Jesus' feet clothed and in his right mind, and how, when Jesus was about to return, he expressed a wish to be allowed to accompany him; that Jesus however did not comply with his wish, but recommended him to go home to his friends, and to tell them of the great things that God had done unto him. This addition in particular, and subsequently the whole narrative, have lately suggested to several critics an allegorical interpretation.† The man who had been just before possessed by a legion of unclean spirits, now sitting decently and in his right mind at the feet of Jesus, appeared to them to be a type of the conversion of the Gentile world, for which the Gadarene, as an inhabitant of a district for the most part heathen, was particularly suited; the legion of demons represented the numerous heathen gods which from the point of view of the

---

* Vita Apollon. iv. 20.

† Baur, Critical Examination of the Canonical Gospels, p. 430 ff. Volkmar, Religion of Jesus, p. 229 ff.

earliest Christians appeared in the light of demons (1 Cor. x. 20 ff.); their elective affinity to the swine represented the moral impurity of heathenism; the refusal of Jesus to retain with himself and the Twelve the man who had been healed, and his command to him to publish among his relations and friends the great things that God had done for him, would be, as it were, the establishment of the heathen Apostolate and its ministry, separated by Jesus himself from the Jewish Apostles. Such an explanation is certainly very obvious in this case; still it can never be anything but conjecture; and how easily it may be pressed too far is shewn by the circumstance that, from the same point of view, the fetters which had been in vain put upon this man were supposed to mean the legislation of the ancient world, which had proved insufficient to restrain it within the bounds of morality.

The object of the third of the miraculous cures indicated above (Matt. xvii. 14—21; Mark ix. 14—29; Luke ix. 37—43), which is described in its simplest form in Matthew, is to prove the strength of the miraculous power in Jesus, not so much by shewing the difficulty of the case in itself, as by pointing out that his disciples proving at first to be incompetent to render assistance, the Master himself does so with ease. A comparison of this kind between the Master and his disciples was involved in the nature of the Hebrew legend. Elisha, to whom we have so often referred as a prototype in the history of Jesus, had sent his servant Gehazi with his staff, for the purpose of raising the dead son of his Shunamitish hostess; but Gehazi not having succeeded at all, Elisha was compelled to go himself in order to raise the youth, which however he does not do without considerable trouble (2 Kings iv. 8 ff., 29—37). Now, though it is a different description of miracle, for it concerns a young man not dead but possessed, this proceeding is in part copied in the act of Jesus, in part surpassed, inasmuch as the latter has no occasion for the busy activity of the prophet, but needs only to threaten the demon, in order to accomplish his object. In Matthew, the cause of the inability of the disciples to heal the sick man is stated to have been their want of faith: Mark refers this want of faith to the father of the youth, and invents upon the strength of it a dialogue between Jesus and him, which we must, undoubtedly, attribute only to Mark himself. In Matthew, next to the want of faith on the part of the disciples, a second cause is stated for their failure; it is, that this kind of demons cometh not forth but by prayer and fasting. This does not exactly agree with all the rest; for if prayer and fasting were necessary to drive out the devil in question, then want of faith was not the cause of the disciples' failure. So Luke skilfully omits the speech about want of faith, and limits himself to that about fasting and prayer. Matthew appears here to have combined together the different attempts made to explain failure in driving out devils, such as must often have occurred in Christian communities, without disadvantage to the cause of Jesus. Still the inability of the disciples to succeed with this sick person in particular, appeared to require some explanation, retrospectively; so even Luke delineates the symptoms of his malady more fully than Matthew, while Mark, as was said above, adds further that he was deaf and dumb, and represents the youth as having been subject to this malady from childhood. As they describe the case, it appears to have been one of inveterate epilepsy: it is contrary to all probability that such a malady should have given way at once and for ever to a word, though supported by the greatest possible dignity on the part of the speaker, and by the greatest possible faith on the part of the sick person; though in a simpler case the circumstance that the disciples may very possibly have failed, and then Jesus himself have stepped in, may very easily have occurred.

It has been already remarked above that this class of the miracles of Jesus, the cures of persons possessed, is wanting in the fourth Gospel. We do indeed find in it the terms

Dæmonion and being Dæmoniac, but they are only used as we find them in classic Greek, and as the Evangelist himself (x. 20) interprets the latter term, that is, as synonymous with being mad or crazy. When Jesus asks the Jews at the feast of Tabernacles, "Why seek ye to kill me?" the people answer him, Who seeks to kill thee? thou hast a devil (John vii. 19 ff.), *i.e.* thou art affected with hypochondriac fancies; as in Matthew (xi. 18) and Luke (vii. 33) it is said of John the Baptist, that because he neither ate nor drank, his contemporaries declared that he had a devil. When, again, on another occasion Jesus declares to the Jews that they are not from God, and therefore they hear not the words of God, but that he who keeps his word will not die for all eternity, they maintain a second time that he must have a devil (viii. 48, 52), *i.e.* be foolish. Now it is true, indeed, that even in classical Greek that expression was understood not merely metaphorically, but an influence of demoniac beings and the like was really assumed; as in John the better class of people meet those reproaches applied to Jesus by asking whether a dæmonion, such as the opponents of Jesus supposed to be in operation within him, could open the eyes of the blind (John x. 21). Still this is not the idea of devils as the causes on the one hand of complaints of different kinds and that occur in other ways as well, on the other of that particular form of malady which is called possession in the strict sense. In the fourth Gospel this conception is not found, and there is no mention in it either summarily or in detail of possessed persons healed by Jesus.

There was a time when this was considered an advantage in favour of John. The Biblical notion of demoniac possession was one of those which were the first to seem intolerable to modern interpretation. How welcome, then, was the absence of so odious a popular belief from the writings of the favourite disciple of Jesus! But we neither find the theory in John, nor the histories with which the theory was connected. It were to be desired that those histories, or others like them, which the Synoptics give us as histories of possessed persons, had been given by John from another and more rational point of view. Instead of this, there are no such stories at all, and their absence is suspicious for the reason that, according to all that we know of that period, possession was the most common form of disease precisely in those districts which were the scene of the events of the evangelical history. From Josephus to Justin Martyr and Philostratus downwards, Jewish, Christian, and in part Heathen Greek writings, are full of notices of persons possessed and their cures. Consequently there is every historical probability in favour of the account of the three first Evangelists that sick persons of this description frequently appeared before Jesus. And when we remember the power exerted by the imagination in diseases of this kind, there is, as has been often remarked before, no form of complaint in which we might more easily suppose a cure to have been performed by the mere word of Jesus than this. Now the fourth Gospel says nothing whatever of such sick persons or such cures, and this omission does certainly not point to an author who was a contemporary of the life and ministry of Jesus, or near to him as a countryman who lived soon after.

No one has felt more deeply than Ewald how nearly this circumstance affects the credibility of the fourth Gospel. He is right in recognising in the histories of possession an element of the three Gospels of a specially historical character, and he sees that if the fourth is to lay claim to historical validity, it ought not to want this component element. And while we are making the best of it, and observing that the fourth Gospel does indeed want this element, and with it a main support upon which its claim to historical validity might be founded—Ewald, on the contrary, says that the Gospel is without it now, but was not originally so; between the fifth and sixth chapters a portion of the Gospel has been lost, which with other matter must also have contained an expulsion of a devil.* We, who are unable to soar after the great Eagle of Göttingen in so bold a flight of authoritative decision, assert, on the contrary, that as the fourth Evangelist says nothing of expulsion of devils, he either knew nothing of them or did not wish to know anything. If he knew nothing of them, the reason cannot have been that occurrences of this kind did not take place, for according to the credible testimony of the synoptic Gospels, they really did take place; but the occurrences must have been unknown to him. This cannot have been the case if he was the Apostle John; moreover, it cannot have been the case if he lived at a later period, but was acquainted with the synoptic Gospels or others connected with them, in all of which the cures of persons possessed played an important part; and there is every indication of his having been acquainted with these Gospels. If, therefore, he says nothing of those histories with which he must have been acquainted from these Gospels, it must be because he did not wish to know anything about them. Baur supposes that he may have found himself unable to extract from them any important support for the point of view in which he places the miracles of Jesus as proof of his Logos-nature.† But the theory of possession, and the cure of it by Christ, would have been sufficiently well adapted to the conflict and antagonism between Light and Darkness, verging as it does upon dualism, and running through the whole of his Gospel, if it had been suited to the ideas of the Evangelist himself and the readers for whom his Gospel was intended. In this point of view, Köstlin has drawn attention to the fact that the belief in demoniac possession, and a power of the Messiah over devils, was eminently Jewish and Jewish-Christian, and that therefore the power of expelling devils is not enumerated by Paul among the gifts of the Spirit practised in the

* The Writings of John, i. 25, note.
† Critical Investigations, p. 255, note.

Corinthian Church (1 Cor. xii. 10, 28); while in the author of the third Gospel and the Acts of the Apostles, the stress which he lays upon this side of the ministry of Jesus belongs to that Jewish-Christian element in him which may be remarked on other occasions.* To this may be added what Bretchneider has already noticed,† that in the second century after Christ the alleged cure of demoniacs by exorcism had become so common, that a reference to these cures was not considered, even by the most uneducated classes, to say nothing of the educated Greeks, any proof of the higher nature of Christ. It is enough to say that demons, and the expulsion of demons, at the period, in the district and the state of cultivation in which and for which the author of the fourth Gospel wrote, were not in good repute: the whole thing, as one may see from Lucian, had, by means of magicians and impostors, come into such discredit, that it appeared most desirable to keep Jesus aloof from the whole of this department.

75. Cures, Involuntary and at a Distance.

So far we have arranged the miraculous cures of Jesus according to the species of maladies to which they were applied. They might also be arranged according to his mode of operation in applying them. Beginning with those in which he availed himself of material means, as saliva or clay, we might pass on to those in which he effected the cure simply by touching, then to those in which he operated by a word alone, and in these again distinguish between the cases in which the patient was present and himself heard the words spoken, and those in which he was absent and the

---

* Origin and Composition of the Synoptic Gospels, p. 241.
† Probabilia, 118.

words of Jesus operated at a distance. From all those cures, which assume a definite individual act of will on the part of Jesus as the cause of the cure, those cases, lastly, would have to be distinguished in which he is touched by one or more sick persons, and the cure is as it were stolen from him without any separate act of will on his part. The miracles of Jesus which we have considered so far, all come under the head of conscious and intentional cures of persons present, sometimes by means of material instruments, sometimes by touching, sometimes by word; on the other hand, involuntary cures, and cures at a distance, have not yet been discussed.

According to several summary statements of the synoptic Gospels (Matt. xiv. 36; Mark vi. 56), Jesus was sometimes besought by sick persons or their connections to allow the hem of his garment to be touched by the former for the purpose of effecting a cure. If he consented, as we must suppose he did, there was, on his part, a definite act of will to effect the cure. If, on the other hand, as we also read (Mark iii. 10; Luke vi. 19), the sick persons came upon him at once, and sought to touch his garment, we do not know whether he could take notice of each individual among those who thus pressed upon him, and specially direct his will towards them. But that the cure did not follow until he knew upon whom it was conferred, we know for certain from what is told of the woman with the issue of blood, whose history is connected by all three Synoptics with that of the raising of the daughter of Jairus (Matt. ix. 20—22; Mark v. 25—34; Luke viii. 43—48).

In this account, however, there is a discrepancy between all three narrators, in which we may plainly see the continued growth of the myth, the increasing materialization of the idea of miracle. In these summary statements, Matthew says (xiv. 36) that the sick persons who touched the hem of the garment of Jesus became whole, Luke (vi. 19) that virtue went out of him which healed all. Now it may indeed be said that these two statements amount to the same thing, as Matthew conceived the cure to be effected, not, as we have supposed in many of these cases, by the power of imagination in the sick persons, but by a miraculous power inherent in Jesus. Still the more cautious or at least indefinite character of the expression of Matthew, compared with the greater concentration and materialism of that of Luke, is not to be mistaken. Corresponding to this difference is the tone of the more lengthened narrative given by each of the case of the woman with the issue, where Mark, as might be expected, is on the side of Luke, and even adds here and there a picturesque touch. Matthew tells that when Jesus, attended by his disciples, was going to the house of the Jewish ruler, in order to raise his daughter who had just died, a woman, who had had an issue of blood twelve years, came behind him and touched the hem of his garment, with the firm conviction that this touch would suffice to make her whole; that Jesus turned round, and, when he saw the woman, said to her, "Daughter, be of good comfort; thy faith hath made thee whole!" And from that very hour the woman was healed. There is nothing here, apart from the accounts of the particular form and duration of the malady, which might not have occurred as is stated. A sick woman may have touched Jesus in a spirit of faith, may have traced an amendment in herself in consequence of this touch, and may have been dismissed by Jesus with a comforting word: it is true that the Evangelist conceives the cause of this amendment in her condition to have been a supernatural healing power inherent in Jesus; but what he says and represents Jesus as saying is quite reconcilable with the belief that it was the faith of the sick person that "made her whole." The meaning of the narrative of the first Evangelist depends principally upon the question as to what it was that made Jesus turn round. This is not expressly stated by Matthew: following his statement, we might suppose that Jesus felt in a perfectly natural manner that some one caught at his garment; for, according to Matthew, he was only attended by his disciples, who did not press on him or touch him, so that as he walked on he might easily feel such a stoppage.

Now it was just at this point that the narrative of Matthew ceased to satisfy the belief in miracles. The woman, it was supposed, must not merely have felt herself cured, but Jesus also must have felt that healing virtue had gone out of him on being touched by the woman, and have turned round towards her for this and no other reason. The pressure of the people, which Luke and Mark add to the attendance of the disciples spoken of in Matthew, only avails to make this turning round of Jesus inexplicable on natural grounds. It was impossible for Jesus, in the crush and pressure of the multitude, to distinguish, in a natural manner, one particular touch of his garment. If he did distinguish it, there must have been something supernatural, there must have been an issue from him of his miraculous power, by which he so distinguished it. This is intended to be shewn by the question of Jesus, the answer of the disciples, and, lastly, by the woman's coming forward in consequence of Jesus' continued inquiries. And as it appeared at the same time that the healing virtue of Jesus had operated on his being touched by the woman in a spirit of faith, without his being aware of the person who was to benefit by it, he appeared no longer merely as one who could produce a cure by his word and his will, but as one in whom the healing power was always present, in whom, to apply a well-known expression in a somewhat different sense, all the fulness of the divine power of salvation and healing dwelt bodily (Col. ii. 9).

From this point it is no great step to those narratives in the Acts of the Apostles of sick persons being healed by the application of handkerchiefs or aprons of Paul (xix. 11), nay, even by the mere shadow of Peter falling upon them (v. 15). Limiting the cases to certain maladies, and for the most part to transient relief only of the sick persons, we would as little deny the possibility of this, as that on the grave of the Abbé Paris, or by the application of relics to faithful Catholics, results have been sometimes attained which might be claimed as cures. But these effects might be produced, whether the bones in which faith was put had really belonged to a saint or a sinner; and likewise in the case of Jesus, whether he were a religious character qualified to give us a standard, or only a prophet in the sense of ordinary Judaism, provided only he knew how to make his contemporaries put faith in him. The case is the same if, as modern theologians are fond of doing, the healing power of Jesus is supposed to have been of the nature of animal magnetism; except that an instantaneous and proportionally healing effect of magnetic power upon sick persons of the most various descriptions, and without continued magnetic relations, is unexampled in the history of animal magnetism.

In involuntary cures of this kind, the healing power of Jesus appears as completely material as an electric fluid, which, on the body filled with it being touched, issues forth upon that which touches it. Conversely, in the cures at a distance, instances of which are also given by our Evangelists, there is quite a spiritual character, as the mere will of Jesus is supposed to have shewn itself in operation upon a sick person corporeally absent. So, as in those other cases, modern theologians are glad to fall back on the analogy of animal magnetism, in these they appeal to that property of spirit in accordance with which we describe it as not being confined to space. "A cure at a distance," says Hase,* "really involves, as a spiritual operation, nothing inconceivable." Certainly, as space is only for corporeal things; and if there were pure spirits, it is conceivable that they should operate upon one another without being bound by the conditions of space. But what is the use of such fancies as these, when, as in the

---

* Life of Jesus, § 55; comp. 81.

case before us, we are concerned not with pure but with embodied spirits? Embodied spirits, such as we have here, not only in Jesus, but in the sick persons, can only operate outside of themselves by means of their bodies, consequently under the conditions of space. Consequently, the appeal to the nature of spirit, in order to explain a cure at a distance, is only a mere form of speech, without any real corresponding meaning.

Of cures of this kind, Matthew and Mark have one in common, Matthew and Luke the other, and John also in a somewhat different form. The first is the healing of the daughter of the Canaanitish woman (Matt. xv. 21—28), the latter that of the servant or son of the captain or king's officer in Capernaum (Matt. viii. 5—13; Luke vii. 1—10; John iv. 46—54). In the first account, the sick person in both Evangelists is a woman possessed; in the other, we have in Matthew a man with the palsy, grievously tormented, in Luke and John a person stated generally to be sick unto death. In the first case, all the stress is laid upon the original refusal of Jesus to use his miraculous power for the benefit of the heathen woman, and his subsequent consent in consequence of the persevering faith of the woman; in the second, everything, at least in Matthew, turns upon the fact that while Jesus is ready to go into the captain's house, the latter declares his confidence that Jesus can perform the cure at a distance. We have already had occasion to consider the first narrative apart from the miracle;* as to the miracle, which is all that remains to discuss, it coincides with the rest of the history.

In this we again see clearly, first and foremost, how, in the repetition and then in the subjective re-touching, it passes through a course of continuous exaggeration. In Matthew, the captain beseeches Jesus to aid his sick boy; Jesus offers to go and heal him; the captain considers this too great a condescension, and also not necessary; Jesus need only speak

* Vol. i. p. 299.

a word and it will take effect, as certainly as when he, the captain, orders one of his subalterns to perform something at a distance; Jesus holds up this faith on the part of the heathen man to his compatriots as an example which may put them to shame. To the captain he grants the cure in which he has expressed his faith, and the cure takes place at the self-same hour. Luke describes the "boy" in Matthew, who might also be possibly a son, as a servant; but in order to suggest a more satisfactory motive for the captain's zealous eagerness for his cure, he also describes him as a particularly valuable servant to his master. All these are unimportant features. But we may recognise in the other discrepancy a more definite object, that discrepancy consisting in the fact that the captain, who in Matthew comes to Jesus in person, sends, in Luke, the elders of the Jews to pray Jesus to come into his house. The object of this change appears in what these elders do; besides conveying the request, they recommend the heathen captain as a friend of the Jews who had built a synagogue for them. If we understand this to mean that Jesus was to be justified, as it were, for putting his miraculous power at the service of a heathen, such a turn might certainly be expected rather in a Gospel of Judaising than of Pauline tendency. If, on the other hand, it is understood to imply a general recommendation of the Heathen to the Jews in words to this effect, See, ye Jews and Jewish Christians, there are among the Heathen persons of so graceful a character and so right-minded as this, and you are very wrong in utterly condemning them—we see how such a turn suited completely the scheme of a Gospel, the object of which was to reconcile Jewish and Pauline Christianity. Exactly in the same way we see in the second part of the work, the Acts of the Apostles (x. 1 ff., 22), also a Roman captain, Cornelius, as a candidate for Christian baptism, recommended by the excellent testimonials given by all the Jews to his fear of God and his benevolence and charity.

In Matthew, the captain had at first only begged, generally, for help for his sick boy, and on Jesus offering to go with him into his house, modestly, and in a spirit of faith, declines this, and only prayed for a Messianic command. In Luke, he sends *first* the elders of the Jews praying Jesus to come to save his servant; then, on Jesus going with them and approaching the house, he sends some friends to meet him, declining his visit and begging for a simple word. The narrative of Matthew is perfectly self-consistent; but in the account of Luke there is an internal inconsistency. If in the first instance the captain has asked Jesus, through the elders, to vouchsafe him a personal visit, what could afterwards have made him change his mind so as to countermand this visit by a second message? The author himself seems to have felt that there was a contradiction here, so he endeavours to reconcile the two messages by the remark put into the mouth of the bearers of the second (ver. 7), that the sending of the first was intended to imply that the captain thought himself unworthy to communicate directly with Jesus, and consequently to be visited personally by him. Nevertheless, he had, in the first message, begged for this visit in plain words, and therefore it still remains a question how he came subsequently to countermand it. In the history of the daughter of Jairus, we find in Luke and Mark, as distinguished from Matthew, a similar deprecating message. In the first Gospel (ix. 18 ff.), the daughter is reported to Jesus by the father as having just died, upon which the process of Jesus visiting the house for the purpose of raising the dead goes on without interruption. In Luke (viii. 41 ff.) and Mark (v. 22 ff.), the maiden is lying in her last agonies, and the father prays Jesus to come and save her life; but as Jesus is going, her death takes place, and the father is met by a message from the house, recommending him not to trouble the Master, as the maiden is dead, and now nothing can do any good. In this case, we may suppose that the father, though he had before begged for the visit of Jesus, did not wish to trouble the latter any more; for, as the state of things in his house had changed in the meantime, he might now have ceased to wish for what he had before gained by his entreaties. On the other hand, in the history of the Capernaum captain, where the circumstances had continued the same, there was no motive for such a change of mind; and the supposition that it has been improperly transferred out of the other history into this seems the more probable, as the visit of Jesus in person is on each occasion declined in the same words.*

The two synoptic accounts have this feature in common, that the petitioner, by his faith, outbids the offer of Jesus, *i.e.* Jesus is ready to do more, but the petitioner prefers less, in the conviction that from Jesus even the less is more than enough. Such a relation between the Logos Christ and a human being is contrary to the ground-plan of the fourth Gospel. According to this, the human being is never to perform more than the God in Man had expected; but, conversely, the latter must always be doing far more than the former could have believed, or even conceived: surprise, outbidding, is here as exclusively on the side of Christ, as on the side of man there is nothing but backwardness in faith and understanding. It was only when remodelled in this spirit that the narrative availed at all; but, so remodelled, it was of much avail for the purposes of the fourth Gospel. The author seems to have compounded the features of his own story from those of the two forms which he had before him in the older Gospels. He takes the boy spoken of in Matthew to have been, not, as Luke calls him, a servant, but a son of the petitioner; on the other hand, he knows nothing of the palsy which, according to Matthew, tortured the patient, but, with Luke, represents him as being on the point of death, without stating the form of the malady. As in Matthew, the peti-

* Luke viii. 49 (daughter of Jairus) : $\mu\dot{\eta}$ σκύλλε τὸν διδάσκαλον. Luke vii. 6 (captain of Capernaum): κύριε, μὴ σκύλλου.

tioner applies personally to Jesus, not with an undefined prayer for aid, but, as in Luke, with a petition still more definitely stated, that Jesus would accompany him for the purpose of healing the sick person. Now here comes in the peculiarly Johannine turn of the narrative. In two of the Synoptics, Jesus readily accompanies him, but is stopped either by the faith of the captain or by his messengers. In the fourth Gospel, on the contrary, Jesus expresses his displeasure at the captain's request, in which, however, the latter perseveres; and while in the other accounts it is the captain who surprises Jesus and ourselves by his faith in the mere word of Jesus as sufficient for the cure of the distant patient, in this, to our surprise and that of the man, Jesus pronounces spontaneously the talismanic word which operates at a distance, and now for the first time, after receiving the rebuke from Jesus, faith in the mere word of Jesus arises all at once in the man's mind.

Had the petitioner been from the first placed in the unfavourable light of a man possessed only of the coarsest notions of the higher power of Jesus, then, in a Gospel which looks upon the heathen world as the proper soil of Christianity, he could no longer be a Roman captain, *i.e.* a heathen; he was therefore transformed into an officer of the king, *i.e.* the Galilean tetrach Herod Antipas, who had also the title of king (Matt. xiv. 9; Mark vi. 14), and, by the expression of Jesus directed to him, "Except ye see signs and wonders ye will not believe," set up as a representative of carnal miracle-seeking Judaism. As one, however, who is led by Jesus to believe in his mere word, he appears contrasted with the stiff-necked Jews in the character of those Galileans who in our Gospel form the transition to the more susceptible Samaritans or Heathen. Capernaum, as stated in the synoptic accounts, is his appropriate dwelling-place; but the fourth Evangelist does not choose that his Jesus should sojourn in this city, which in the Jewish-Christian tradition appeared as the proper seat of his ministry (comp. ii. 12); the place of his Galilean performance of miracles is here, on the contrary, Cana (iv. 46): and by this arrangement in the present case, as the sick person lay at Capernaum, an increase of the distance, and consequently an exaggeration of the miracle, was gained.

We see from another feature that, among other things, the author of the fourth Gospel had in view in a general way to give more emphatic importance to the supernatural element in the occurrence, and to accredit that element to the utmost of his power. In Matthew, it is said that after Jesus had pronounced the words that guaranteed the cure, at the self-same hour the boy was healed; in Luke, that when the messengers came back into the house they found the sick servant recovered. Here certainly, from the nature of the case, no circumstantial investigation into the moment at which the cure took place was required, as in Luke the messengers found Jesus already in the neighbourhood of the house, and in Matthew the captain himself came upon him in a street of the same little town in which his house was: it was, therefore, a matter of course that when he or his messengers on returning home found the sick person recovered, that the recovery must have followed the words of Jesus. In John, on the contrary, on account of the distance between Cana and Capernaum, it is not until the following day that the father comes home, and there was therefore room for the investigation as to whether it was not until that day or on the day before, and at what hour on the day before, that the amendment in the health of the sick person took place. This inquiry is now actually made by the father of the boy, and it is found that the hour of the amendment coincided accurately with that in which Jesus spoke the word of life for the benefit of the son. Now the laboriousness of this investigation and settlement of the time, if we compare it with the simple account of Matthew, gives to the statement of the fourth Gospel a very secondhand character, and proves it in this case also to be the latest subjective re-touching of the matter of the Synoptics.

In the case of this history it is particularly clear that between the view of the strongest believer in miracles and that of Reimar, so long as the evangelical accounts are considered historical, there is no intermediate point. For every natural or even half-natural explanation of the result is excluded, because as the patient is at a distance from the performer of the miracle, it is impossible that faith should have been excited in the former by the personal impress of the latter. If, according to Matthew, Jesus said to the captain, "Go thy way, and as thou hast believed, so be it done unto thee;" or, according to John, to the officer of the king, "Go thy way, thy son liveth!" he must either have felt conscious that he could effect such a cure, *i.e.* he must have been a performer of miracles in the sense of the most decided supranaturalism; or, if he attributed to himself such miraculous power as this without any ground, he was a wild enthusiast; while, if he ascribed it to himself with the consciousness that he did not really possess it, he was an audacious cheat and impostor. To understand the words, "Thy son lives," as Ewald does, and explain them away to mean that Jesus only intended to say to the father that his son would not die, and then to speak of a miraculous (*i.e.*, in plain words, accidental) coincidence between the time at which the words were uttered and the hour of the amendment, is an evasion and of no use. For no one but either a charlatan who was as inconsiderate as he was shameless, or a man who was conscious that he could put an end to an illness, would declare that a sick person at a distance, represented to him as dying, would not die. In this case, if in any, criticism alone points out a mode of escape from a superstitious belief in miracles to which we cannot bring ourselves, and a naturalistic pragmatism altogether unsatisfactory. We have not here a history, but a Messianic myth, which has grown out of the myth of the prophet in the

Old Testament. The attribute ordinarily ascribed to a prophet was the power of healing on the spot by bodily contact; it was this that the leprous Naaman (2 Kings v. 11) says he expected of Elisha; and when, instead of this, the prophet, without quitting his house, tells him he is to wash seven times in the Jordan, he considers himself mocked, because he expects no result in doing so. Still he allows himself to be persuaded to follow the advice, and is healed; *i.e.* the prophet has performed a miracle at a distance, as the bathing in the Jordan, as in the case of the Johannine cure of the blind man the washing in the pool of Siloa, is only the form with which it was his pleasure to connect the operation of his word. The Messiah could not be supposed to have fallen short of such miraculous power; and, above all, the Being in whom the Creative Word of God had become flesh, what would such a Being require but a mere word to operate in the furthest distance so as to heal and restore to life?

76. Cases of Raising of the Dead.

Turning now from those cures effected by Jesus which we do not find mentioned in the list of miracles, Matt. xi. 5, to the order of the miracles there enumerated, we find, in the next and last place, raising of the dead to life. Neither the cures of leprosy nor these cases are taken from the prophetic passage (Isaiah xxxv. 5 ff.), as are the other Messianic signs to which Jesus appeals in Matthew, but still the raising of the dead was suggested by the prophetic prototype. Elijah (1 Kings xvii. 17 ff.) and Elisha had raised the dead, and among the divine acts which, in accordance with this prototype, the Jews expected at the time of the Messiah, raising of the dead is particularly mentioned.*

Added to this there was an element involved in Christian-

---
* See above, Vol. i. p. 204 ff., the passages quoted from Tanchuma.

ity itself. It was Jesus who had brought life and immortality to light (2 Tim. i. 10); the Christians were not like other men who have no hope beyond the grave (1 Thess. iv. 13); Christianity was the religion of the resurrection and of immortality. A future resurrection of the dead to a new and immortal life was, indeed, according to Daniel, xii. 2, also the doctrine of later and especially of Pharisaic Judaism (2 Macc. vii.); but as it was not found in the books of Moses and of the older prophets, but required to be foisted upon them by means of artificial interpretation, it was not recognised by the Sadducees, and continued as an apple of discord between the schools, and little else but a scholastic opinion. The raising of the dead was expected to be brought about, sometimes by God himself, sometimes it was represented as to be undertaken by the Messiah, according as the conception of the latter took a form more or less supernatural; and indeed this conception was itself uncertain and indefinite until the appearance of Jesus, from whom it received its due precision and living spirit. From the time of his ministry it was known, *i.e.* his adherents knew, what conception was to be formed of the Messiah; from the time of his departure they knew—they knew it because they wished it, and knew it for certain because they wished it ardently—that he would return immediately, in order to fulfil all those Messianic functions which on his first presence upon earth had been left in arrear, among them the raising of the dead. In view of this immediate raising of the dead by Christ, death appeared to Christians nothing but a sleep, and the expression of Jesus over the daughter of Jairus (Matt. ix. 24), "She is not dead, but sleepeth," apart from the miracle with which it is here brought into connection, contains the early Christian view of death generally. The faith in the resurrection of Christ, *i.e.* in the fact that he had been raised to life by God (1 Cor. xv. 12 ff.), involved, indeed, the principal guarantee for the future resurrection; but together with this passive resurrection, men desired to see also active proofs of the exercise of this power on the part of him who was to raise the dead; he must not merely have been raised from the dead himself, but have also himself raised the dead.

If the answer to the message of the Baptist, which in the present section we are making the basis of our discussion, was really spoken by Jesus, he attributes to himself, together with the restoration of the blind to sight, &c., also the raising of the dead; not indeed in any other sense than that in which (Matt. viii. 22) he replied to the man who wished first to bury his father, commanding him to leave to the (spiritually) dead the task of burying the (corporeally) dead, the symbolical sense, that is, that he is able to quicken anew the dead mind of man with a feeling for something more exalted, and fill it with a new moral aim. In this sense the fourth Evangelist, in particular, framed the Christian expression, making his Jesus say (xi. 25), "I am the resurrection and the life; he that believeth in me, though he were dead, yet shall he live;" or (v. 21), "As the Father raiseth up the dead and quickeneth them, even so the Son quickeneth whom he will." In these expressions we must, indeed, understand to be implied the future resuscitation of those who are corporeally dead, and at the same time that spiritual quickening which proceeds from Jesus.

But whatever was the theory of the early Christian circle, this present spiritual awakening could not suffice as a guarantee for the future corporeal resurrection of the dead. Jesus, during his life on earth, must also have raised the corporeally dead, at least in some cases. Then, and not before, could it be known for certain that there dwelt in him a power to recal all the dead to life on his more glorious second coming. And now the legend of the prophets came in opportunely. As Elijah and Elisha had each raised a dead body to life, so Jesus the Messiah must at least have done as much. Matthew and Mark are satisfied with one history of this description, the raising of the daughter of Jairus (Matt. ix. 18 ff.; Mark v. 22 ff.); Luke gives two of them, namely, together with the one just mentioned (in him, viii. 41 ff.), that of the youth at Nain (vii. 11 ff.); John only one indeed, the raising of Lazarus (chap. xi.), but one of such a character that it stands for all, and that, in comparison with it, every other is simply superfluous.

The theme of the first account of a raising of the dead, common to the three synoptic Evangelists, is, as has been already remarked, the text, "She is not dead, but sleepeth;" *i.e.* the fundamental Christian view of death as merely a sleep. We find this theme here embodied in the form of a miraculous history, and indeed in its simplest form in Matthew. The father of the maiden, described indefinitely as a ruler, announces to Jesus the death of his daughter as having just occurred, petitioning him to come and lay his hand upon her, so will she become alive again. Jesus, attended by his disciples, goes with him. The interlude of the woman with an issue of blood having taken place, they come into the house of mourning, and here they find, in accordance with the bad habit of the Jews at that time, the burial of the dead body of the girl about to take place in a few hours, the musicians already on the spot, and a noisy crowd of mourners of other kinds whom Jesus orders out, alleging as a reason what we have just described as the theme of the narrative; whereupon, however, he is ridiculed by the people. The new Christian view of death is here immediately contrasted with that of the old Jews as a heathen view. Even the Jew of the old style, with his faith in a resurrection, not grounded on the principles of Moses, but wavering in the midst of the conflicts of the schools—a resurrection, moreover, which lay in the distant background of a long life amid disembodied shades, belonged no less than the heathen to those who have no hope; the noisy death-wail might therefore suit their notion, but, on the Christian point of view, it had to be put aside as something altogether inappropriate; while, conversely, Christian confidence in death appeared to Jews, as well as to Heathens, a ridiculous delusion.

It is Christ who has put an end to the inconsolable sorrow for the dead felt by the ancient world, in reality by the fact that the hope of a resurrection, not long to be delayed, and of a happy life with him, was connected with faith in him for all who believed; here, on the other hand, where this relation is put in the form of a miraculous history, the object of the history is attained by his recalling, on the spot, to earthly life the maiden for whom the death-wail was intended. After having put out the profane multitude, he accomplishes this simply by taking the hand of the maiden, who immediately rises; in complete contrast with the instances of raising the dead by the prophets, which were not effected without long exerted efforts by the performers of the miracles.

Now it is certainly a proof of great simplicity and naiveté, that, according to Matthew, the father at once assumes that Jesus need only come and lay his hand upon the body of the child, and she will immediately come to life again. By his looking upon it thus as a matter of course, so extraordinary a miracle as a raising of the dead is, appeared to be degraded to the level of an ordinary thing, or at all events to something short of a miracle. It appeared greater if it was not expected, but nevertheless took place. If indeed the father accosted Jesus, as he is said in Matthew to have done, with a petition to come to his daughter who was dead, he must have considered her recal to life as possible. On this account Luke and Mark represent him as going to Jesus before the girl is dead. The laying on of hands, for which he petitions, is supposed to heal only those who are dangerously sick; it is not assumed that it is also sufficient to resuscitate a person already dead. But it was necessary that Jesus should have raised a person in that state. So in Mark and Luke the girl dies in the interval between the father's con-

versation with Jesus, and his arrival at the house of mourning, and now the supposition that the assistance of the performer of miracles comes too late, is enunciated by people who come out of the house, and recommend the father, now that it is all over with the child, not to trouble the Master any longer. Whether, on receiving this intelligence, the father himself also abandoned all hope we are not told, as Jesus anticipates anything he might say by the encouraging exhortation not to fear, but only to believe, and his child shall be saved. By this the way is prepared for the subsequent declaration that the maiden is not dead but only sleeping, but this declaration does not produce so striking an effect as in Matthew, where it comes in without any such introduction. Moreover, we see clearly, on comparing the form in which the history is given in Luke and Mark with that in Matthew, that the raising of the dead is here brought in supplementarily, and placed as it were upon a pedestal. The mode in which the two middle Evangelists introduce it, is only the objective statement of the reflection that cures of the sick by word and laying on of hands are indeed marvellous enough, but still something conceivable by the human mind, while the raising of the dead transcends all human thought and intelligence. Luke and Mark limit more accurately the father's office of "Ruler," by stating that he was ruler of a synagogue, and they also give his name. But this fact is no advantage to their account over that of Matthew, as the first feature might be an addition from the narrator's own invention, while the name of Jair might be chosen simply on account of its meaning in the language.*
Another feature peculiar to Luke, that, namely, of the girl

---

* The Hebrew word Jair (which is moreover the name, among others, of a son of Manasseh, the son of Joseph, 4 Mos. xxxii. 41 ; Josh. xiii. 30) means, *he will enlighten.* In Ps. xiii. 4, it is said, the same word being used, Lord, lighten thou mine eyes, that I sleep not in death. The father might have got this name because this quickening enlightenment shewed itself in his daughter.

having been her father's only child, only serves the purpose of making the scene more pathetic, and appears to be taken from the history of the son of the widow of Nain, where Luke likewise has it, as the account in him and Mark, that the girl was twelve years old, is probably introduced in consequence of the interweaving with the history we are considering, the narrative of the woman with the issue of blood, the period of whose illness is fixed by all the narrators at twelve years. Matthew is the only one who states that Jesus ordered out the people, who could do no good, before setting about the performance of the miracle; he says nothing of his having also excluded some of the disciples. On the other hand, according to Luke and Mark, Jesus takes with him, besides the parents of the girl, only a very small and select number of his disciples, Peter, James, and John; and in their account, in addition to the stretching out of the hand, by means of which Matthew represents the raising of the girl as having been effected, there comes the word of command, "Damsel, arise," which Mark repeats in the original Aramaic, which Jesus used. In this case also, as in that of the cure of the deaf and dumb man, which is peculiar to Mark, the object of this last-mentioned feature can only be to invest the miraculous act with greater mystery; and this is also the object of the exclusion of the disciples, with the exception of that triumvirate, and of the command, at the conclusion, not to publish the occurrence, while Matthew represents it as having been, without hesitation, proclaimed abroad over the whole country; the command of Jesus in Mark and Luke to give the damsel something to eat, is a feature which adds vividness to the scene, and one which the natural explanation in vain endeavours to turn to its advantage.

As a parallel to the history of the raising of a damsel, there arose another, the object of which is a boy or youth. The formation of such a parallel was suggested by the Old Testament prototypes, as Elijah and Elisha were said, each of them, to have raised the young and only son of a mother, who, moreover, in the history of Elijah, is a widow. We find all these elements, calculated as they are to excite sympathy, repeated in the history of the youth of Nain as given in Luke, and which, moreover, in this respect stands in the relation of an exaggerated account, as compared with that of the daughter of Jairus. The mother, the widow, accompanying to the grave her only son, has a stronger claim on our sympathy than the father whose daughter (as to whom, moreover, we only learn from the narrator of our history that she also was an only child) has died; in that account the mourners are especially mentioned as hired attendants, whose conduct is only disgusting; in this it is the bereaved mother who, by her tears for her only son, moves the compassion of the performer of miracles. Thus we find also in the address of Jesus to the widow, when we compare it with that to Jairus, the same substantive meaning, only changed from the objective into the subjective. If, as Jesus had said to Jairus, it is really the case that death is only a sleep, the inference is, what Jesus says to the widow of Nain, and Luke had already introduced in the history of the daughter of Jairus, that the dead are not to be wept for. On the point of view of the early Christians, this follows even if they continue dead, as their resurrection is at hand with the second coming of Christ; in the miraculous history, indeed, the consolation appears to be founded upon the fact that the dead person is to be immediately recalled to life on earth. But that such a bringing out of the sympathetic side is quite in the character of the third Gospel, any one may see who remembers the principal parables peculiar to him, as distinguished from those of Matthew.

But even as regards what actually took place, this case of raising the dead is an exaggeration, as compared with that considered above. The daughter of Jairus had just died, and was lying, as we must suppose not yet cold, upon her bed.

If her recal to life was used as a proof of the miraculous power of Jesus, how obvious it was for the unbelievers to suspect that the damsel was not really dead, but had only fainted, and would have come to herself again, even without the intervention of Jesus. The case was different with a dead person who was already being carried to the grave; he was beyond comparison more certainly, was, so to say, notoriously dead. It was, indeed, the custom among the Jews at that time, as has been already mentioned, to bury the dead very soon after death, usually within four hours; but still some test of death was instituted which had power of proof, at least for contemporaries. Consequently Philostratus also, in his biography of Apollonius, the Neo-Pythagorean performer of miracles, has copied, in particular, this history.* He represents his hero as meeting the bier of a bride, whom he recals to life by a touch and a few words. In the case of Jesus, it requires only the command to the youth to rise up; the touch had been only for the coffin, to make the bearers stop. Then, when the dead upon the bier had raised himself into a sitting posture, it is said that Jesus gave him to his mother. And this is described in exactly the same words as the act of Elijah with reference to the son of the widow of Sarepta raised by him (1 Kings xvii. 23).

It may, however, be conceded to the natural explanation that in this case, in which the person to be raised is already being borne to the grave, there is not, considering the Jewish custom of early burial, any absolute security that the person believed to be dead was not only apparently so. So much the more certain is it that Jesus, when he forbids the mother to weep, orders the bearers to stop and the young man to rise, does not at any moment conduct himself as if he recognised in the condition of the body an apparent death, but as if he had the power and the will to restore to life one really dead.

---

* Comp. Baur, Apollonius of Tyana and Christ, p. 145.

Quite as little can the astonishment of the people, amounting almost to terror, their praise to God that he had visited his people by sending a great Prophet among them, be looked upon as the mere discovery of an apparent death. Consequently the history, as narrated by the Evangelist, is intended as a real raising of the dead. If we cannot conceive the occurrence of such an event, then we have remaining, not a natural history, but no history at all, and we shall have to look for the elements out of which the narrative has arisen, in the same department in which the impossibility lies of looking upon it as a history,—in the conceptions of God and his revelation in nature and the world of mankind, which among the Jews and the most ancient Christians were different, and produced different effects from what they produce among ourselves.

77. THE RAISING OF LAZARUS.

It was felt, however, that the forms in which the miraculous act of raising the dead appears in the history which we have just been considering, did not put an end to all doubt, and that the proof which it was intended to establish was still imperfect. And this was the case, not in the first instance with the rationalists of modern times, or the ancient opponents of Christianity, but from the very beginning, within the Christian circle itself. What men wished to be most certain of by these histories of the raising of the dead, was the future resurrection of the dead by the power of Christ on his coming again. Now this second coming was, in the first years of Christianity, considered so near, that the Apostle Paul, for example, still hoped to live to see it (1 Cor. xv. 51 ff.; 1 Thess. iv. 15 ff.). But still, taking only Christians into consideration, a considerable number of these, and the longer time went on the more the numbers increased, had long since died, been buried and had seen corruption, and though he in his lifetime had recalled to life certain persons, who were scarcely dead and not yet buried, it was by no means sufficiently established from this fact that the re-awakening power of Christ on his return would extend to the former. It was necessary that the miracle of the past, which should guarantee the future, should stand to that future in a more direct relation, as a proof that some time or other all who should be lying in the grave should hear the voice of the Son of God and come out of it (John v. 28 ff.); it was necessary that during his earthly pilgrimage he should have called forth out of the grave, with a mighty voice, one who had already been lying in it for some time, and been given up to corruption (John xi. 17, 39, 43). This is the origin of the Johannine history of the raising of the dead, in which, moreover, all the threads coincide that constitute the peculiarity of the Gospel. Among all the three raisings of the dead mentioned in the Gospels, that of the daughter of Jairus, which is common to them all, has been described as the positive, that of the youth of Nain as the comparative, to which the narrative of the raising of Lazarus, peculiar to John, forms the superlative; but this is exactly the relation in which the Gospels of Matthew, Luke, and John, also stand, in general, to each other. In Matthew, the miraculous element appears throughout in simple solidity, as if it could not be otherwise; in Luke, the principle from which it proceeds, and the effect upon the mind, are each in a degree brought more fully to light; in John, lastly, everything, principle and miraculous act, mental impression and spiritual meaning of the miracle, are all raised to their highest expression, and these different sides at the same time brought into a unity which does not fail to produce its effect even after the contradictions involved in it have been long discoverable by the unprejudiced eye.

In order that our sympathies might be engaged from first to last, it was necessary that the subject of the miracle should be, not an unknown person, but a friend of Jesus, and the female heart that sorrowed for his death, not that of an ordinary mother, but the tender sister hearts of Martha and Mary, that Mary who hung upon Jesus with such enthusiastic worship peculiar to herself. Nor has the narrator in the fourth Gospel left out of sight that more subtle characteristic by which, in the history of the raising of the daughter of Jairus, Luke was distinguished from Matthew. In order to get a step from the lower to the higher, he also represents the person subsequently raised as having been announced at first to be not dead but only sick. In the first case the father goes himself; in this the sister sends to Jesus a message with the intelligence of their brother's illness: it is not said, but appears nevertheless from what follows (ver. 21, 32), that their intention was that he should come and heal him. Jesus was at that time, not, as in the case of the former miracle, in the same city with the sick man, but in the province of Peræa, on the other side of Jordan, while Lazarus lay at Bethany, near Jerusalem. Nevertheless, instead of going without delay to the house of the sick man, he remains here two days, without making preparations for his journey.

How was this, when, on the one hand, the distance, not inconsiderable—on the other, the close relations between the parties—must have urged him to redoubled haste? In the other case, there is a plain statement, implying that Jesus hastened to a sick person, but that she died, contrary to his expectation, before he reached the house. But this defect of knowledge in no way derogated from the dignity of the Messiah, having as he had the power to awaken from death at once the damsel who had died unexpectedly as far as he was concerned. But with the divine Logos incarnate it was a different thing. In him there could be no defect of knowledge of any kind. The Johannine Christ knew what he was doing when he stayed two days longer in Peræa, after receiving the message about the illness; he knew that Lazarus would die in the interval, and it was his will that he should do so. When, on the arrival of the message, he said that the sickness was not unto death, but for the glorifying of God and of his Son, it is the greatest misapprehension to understand this to mean that at that time Jesus himself did not expect a fatal issue of the illness of Lazarus; the meaning is only that the intervening death will not be the last result, but that by means of the resurrection of the dead all will end in the glorification of God and his Logos-Christ. For when the two days are over, and he is starting on his journey to Judea, he says, without having received meanwhile any further intelligence, consequently from his higher knowledge which penetrates into the distance, that Lazarus has gone to sleep, but that he goes to awaken him. This speech gives occasion to the Evangelist to bring in one of his regular misunderstandings. The disciples understand the sleep literally, Jesus having meant it figuratively of death, which was soon, like a light sleep, to yield to his word of command. Here, also, is the contrast between the Christian view of death and the ordinary one which all persons except himself entertained. And now, also, Jesus discloses the object of his delay; he rejoices, he declares to the disciples, that for their sake he had not been present to prevent the death of their friend, because what he is now intending to accomplish, namely, his restoration to life, will serve to strengthen their faith far more than a mere healing of the sick. It requires scarcely a word to point out that such a mode of proceeding on the part of any one—that is, of preferring to allow a friend to die, when he might have saved him, in order afterwards to have the power of reviving him—is as appropriate to a being of the imagination like the Johannine Christ, as in the case of a real man, even the most divinely endowed and most closely united with God, it would be inhuman and revolting.

But Jesus had lingered not merely on this account, and not merely so long as was necessary for the death of Lazarus to have occurred before he arrived at Bethany, but it was requisite that time enough should have passed for Lazarus to have lain four days in the grave (ver. 17), so that Martha might say that by this time he stinketh (ver. 39), and that corruption had already begun. It is not indeed said that when the cave was opened the latter was the case, or the contrary: it was believed among the later Jews that for a space of three days* the soul hovered round the dead body, and departed on the fourth, leaving it to corruption. This feature was obviously intended to make the condition of the person who was to be raised as near as possible to that of those whose future resuscitation by Jesus was expected on the last day.

In the history of the daughter of Jairus, when Jesus had arrived in the neighbourhood of the house, one or more persons go out and inform the father of the death of the damsel, which had occurred in the interval, and do not wish to have the Master troubled further. In like manner, in this case, on hearing that Jesus is coming, Martha goes out of the village to meet him. She speaks of the death of her brother as if she knew that Jesus was already acquainted with it, and that it would not have happened if Jesus had been present. The fact, however, of its having occurred had not, as was the case with the people of Jairus, deprived her of all hope; even before the disciples in our narrative, who had been averse to the journey of Jesus to Judea, she has a sort of foreboding that all is not over with her brother's death, that even now Jesus need only pray to the Father in order to obtain what he wishes. But however impressible the sister of Mary, the member of that devoted circle of Bethany, may

---

* Gfrörer, The Sanctuary and the Truth, p. 319 ff.

be represented as being, still it was considered right to represent Jesus as surpassing her understanding and expectation. So she immediately exposes the indefiniteness of her presentiment and the weakness of her intelligence by taking the assurance of Jesus that her brother shall rise again, to apply only to the resurrection on the last day, and, so far, not very consolatory. But on Jesus referring that assurance to its general principle, by explaining that he is the resurrection and the life, and that he who believes in him shall live even though he die, she confidently declares her faith that he is the Christ, the Son of God, that cometh into the world, a faith devoid as yet of any intelligent meaning, but from which, however, the germ of such a faith might be developed. Moreover, the proposition, "I am the resurrection and the life," &c., forms the theme of the Johannine account of a resurrection, exactly as the text, "The damsel is not dead, but sleepeth," forms that of the account common to the Synoptics, and the addition of "weep not" had formed that of the history in Luke particularly. The Johannine theme is distinguished from both by the characteristic by which the Johannine Gospel generally is distinguished from those of the Synoptics. That characteristic consists in the assumption of the principle that, in the first place, Christ appeared not merely actually as One who makes death nothing but a sleep, and dries men's tears for the dead, but that, as the Son of God in the higher sense of this Gospel, he exists expressly as an object of faith, and establishes this faith, moreover, as a condition of our participating in eternal life; and that, in the next place, by the life spent by him is understood neither the future life in general, nor the bodily resurrection to be now granted exceptionally to any single individual, but, at the same time, the new spiritual life that proceeds from him.

Martha, having confessed this faith, goes to fetch her sister, who not only comes herself, but a host of sympathising and sorrowing Jews with her. These weeping Jews play in the history of Lazarus the same part as the musicians and the noisy assemblage of mourners in that of the daughter of Jairus: they bring out into relief the contrast between the old Jewish and Heathen view of death on the one hand, and the new Christian view on the other. But how much higher above the former point of view the Johannine Christ stands than the Christ of the Synoptics, is seen in his conduct. To the synoptic Christ, the noisy wail of the people appears unsuitable, and therefore he orders them out: here, in John, no wailing is spoken of; the people only weep, and Mary weeps with them; but Jesus, instead of forbidding them to weep in a kindly tone as he forbid the widow of Nain, "is troubled" (angry) in spirit at their proceedings. That he had no reason for this from a human point of view is clear; but all attempts to give to the word by which the Evangelist repeatedly describes* the emotion in the mind of Jesus any other meaning than that of anger, or any application except to the tears of the Jews and of Mary, are useless. The Logos-Christ is angry that the people and even Mary can weep at the death of Lazarus, while he, the principle of life, is at hand. This blindness of men to what they have in him excites displeasure in him, followed immediately by pain; for even the tears into which he now bursts as he goes to the grave, cannot, if the description is to be consistent with itself, be tears of sorrow at the death of Lazarus, whom he is on the point of awakening to life, and they are not to be considered so because they are so understood by the Jews, who, in the fourth Gospel, always misunderstand Jesus. If we look for a parallel in the evangelical history, the only other occasion on which the tears of Jesus are spoken of is that (Luke xix. 41) when he weeps on beholding the city of Jerusalem, when he thinks of the awful days which shall

---

* Ver. 33, ἐνεβριμήσατο τῷ πνεύματι; ver. 38, πάλιν ἐμβριμώμενος ἐν ἑαυτῷ.

come upon her because she knew not the time of her visitation. This time of visitation for the Jewish people was in the days of the ministry of Jesus, which was at this very time to reach its culminating point in the miracle of the raising of Lazarus, without, however, bringing the Jews to faith and knowledge. Therefore it is that Jesus weeps, and therefore also his tears give way to displeasure when the Jews give utterance to the question as to whether the man who a short time before made the blind to see, could not also have hindered the death of Lazarus. For in this question was involved, in part a reproach against him, and in part an absence of all presentiment that here they have before them, in person, the resurrection and the life.*

The sepulchre, to the front of which we are immediately taken, is described in almost the same terms as, afterwards, the sepulchre of Jesus. It is called a cave, as the sepulchre of Jesus was, according to the Synoptics, hewn in rock, and consequently a sort of artificial cave, and it is closed, like the sepulchre of Jesus, by a stone rolled to the mouth of it. The grave-clothes also in which the body was wrapt are spoken of exactly in the same manner as in the case of Jesus (xx. 6 ff.). The raising of Lazarus by Christ was to be not merely a guarantee for the raising of all the dead by his means, but a type of his own resurrection that was close at hand. And now, notwithstanding Martha's remonstrance on the ground of the probable stench from decomposition, the stone is removed from the sepulchre. This being done, the Johannine Christ, instead of proceeding as the synoptic Christ does in the two previous accounts of raising the dead, that is, simply uttering his word of command, considers it right to preface

* Hilgenfeld's explanation is (Gospels, p. 296, note 1), that the displeasure of Jesus applies to the sorrow which here threatens to tear the human personality out of its unity with the divine Logos. I am unable to agree with this, because everywhere else in this Gospel, and especially in the following chapter immediately after (xii. 27), the unity of these two personalities appears undisturbed.

his act with a prayer to his Father. Not, indeed, a prayer containing a petition, such as Elijah offers on raising the dead, and which could not be necessary for the Son who was One with the Father, but a prayer of thanksgiving for the hearing which had been already vouchsafed. Consequently he had at first prayed in silence, but with the certainty of being heard; as prayer and hearing, or, looked at from the other side, command and execution, between the Father and him are to be considered, not as a series of individual acts, but as a state of constant correlation subject to no change. In a strict sense, therefore, the notion of an individual act of thanksgiving to the Father can be as little entertained as a prayer; and if Jesus condescends to anything of the kind, this must be solely from accommodation to the bystanders, in order to draw their attention to God, who has given such power to the Son (ver. 42). But if an accommodation is to have the desired effect, the person so accommodating himself must not say that it is only accommodation; and, on the other hand, a prayer which is only uttered in a spirit of accommodation is an absurd mockery. It has been thought an acute remark, in opposition to the view of criticism that the Johannine Christ is only a personified dogmatic idea, that an idea does not go to a marriage, does not feel sympathy, &c.* Conversely we may say, no real human being acts as the Johannine Christ is said to have acted at the tomb of Lazarus, even though he were a human being with a divine nature, but only an embodied idea, and moreover an idea compounded of two contradictory elements. The Johannine Christ, being on the one hand the everlasting creative Word, one with God, has no need to pray the Father for anything particular, or to thank him for anything particular, as his whole conduct is only a constant effusion of that which is being infused into him from the Father. On the other hand,

* Luthardt, The Peculiar Character of the Gospel of John, i. 96.

however, he walks among human beings as a human being who is to lead them to the Father, to refer them to the Father on every opportunity, and who could least of all omit to do this on occasion of an act in which, as the raising of a dead man, the glory of the Father so especially reveals itself. Consequently he offers aloud a prayer to the Father, preferring indeed a prayer of thanksgiving to one of petition, which might be more liable to be misunderstood as bearing an appearance of uncertainty of being heard. But since, in his human character, he is at the same time the Logos incarnate, prayer with him is a mere accommodation, and since he wishes to be recognised also as the Logos, he declares himself that he has uttered the prayer, not out of and for himself, but solely for those who are standing around. Considered as a real Being, as a Man, the Christ of the fourth Gospel appears in this prayer of accommodation as an actor, and in his confession that his praying is only an act of accommodation, an awkward one as well; but considered as an idea personified, he exposes in a particularly marked manner the contradictory elements which in him are compounded into an inconceivable union.

The loud voice with which Jesus immediately calls into the sepulchre and orders the dead to come forth, plainly typifies the voice of the Son of God, which hereafter all men who are lying in their graves shall hear, and thereupon come forth out of them (John v. 28 ff.); it is the word of command for the resurrection, which in other passages the archangel, as the herald of the Messiah, is commissioned to pronounce, and which is accompanied by a loud sound of a trumpet (1 Cor. xv. 52; 1 Thess. iv. 16).

We have considered the history of the raising of Lazarus, as well as the two other evangelical histories of the raising of dead persons, as an unhistorical emanation of the imagination of the first Christians, as an illustration of the same dogmatic theme, only more conscious and more artificial.

We have felt ourselves bound to take this view by the consideration that the narrative is as inconceivable historically as its origin is capable of easy and complete explanation from the dogmatic theories and peculiar character of the Johannine Gospel. There is still another circumstance to be considered. The fourth Gospel makes no mention of the two other cases of raising of the dead. It is intelligible that it should not do so, and no one would think of impugning its historical character on the ground of its silence about them. For even supposing that they had actually taken place, everything that gave them importance was involved in the history of Lazarus to such a high degree, that in a history which besides was under the necessity of proceeding electively, the addition of the former to the latter might be fairly dispensed with. The case is very different if it is asked, conversely, how it is that the Synoptics say nothing of the raising of Lazarus—a history so much more important; why, instead of those cases which they do report, so much less important and convincing, they did not choose in preference that of Lazarus? It has been said that this is all the worse for the authors of the three first Gospels; that it proves that none of them, not even Matthew, was an Apostle, or, otherwise, an eye-witness of the life of Jesus; for that to any one who had been so, it was impossible that the raising of Lazarus could have been unknown, and if it had been known he must have given an account of it; but that if none of them was an eye-witness, and all only collectors of traditions, the raising of Lazarus might have taken place, and yet no account of it been given to them. It might, at the time at which they wrote, have either dropped altogether out of the tradition, or at all events lost some of its importance. This importance, it is said, consisted principally in the effect which it had upon the development of the destiny of Jesus,* inasmuch as it raised the

* Schleiermacher, in particular, Introduction to the New Testament, p. 282 ff. Comp. Lücke, Commentary on the Gospel of John (third ed.), ii. 476.

animosity of his enemies against him to such a point, that they laid that regular plot against his life which ended in his destruction. It has been already pointed out what the real importance of the raising of Lazarus was in this respect.* The offence occasioned by a miracle was as little required to produce the crucifixion of Jesus as in the case of Socrates, where, in the opposition to the popular standpoint and the popular interests, there were natural causes enough, and over enough, to account for the result. Quite as little did the raising of Lazarus require this sort of importance in order to appear in the character of an event which, if it really happened, could not be passed over in a Gospel containing any sort of details or having any intelligent purpose. It was the miracle of miracles, and as such it is evidently represented by the fourth Gospel. We cannot trust our eyes when we read in Schleiermacher the assertion that, as regards the doctrine, the history of Lazarus has no great value. What! a history no great didactic value, in which, more than in any other, Jesus proves himself to be the resurrection and the life; and not only proves himself practically, but also extracts the doctrine out of the history? But Schleiermacher has traced out another cause which may have occasioned, at an early period, the history of Lazarus to drop out of the evangelical tradition. He draws attention to the fact that there is no mention at all in Matthew and Mark of the relation of Jesus to the family which is the subject of the history; that in Luke, who is acquainted with the sisters, the brother and the place where they lived are lost. This, he says, may have arisen from the circumstance that when the traditions upon which the accounts of the Synoptics rest were collected, the family of Lazarus, perhaps by reason of persecutions which they had gone through, was no longer to be met with in Bethany. As if the fame of an event so extraordinary, if it really took place, would not

* Vol. i. p. 344.

necessarily have survived in the district, whether the family whom it immediately concerned had emigrated, or died out, or not. The silence of the older Evangelists is intelligible only on the supposition that the fourth Evangelist composed the history in the second century.

But we need not lose sight of Schleiermacher's hint, with regard to different relations of the Evangelists to the family at Bethany, even though we are led by it to a different result from that at which the acute friend of John arrives. The three first Evangelists certainly knew nothing of a family at Bethany, towards which Jesus stood in a relation of intimate friendship. The two first (Matt. xxvi. 6 ff.; Mark xiv. 3 ff.) represent him as having been anointed a few days before his last Passover in Bethany, but in the house of one Simon, called the leper, and by a woman whose name is not stated. Luke represents an anointing of Jesus as having been performed still earlier in Galilee, not mentioning the name of the place, but in the house of a Pharisee called Simon, and he describes the woman who anoints him, whose name he also omits, as a sinner (vii. 36 ff.). On the other hand, he represents Jesus at a later period, on the journey from Galilee to Jerusalem, but while still far from his destination, and in a village which he does not name, as turning in to lodge with a woman of the name of Martha who has a sister Mary. Here an event takes place which is the subject of a well-known history, the cream of which consists in the words, "One thing is needful" (x. 38 ff.). The fact that we find not only the history but the names of the two sisters for the first time in Luke certainly excites suspicion, but does not decide against the historical value of the account. Martha, who is troubled about many things, and who is dissatisfied with her apparently idle sister Mary, who sits listening at the feet of Jesus, but who, in his judgment, has chosen the better part, are personifications of Jewish Christianity with its zeal about works, and Pauline

Christianity with its inward faith.* But it is intelligible that this should be so, even though two such sisters really lived and stood in some such relation to Jesus.

Consequently in Matthew and Mark we have in Bethany a woman who anoints, but without a name; in Luke, on the one hand, a female sinner who anoints, likewise without a name, and not in Bethany; on the other hand, the sisters Martha and Mary, likewise not in Bethany, and different from the woman who anoints. In John these threads are combined (xii. 1 ff.). The woman who anoints is Mary, and since the anointing took place, according to the tradition, in Bethany, Mary with her sister are dwelling in Bethany. Even in Luke the reception which Martha accords to Jesus betokens, certainly, friendly feelings, and the conduct of Mary points to a still deeper susceptibility; but a relation of intimate friendship between Jesus and the family is first spoken of in John (xi. 3, 5, 11, 36). For the rest, the characters of the sisters appear in the fourth Gospel exactly as they are described in the third. At the meal, which is followed by the anointing, Martha waits, exactly as in the narrative of Luke she gave herself much trouble with the waiting; even her hastening to meet Jesus on hearing of his arrival, after her brother's decease, is quite in character. So also on the side of Mary, her falling at the feet of Jesus, and, subsequently, her pouring out the costly ointment on his feet, is in accordance with the behaviour of the person who, sitting at Jesus' feet and listening to his words, forgets all besides. And now arises the question—whether is it more probable that all should in reality have taken place as John represents, that, therefore, it was Mary who anointed Jesus, that she and her sister lived in Bethany near Jerusalem, and that this house afforded a friendly asylum to Jesus on his last journey to a feast, but that the tradition was lost, that the name of Mary as the

---

* Zeller first drew attention to this, Theological Annual, 1843, p. 85.

woman who anointed had disappeared, that of her and her sister's household in Bethany, which, even though the place was destroyed, must have continued to survive as a sanctuary in the memory of Christendom, no one in the district knew anything after only a few decades of years—or that, conversely, the true state of the case was what appears in the Synoptics, that in the house of a man at Bethany, who stood in no very close relation to Jesus, a woman, otherwise unknown, anointed Jesus, and that in another locality, perhaps in Galilee, there lived a pair of sisters, with whom Jesus found a hospitable reception and readiness to listen to his doctrines; but that the fourth Evangelist adroitly combined these accounts, transferred to the listener at Jesus' feet the anointing of his feet, to the busy Martha the task of waiting on that occasion, took the two sisters to Bethany and settled them there, placing them in that relation of intimate friendship to Jesus which meets us in the history of Lazarus? If we put this question to ourselves, we may reply that, according to the discussion, as far as it has gone already, the first alternative of the two is sufficiently improbable; but still we would not decide until we have taken a more comprehensive view of both.

We have, so far, left out of consideration the brother of the two sisters, Lazarus, with whom, however, we commenced. In the first case, therefore, the synoptic tradition must likewise have forgotten him, which, considering the perfectly unique miracle connected with his name, is scarcely conceivable. But, it might be said, the tradition did not forget him. There is a Lazarus, too, in Luke. Not, indeed, a real Lazarus, only an allegorical one, the beggar Lazarus, who lies, in this life, covered with sores and suffering hunger, before the rich man's gate, and then, lying after death in Abraham's bosom, excites the envy of the rich man, who is tormented in hell (xvi. 19 ff.). There is, in fact, a connection between the two men called Lazarus. The Johannine Lazarus is not, indeed, like the allegorical Lazarus of Luke, a poor man, but he also is sick, and even the introductory words of the two narratives have a remarkable resemblance. "Now there was a certain sick man, Lazarus of Bethany," John begins: "There was a certain poor man of the name of Lazarus," Jesus begins his parable in Luke. Moreover, these two men die and are buried. The difference is, that the one does indeed return from the tomb to life, while the other might at least have returned; it is desired, but not allowed. And why, in the parable, is the prayer of the rich man not granted by Abraham, to send Lazarus unto his father's house in order to convert his five brethren? For the reason that Abraham foresees that, not believing Moses and the prophets, they would not believe even if one rose from the dead. And how true was the foresight of Father Abraham in this case! One really did rise from the dead, namely, Jesus, but did the Jews therefore believe? Nay, a Lazarus, exactly as the rich man would have wished, did rise from the grave, but still the Jews did not believe, but then first formed a regular design to put Jesus to death.

Well, then, are we to assume that the historic Lazarus became in the tradition the allegorical one, that the miraculous history became the parable, the event that really took place (the return of one dead) a merely hypothetical case? Whoever has any conception of the mode in which such narratives are remodelled and extended, will feel that the converse is the more probable. The fourth Evangelist adopted into his scheme, out of the third, the two sisters who lived in one village, and who entertained Jesus in their house. He adopted them into his scheme, as the one of them seemed to him a person adapted to have attributed to her the well-known anointing, the other the attendance at the meal during which the anointing took place. If he was obliged, for this purpose, to transplant them to Bethany, where, according to the tradition, the anointing had taken place, he saw that there was no place better suited for the history of the raising of the dead, which he wished to tell, than just this very Bethany. This, as the miracle of miracles, was to close the career of Jesus as the performer of miracles; it was, further, to bring to a head the animosity of the dominant party of Pharisees and High-priests in Jerusalem; it was necessary, therefore, that it should take place at a later period, and either in, or at all events near to, the capital. To place it, however, in the capital itself, would have been contradictory to the view of the fourth Gospel, according to which Jesus, during the last period, chose to avoid Jerusalem on account of the plots of his enemies, and, if he was there, had every reason for being cautious: consequently, a village near was a better place, and, from the history of the anointing, Bethany was already *given*. And if the two sisters were transplanted to that place, they might be considered as attending upon their brother, who is consequently assigned to them as Lazarus. That the fourth Evangelist came to represent the occurrence as he does by first taking the sisters out of the third Gospel, and then associating the brother with them, is plainly shewn by the manner in which he introduces the three relatives for the first time (xi. 1 ff.). "Now a certain man was sick, named Lazarus, of Bethany, the town of Mary and her sister Martha. It was that Mary which anointed the Lord with ointment, and wiped his feet with her hair, whose brother Lazarus was sick." A brother is only described thus when his sisters are better known than he. Mary and Martha were so, in consequence of the story in the third Gospel of Jesus' reception by them, to which also the expression in the fourth, "the town of Mary and her sister Martha," refers; for Luke begins his narrative with the statement that Jesus, on his journey, came to a village, and that there Martha received him. And the fourth Evangelist further adds, that it was that Mary which anointed Jesus, a circumstance which he does not speak of until afterwards: his noticing it here beforehand looks exactly as if he wished to put this notice in circulation for the first time. He shews still more plainly that in his Lazarus he is introducing a new figure into evangelical history; for surely he was not "a *certain* man," a brother of more famous sisters, if Jesus had performed on him the greatest of his miracles, he being beloved by Jesus as well as his sisters.

Consequently, the fourth Evangelist had transplanted the two sisters to Bethany, and for a crowning miracle, such as a raising of the dead was to be, Bethany was, in his opinion, the most appropriate theatre. It was, at all events, an obvious proceeding to associate, in the capacity of brother, one who was to be raised in the flesh, with the sisters who were awakened in the spirit. The two Synoptics were of no avail to him for the further setting forth of his history of a raising of the dead. He wished to have one who was most certainly and surely dead, one who was at least buried, neither of which was the case with the daughter of Jairus, or the son of the widow of Nain. On the other hand, there was, in Luke, a man dead, only indeed in a parable, but who was buried and certainly dead, for his soul was now carried in Abraham's bosom. He also might have returned to earth, but was not permitted to do so, because it would have been in vain, as he would not have converted the brothers of the rich man. But for this very reason it was, in the opinion of the fourth Evangelist, worth the trouble to represent the dead man as having really returned, in order fully to confirm the fact of the incorrigible unbelief of the Jewish people. Accordingly, no figure in the synoptic tradition was more adapted in every respect for a hero of a history of a raising of the dead, which the fourth Evangelist wished to give, than the Lazarus of the parable in Luke. And as we see from this whence the fourth Evangelist gets his Lazarus and the attendant circumstances, quite as clearly as we are unable to conceive what the other Evangelists can be supposed to have done with him, if he really existed and was raised by Jesus, we may, it would seem, look upon the investigation upon this point as concluded.*

We shall not, however, consider it as too much trouble to examine the explanations of the history of Lazarus by which others have endeavoured to satisfy themselves. In this case, also, Schleiermacher's theory has given the rule to modern theology.† The two dead persons, of whose raising by Jesus we read in the Synoptics, were looked upon by Schleiermacher, without hesitation, as cases of sham death only. In the instance of one narrative, adopting the most miserable form of exegesis, he takes Jesus at his word, that the damsel is not dead but sleepeth: he remarks also that the youth of Nain, considering the Jewish custom of speedy burial, may very easily have been only in appearance dead. But it was the fourth day of Lazarus' lying in the tomb. So decomposition might, indeed, have already begun. But, says Schleiermacher, it need not have done so; what Martha says is only surmise on her part. In any case, Jesus does not ascribe this act to himself as his own. Indeed, it cannot be conceived as having been so, without the destruction of the unity and continuity of his human life by such a creative act. But he obtains the result by prayer to God, and thanks God for it, as the immediate act of the latter. Now what, in plain German, does that mean? Lazarus also, though, from the longer time that he

* This investigation owes most to Zeller, who was the first to trace, as is here done, the Johannine Lazarus to the Lazarus of the parable (Studies in New Testament Theology, in the Theological Annual, 1843, p. 89. Comp. also Baur, Critical Investigations, p. 248 ff.). I had already, in the year 1833, thrown out the supposition that the two are identical in a notice of the treatises of Paulus and Hase on the Life of Jesus, a paper which I sent, at their request, to the Society for Scientific Criticism in Berlin; from which body, however, I received it back, because they observed in it the frons turgida cornibus. But as I had not found the key of the connection, the change of the hypothetical return of one who was dead into a real one, the supposition, as being too bold, was left out of my Life of Jesus.

† What follows is from his lectures on the Life of Jesus.

had lain in the grave, the case was a more uncommon one, had been only apparently dead, and that Jesus was the instrument of his resurrection was a mere accident, in which the action of a higher Providence is not to be mistaken. We now understand how Schleiermacher could say that the history of Lazarus has no great doctrinal value. So far from having any great value, it has, from his point of view, none at all.

Schleiermacher has wisely omitted to grapple with the more immediate question of the conduct of Jesus as described in the Gospel of John. And yet it is impossible to avoid asking the question: if it was only accident, only the improbable possibility that Lazarus, who had been buried four days, might be only apparently dead, upon which Jesus counted—how could he, while still at a distance—how, by the very side of the tomb, utter speeches which must be characterised as mere trifling if not backed by the certainty that he could restore his friend alive to his relations? It is necessary, says Schweizer,* to take into consideration the whole practical and psychological condition of Jesus. At that moment, having avoided the persecutions of the authorities at Jerusalem by going to Peræa, he was in a state more depressed than he had ever been before. But still his Messianic consciousness was unbroken. What must the result have been?† The most confident hope, answers Schweizer, that God will not desert him in such a condition. "For him," explains Hase (for in these cases one good turn always meets with another), "before whom Jairus' daughter "had been awakened" (from her apparent death), "the wish

---

* The Gospel of St. John, according to its Internal Value, &c., p. 156 ff.

† "There are powers," adds Schweizer, with obvious reference to the present writer, "which a Life of Jesus must discover, and use as a key for the understanding of particular acts, before it can deserve the name of a Life of Jesus." Very good, replies the writer, if the alleged facts are critically established. Until they are so, psychological pragmatism is ill applied in opposition to mere legend.

"might become a presentiment, or in his distress a bold con-"fidence, that in this case, in which his individual inclination "coincided with the glorifying of the kingdom of God, God "would hear his prayer for the life of the man beloved by "him."* If, then, continues Schweizer, an external event corresponds to such confidence, an event which is in itself no real miracle, there arises a miracle notwithstanding, namely, that of confidence in God justified. So in this case, the miracle is not really the return of the life which had only retreated, but the coincidence of that return with the confidence of Jesus and the opening at his command of the tomb. Why then, concludes the æsthetically educated theologian, should not, sometimes at least in the life of Jesus, a striking result have corresponded with his bold confidence—if there is any truth in the words of the poet, "There exist moments in the "life of man"? &c.† That is real sublimity, for Theology to deck herself out with the pens of modern poets, applying them, too, in an improper manner. Thus in this case she does not remember how ill the false application of the truth contained in these words suits the hero who utters them. He had settled it arbitrarily in his own mind that the first person who came to meet him the next morning with a token of friendship must be his truest friend, and that very person was his betrayer. The friend whom he found dead, must be, as surely as God would not desert him, not really dead, but at his call return to life—Jesus had got this into his head, and the result corresponded to so wild a notion. Ebrard remarks, with perfect truth, that such an explanation, according to which the Lord would have tempted God in the most extravagant manner, contains ten times as many inconceivabilities as twenty writers can find in the account of the Evangelist.‡ This is not enough; what he should have said

* Life of Jesus, § 94.
† Schiller's Wallenstein, Coleridge's translation; Piccolomini, Act v. Sc. 3.
‡ Scientific Criticism, p. 463.

is, that it abases Jesus as only naturalists and mockers have abased him.

The theory is not made much better by following Renan, and taking the raising of Lazarus to have been an intrigue of the family at Bethany, instead of a wild enterprise on the part of Jesus. Mortified at the ill reception which their adored friend had met with in Jerusalem, his worshippers at Bethany attempted to do something which might give a new impulse to his cause in the unbelieving city. That, they thought, must be a miracle, if possible the raising of a dead man, and above all a man well known in Jerusalem. Now during Jesus' absence in Peræa, Lazarus is taken ill. The sisters, becoming alarmed, send for their absent friend. But before he arrives, the brother has become better; and now an excellent idea occurs to them. Lazarus, still pale from the effects of his illness, permits himself to be put into a winding-sheet like a dead body and shut up in the family tomb. When Jesus arrives, Martha goes to meet him, and leads him to the tomb. Jesus wishes to see his departed friend once more, but on the stone being removed, Lazarus comes forth alive to meet him with his winding-sheet and napkins. In this all the bystanders behold a miracle. But Jesus? Did *he* permit himself to be blinded by so coarse a trick? Or, still worse, was he a party to the deception? He might, says Renan, have been as little able to control the thirst for miracles on the part of his adherents as St. Bernard, as Francis of Assisi. He allowed the miracles which were wanted of him to be forced upon him, rather than that he performed them himself. In despair, and reduced to extremities, he was no longer his own master. After a few days, moreover, death delivered him from the distressing weight of a character which daily made greater claims upon him, was daily more difficult to maintain.*

In fact, as soon as we cease to consider the history of Lazarus as a miracle, in the true sense of the word, nothing

* Renan, Vie de Jesus, 359 ff.

remains but either to follow the explanations last described, and to sacrifice the honour of Jesus to the truth of the account, or the truth of the account to the honour of Jesus and common sense. Ewald is entitled to commendation for having preferred the latter, though he has done so certainly with all sorts of evasions peculiar to himself. So far is he from maintaining the whole of the Johannine narrative, with all its attendant circumstances, to be historical, that he considers only the most general result of it to be so. "That " Lazarus was really raised by Christ from the grave" (observe, Ewald does not say, from the dead), " we cannot doubt, but " it would be equally unreasonable and perverse to overlook " the spirit of more elevated life which swells the bosom of the " Apostle, and inspires the narrative with the most miraculous " character. The recollection of a raising of the dead, which " he had once really lived to see, became to him the sign and " token of that great general resurrection at the end of the " world, that introduction into a new life which the whole " apostolic age expected with joy and exultation; all the " several circumstances accompanying it, which he could still " remember, had become in his view parts of this most sublime " truth, and it was only when seized with the glow of infinite " hope that he now looked back upon that which he had once " experienced and seen with his own eyes, in order to write " down with the same most fiery vividness all that he could " remember of this material image of heavenly assurance."*
So the Apostle John wrote down what he could remember in his old age of the raising of Lazarus; but he wrote it down with all the glow of feeling and imagination excited by the hope of the future general resurrection through Christ—his description of the past was, as Ewald expresses himself, "glorified" by the light of the future. Now this may and indeed should at first sight be understood to mean, that by this prospect of the future only the form o the Johannine

* The Johannine Writings, i. 314 ff.

narrative is affected, that the description has become more vivid and pathetic, but that the substance consists only of what the writer actually remembered. But then much more of the narrative must be maintained to be historical than is allowed by Ewald; that Lazarus was really raised from the tomb by Christ, or, as he expresses it on another occasion, that Christ saved "him that was lost."* For this last expression, however ambiguously and cautiously selected, clearly shews us that Ewald's view of this miraculous history simply extends to this, that Lazarus would have been "lost" if Jesus had not, by the command which he gave, we know not why, to open his tomb, "saved" him, *i.e.* made it possible for him to wake from his death-like trance, and to return to life. Everything in the conduct and speeches of Jesus that goes beyond this natural and probably merely accidental fact, which implies the exhibition of a miracle performed by Jesus, more convincing than any other as regards his dignity as the Son of God, would be an addition on the part of the Evangelist arising from his inspired expectation. What an Evangelist, in whose mind, supposing his life to have been as long as we will, a history could change into something so completely different! What real value could his testimony have? If the real Christ stood to his Christ in the same relation in which, according to Ewald, the historical basis of the account of the raising of Lazarus is supposed to have stood to what John has made of it, how much of the real Christ have we left in that of John? No! we have here the miserable remnant of a probably natural event, not worth further discussion, but which, if only it and nothing further is supposed to have been the historical basis of the evangelical narrative, either makes Jesus a madman, or the Evangelist a dotard. So let us quit this characterless and isolated thing, and openly admit that we are here concerned only with an ideal image, an arbitrary invention of the Evangelist, from which we learn nothing whatever

* History of Christ, 358.

of the real Christ, but only the extent to which the conception of the higher element in Christ, first much changed in the Jewish-Christian circles, and afterwards in those of the Pauline Christians, was now completely reflected in the mind of a Christian who had had an Alexandrine education.

78. Sea Anecdotes.

As the dwelling of Jesus was situated on the Sea of Galilee, and his ministry, for the greatest part of the time, was confined to its shore, it was natural that there should be a connection between the sea and a portion of the miraculous histories circulated about him. Of these anecdotes, we may describe one-half more immediately as Fishing legends, the other as Sailing legends, in so far as the one class refers to fishing as the trade of a portion of the disciples, the other to the element of water as a means of transport. Of the anecdotes of the first class we have that of the miraculous draught of fish by Peter in Luke. Of this we have already spoken, because it is connected with his call to be a fisher of men, and we combined with it, in consequence of the internal connection, notwithstanding its occurrence at a period so much later, the draught of fishes in the supplement to the Johannine Gospel. There remains yet the history of the piece of money, which, as advised by Jesus, Peter is supposed to have found in the mouth of a fish (Matt. xvii. 24—27).

By this miraculous history, which is peculiar to Matthew, all explanations appear to be put to shame. The believers in miracles cannot answer the question when asked, where was the necessity or even the good of so strange a miracle as that of bringing to Peter's hook a fish with a piece of money in its mouth, and how, without a second miracle, the fish, when opening its mouth to snap at the hook, could still have held the coin in it. The natural explanation which represents the piece of money, not as having been found immediately in the mouth of the fish, but earned by the sale of it, offends too much against the text, which connects the finding of the coin immediately with the opening of the mouth of the fish. As the Evangelist only mentions the recommendation given by Jesus, but does not say that Peter followed it and really found a piece of gold in the mouth of the fish, there has been lately an inclination to understand the expression of Jesus merely figuratively and proverbially, as when we say of the dawn that it has gold in its mouth; but the execution of an order of Jesus, and the correspondence between a prediction of his and the result predicted, are taken in the Gospel as a matter of course. And even the mythical explanation does not appear altogether suitable to an account of a miracle which has neither the character of a fulfilment of a Messianic expectation, nor an embodiment of an original Christian conception, but of a capricious result of an uncontrolled imagination.

Meanwhile, if we examine the case more accurately, the narrative in question has the character of a miraculous history only at the conclusion. At the beginning and in the middle it looks exactly like one of those discussions, several of which are contained in the three first Gospels, and among these it has an unmistakeable connection with that about the tribute-money (Matt. xx. 15—22; Mark xii. 13—17; Luke xx. 20—26). In each case the discussion refers to a tax; in the former case, the tribute to the Romans, and the question is asked whether it is right for the Jews to pay it; in this case the tribute is for the Temple at Jerusalem, and the question is whether Jesus and his disciples are bound to pay it. In the former case, Jesus decides the question in the affirmative, after ordering the tribute-money, a denarius, to be shewn to him; in this case, after deciding the question negatively, he himself miraculously provides the tribute-money, a stater, in order to settle the matter amicably.

As the dispute as to whether the people of God were free from sin in recognising in the Romans any supreme authority besides them, had continued among the Jews since the days of Judas the Gaulonite, it is possible that a question bearing upon this dispute may have been at some time or other put to Jesus. It is, on the other hand, less probable that the question as to his obligation, and that of his followers, to pay tribute to the Temple at Jerusalem, was mooted in his lifetime. It was not until a considerable time after his death, when the Christian community had separated itself more and more from the Jewish, that the question could arise as to whether the Christians were bound to contribute to the expenses of the Temple at Jerusalem. And from the Christian point of view, the most correct answer was, that in the abstract neither the Messiah, as being greater than the Temple (Matt. xii. 6), nor his adherents as the Royal Priesthood (1 Peter ii. 9), could be amenable to the tax, but that still, for the sake of precious peace, they would not refuse to pay it; a decision which, like so many other results of later development, was attributed to Jesus himself, and very probably in direct imitation of the history of the civil tribute-money.

But now the miracle? Jesus, it was thought, was not to prejudice himself at all by that admission—by that acquiescence in the payment of a tax which the Messiah was not called upon properly to pay. While he submitted to it, he must (it was considered) at the same time shew himself raised above it; he must himself provide the token of his submission in a manner which placed him above all these relations. Thus a miracle was required in this case more than in any other.

But why especially this miracle? And as on so many other occasions, so also on this, the disciple Peter is brought forward as the spokesman. It is to him that the collectors of

the tax apply with the question as to whether his Master
pays the tribute to the Temple; it is he whom Jesus catechises,
on entering the house, with a series of questions, which lead
to the conclusion that, strictly speaking, they, as children of
God, are not subject to any tax for the support of the house
of God; it was with him, therefore, that the miracle was
most appropriately connected, which was to put into its
proper light the discharge of this claim on the part of Jesus
and his followers. Peter, in the original Christian tradition,
was the fisherman. He had been, before all, called away
from his net to undertake the office of a fisher of men; it was
to him that the rich draught of fishes was vouchsafed as a
type of his apostolical ministry. Jesus might now again
have granted him another such, which, turned into money,
would have made up the amount of the Temple-tribute. But
this was an unnecessary resource. On the occasion of the
former miraculous draught, the case had been different: then
the question had been, not about an amount of money, but
about a symbol of the apostolic ministry. So in that case
only ordinary fish, only in great numbers, had been caught.
In this case, on the other hand, the question was about the
tribute to the Temple, payable by two persons, amounting to
four drachms, or a stater. As this was to be provided miraculously, why not at once in ready money? and as it was to
be provided by the fisher-Apostle, why not by a fish bringing him a stater? Consequently, as on this occasion only
one fish is wanted, it was not necessary for Peter to throw
out his net, but only his line; and because when the fish
was caught it was necessary to open its mouth in order to
extract the hook, it was necessary that the fish should have
the stater in its mouth. But here the narrator, while he endeavours to make matters easy for Peter, makes the task of
the fish far too difficult. Since the times of Polycrates, it has
often happened that fishes have swallowed treasures and
kept them in their stomachs; but for a fish, and one too

caught by a hook, to have kept a piece of money in its mouth together with the hook, is without example in the history of the world.

Our Evangelist made light of difficulties of this kind. We need only remember the two asses upon which he makes Jesus ride on the entrance into Jerusalem. Still it would be a great mistake to consider the miracle—one certainly of a fabulous character, and told by Matthew alone of all the Synoptics—as a proof that he was at all events the latest of them. On the contrary, the omission of it by Luke and Mark marks them as later than Matthew. The question as to the obligation of the Christians to pay the tax for the Temple, could only be of interest as long as the Temple stood.* Consequently this history does not belong even to the latest portions of the Gospel of Matthew. When this was worked up into the whole which we now have before us, the Temple was, indeed, already destroyed; but the antecedent circumstances, especially in Palestine itself, were still fresh in men's recollection. When at a later period Luke and Mark wrote in another country, the subject of the narrative of Matthew appeared to them as no longer of importance, and perhaps even the solution of it too favourable to the Jews to admit of their admitting it among their evangelical narratives.†

In the same manner as the fishing anecdotes go so far as to say that Jesus granted to his disciples a rich and valuable draught of fish, so the sailing anecdotes assert that he rescues

---

* Comp. Köstlin, Synoptic Gospels, p. 31, note. Hilgenfeld, Gospels, p. 91.

† Volkmar, The Religion of Jesus and its First Development, p. 265, refers the history to the poll-tax, which, after the destruction of Jerusalem, the Jews, and consequently the Jewish Christians also, had to pay to the Romans, upon which he thinks the question arose as to whether the Heathen Christians also had to pay it. But in that case, as in that of the tribute-money, the narrative must have spoken of a tribute to the emperor. It would have been too absurd to take the Jewish tribute to the Temple as an example of the later poll-tax payable to the Roman treasury.

them out of the distress and trouble into which wind and waves have brought them. On one occasion, he is himself present in the ship; on another, he walks from the shore over the lake and comes to them.

The first history (Matt. viii. 23—27; Mark iv. 36—40; Luke viii. 22—25) describes throughout what might easily have happened. After a laborious day, Jesus may have started from Capernaum with his disciples, gone to sleep in the ship, a storm, alarming the disciples, may have broken out while he slept, they may have awakened him and begged his assistance, and he may have rebuked their timidity—but he cannot, as the Evangelists report, have also rebuked the winds and the sea, unless he was either conscious of unconditional power over nature, or a miserable braggart and impostor—the first of which is altogether inconceivable, the second excluded by all that we credibly know of Jesus. A Psalm (cvi. 9, with the same expression in the Greek translation) says, he "rebuked" the Red Sea also, and it retired, and let the people pass dryshod through its waves. And we may certainly suppose that to the Messiah also, as God's representative, the power might be attributed of setting limits to the raging of the sea.

But we can only understand this narrative completely when we take the ship and the disciples into consideration as well as Jesus. In this, as well as in the other history, the Fathers have seen in the battling with the waves a figure of the Christian Church, in the tempest and the surges an image of the assaults to which the Church is exposed in the world. A scholar, distinguished for his knowledge of Judaism, has shewn, with praiseworthy industry, that this symbolism did not come first out of the history we are considering into the circle of Christian ideas, but was already in existence among the Jews. Hengstenberg* has drawn

---

* In the preface to the series of the Evangelical Journals for the year 1861, p. 4 ff. Comp. his Commentary on the Gospel of John, i. 352 ff.

attention to the mode in which in Psalm cvii. the restoration of the people out of captivity is described under the image of seafaring men, who are happily brought to land by Jehovah, and saved from the billows and the tempest. "He commandeth," it is said (xxv. 28—30), "and raiseth the stormy wind, which lifteth up the waves thereof. Then they cry unto the Lord in their trouble, and he bringeth them out of their distresses. Then are they glad because they be quiet; so he bringeth them unto their desired haven." Now Hengstenberg thinks that it was with reference to this Psalm and its symbolizing imagery that Jesus really undertook the miraculous calming of the tempest, in order thereby to give a practical prophecy of the protection which he purposes to give for the comfort of his Church in all its distresses and perils, till the end of time; and Hengstenberg even says generally that the symbolical acts of the Lord in the New Testament usually rest upon figures in the Old. In so far as these symbolical acts are understood, as in the present instance, to comprise miracles, we are in perfect agreement with the proposition of Hengstenberg, even though we take it in a somewhat different sense from him. Hengstenberg's opinion is, that an Old Testament writer was inspired with an image, and that then this image was realised by Jesus: ours, on the contrary, is, that images of this kind were in the later legend fictitiously converted into acts which never were really performed as they are represented to have been.

We know from the Epistles of Paul that the first Christians, when they met together, were accustomed, among other things, to edify each other with psalms and spiritual hymns (1 Cor. xiv. 26; Eph. v. 19; Col. iii. 16). In the Acts (iv. 24—30) such an effusion is preserved, which is, indeed, in other respects an arbitrary composition, but still only an application of a passage in a Psalm quoted in it (Ps. ii. 1 ff.). There is no doubt that whole Psalms were thus sung and applied to Christian circumstances, and for this purpose there were scarcely any more appropriate than that pointed out by Hengstenberg, the 107th. According to ver. 2, it is to be understood, they say, of the redeemed whom the Lord has redeemed out of the hand of the enemy, and whom he has assembled together out of all lands, from the East and from the West, from the North and from the sea. In these words the Christians could not fail to recognise themselves, called as they were from the East and from the West, from the North and from the South (Matt. viii. 11; Luke xiii. 29), and redeemed by Christ out of the hand of the enemy—by whom the devil and his angels were now understood (Luke i. 74). But further on in the Psalm tempests at sea were spoken of, out of which those assembled together had been saved. And these tempests were now no longer referred to the misfortunes of the ancient people of God, but to the persecutions which the new Church of the Messiah had to undergo at an early period, and the Lord, to whom they called, and who commanded the storms and waves to rest, was no longer Jehovah, but Christ. And thus a point was attained at which the image became, almost necessarily, history, and indeed miraculous history. Jesus had once lived on earth as a real man; hence the calming of the storm was looked upon as his real act, and those whom he saved out of it must have been his Apostles, the original society who surrounded him during his pilgrimage on earth. It is still possible, as was remarked above, that, in company with his disciples, he did really experience a storm on the Sea of Galilee, during which he was at first asleep, and then, having been awakened, displayed great presence of mind; but the miraculous story would have been told of him, founded upon the passage in the Psalm and the early Christian symbolism, whether any event in his real life supplied a point of connection or not; and thus, while we are compelled to declare the miracle in the evangelical narrative to be decidedly fiction, we are, as regards the natural remainder of it, at all events without any guarantee for its historical character.

However valuable this history must have been to the Christendom of the earliest time, by reason of its consolatory figurative meaning, still it had one defect. The distress falls upon the disciples while Jesus is with them in the ship. Can the Church be attacked by any distress in the presence of its Lord? He was indeed sleeping, but the guardian of Israel slumbers not nor sleeps (Ps. cxxi. 4). No distress attacks the Church except while and during the time that Christ is absent; indeed he is with her until the end of the world (Matt. xxviii. 20), but only spiritually; he has withdrawn from her his bodily presence, and in order to sift and prove her has left her to the battle with the world. But that even then his arm is not shortened, that when the distress of his followers is greatest he is able to help them—this it is of which they would wish to assure themselves, which they would wish to behold in the history of a miracle. On this occasion (Matt. xiv. 22—33; Mark vi. 45—52; John vi. 16—21) they embarked alone, and without Jesus; a somewhat far-fetched reason for his remaining behind is given in the statement that he did so in order to send the multitude away after the miraculous feasting. When he had completed this task, he ascends the mountain for the purpose of solitary prayer; according to Mark, he saw from there what in Matthew is only mentioned as having taken place in the meantime—the ship, now in the middle of the sea, battling with the waves after nightfall, in consequence of the wind being against it. He allows it thus to battle for some time, and it is not until the fourth watch of the night, *i.e.* towards daybreak, that he bestirs himself to help them. More than once (Matt. xxiv. 42, xxv. 6), according to the evangelical narrative, and on one occasion even with direct reference to the division of the night into four night watches, he gives it as a motive for watchfulness that they cannot know when the Lord cometh, whether in the evening, or at midnight, or at cock-crow, or in the morning (Mark xiii. 35); equally unknown is the hour he has determined for appearing to render assistance; it may, as in this instance, be the latest, the fourth watch of the night.

But again, how will Jesus leave the shore without a boat, and render assistance to the disciples while sailing in the very middle of the sea? It is impossible that this can cause any difficulty to the Messiah: the only question is, what kind of miraculous passage is the most appropriate for him. Flying, by means of which Abaris the Hyperborean traversed sea and rivers, was not traditionary in the Hebrew legend, and in that of the first Christians it was only attributed to the wicked magician Simon. The miraculous heroes of the Old Testament, when they wanted to cross a piece of water, had a wand in their hand, which they had only to stretch out (2 Mos. xiv. 16), or a cloak, with which they had only to strike the water (2 Kings ii. 14); in other cases, the bearers of the ark had only to step into the water (Josh. iii. 13—17); this done, it parted and gave them a road, so that they could pass over on dry ground. This celebrated resource from the history of Moses, Joshua, and Elisha, was, unfortunately, not applicable in this case. Jesus did not wish to reach the opposite shore, but to get on board a ship sailing on the surface of the lake, so that it was of no use to lay the bottom dry and walk upon it. So the only way that was left was to walk upon the water itself, and in fact no more appropriate mode of transit could be imagined for the Messiah, for whom the idea of difficulty was altogether impossible. It was the method of Jehovah himself. The march of Israel through the Red Sea, on which occasion Jehovah himself formed the rear-guard in the pillar of fire, was sometimes poetically so described that he himself was represented more as one walking upon the sea than through the sea. When it is said in Isaiah (xliii. 16), "Thus saith the Lord, which maketh a way in the sea, and a path in the mighty waters," we are quite on the ground of the Mosaic narrative; but when the Psalmist says (lxxvii. 19), "Thy way is in the sea, and thy path in the great waters, and thy footsteps are not known," it is but a step from the last description to that in the Book of Job (ix. 8), where God is described as he who treadeth on the waves of the sea, or, according to the Greek translation, who walks upon the sea as upon firm ground. That the Messiah should pass over the water in the same way as Jehovah, was certainly the most appropriate thing that could be said of him.

We must here glance at the mode in which the peculiarity of the several Evangelists shews itself in the narrative. The statement of Mark, already mentioned, that Jesus saw from the mountain the ship driven in the midst of the sea, although the coming on of darkness creates some difficulty, is still not altogether untenable. The more suspicious, after the words (ver. 48), "About the fourth watch of the night he cometh unto them, walking upon the sea," is the addition of the same Evangelist, "and he would have passed them." When Ewald maintains* that these words can mean nothing else but that Jesus would have come to them over the sea, he only says what he wishes his friend Mark *had* said; but in fact he does not say so, but he says that Jesus wished to have passed by them, and also that he would have done so if they had not cried out and so caused him to take notice of them. From first to last, when Jesus sees their distress, and at last bestirs himself to go to them, the narrative of Mark might be understood to mean that the bark of the disciples had been the object of Jesus walking upon the sea; but by that addition we are taught something else, which is, that Jesus would have continued to leave the disciples to themselves, and only have passed over the sea on his own account,

---

* The Three First Evangelists.

for which purpose the way across the surface was as passable for him as the road round the shore would have been for another person. As in this point of view the walking on the sea appears to be a thing which Jesus performs not merely for the sake of the miracle, but as quite an ordinary act, he becomes a Being perfectly supernatural and foreign to us, and the Evangelist indulging in such a conception of Jesus cannot, to us at all events, appear in the character of the original Evangelist.

Moreover, we find a not less remarkable feature in the corresponding passage in John. After describing the start of the disciples, he continues (ver. 17), "And it was now dark, and Jesus was not come to them." But could the disciples have expected that he would come to them in the midst of the sea? They could only have done so if he had either promised them to come, of which nothing is said, and then when he came they would not have been afraid, or if passages of this kind were customary with him, as the addition of Mark supposes. So that we may in this case again see a trace of the fact that the fourth Evangelist, in his miraculous histories, is glad to follow the second.

When Jesus had come near to the ship, and the first alarm of the disciples had been pacified by his "It is I," Matthew has something peculiar to himself in an interlude with Peter. As if to prove that the apparition approaching him on the waves is not a spirit, but the Being whom it professes to be, Peter calls out to him to be allowed (and at the same time to have power given to him to enable him to do so) to go over the water to him. Jesus directs him to come; Peter makes the attempt, succeeds for a moment, but is soon terrified by the strength of the wind; he begins to sink, and appeals to the Lord for support, who, with the words, "O thou of little faith," seizes him by the hand, and takes him with him into the ship. In any case, we have here in this addition of Matthew an extremely ingenious feature, not one merely extravagant, like that in Mark which we have just remarked upon. Eckerman tells us that Goethe* considered this narrative as one of the most beautiful, and, to him, most valuable of legends, inasmuch as in it is illustrated the lofty truth that man, by faith and courage, is victorious in the most difficult undertaking, and, on the other hand, is inevitably lost when the slightest doubt arises in his mind. In order, however, to understand its origin, we must go back to the Old Testament, and moreover to the history of the passage of the Israelites through the Red Sea. There the Israelites who passed through in safety are contrasted with the Egyptians who would have pursued them, but were drowned in the returning waters. And why? "By faith," says the author of the Epistle to the Hebrews (xi. 29), "they (the Israelites) passed through the Red Sea as by dry land, which the Egyptians assaying to do were drowned." They were drowned because they had not faith, as on this occasion Peter was on the point of being drowned because his faith deserted him. If it was wished, in order to make the Mosaic parallel complete, to have a counterpart to the unfaithful who were drowned out of the circle that surrounded Jesus, there was Peter, whose faith in the hour of danger was nearly extinguished, and who was only preserved by the intercession of Jesus (Luke xxii. 31 ff.); and thus in this he does not actually sink as the Egyptians did, but only begins to do so, and is saved by Jesus. The two middle Evangelists omit this episode, as they do much beside which concerns only Peter in particular; only the author of the supplement to the fourth Gospel, which, for a reason above explained, has more to do with Peter, incorporates it with a narrative which we have discussed above, but in a form essentially different.†

According to Matthew and Mark, Jesus now joins his disciples in the ship, whereupon the wind drops, and they accom-

---

* Dialogues with Goethe, ii. 263. † See above, § 69.

plish the remainder of the passage to the other shore without further delay. The distance must have been considerable, as when Jesus set out upon his miraculous walk they had only just arrived at the middle of the lake. According to the fourth Evangelist, on the contrary, they wished, indeed, to take Jesus on board, but found themselves at the same moment already close to the shore to which they were bound (ver. 21). Consequently, Jesus did not go on board. What, therefore, Mark represents him as only intending to do, that is, to pass the disciples and cross the lake, he actually accomplishes in John. Without availing himself of the ship, he comes to the opposite shore, and possibly, moreover, accelerates in a miraculous manner the speed of the vessel.* Accordingly, in this instance also the fourth Evangelist treads in the steps of the second in the exaggeration of the miracle, but only, as in so many others, to attain, in our time at least, the opposite of what he wishes. For as he represents Jesus as not meeting with the disciples until they were close in shore, even theologians† who believe in John conclude from this, awakening again the shade of old Paulus, that Jesus did not walk over the sea, but passed by land round its northern point, and that the disciples, in the mist of the morning, only imagined that they saw him walking over the water; so that even John does not say, as the others do, that Jesus walked upon the sea, but only that the *disciples saw* him walking on it. But this does not mean in the least that they merely imagined what they saw, but comes to exactly the same thing as the two Synoptics say. In this case it is not easy to see what meaning the whole narrative is to be supposed to have if Jesus came to the disciples in a natural manner.

That it is not the intention of the fourth Evangelist to

* Comp. Meyer's Commentary on the passage.

† Bleek, Contributions, i. 103 ff., in remarkable agreement with Gfrörer, The Sacred Legend, i. 218 ff. In this case also, as in all subterfuges of the same kind, Schleiermacher has set the example, in his Lectures on the Life of Jesus, though only in passing allusions.

represent the passage of Jesus as a natural proceeding, is clear from the pains which he takes to describe the investigation carried on on the part of the people into the mode in which Jesus crossed the lake. When the people who had been collected around Jesus on the eastern shore for the loaves and fishes, find him on the next morning no longer in the spot or in the locality, they calculate that he cannot have sailed across, because (*a*) he had not embarked with the disciples on board their ship, and (*b*) there had been no other ferry-boat there. But neither could he have gone by land, as the people, returning by water, find him already there (ver. 25), and he could not have arrived in so short a time if he had taken the circuit of the shore. Thus all natural modes of transit having been cut off, there remains only a supernatural one by which Jesus could have crossed, and this is the inference drawn by the people themselves in their question of surprise (ver. 25) as to when he came hither, *i.e.* back to the western shore. In order to make this process of investigation into his quick passage possible, the Evangelist provides "other boats" (ver. 23), *i.e.* fishing boats, which he gets out of the history of the calming of the storm in Mark (iv. 36), of which, however, a whole fleet would not have sufficed to transport the five thousand men, with their wives and children. John, therefore, here narrates a miracle if any one ever did, and whoever does not choose to believe him, but nevertheless considers him to have been an eye-witness, has no resource left but, with Hase,* to admit that here is another occasion on which he was absent—that is, to make a second hole in the theory of the school of the fourth Gospel, in which there are already holes enough.

* Life of Jesus, § 75, comp. with 74.

79. THE MIRACLE OF THE LOAVES AND FISHES.

In the Psalm which describes the distress of the Israelites during their captivity by the image of a storm at sea, and their preservation out of it as a calming of the tempest by Jehovah, we find, just at the beginning, the same thought expressed by the image of a famine, out of which Jehovah saved them. "They wandered," it is said (Psalm cvii. 4—9), "in the wilderness in a solitary way; they found no city to dwell in. Hungry and thirsty, their soul fainted in them. Then they cried unto the Lord in their trouble, and he delivered them out of their distresses. And he led them forth by the right way, that they might go to a city of habitation. Oh that men would praise the Lord for his goodness, and for his wonderful works to the children of men! For he satisfieth the longing soul, and filleth the hungry soul with goodness."

But famine in the wilderness, as we may remember from the history of the temptation, not merely figuratively, but as real hunger, had been among the trials which the people of Israel had had to undergo during their exodus from Egypt, and the mode in which Jehovah had relieved them was among the most famous miracles described in the original history of the Hebrews. He had relieved them by manna, as a substitute for bread; and besides this, as they wished for flesh as well, by quails. And, according to the Rabbinic text, taken from 5 Mos. xviii. 15, as was the first Saviour, so is the last Saviour, a new edition of the gift of manna was especially expected from the Messiah.*

In famines, too, the prophets had proved their divine mission by sending miraculous relief. When, during the great drought under Ahab, Elijah lodged with the widow of Zare-

---

* See the passage from Midrasch Koheleth, above, p. 204.

phath, Jehovah's miraculous operation in favour of his prophet prevented the barrel of meal wasting or the oil failing in the widow's cruse, so long as the scarcity lasted (1 Kings xvii. 7 ff.). Likewise, when in the days of Elisha a famine occurred, and the hundred disciples of the prophets whom he had with him were in want, twenty barley loaves and some ears of corn in the husk were so completely sufficient at Jehovah's word to satisfy them, that something thereof was left (2 Kings iv. 38, 42—44).

Thus, in the history of the prophets, in accordance with the change of circumstances, the form of the miracle had so far changed, that a new aliment from heaven was no longer given, but common and earthly nourishment was made sufficient for a far longer time, or for far more persons, than it would naturally have maintained. And therefore it was natural that the Messianic hope, while keeping that strict Mosaic form in view, should also appear in another, in which, connecting itself with the history of the prophets, it expected* of the Messiah only a miraculous increase of means of nourishment already existing; only that, in order to excel the prophet, the Messiah must feed a larger number with a less amount of provision.

But the fact that a miraculous supply of food, such being considered an appropriate act for the Messiah to perform, was attributed to him, not in the form of a shower of manna, but of a distribution of bread, depends also upon a further consideration. The most important rite of the new Church of Christ consisted in a distribution of bread. After the Pentecostal speech of the Apostle Peter, the first believers assembled for the breaking of bread and prayer (Acts ii. 42,

---

* Thus in the passage above quoted from Midrasch Koheleth, Ps. lxxii. 16 is brought forward as referring to the manna to be given by the latter Saviour. In that Psalm only a superabundance of bread-corn is spoken of, which is to be in the land in the days of the king eulogised in the Psalm, who is, according to the later explanation, the Messiah.

46); it was at the breaking of bread that the disciples going to Emmaus recognised Jesus after the resurrection (Luke xxiv. 30, 35); for, it is said, he took the bread exactly as at the last supper, gave thanks over it, broke it in pieces, and distributed it to his disciples. And when Paul (1 Cor. x. 3) says of the Israelites under Moses, that they had been all baptized in the cloud and in the sea, had all eaten the same spiritual meat, and drunk the same spiritual drink, he considers the manna and the water out of the rock likewise as signs prefigurative of the bread and wine in the Supper of the Lord, in the same way as he considered the wetting by the cloud and the sea as a type of Christian baptism. Of the last supper, indeed, the Christians told each other of the mode in which Jesus instituted it on the last evening he spent on earth; but it admitted also of being represented as a counterpart to the feeding with manna under Moses, and moreover in the character of a miraculous feast: hence our evangelical history of the Loaves and Fishes. It does not contain a feature which may not be derived from the Mosaico-prophetic type on the one hand, and the antitype of the Christian supper on the other.

In the account given in the books of Moses there is this peculiarity, that the feeding of the people with quails is told twice over. So also the manna is twice spoken of (2 Mos. xvi.; 4 Mos. xi.). And it would seem to have been thought necessary to imitate this peculiarity in the Gospels. At all events, the two first of these have each two accounts of feeding respectively. These accounts are, in each instance, similar in the main, but differ in detail (Matt. xiv. 13—21, and xv. 29, 32—39; Mark vi. 30—44, viii. 1—10). On the first occasion Jesus withdraws into a wild region on the eastern shore of the Sea of Galilee; on the second, to a mountain in the neighbourhood of the same Sea, which is also described as Wilderness;—on the first, the multitude that followed him stayed with him a whole day until evening; on the second, three days;—on the first, the multitude, without women and children, amounted to five thousand; on the second, to four thousand men;—on the first, it is the disciples who at first recommend Jesus to dismiss the multitude, that they may buy food; on the second, it is Jesus who declares to the disciples that he will not send the people away fasting;—on the first, there are five loaves and two fishes; on the second, seven loaves and a few fishes;—on the first, there are twelve baskets remaining; on the second, seven baskets of fragments. But everything else,—the hunger, which threatens the numbers that have flocked together, by reason of their prolonged stay, the doubt of the disciples as to the possibility of providing sufficient nourishment for them, the question of Jesus as to the provision in hand, the command to the people to sit down, then the prayer, the distribution, the satisfying of the hunger, and gathering of what remains,—all these are told exactly to the same purport in both, in part in the same terms. Still, in both Gospels, reference is expressly made to the two narratives as relating two different events (Matt. xvi. 9 ff.; Mark viii. 19 ff.). Now this indeed can scarcely be an intentional imitation of the double narrative in the Old Testament, but may easily be explained from the same cause, namely, that the author of our first Gospel, as well as the compiler of the Pentateuch, found the same history in two different sources given with somewhat varying details and in a different connection, and took, in consequence, the double narrative of the same history for two histories, and placed them unhesitatingly close to one another. In this, Mark followed Matthew; Luke, as elsewhere in similar cases, only gives the first history (ix. 10—17), and omits the second; while John, likewise quite in his own manner, compounds his narrative out of features of both histories (vi. 1—15). He takes the five loaves and two fishes, the five thousand men and the twelve baskets of fragments, from the first history of the feeding; on the other hand, he transplants the occurrence, as Matthew and Mark do the second feeding, to a mountain, represents moreover, as is done in the latter, the scene as being opened by an address of Jesus to the disciples; and to his account, moreover, as to the second of the two first Synoptics, there is subjoined the demand for a sign from heaven and a confession of Peter (vi. 30 ff., 68, comp. with Matt. xvi. 1, 16).

If, after these preliminary remarks, we go through the several details of the narrative, we shall find that the locality in which the miracle takes place, the wild district remote from human habitations, supplies, on the one hand, a motive for the performance of it, while, on the other hand, as in the case of the history of the temptation, it already existed in the Mosaic type. So also the time of day, the late evening, does indeed supply a motive for what was to follow, but it points not backwards into the Mosaic, but forwards into the Christian history. The mode in which the disciples draw the attention of Jesus to the day being far advanced, and as a reason for either dismissing the people, or, which is the alternative *he* adopts, feeding them, reminds us of the request of the disciples going to Emmaus to stay with them, because it was towards evening and the day was far spent, whereupon follows the breaking of bread already mentioned (Luke xxiv. 29); it reminds us moreover of the evening when Jesus sat at table with the Twelve to eat the Passover and to institute his holy Supper. Jesus' meal of love and miracle is a supper.

The beginning of the miracle creates no difficulty on any supposition, whether, that is, it is introduced, as in the first account given by the Synoptics, by a suggestion of the disciples, or, as in the second, by Jesus himself expressing his compassion for the multitude, who have already been with him three days without sufficient food. On the other hand, it is unintelligible how Jesus, according to the narrative of the fourth Gospel, the very moment he sees the multitude coming to him, can ask Philip, "Whence can we buy bread that these may eat?" The people came, not to eat, but, according to the Evangelist's own statement, on account of the healing of the sick, and it was certainly not the business of Jesus, before anything else and without any necessity, which, according to the Johannine narrative, did not exist, to look after the bodily support of the people. In fact, on reading the additional words of the Evangelist, that Jesus put that question to Philip in order to tempt him, we might understand the purport of the speech to be exactly the same as that of his speech at Jacob's well in Samaria, when the disciples had fetched means of support for him out of the city, and called upon him to eat. Then he said that he had food of which they knew nothing. This the disciples understand of real food, which some one might have brought for him during their absence, while he is alluding to his performance of the will of God and the execution of his work (John iv. 31—34). Thus, it might be supposed, on this occasion also Jesus has in his mind a spiritual feeding of the people, and so the answer of Philip, that five hundred pennyworth of bread would not suffice for such a multitude, would be only one of the regular misunderstandings in John, and the solution would be involved in the subsequent discussions contained in the sixth chapter about the Logos as the bread of life given by God to men. But, as usual in the Gospel of John, this flight into the region of the spiritual meets with an obstacle which brings it to the ground; in spite of the ideal elements introduced, the material miracle goes on, and this, after being performed in all its material breadth, is again remodelled and invested with a spiritual character. But the Evangelist has this ideal perspective in view from the very first; it is because he knows what he intends at last to make of the history of the feeding, namely, without prejudice to its natural reality, a symbol of the spiritual nourishment of mankind by the Logos, it is because the material element in the history is, as it were, transparent to him, that he represents

Jesus as putting this question at the very outset, a question which, unless we place ourselves exactly upon his point of view, must appear absurd.

The objections which, in the first account of the feeding, the disciples make to the request of Jesus to them to give food to the people—in the second, to his declaration that he cannot send the people away fasting, expressed in the one case by their pointing to the small quantity of their provision, in the other by the question as to where sufficient nourishment is to come from in the wilderness, are indeed of the same description as the narrators of every detailed miraculous history are fond of introducing, in order to give relief to the accounts, but at the same time are prefigured both in the Mosaic and also in the prophetic history. Jehovah declares to Moses his intention of feeding the murmuring people with flesh for a whole month even to satiety. He is met by Moses first with an objection founded upon the number of the people, and then attention is drawn to what would be required to satisfy so large a host with meat for so long a time. In like manner when Elisha's servant is commanded by his master to set before the sons of the prophets the twenty barley-loaves, the latter is met by the question, "What! should I set this before a hundred men?" (2 Kings iv. 43). Here also we see the fourth Gospel going further in the steps of the second. It is only in these two that the disciples name a sum which would be required to provide food for the assembled multitude, and moreover the same sum, two hundred pence, doubtless as an amount which would exceed that in the treasury of the society; only that Mark says that this amount would certainly be wanted, John, on the contrary, that so much would *not* suffice for each to have but a small quantity. On the other hand, the assignment of the conversation, which in the other Evangelists the disciples carry on in common, to Philip and Andrew, together with the introduction of a lad as the bearer of the loaves and fishes, is to be laid to the account of that dramatically picturesque manner of the fourth Gospel with which we are already acquainted.

The provision in hand consists principally of bread. This is the result partly of the ecclesiastical tradition, partly of the Mosaic, and also of the prophetical type. For manna takes the place of bread, and is frequently so called. The fact that the bread is in the form of barley-loaves, that is, the cheapest kind of bread, and that John speaks of this alone, may be taken from the history of Elisha. The circumstance that an accessory consisting of meat is added to the bread, corresponds to the Mosaic precedent, according to which, besides the manna, quails are also given to the people; and that in the evangelical narrative the accessory consists of fish,—this might be derived, though not very satisfactorily, from the remembrance of the murmuring of the people for the fish which they had for nothing in Egypt, and from the expression of Moses, that to feed so many people with flesh all the fish of the sea must be gathered together. If we look to the other of the types to which we have drawn attention, the Christian supper, the fish, and the accessory of flesh at all, might even excite surprise. It would not, indeed, have suited the disciples' mode of life, in their travels into the desert, to have carried wine as well as bread with them; it is therefore quite intelligible that in the history of the loaves and fishes the other element should be unrepresented, but where the fishes came from is a question that from this point of view is still enigmatical. We might, apart from the Supper, and supposing the miraculous legend to have had its origin in Galilee, look upon the fishes as a local feature, as in these lake countries fish was a main element in the food of the people, and indeed among the proofs of his resurrection which Jesus gives to his doubting disciples, the consumption of a piece of broiled fish occurs; we might, moreover, remember that the Apostles, some literally and all figuratively, were fishermen, consequently the fishes were the most obvious things to connect with the bread.

But we are at once, and necessarily, taken back to the Supper, when we look at the description which the Evangelists give of the distribution of the bread and the fishes by Jesus. It might, indeed, be said that the fact of Jesus, on this occasion as well on that of the institution of the Supper, first blessing the bread with a prayer, was a part of the Jewish custom, and still more, here, of the intention to perform a miracle; that his breaking the bread twice arose from the nature of it; his distributing it twice, from the circumstances of the case; so that, consequently, no conclusion should be drawn from the similarity of his proceedings in both cases as to an internal relation of the one narrative to the other. But why then is the resemblance of the conduct of Jesus on one occasion to his conduct on another so frequently and so industriously brought forward? Why is the mode in which he acted on these occasions represented as a test by which he might be recognised? As in this instance it is said of him that he took the five loaves and the two fishes, looked up to heaven, gave thanks, broke the bread and gave it to his disciples, so it is said, not merely at the institution of the Supper, exactly in the same terms, that he took the bread, gave thanks, broke and gave it to his disciples (Matt. xxvi. 26);* but also in the scene at the sea of Galilee after the resurrection, Jesus takes the bread and gives it to them, likewise also of the fish (John xxi. 13);† and likewise after the resurrection, with the disciples at Emmaus, "He took the bread, blessed it, broke it, and gave it to them;" and it was by this, "by the breaking of the bread," that he, who

* It is said in Mark of the fishes, vi. 41, Καὶ τοὺς δύο ἰχθύας ἐμέρισε πᾶσι, as in Luke xxii. 17, it is said of the cup that Jesus gave it to his disciples with the words, Λάβετε τοῦτο, καὶ διαμερίσατε ἑαυτοῖς.

† Here also the words, καὶ τὸ ὀψάριον ὁμοίως, remind us of the ὡσαύτως καὶ τὸ ποτήριον (in Justin, Apol. i. 66, καὶ τὸ ποτήριον ὁμοίως), in the history of the institution of the Supper, Luke xxii. 20; 1 Cor. xi. 25.

up to that time had been unknown to them, was recognised by them as Jesus (Luke xxiv. 30 ff., 35). This, therefore, was the act in the performance of which the members of the Church took most pleasure in conceiving Jesus as being engaged; it was that in which he continued to survive in the holy custom of the Supper; and it was upon this conception, independent of the act of instituting the Supper, that similar acts were referred partly to the days of his resurrection, partly to those of his natural life. And there is one point in which our history of the loaves and fishes prefigures the ancient Christian rite of the Supper even more accurately than the history of the consecration itself. In this, Jesus was only in the company of his disciples; he therefore distributed the bread and wine to them alone: on the other hand, at the Supper, in the most ancient Churches, there existed a double gradation, the bread and wine being delivered by the chief to the deacons, and then by them handed to the several members of the congregation,* exactly as in the history of the feeding, bread and fish is first given by Jesus to the Apostles, and then by them to the people.

The absence of wine at these preliminary semblances of the Supper admits of the same explanation as the circumstance that the celebration of the original Christian Supper is sometimes only described as "breaking of bread" (Acts ii. 42, 46, xx. 7). The bread was always the substantial part of the repast. And the circumstance that here, as in John xxi., the bread is accompanied by fish instead of wine, may perhaps be explained from this, that with the Supper, in Christian antiquity, common meals, the so-called *agapæ*, were connected. An allusion to these meals, properly so-called, exceeding as they did the simple elements of the Supper, may be found in the fishes; so that the history of the feeding would have a reference not merely to the Supper, in the

---

* Justin Martyr, Apol. i. 65.

more restricted sense, but to the custom of the Christian love-feasts generally, the Supper included. The comprehensive nature of Christian love, which at these feasts fed also the poor members of the Church, was represented in the history of the feeding as a product of the miraculous power of Christ, which richly provides food for all. Perhaps also from the custom which prevailed at these ancient Christian meals may be explained the feature that, in the first account of the feeding, Luke represents the people as sitting down, some in fifties, some in hundreds: this may be an allusion to the *masses* into which a large company might divide itself at the love-feasts.

That a miracle is involved in the history of the feeding is shewn unmistakeably by the fact that Jesus distributes the broken pieces of five or seven loaves, and of two, or at all events only a few fishes, and that by these pieces four or five thousand men, together with the women and children belonging to them, are not merely satisfied, but besides this, on one occasion twelve, on another seven, baskets of fragments, *i.e.* a larger quantity than was originally there for distribution, remain. But it is not stated at what moment the miracle really took place. Schleiermacher thinks that an eye-witness would have told us this for certain: we add, yes, if there could be an eye-witness of an impossible event. If we endeavour to put the thing plainly before us, especially the moment of the miraculous increase, we see the pieces, before coming into the mouth and stomach of the people, pass through three sets of hands—the hands of Jesus, then those of the Apostles, lastly those of the multitude to be fed—and the miraculous increase may be supposed to have taken place under any one of these three processes. Supposing the fragments of five loaves to have come into the hands of more than five thousand men without preceding increase, so as to grow in their hands, not having done so before, then only very small crumbs must have been carefully distributed by the disciples to the people; a conception that involves an amount of trifling which certainly was not in the mind of the Evangelists. There remain, therefore, only the hands of Jesus or the Apostles, and it appears to be most in accordance with the spirit of the narrative to suppose that it was in the hands of him who looked up to heaven and blessed the little store that the increase of it also took place. We may conceive this increase to have taken place in one of two ways: that either when Jesus had finished with one cake of bread or one fish, a fresh one and then again a fresh one came out of his hands; or that each of the five loaves and two fishes grew under his hands, that is, threw off new pieces, until in the case of the loaves a fifth part, in that of the fishes a half, of the multitude was provided for, and that then another loaf and the second fish came into the series. And as John, certainly in the sense of the other narrators, says that the baskets of fragments were collected from the five loaves, the occurrence must have taken place, according to their notion, in the manner last described, for in the first case the fragments would not have come from the five loaves, but each loaf would itself have been multiplied.

But whatever conception we may form of the miracle, it involves, in any case, something so extravagant, that we cannot be surprised if modern theology is anxious to get rid of it at any price. But in doing so, the theologians should set about the task fairly and openly, admitting that the Evangelists here intend to describe a miracle, but that *they* do not believe it, and inasmuch as similar cases are constantly recurring in the Gospels, they are unable to look upon these, generally, as historical compositions. Instead of this, we see in the passage in question a set of miserable shifts and delusive evasions contending with each other for the mastery. Schleiermacher, who in this case also takes altogether the ground of Paulus, finds in the words of Jesus in John (vi. 26), that the people had followed him, not because they had seen miracles, but because they had eaten of the loaves, an indication that the increase of the bread had been a natural process. But as to what the miracles had been which the people saw, and what had happened to the loaves—upon this point, with more cunning but less candour than Paulus, he avoids every explanation. Naturally—because on a nearer examination of the question he cannot avoid seeing that even his eye-witness John describes the occurrence as a miracle, and understands the speech of Jesus to mean that the people looked upon the miracle which they had seen as important, not because it was a miracle, that is, a proof and reflex of his higher power, but only on its material side, as a distribution of bread. The hypothesis that a hospitable meal, provided by Jesus not through his own miraculous power but in a perfectly natural manner, for the purpose of setting an example of a man's sharing his own provision with others, operated upon by popular recollections and expectations, quickly took the form of a legend about a miraculous feeding—this hypothesis, according to Hase,* is only opposed by the fact of John's having been an eye-witness. But what is to be done, as, according to the admission of the same theologian, "the possibility of an increase in a quantity of nourishing substance, without cause assigned, is undeserving of serious thought"? We know already what the scientific investigator of the life of Jesus will do: he dismisses the unwelcome eye-witness, whose presence, moreover, on the occasion of Jesus' walking on the water (the narrative of which immediately follows, and which we have already discussed), would place him in a difficulty. It is true, indeed, that according to the express account of the two middle Evangelists (Mark vi. 30; Luke ix. 10), the Apostles, *i.e.* the twelve who had been sent out (Luke ix. 1; Mark vi. 7), had just before returned; but the dreamer John must have been behindhand, and on meeting afterwards with Jesus, and hearing the

* Life of Jesus, § 74.

history spoken of, cannot have taken the trouble to examine into the actual circumstances. According to Ewald,* it is impossible now to state with accuracy what was the original occasion of the narrative, in which he sees simply an embodiment of the doctrine that where true faith is combined with genuine love, infinite effects may be produced by the smallest external means. When the meaning of a miraculous history is understood to be so abstractedly moral as this explanation implies, we certainly require, if the origin of the evangelical narrative is to be made intelligible, a special external occasion. In Ewald's explanation, this occasion is simply an immaterial nonentity. We, who have definitely accounted for the origin of all the individual features of the narrative, are formally exempt from the necessity of suggesting this external occasion.

Of these features there still remain only the gathering together of the fragments and the number of the baskets. The *gathering* of fragments generally may appear on the one hand to be simply an imitation of the history of the manna, which is also *gathered* from first to last, and not merely the remnants. There is, however, a more definite antitype in the history of Elisha, who causes the twenty loaves to be set before the hundred prophets, with the explanation, "for thus saith the Lord, They shall eat and shall leave thereof." Then the writer continues, "So he (the servitor) set it before them, and they did eat and left thereof, according to the word of the Lord" (2 Kings iv. 43 ff.). On the other hand, this gathering up of the remains of the miraculous feast, especially when the reason for it given by the Evangelist is taken into account, "that nothing may remain," reminds us of the horror which the ancient Church had of any of the clements of the Supper dropping to the ground or being otherwise lost.† The fragments are gathered

* Three First Evangelists, p. 260.   History of Christ, p. 320 ff.
† Tertull. de Cor. Mil. 3.   Orig. in Exod. Homil. xiii. 3.

into baskets. This was partly a matter of course; but the manna was also gathered into measures of a homer each. In one account the number of baskets is exactly twelve. This number may be copied from that of the Apostles who gather. In the other, the number of baskets, seven, might seem to be taken from that of the seven loaves mentioned in the account, possibly also from that of the seven deacons employed* at the celebration of the Supper. (Comp. Acts vi. 1 ff., xxi. 8.) In the first number, as well as in that of the twelve Apostles, an allusion to the twelve tribes of Israel may at the same time be found; but whether, because only the remnants of the meal are collected into the twelve baskets, those who had already feasted are to be understood as Heathen and the feast as the great Supper of the Heathen, by which the number of the twelve tribes of the Jews was to be by no means diminished—is a question but few readers would answer in the affirmative.†

80. The Miracle at Cana.

In the history of Moses (2 Mos. xvii.; 4 Mos. xx.), the gift of manna or bread is accompanied by a miraculous gift of water, and this also, in the expectations of the Jews, was transferred from the first Saviour to the second, the Messiah. Metaphorically also, in speaking of spiritual nourishment, the bread of understanding was placed by the side of the water of Wisdom (Ecclus. xv. 3); in the Apocalypse, the water of life to which the Lamb leads his followers, whose stream

---

* Comp. the passage from Justin quoted above.

† Thus Luthardt, The Gospel of John, ii. 44, to the effect that Jesus meant to imply this by the command given, at the conclusion of his miracle, to gather into twelve baskets; Volkmar, Religion of Jesus, p. 232 ff., supposes a fiction, alluding to the ministry of the Apostle of the Heathen.

springs forth from the throne of God and the Lamb, plays a great part (vii. 17, xxi. 6, xxii. 1, 17); and even in the Gospel of John, Jesus speaks of a living water which he gives to men and which appeases thirst for ever (iv. 10, 13 ff.).

On other occasions Jesus prefers to compare what he offers to mankind to wine, and moreover to new wine which should be put into new bottles (Matt. ix. 17). And in consequence of his mode of life he found himself contrasted in many ways, and not much to his advantage, as a drinker of wine, with the Baptist who drank water (Matt. xi. 18 ff.). Moreover, the frequent comparison of the joys of the kingdom of the Messiah to a feast (Matt. viii. 11, xxvi. 29; Rev. iii. 20), to a marriage-feast, at which the Messiah appears as a bridegroom (Matt. xxii. 1—14, comp. ix. 15; John iii. 29; Rev. xix. 7, xxi. 2, 9, xxii. 17), suggested the idea of wine that rejoices the heart rather than that of sober water.

John's calling was to baptize with water; he was to be followed by the Messiah with the baptism of the Spirit and fire (Matt. iii. 11; Luke iii. 16; John i. 26, 33). According to the accounts given in the Acts, the pouring out of the Holy Spirit upon the disciples of Jesus did actually manifest itself by tongues of fire, resulting in phenomena which were ascribed by mockers to those men being filled with sweet wine (Acts ii. 13), the phenomena being on the contrary the effects of the Holy Spirit. But if, on this occasion, being filled by the Spirit gave the impression that the effects of the Spirit were those of the heat of new wine, conversely a gift of wine might easily be taken as an image of the communication of the Spirit.

The Baptist belonged to the old covenant; his baptism by water was but the last of those purifications, those works of the law by which, since Moses, the Jewish people had in vain attempted to gain the favour of God. The contrast between the new element that had come in Christ and the old element, between grace and the law, between the Son of God and Moses, implying that it was only under the first conditions of this series that satisfaction and happiness are to be attained, under the last nothing but imperfection and dissatisfaction, is especially involved in the principle of the fourth Gospel, "For the law," it is said at the conclusion of the preface, "was given by Moses, but grace and truth came by Jesus Christ." "And of his fulness," it had been said just before, "have all we received, and grace for grace" (i. 16 ff.). It has been correctly remarked,* that in the narrative of the gift of wine at Cana, exactly the same principle returns in the form of a fact that had been enunciated in that passage of the preface as to the relation of Moses to Christ, of the law to grace.

If, as a parallel to the miraculous gift of food, a similar gift of drink was to be ascribed to Jesus as the second Moses, or the divine Wisdom personified, all these considerations must have concurred in causing that drink to be represented as consisting rather in wine than, as in the case of its antitype, in water. And then there came in the additional consideration which had principally contributed, in the case of Jesus, to change the gift of manna into a gift of bread. It was impossible that a miraculous gift of food should be attributed to Jesus without an allusion to the bread at the Supper. Quite as impossible to describe him as having, like Moses, miraculously supplied drink as well, without thinking of the wine at the Supper. Thus Paul (1 Cor. x. 3 ff.), in speaking of the water out of the rock in the wilderness, considers both it and the manna as types of the two elements of the Supper. But if the matter employed at the miraculous feeding was the same as one of the elements of the Supper, it was obvious to represent the matter of the miraculous supply of drink as corresponding to the other element of the Supper, consequently as consisting of wine. Moreover, it is intelligible from this why the narrative of the miraculous

---

* Luthardt, i. 354.

gift of wine is found only in the Gospel of John. The three first Evangelists were satisfied with the history of the feeding as prefiguring the Supper, as they all give a special account besides of the institution of the Supper, in which, together with the bread, its other element also, wine, has its proper place. On the contrary, as the fourth Evangelist had, as is to be explained below, his reasons for avoiding all mention of the scene of the institution of the Supper, he was called upon, in order that both the elements might be spoken of, at all events indirectly, in his Gospel, to place a miraculous supply of drink by the side of a miraculous supply of food, a gift of wine by the side of a gift of bread.

He makes it the beginning of the miracles which Jesus did (ii. 11); it would seem as though he had felt himself compelled, after having illustrated the propositions of his preface with regard to the purpose and testimony of the Baptist, to bring upon the stage, as a sort of a prologue to his whole Gospel, the passage quoted as to the relation of Jesus to Moses, of grace to the law. On this principle, perhaps, the form which he gives to the miracle may be explained. It would have corresponded to the evangelical miracle of the feeding, as well as to the Old Testament miracle of the oil performed by Elijah, if Jesus had increased a small quantity of wine, had made it sufficient for a considerable time, or for many men. Instead of that, he changes water into wine. Moses also had opened his miraculous career by a change of water; only it had been the vindictive change of all the water in Egypt into blood. The first-fruits of the miracles of Jesus could not, indeed, be a miracle of vengeance; the blood into which he changed the water must not be real blood, but only the noble blood of the grape (1 Mos. xlix. 11 ; 5 Mos. xxxii. 14), which indeed, as taken at the last Supper, is the sacrificial blood of the Messiah (Matt. xxvi. 28), the life-giving blood of the Son of Man who came down from heaven (John vi. 53—58).

If, after these preliminary remarks, we examine more closely the Johannine account of the miracle at Cana (ii. 1—11), we find that the scene where it takes place, a marriage feast, is fixed by the conception already mentioned, of the kingdom of the Messiah under the figure of a feast, and, more especially, a marriage feast. Had the scene of such a feast been transplanted into the future, or the description been intended to be a mere comparison, as in Matt. ix. 15, xxii. 1 ff., John iii. 29, then, by a figure probably taken from the Song of Solomon, Jesus himself might represent the bridegroom whose bride is sometimes represented to be the Church (Ephes. v. 25—27, 29, 32, and the passages from the Revelations above quoted). On the other hand, in the case of a scene placed as an historical occurrence in the life of Jesus, the representation of it could not be given; the bridegroom must be a different person; Jesus himself can only be a guest at the marriage; but still he is the person from whom, in the end, the enjoyment of the feast proceeds. For the natural bridegroom (this is necessary as a motive for the miracle) has not provided, or has not been able to provide, a sufficient quantity of wine.

The mother of Jesus points out to her Son the deficiency that has occurred, as in the first account of the loaves and fishes given by the Synoptics the disciples call his attention to the fact that it is time to send the people away that they may buy food. But, as is clear from his answer, the mother of Jesus gives him this information intending to make a demand upon his miraculous powers. The ensuing miracle being the first, according to the Evangelist's own account, that Jesus did, and no account having been given of the miraculous events of his infancy, it appeared to the narrator suitable that the mother of Jesus should have been from the first aware of, or at all events have suspected, the existence of her Son's exalted nature. But while he exalts her by implying this, he degrades her on the other hand far below her Son's unapproachable dignity, by the abrupt retort which

Jesus makes. By the cutting words, "Woman, what have I to do with thee?" the fourth Evangelist appears to have intended to outdo the question of Jesus to his parents, "Why sought ye me? Wist ye not that I must be about my Father's business?" which the third Evangelist puts into the mouth of Jesus at twelve years of age (Luke ii. 49); but that this is too abrupt for him, will be the opinion of every one who does not consider that what we are dealing with here is not a condition of natural humanity, but the relation between the creative Word incarnate and every human authority, and that even that authority which is otherwise most sacred must be repudiated by that incarnate Word. Jesus adds, as a special ground for this repudiation, that his hour is not yet come. That of the day and hour of the second coming of the Messiah, and the end of the present period of the world, no man knows, but only God the Father alone—this is the concurrent view of the three first Evangelists (Matt. xxiv. 36, xxv. 13; Mark xiii. 32; Acts i. 7), of whom the second extends that ignorance to the Son, the Messiah. There, God alone is the Being who knows, men (the Messiah being more or less expressly included) do not know; in the fourth Gospel, a most important point in favour of its fundamental view, the Son of God, the incarnate Logos, is contrasted as the only Being that knows with men who do not know, and the day and the hour in question are not those of his future return but of his present glorification, first by miracles and lastly by his death. It is the latter that is implied when, as is frequently the case, it is said that the persecution of his enemies had no result because his hour was not yet come (vii. 30, viii. 20), and subsequently that he knew and declared that his hour was now come (xii. 21, xiii. 1). On the other hand, with regard to the time for his public entrance into Jerusalem, he maintains, in opposition to his brethren, that it is not yet come (vii. 6, 8), as he here objects to his mother that it is not yet the hour for him to perform miracles: although in this case, as well as in the former, he does really and after a short interval acquiesce in the demand made upon him before the time. Mary knows beforehand that he will do this, and upon this knowledge directs the servants to do as her Son shall direct them. Thus she is again exalted. For though she bears in mind the distance between herself and him who is above all (iii. 31), still, knowing what she does, she is not embarrassed or perplexed.

The symbolical meaning of the six water-pots of stone, which, according to the custom of the Jewish ablution (of the hands before eating, Matt. xv. 2; Mark vii. 2 ff.), stood at hand, cannot be mistaken. Jesus orders them to be filled with water, thus getting the basis for his miracle. The statement of the capacity of the pots, which was considerable, and their being filled to the brim, is intended to imply that Jesus was he who gives of his fulness (i. 15), who, like God himself, gives not his gifts with scanty measure (iii. 34).

The pots, therefore, are filled with water; then the servants, at the order of Jesus, draw out and bear to the Master of the feast, who, having tasted the liquor, recognises it as wine, and better too than had before come to table. When, on this, the Evangelist uses the expression, "the water that became wine," and, further on, describes Cana as the place where Jesus changed the water into wine (iv. 46); when, moreover, he calls this change of water a miracle, in consequence of which the disciples believed in Jesus (ver. 11), and ranks it as the first Galilean miracle, with a cure at a distance as the second (iv. 54);—when he does all this, he describes the act of Jesus unmistakeably as a miracle, and the interpretation of believers is justified in the remark that any explanation that does away with the miraculous element is not merely opposed to the words and the view of John, but also depreciates his credibility and capacity for observation, placing even the character of Jesus in an equivocal light.[*]

[*] Meyer, Commentary on the Gospel of John, p. 108 of the third edition.

If we believe in John, we must believe in the miracle; if we cannot do the latter, we must refuse to believe in the Evangelist, and that not only here, but as he narrates a series of miracles not less incredible; nay, as almost every word uttered by his Christ is as incredible as this miracle, we must do so throughout, and particularly as regards his giving us to understand that he is the Apostle John. The application in this case of Hase's solution, which supposes him to have been absent,* is the more ridiculous, as, according to ver. 2, the disciples of Jesus were invited with him to the marriage, and in the unnamed disciple who appears among those before engaged by Jesus (i. 35, 41), Hase himself recognises John; the appeal of Schleiermacher and his followers† to the fact that nothing is said of the impression made upon the guests by the alleged miracle, and that the narrative generally is not vivid enough, is a weak juggle about an account which no honest reader can misunderstand; while Neander's‡ attempt to substitute a mere potentialization of the water for vinous properties, for the change of water into real wine, can only be called a result of imbecility of thought, as well as of faith, which deserves our compassion.

There now follows a speech of the master of the feast which has caused the expositors much trouble in the attempt to shew that the custom which is described in it as common existed somewhere or other in the world. The master of the feast says that every man puts before his guests the good wine first, and then, when they have well drunk, that which is worse. But, on the contrary, no man does this, because it contradicts the nature of the operations of the human mind, which requires a gradation of pleasure in the ascending scale. The Evangelist simply invented this alleged custom altogether, or rather appropriated it from a synoptic expression

* Life of Jesus, § 50.
† Among whom, in this case, Ewald must be numbered, The Johannine Writings, i. 149 ff. ‡ Life of Jesus Christ, p. 271.

of Jesus. In composing his narrative, he had floating in his mind that speech of Jesus in which the latter compared what he offered to mankind with new wine. And in Luke he found appended to it (v. 39) the words: "No man also having drunk old wine, straightway desireth new: for he saith, The old is better." This passage in the third Gospel is intended to apply to the attachment of men to what is old (in this instance, Judaism and the Jewish customs), and to their prejudice against what is new; and practical experience is appealed to in proof of the assertion: our Evangelist intends, conversely, to shew that the new element offered by Jesus is preferable to the old, and that consequently in the miraculous narrative the wine that was given last tasted better than that before placed upon the table by the bridegroom. He endeavours, in his own peculiar manner, to illustrate this by a contrast; but inasmuch as the question does not, in his narrative, as in the passage of Luke, concern the difference between wine that is old, *i.e.* grown in an earlier year, and new, *i.e.* of a later growth, but only that between wine put on the table sooner or later, that natural and frequently heard phrase in Luke, The old is better, is converted into the pretended custom, but one which cannot be proved to have anywhere existed, of first setting on the better wine, and the fact that immediately after the old the new has no taste, into the imaginary usage of putting the worse wine before the guests after the better.

Such is the symbolical view of the miracle at Cana, in the form in which it was some time since brought forward by Herder, without impugning its historical validity, most lately by Baur in particular, who expressly rejects the latter. On critical grounds, the only objection to be made to it is that the Evangelist does not say a word pointing to such a purport of the narrative, and especially that he does not, as he does, *e.g.* in the case of the miracle of the feeding, connect with it speeches of Jesus illustrative of this meaning. But this very reference to the miracle of the feeding, assists us in the solution of this difficulty. The two miracles of the gift of bread and the gift of wine are so essentially connected in form and substance, as well as by their common reference to the Supper, that the meaning of the one cannot be explained without that of the other; but the question was only this, whether the higher meaning of the miraculous gift of food should come under discussion on the occasion of the miraculous gift of drink, or the meaning of the latter on occasion of the former. The miracle of food appears in the Synoptics nearly in the middle of the narratives about Jesus, and its position was assigned to it by reason of the connection in which it appears. And if the fourth Evangelist had reasons for placing the gift of wine at the beginning of his Gospel, it is easily intelligible that he might not be inclined to subjoin to the very first miracle described by him that lengthy sort of illustration. In order to introduce a gradual ascent into his Gospel, he gives of the two first miracles (ii. 1 ff., iv. 46 ff.) a short and simple description; the third is the first to which he annexes long dissertations, and these, in the case of the fourth, the account of the loaves and fishes (the walking on the water is treated more as an appendix to this), increase in importance, until they culminate in the case of the last, the raising of Lazarus, though here, in consequence of the dramatic character of the scene, they are carried on only in the form of a dialogue. In the discussions annexed to the account of the loaves and fishes, it was natural that Jesus should represent himself as the spiritual food of mankind in every sense, his flesh as their meat, his blood as their drink, and should also allude to the wine given at Cana, at least in its reference to the Supper. But the relation between the old and new, Judaism and Christianity, as it was involved in the change of water into wine, had been already expounded beforehand in the passage of the preface discussed above.

81. The Cursing of the Fig-tree.

The miracle of the cursing of the fig-tree (Matt. xxi. 18—22; Mark xi. 12—14, 20—23), which we have left to the last, being, as a vindictive miracle, the only one of its kind in the evangelical history (the Book of Acts has several such), is indeed as such a particularly difficult one, but still on other accounts remarkably instructive. For in the case of this miracle, not only, as in that of others, may the elements be pointed out of which it is compounded, but also the different shapes which it had to pass through before becoming a miraculous account; its changes, as it were, from the chrysalis to the butterfly, or from the tadpole to the frog, are still co-existing in the Old and New Testament.

In a retrospect of the past ages of Israel, the prophet Hosea, the prophet who has, soon after, the passage about the Son or favourite of God, represents Jehovah as saying (ix. 10), "I found Israel like grapes in the wilderness; I saw your fathers as the first-ripe in the fig-tree at her first time; but they went to Baal-peor," &c. That is, they requited the care which he bestowed upon the isolated and unprotected horde by falling away into idolatry. The same image is found with a different turn given to it in Micah (vii. 1 ff.), when he exclaims, "Woe is me! for I am as when they have gathered the summer fruits, as the grape gleanings of the vintage: there is no cluster to eat: my soul desired the first-ripe fruit (*i.e.* fig). The good man is perished out of the earth; and there is none upright among men ... the best of them is as a briar," &c. &c. Here the people is not, as above, the grape or early fig, but the fig-tree or the vine-branch, which, like the stripped stem after the vintage, gives no more fruit; degenerate Israel, throwing out no more good shoots, is a fig-tree barren of fruit.

Whether such a tree means a whole people or a single man, we are told in the New Testament what its just fate is to be, first by the Baptist (Matt. iii. 10), then by Jesus himself (Matt. vii. 19). "And now also the axe is laid unto the root of the trees; every tree which bringeth not forth good fruit is hewn down and cast into the fire." And in connection, as it were, with the passage of Micah (and also with the parable of the Vineyard in Isaiah, chap. v.), Jesus on another occasion brings forward a parable of a man who had planted a fig-tree in his vineyard, upon which for two years he sought fruit in vain. In the third year he again finds none, and then he commands the gardener to cut down the useless tree that only burdens the soil; but the gardener prays for a respite for this year, during which he will try every means to make the tree fruitful; if then it does not answer to their expectation, it may be cut down without further grace. Now it is remarkable that Luke, who alone has this parable of the barren Fig-tree, passes over the history of the cursing of the fig-tree. Does he not appear to have been conscious that he had already communicated the essential substance of this history in that parable, and in a less offensive form than that of a vindictive miracle performed by Jesus might appear to the Evangelist, who likewise is the only one who represents the demand made by certain disciples for a vindictive miracle as having been rejected by Jesus (Luke ix. 54 ff.)?

But the motive was there. No sooner was a word or an image of this kind found in the original Christian tradition, than it became, if possible, a miraculous history. The severe possessor of the vineyard in the parable was God; the patient gardener, Jesus the Messiah; the year's respite which he obtains for the tree, the acceptable year of the Lord (Luke iv. 18), the period of the ministry of Christ in Israel. But, as is well known, the time of this respite expired without result; if it did so, the gardener was ready to leave the tree to its fate; nay, the Messiah whom he represents was himself, according to the Christian view, returning in the clouds of heaven to execute this punishment in the place of God. If Jesus was supposed to have done this prefiguratively during his earthly life to a tree which symbolised unfruitful Israel, still the axe, according to the words of the text, could not appropriately be put into his hands, so that he might be represented as cutting down the tree like a day-labourer, but the proceeding was brought into connection with his miraculous power, and the barren fig-tree was withered by a word from him. This is the form in which the history is given by Matthew and Mark, and put into a connection which on the one side bears traces of its original import, while on the other these traces have entirely disappeared. For it is in the last week of the life of Jesus, on one of his last walks from Bethany to Jerusalem, that he is said to have noticed the barren tree, and to have passed judgment upon it. This is connected with the meaning of the history, in so far as that at that time the incapacity of Israel for the salvation offered by Jesus was fully proved. On the other hand, the dialogue between Jesus and the disciples, which both the Evangelists append to the miracle, shews that in view of the miracle itself they had altogether lost sight of the original meaning of the narrative. For, on the disciples observing with surprise how soon the fig-tree was withered away, Jesus replies, that if they have faith and doubt not, they shall not only do what had been done to the fig-tree, but also if they say to a mountain (Luke, in a similar speech, on another occasion introduces a sort of fig-tree, xvii. 6), "Be thou removed and be thou cast into the sea, it shall be done." These speeches, which only obscure the real meaning of the narrative, might have been added to it when it begun to be looked upon only as a miraculous history; Luke has preserved for us, in connection with his parable of the Fig-tree, the sort of speeches which did originally belong to it. There

(xiii. 1) Jesus is speaking of the Galileans, whose blood Pilate had mingled with their sacrifices, and of the eighteen upon whom the tower of Siloam fell, and asks the Jews whether they thought that this had happened to those people because of any particular guilt. No, he answers, but unless ye repent ye shall all likewise perish ; and then he connects with this the parable of the Fig-tree. Only this would also be the moral of the history of the accursed fig-tree, and then it would have been addressed, not to the disciples, but, as in the first case, to the Jews, to the effect that except they repent they would all perish like the fig-tree.

If then, in this case, as we have found in several others also, and as is natural when we consider the numerous different sources open to him and Matthew alike, Luke has preserved in his parable the pure and original form of this narrative, it appears on further consideration, if we look at the account as that of a miracle, and compare the description of it in Matthew and Mark, that Matthew's is from two points of view the more original. In the first place, he represents the fig-tree as withering in a moment at the command of Jesus; and this, in the case of miraculous narratives, is the only test of real simplicity. If the performer of a miracle can produce the withering of a tree by a word, he can as easily make the effect apparent immediately after the word has been spoken. Separating the two in the way in which Mark represents the tree as being cursed by Jesus on one morning, and then its decay as being observed by the disciples on the next, and not before, is pedantry and pragmaticism. It did not indeed occur to the Evangelist, that the event might thus be made capable of explanation on natural grounds, a purpose for which his representation has been employed ; all that he had in view was to make the thing more vivid and dramatic; but, as by other similar modifications, he has only by this attempt weakened the strong and original form of the miraculous account.

But he has made a still greater mistake by his addition of the words, that the time of figs was not yet. Not that he was wrong in saying so, if we take the history by the Calendar. That time, the week before Easter, is not yet the time for figs; for the early fig was not ripe till June, the regular fig not till August; and when Josephus says of the shore district of the Sea of Galilee that it bears figs* ten months in the year, this proves nothing for the rocky region of Judea. Mark adds these words in order to explain (what in the case of a particular tree may easily be explained, even in fig-time, by disease or from local causes) why Jesus found no figs upon it; but in his eagerness to explain, he overlooks the fact that he thus makes the act of vengeance performed by Jesus unintelligible. If it was not yet the time at which a healthy tree should have had fruit, the cursing of it by Jesus had no meaning. So in this respect also Matthew takes the better course in not explaining the barrenness of the tree, *i.e.* not mentioning that at that time no fruit whatever could properly have been on a fig-tree, and thus leaving open the possibility of explaining, at least from a certain point of view, the conduct of Jesus with regard to it. In the moral precept and parable upon which our history is based, no time of year is named, but the period at which fruit was sought in vain upon the tree is naturally supposed to have been that of the fruit-harvest. In the form of a miraculous history it was transplanted into the last day of the life of Jesus, and the cause of this, as we have seen, was probably a faint remembrance of its original meaning. But the narrators who repeated the story, and who were thinking only of its miraculous character, did not consider that by thus placing the occurrence they brought it into the spring, a season unsuited to it if looked upon as a subject of real history.

* Bell. Jud. iii. 10, 8.

FOURTH GROUP OF MYTHS.

THE TRANSFIGURATION AND ENTRANCE OF JESUS INTO
JERUSALEM.

82. THE TRANSFIGURATION.

IN a Jewish work* we read in the narrative, 2 Mos. xxxiv. 29 ff., "Behold, Moses our Teacher, of blessed memory, who was a mere man, God having spoken to him face to face, obtained so shining a countenance, that the Jews feared to approach him; how much more must this be assumed of the Godhead itself, and the face of Jesus must have shone from the one extremity of the world to the other! But he was not endowed with brightness of any kind, and was altogether like other men. Hence it is clear that we are not to believe in him." This is indeed from a late post-Christian writing; but the inference it draws is that which a Jew must have drawn in the earliest Christian times so long as he saw, on the part of him who was held up as the last Saviour, nothing corresponding to the shining countenance of the first Saviour. Now it could not indeed be said of Jesus, as it was of Moses, that when he spoke with the people he was obliged to put a veil over his face on account of its brightness—because this was notoriously not the case. But so celebrated a feature in the history of Moses could not be left without a parallel in that of Christ; all that was required was to give it the proper character.

Now we find, first of all, in the Apostle Paul, in a passage (2 Cor. iii. 7 ff.) where he is giving utterance to his exalted feelings, as a servant of the New Covenant, of the Spirit that giveth life, the words: "But if the ministration of death,

* Nizzachon Vetus, p. 40.

written and engraven in stones, was glorious, so that the children of Israel could not steadfastly behold the face of Moses for the glory of his countenance; which glory was to be done away; how shall not the ministration of the Spirit be rather glorious? In this passage, indeed, it is not Christ but the Apostles who are contrasted with Moses, and the glory of the latter only understood in a spiritual sense. But when it is said further on (ver. 13, 18), that they, the ministers of the New Covenant, do not as Moses did, who placed a veil upon his face, "But we all with open face beholding as in a glass the glory of the Lord, are changed into the same image from glory to glory;" Christ himself also is brought into the comparison as the Being from whom the glory of his ministers is reflected, and moreover allusion is made to the outward transfiguration which the risen Christ has undergone, and which on his return his followers also shall undergo (1 Cor. xv. 43—49).

Now it was always a subject of possible objection on the part of Jewish opponents that so much that was expected of the Messiah had not been performed by Jesus during his earthly life, and must consequently be deferred to his second coming. And in order to guarantee this future performance, some preliminary proofs of it, as, *e.g.* of the raising of the dead by the Messiah, were mythically referred to the bygone life of Jesus upon earth. Thus a necessity may have been felt of representing also the glory of that Christ who had risen again, and was to return in the clouds of heaven, as having appeared through the veil of his humanity, though transiently only, during his first presence upon earth. This, on one side at least, is the mode in which the history of the Transfiguration, as given in the New Testament, arose (Matt. xvii. 1—13; Mark ix. 2—13; Luke ix. 28—36). This history could not be unknown to the Jewish writer quoted above, but no notice is taken of it, no doubt because it does not speak of a permanent glory of the countenance of Jesus, like that of Moses in the Old Testament narrative. Instead of this, as we shall see, pains are taken in other respects to outdo the Mosaic history.

The imitation of this in the evangelical narrative is plain, and indeed the events mentioned in 2 Mos. xxiv. 1 ff. and xxxiv. 29 are combined. The theatre of the representation, both in the New Testament and the Old, is a mountain. In the latter, it is Sinai; in the former, as elsewhere in the history of the New Testament, a mountain without a name, but described, as in the history of the Temptation, as a high mountain. The number of persons whom Jesus takes with him for a nearer view of what was to happen to him is three, and they are those who form that small committee, with which we are well acquainted, of the apostolical college: as Moses had taken with him to the mountain, besides the seventy elders, three men in particular, Aaron, Nadab and Abihu (2 Mos. xxiv. 1, 9). The evangelical narrative is connected with the preceding events by the date "after six" (in Luke, eight) "days;" as it is said of Moses, that after the cloud had for six days covered the mountain, he was called up to it by Jehovah on the seventh (2 Mos. xxiv. 16). Moreover, there is in each case some resemblance in what follows the scene upon the mountain. When Moses, after his call, comes from the mountain with the three men, from whom the triumvirate that accompanies Jesus is copied (the illumination of his countenance is indeed spoken of subsequently), the first thing that meets his eyes is the sight of the people dancing round the golden calf, and his first emotion is one of anger at the incapacity of the representatives he had left behind him (2 Mos. xxiv. 14), of whom Aaron had been even an accomplice in the preparation of the idol (2 Mos. xxxii. 15 ff.). When Jesus comes from the mountain, his first sight is the boy possessed with a devil, and his first feeling one of displeasure at the inability of his disciples to drive it out.

In both cases, the glory of the countenance is developed upon the mountain itself; for that of Moses also had become shining upon the mountain during his conversation with Jehovah, though this was not noticeable until he had descended again to the people. The cloud, moreover, and indeed a bright cloud, because the glory of God must be supposed to have been in it, is likewise a feature taken from the Mosaic history (2 Mos. xix. 16, xxiv. 16, 18). But in the case of Jesus there is this addition, that besides his countenance, his clothes also became shining; and especially that he, as a glorified Being, takes the place of Moses; while the latter, with Elijah, stands at his side in a subordinate position, nearly in the same manner as the two accompanying angels at the side of Jehovah in the history of Abraham.

The object of Moses' ascent of the mountain was to hear the laws from Jehovah, and to receive the tables which he was to hand over to the people. No such instruction could be required by the Messiah: he, in whose time the law was to be written in the hearts of men by the pouring out of the Holy Spirit (Jer. xxxi. 31 ff.; Ezek. xi. 19 ff., xxxvi. 26 ff.), must, above all men, carry it in his heart; in his case the ascent of the mountain was only intended to exhibit him to his followers penetrated by supernatural light, and in communication with exalted personages of Jewish antiquity, and moreover, as had already been done at his baptism, to be declared by God to be his Son. The presence of Moses was naturally called for by the similarity of what was now occurring to Jesus to that which had once occurred to the Lawgiver, and, generally, by the connection between the office of the Messiah and his own. The Messiah was, indeed, according to the interpretation of that time (Acts iii. 22, vii. 36), he whom Moses had once proclaimed in the words (5 Mos. xviii. 15), "The Lord thy God will raise up unto thee a Prophet from the midst of thee, of thy brethren, like unto me; unto him ye shall hearken." Moreover, if Moses was now seen in friendly conversation with Jesus, it was proved that the former saw in him, not, as was the view of Jewish wranglers, the destroyer, but the fulfiller of the law.

But, besides the Lawgiver, there appeared upon the mountain of the transfiguration a prophet as well—Elijah. According to the prophecy of Malachi (iii. 23 ff., comp. Ecclus. xlviii. 10 ff.), Jehovah was to send him before the coming of his terrible day of judgment, to move, if possible, the people to repentance. Hence it was a dictum of those learned in the Scriptures that Elijah must first come and restore all things, and that until the forerunner had appeared, the Messiah was not to be expected (Matt. xvii. 10). It is well known how Jesus himself (more probably the defensive tactics of the first Christians) was said to have endeavoured to weaken the proof drawn from the non-appearance of Elijah against his own Messiahship, by representing John the Baptist to be this Elijah (Matt. xi. 14; Mark i. 2; Luke i. 17): they were satisfied with an imaginary Elijah, as the real Elijah was not to be had. But it is in the highest degree remarkable that, according to the evangelical narrative, Jesus should, just after the appearance of the real Elijah, have referred his disciples to the unreal one, and moreover have referred to the latter because they looked for an appearance of the former. For after they descended from the mountain of the transfiguration, his disciples are said to have asked him, How then do the scribes say that Elijah must first come? To which he answers, Certainly Elijah must first come; but in fact he has already come (that is, in John), and not only not been recognised, but in fact maltreated and put to death, which shall be also the fate of the Messiah himself (Matt. xvii. 10—13; Mark ix. 11—13). The question of the disciples can only mean—If, as we are convinced (comp. Matt. xvi. 16), thou art the Messiah, what then becomes of the maxim of the scribes, that Elijah must precede the Messiah, seeing that he has not preceded thee? It is impossible that the disciples should have asked this question if Elijah had appeared just before, and quite as little, supposing them to have asked it, would Jesus have referred them to the Baptist, and not simply to the real Tishbite whom they had just seen. On the other hand, that question of the disciples would have come in extremely well after the foregoing history of the confession of Peter; and it has therefore been surmised that Matthew found it in this connection, and inserted, on his own responsibility, the history of the Transfiguration.* It is, however, quite in the manner of our synoptic Gospels, simply on account of a common subject, in this case the word Elijah, to put together two narratives, as frequently on other occasions two texts, which in point of meaning have no connection. In this instance, indeed, not merely is this done, but the two histories formally exclude each other. Had Elijah just appeared, as is said, the disciples could not ask the question they are said to have done; if they did ask the question, Elijah could not have appeared just before. It is indeed a very naive proceeding to connect two such histories; but it is exactly like Matthew to do so.† We can here distinguish plainly between two layers of the tradition. The doubt of the truth of the Messiahship of Jesus, arising from the prophecy of Malachi, was first met by investing the Baptist with the character of Elijah; then, when a pressure was put upon the literal meaning of the prophecy, an attempt was made to exhibit the real Elijah. He could not be represented as appearing publicly to all men, but only apart to one or two

---

* Köstlin, Synoptic Gospels, p. 25.

† Baur starts with John, and thus his sense of the simplicity of the Synoptics becomes obscured. So he tries to introduce a meaning into this conversation by artificially interpreting the question of the Apostles to imply that after the appearance of Elijah it was only their expectation that he would remain that was disappointed (Review of the latest Investigations into the Gospel of Mark, Theological Annual, 1853, p. 78). But their words imply that it was not his stay they were disappointed of, but his coming at all, of which, according to the preceding history, they could not have been disappointed.

For this purpose the history of the Transfiguration and the grouping with Moses naturally suggested itself.

The two first Evangelists do not say what formed the subject of the conversation between Jesus and the two departed personages. Moreover, nothing depended upon it, as the object of the meeting was only to exhibit Jesus in agreement with the Lawgiver, and not without the Prophets associated with him. Luke says that these personages announced to him beforehand the death which awaited him in Jerusalem. But this was superfluous, as he had already himself prophesied this death (Luke ix. 22). But there is no doubt that the purpose of the Evangelist is to represent the death of Jesus, that great stumbling-block to the notions of the Jews, as founded on the divine counsels of which his two associates were considered as the depositaries. The proposal of Peter to build tabernacles for Jesus and the two forms from the kingdom of Spirits, to detain the grand supernatural apparition as something natural and material, is described by Luke and Mark as a misunderstanding, and the former represents all three disciples as overcome with sleep, as they appear subsequently in Gethsemane. By this, on both occasions, the distance between them and Jesus is intended to be indicated. While their Master is in the most elevated and mysterious of states, they were lying on the ground with their senses paralysed.

On the mountain of the transfiguration, as formerly in Sinai, there was a cloud containing the glory of God, who could not be supposed to have been silent on this occasion, any more than on that. His words were then directed to Moses, which the latter was commissioned to convey to the people; now, in accordance with the different objects of the scene, they are addressed to the disciples as a divine testimony to Jesus. They are the words from Isaiah, xlii. 1, comp. with Psalm ii. 7, which had already sounded from heaven on the occasion of the baptism of Jesus, only that on this occasion, as having a manifest reference to the history of Moses, the call to hear him is added to them, from the passage in which the Lawgiver promises to the people a Prophet like unto himself (5 Mos. xviii. 15).

After this account of the origin of the history of the Transfiguration, there is only one view of it which need be considered with respect. It is that which sees in it an objective and miraculous occurrence, which believes in a supernatural brightness of the face and garments of Jesus, a real appearance of the two personages who had been long dead, and an audible voice of God from out the cloud. Whoever can admit these things seriously—whoever, being himself convinced, stands on the same point of view as the Evangelist— to him indeed this narrative presents no difficulty, and we have nothing to say against him, except that we doubt as to whether he really is what he believes himself to be, and does not merely imagine it. On the other hand, all those explanations which attempt to represent the occurrence as half natural, or entirely so, are too miserable and absurd to make it worth while to dwell upon them. Who could suppose that in the change of the figure of Jesus and the brightness which shone around him, even Schleiermacher* sees an optical illusion, of which, however, no more account can be given, *i.e.* he will not allow the point to be more accurately investigated, because he is well aware that all closer investigation can only expose more fully the absurdity of the whole view: the two personages, whom the Evangelists suppose to have been and consequently describe as Moses and Elijah, were, he imagines, secret adherents, connected, perhaps, with the Sanhedrim, an idea corroborated by the statement that they foretold his death to Jesus, as the deadly hatred of that body against him might be known to men of this description; an actual voice, indeed, is not supposed to have been heard at

---

* In his Lectures on the Life of Jesus. Likewise Hase, Life of Jesus.

all, but the disciples, after the manner of the Jews, looked upon the optical illusion as a divine revelation about Jesus, and later Hellenistic narrators misunderstood this revelation to have been expressed by an actual voice. Thus, after the example of Paulus and Venturini, all the main points of the evangelical narrative are happily set aside; Jesus was not really transfigured, Moses and Elijah did not appear, no voice from heaven spoke over his head. But then we are at a loss to know what, or whether anything of the sort, did occur to Jesus. Ewald appears to be of this opinion when he says,* that we are now unable to state of what lower materials this description is formed, but that its inward truth is plain, and that the higher materials, of which this inward truth avails itself for its representation, are in no way doubtful. By lower materials are meant, in the mysterious language of Ewald, the natural and historical foundations of a narrative; by higher materials, the Old Testament conceptions and events, from which the narrative is copied, the inward truth is the idea. So that Ewald means to say, that we cannot now know what historical element is at the bottom of the history of the Transfiguration, but that its ideal truth is evident, and the Old Testament antitypes upon which it was formed unmistakeable. This is nearly the same thing as we say; only that we are not concerned to find a professedly natural occasion for what never took place; and as to ideal truth, all that we see in the narrative is the Jewish opinion that Moses and Christ were antitypes of each other, and that a connection existed between Elijah and the latter.

It is because of the Jewish-Christian character of the history that the fourth Evangelist omits it, or only adopted it in a form so changed that we cannot recognise it. Of this we cannot speak until we come to it further on.

* Three First Evangelists, p. 274. Comp. History of Christ, p. 338 ff.

83. The Entrance of Jesus into Jerusalem.

The history of the Transfiguration is followed in all the Synoptics by only a few speeches of Jesus. They represent him then as entering upon the eventful journey to the Passover at Jerusalem. We have already spoken, in an earlier part of the work, of the mode in which, on the subject of this journey, the three first Evangelists differ, partly from one another, partly from the fourth. Here we are only concerned with the conclusion of it (Matt. xxi. 1—11; Mark xi. 1—10; Luke xix. 29—34; John xii. 12—16).

Among the contrasts which resulted from a comparison of passages of the Old Testament, so different in their character, but all referred to the Messiah, there was one referring to the mode of his advent. According to Daniel, vii. 13, he was to come with the clouds of heaven; according to Zechariah, ix. 9, to enter upon an ass. This passage, in which in point of fact an ideal Prince of Peace was alluded to, was, more correctly than many others, referred to the Messiah. "What says the Scripture of the first Saviour?" it is said in that Rabbinical passage which we have already quoted so often.* Answer: "2 Mos. iv. 20, we read: And Moses took his wife and his sons, and set them upon an ass. So also the last Saviour, Zech. ix. 9: Poor, and sitting upon an ass."† This contradiction between the description taken from Zechariah and that from Daniel, was reconciled by the Rabbis, by explaining that in case the Israelites should prove worthy, their Messiah was to appear majestically in the clouds of heaven, but if they were unworthy of him, he should ride in upon an ass in a poor and needy condi-

---

* Midrasch Koheleth, 73, 3. See above, Vol. i. p. 204.

† This ass of Moses and the Messiah is supposed to have been the same as Abraham had saddled when he was preparing for the sacrifice of Isaac. Jalkut Rubeni, 79, 3.

tion.* The Christians reconciled the contradiction otherwise. They assigned the riding upon the ass to the period of the first presence of their Messiah upon the earth, that is, to the earthly life of Jesus, expecting his coming with the clouds of heaven on the occasion of his future second advent. Since in the passage of Zechariah, in so far as it represents the King as entering meekly seated on the animal of peace (nothing is said of poverty), there seemed to be involved an opposition to the expectation of the Messiah current among the Jews, in which he was represented as a mighty warrior, it might indeed be supposed that Jesus on entering the capital had chosen to ride upon an ass, with the intention of recalling the passage of Zechariah to men's minds, and by this palpable demonstration to divest himself of the character of Messiah who was to be a warrior and a politician. For we have above explained that the royal dignity attributed even in Zechariah to the coming Personage, did not necessarily carry a political meaning. If, therefore, we are unable to do what has lately been often done, that is, reject as unhistorical the whole of the entrance of Jesus into Jerusalem upon an ass, we shall certainly soon discover thus much, that the evangelical narratives about it are formed, not so much upon a given fact, as upon Old Testament passages and dogmatic ideas.

The clearest proof of this lies in the description of the first Evangelist, whose account of the entrance of Jesus contains an impossibility which he cannot have taken from any source of information about a real fact, however much distorted, but only from a passage in a Prophet which he himself misunderstood. He tells us that the two disciples sent by Jesus to Bethphage, brought from that place, in accordance with his directions, an ass and its colt, spread their clothes upon both animals and set Jesus thereon. Now, if we are to imagine how Jesus could have ridden upon both beasts at the same

* Gemara Sandhedr. f. 98, 1.

time (and considering the shortness of the distance the notion of a change from one to the other is quite inadmissible), our understanding is paralysed, nor does it recover itself until we look more accurately at the passage of Zechariah quoted by the Evangelist. "Rejoice greatly, O daughter of Zion (the words, Tell ye the daughter of Zion, in Matthew, are from Isaiah lxii. 11); behold, thy King cometh unto thee; he is just and having salvation, lowly, and riding upon an ass, and upon a colt the foal of an ass." Now, every one who has the least acquaintance with the poetical language of the Hebrews, knows that by these words not two animals are meant; but the same animal, which in the first part of the verse is called an ass, is in the second more accurately defined as the foal of an ass. There is no doubt that, in general, the author of the first Gospel knew this as well as we do; but as he saw in this passage a prophecy of Christ, he thought that on this occasion he must understand it literally, and understand the words as applying to two animals. Having thus, as he thought, done full justice to the prophecy, he considered that his task was accomplished, and did not set himself the further problem of realising to his own mind the possibility of one Messiah riding upon two asses.

In this Luke and Mark do not follow him, but are satisfied with one animal. Their description does not on this account approve itself as the more original, for the feature in question comes from the passage of Zechariah, and to this Matthew keeps closer than they do, following it as he does literally and blindly, while the two others, doing the same, do it with a certain amount of reflection. Of the two animals spoken of by Matthew, they choose for the use of Jesus not the dam but the foal. But this, again, is the result of an unhistorical reflection which they betray by the addition that Jesus ordered them to bring a foal upon which no man had sate. This condition was not brought out in the passage of Zechariah, but the foal of which the passage speaks might be understood to be of that description, and moreover met the view that, as subsequently only a tomb in which no man had been laid (Luke xxiii. 53) was worthy to receive the sacred body of the Messiah, so now only an animal on which no man had sate was worthy to carry him. Moreover, it is self-evident that this is a reflection far more suitable for a subsequent narrative than for Jesus himself, who, if he rode an animal never ridden before, could only expect the procession to be disturbed, and the impression which he wished to make destroyed.

But the original Christian legend was not satisfied with a general fulfilment of the prophecy of Zechariah by Jesus riding into Jerusalem upon an ass; the ass of the Messiah, it was supposed, must have been destined for his use by a higher Providence, and, as the Messiah, he must have known where the ass intended for him was standing bound, and had only to be fetched away. He must have known this all the more, as in an Old Testament prophecy the Messiah was expressly described as he who binds up his ass. In the blessing of Jacob, the dying Patriarch says of Judah, but in terms that might apply to Shiloh, so often understood of the Messiah (1 Mos. xlix. 11): "Binding his foal unto the vine, and his ass's colt unto the choice vine;" thus Matthew had here again his two asses, the older one and the young one, while all had the tethered ass which Justin Martyr does, in fact, in accordance with the prophecy, represent as being tethered to a vine at the entrance of the village.* The Evangelists have nothing about the vine, but represent Jesus as only saying to the two disciples whom he despatches, that when they come into the village before them, they will find an ass bound. The passage from Jacob's blessing was not so present to their minds as that from Zechariah, but it

---

* Apol. i. 32.

very naturally occurred to that of the Martyr, as it is certain that the beginning of the evangelical narrative was originally as much taken from the former as the rest of it was from the latter. Properly speaking, it might certainly have been expected that, in accordance with the passage from Genesis, the Messiah would have bound his ass to the vine on dismounting; but the assumption that it was already standing bound gave at the same time an opportunity of a proof being afforded of the supernatural knowledge of the Messiah, and in addition of the power of his Messianic calling, if the disciples had only to say to the owner of the ass, that the Messiah had need of it, to obtain the loan of it without opposition. The fourth Evangelist avoids all these details, and simply says that Jesus found a young ass and mounted it. But this is only because, when he notices the prophecy of Zechariah, he is only concerned with the retrospect of the raising of Lazarus, to which he passes on immediately after (ver. 17 ff.).

But the prophecy of Zechariah did not merely assert that the Messianic Ruler should enter Jerusalem upon an ass, but also called on the capital on this occasion to shout and rejoice; as also the passage of Isaiah which the first Evangelist, in consequence of its resemblance, combines with that of Zechariah, commands that the daughter of Zion should be told that her Saviour cometh. According to the description of the three first Evangelists, this is the character which the multitudes that accompany him give to Jesus, by the cry, "Hosanna to the Son of David, that cometh in the name of Jehovah!" and by spreading out their garments and strewing the road with palm-branches; the capital, in which, according to the history as given by the Synoptics, Jesus is as yet unknown, is thus thrown into confusion, and the people ask who this is; upon which he is represented to them to be Jesus, the Prophet from Nazareth in Galilee. According to John, on the contrary, the crowds are from the city itself, and on hearing of the approach of Jesus, who was not unknown in Jerusalem, go to meet him with that shout and those offerings of homage, and the reason that is alleged for this solemn introduction is the raising of Lazarus. With the exception of this last feature, including even the offence taken by the Pharisees and the reply of Jesus, of which the account given by the Evangelists is not uniform, all that is here told might have so happened: but even if nothing of it had happened, the narrative was a natural result of the prophetic passage taken in a Messianic sense.

THIRD CHAPTER.

MYTHICAL HISTORY OF THE PASSION, DEATH, AND RESURRECTION OF JESUS.

FIRST GROUP OF MYTHS.

THE MEAL AT BETHANY, AND THE PASCHAL MEAL.

84. THE MEAL AT BETHANY AND THE ANOINTING.

It is one of the most ancient of the evangelical traditions that Jesus, shortly before his Passion, was anointed with precious ointment by a woman on the occasion of a supper at Bethany (Matt. xxvi. 6—13; Mark xiv. 3—9; John xii. 1—8). This history was especially valuable to the Christendom of the earliest ages, as is shown by the words which Matthew and Mark put into the mouth of Jesus at the time : " Wherever in the world this Gospel" (but it is scarcely possible that Jesus should thus have spoken of a " Gospel," meaning thereby his own history) " shall be preached, there shall also this be told for a memorial of this woman." According to this we might have expected that the two first Evangelists would have preserved for us the name of the woman, or something more definite about her; as this is not the case, it is clear that the earliest Christendom was not so much concerned to know who had anointed Jesus, as that he had been anointed. And, therefore, not only is Bethany named as the locality, but the house in which the occurrence took place and the owner of it. The reason of so much stress being laid upon the fact that Jesus was anointed before his passion, is given us by the narrative in the expression which it likewise puts into the mouth of Jesus, that in that she poured that ointment on his body, she did it for his burial; or, as Mark rightly explains the expression of Matthew, that she came beforehand to anoint his body to the burying, while the turn given to the words in John, that she had preserved the ointment for the day of his burial, obliterates the original meaning of the words till they are almost unintelligible. But the importance thus attributed to this anticipation of the anointing can only be satisfactorily explained upon the supposition that the anointing of the body of Jesus at the proper time, that is, on the occasion of his burial, did not in fact take place. This, according to Matthew and Mark, was really the case; according to Luke, it was intended but not done; and John is the only one who asserts that it was actually performed at the expense of an entire hundred-weight of spices. These statements involve questions to which we shall return at the proper place.

But these utterances of Jesus only form the conclusion of the scene which has been introduced by the appearance of the woman with the box of ointment, which she pours out upon the head of Jesus. This act is first censured by the disciples, who point out how much good might have been done to the poor for the value of the precious ointment; it is then defended by Jesus as a virtuous deed, as the poor are always there, and opportunities of doing *them* good, while he, and with him the possibility of shewing him love and honour, will soon be withdrawn from them. It is not impossible that all this may have been really said as it is recounted. But the next speech of Jesus, explaining the anointing by the woman as an anticipation of the anointing of his dead body, looks very much as if it were evolved out of the consciousness of the Christendom of the earliest period, which was pained at the fact that there had been no anointing of the body of the Master on the occasion of his burial. A similar supposition, therefore, as regards the preceding speech naturally suggests itself. We may suppose the existence in the earliest times of Christianity of an exaggerated feeling for the poor, which looked upon benevolence towards them in the shape of almsgiving as the only really good work, and on the other hand rejected as waste all ornament or decoration in worship. This unimaginative Ebionitish tendency was here met by a feeling of the necessity of a personal worship of Christ—and it is significant that it is the fourth Evangelist who goes so far as to see mere hypocrisy in the objection taken to such expenditure on the ground of the poor, that it is he who considers avarice to have been the real motive for it, and accordingly, instead of the disciples generally, into whose mouth Matthew puts it, Mark having mentioned indefinitely some of them, he attributes it to Judas, the thief of the treasury and subsequent traitor. Naturally; if the censure passed upon the expense incurred for the person of the Jewish-Christian Messiah was inadmissible, it can, as against the divine creative Word incarnate, have only been passed by the representative of abandoned profligacy.

But, impossible as it was, on the standpoint of the fourth Gospel, that any one of the weak but honest eleven should begrudge the ointment—only the abandoned twelfth could do this—quite as impossible was it that an act so graceful, so appropriate to the dignity of the Son of God, should be performed by an unknown person: it must have been performed by the most hearty and cordial worshipper of Jesus. Such a person was, as we have seen above, suggested by the author of the third Gospel to that of the fourth, in that Mary, the sister of Martha, who in Luke indeed is neither represented as living in Bethany nor as taking part in the anointing, but while her sister is preparing a hospitable reception for Jesus on his journey, sits at his feet listening to his words, is complained of to Jesus by her busy sister for doing so, and is defended by him (Luke x. 38—42). She, and no one else, must have been the woman who anoints him; as on that occasion she sate at Jesus' feet, so also on this, she must have anointed not his head, as Matthew and Mark say she did, but his feet: she must have used for that purpose not merely an indefinite quantity, but a whole pound of costly spikenard to the value of three hundred pence. In giving a more definite description of the ointment, as well as in the statement of its value in figures, the fourth Evangelist here takes as his copy the representation given by the second, as he frequently does in the introduction of features that tend to realise and strengthen his account.

John, following Luke, chap. x., had, as we have seen above, associated with the two sisters Lazarus as their brother, and thus Simon the Leper is excluded from the narrative of the Supper, and Lazarus, who had been dead and raised again by Jesus, is substituted for him. But he is not put altogether in the place of Simon; he does not appear as Simon does in the character of the master of the house and host, but only as one of those who are sitting at table; Martha waits, in the same way as she had, in the narrative in Luke, busied herself much with waiting. We see here that the fourth Evangelist does not intend exactly to contradict the traditional account which connected the anointing with the house of Simon, so he leaves him out and names Lazarus, but without quite putting him in the place of the former, so that we do not know, on reading his account, who it was that really gave the feast to Jesus, and can only guess from Martha's waiting that, according to Luke, it was her household or that of her brother in which Jesus was entertained.

But the fourth Evangelist has one feature pointing in a direction quite different from that of the anecdote about Mary and Martha told by the third. The fact that he differs from the two first in representing Mary to anoint not the head but the feet of Jesus, might, in default of any other, admit of the explanation that it is founded upon the statement of Mary's having sate, according to Luke, at Jesus' feet; but she also dries his feet with her hair, and this is a feature of so peculiar a character that we are compelled to ask what it means and whence it comes. As regards the first, we might look upon it as a sign of heartfelt and meek submission, and thus, possibly, as the result of the Evangelist's own imagination: but if it is found in another evangelical narrative, we shall be compelled to assume a connection between the two; and if it appears to be more essentially a part of the other account than it is of this, we shall be further compelled to assume that the former was the source from which ours is taken. In fact, it is found, and found with every mark of originality, in the account of the anointing of Jesus by a sinful woman, which is peculiar to Luke alone (vii. 36—50). There are many indications from which we may gather that this history is not foreign to that which we are considering, *i.e.* is not, as is commonly supposed, the narrative of an entirely different occurrence. It must strike us at once that Luke knows nothing of any other anointing; that therefore, in him, this anointing by the sinful woman, which he does not indeed place at Bethany and in the last days of Jesus, but in the period of his ministry in Galilee, takes the place of the anointing at Bethany. In Luke, moreover, it not only takes place on the occasion of a supper, but the master of the house and giver of the feast has the same name as he of Bethany in Matthew and Mark, namely, Simon, only that he is described not as a Leper but as a Pharisee, as befitted the part he had to play in contrast with the sinful woman. Moreover, as in Matthew and Mark, the woman carries her ointment in an alabaster box; as in their account she is attacked, not indeed aloud by the disciples, but by the master of the house in a murmur to himself, and defended by Jesus, though the attack as well as the defence, in accordance with the change in the personality of the woman, are each quite different.

But how can this change be explained; and is it conceivable that of the woman who is the subject of much praise, who, from a feeling of profound reverence, emptied her box of ointment on the head of Jesus, either tradition or modification by a writer should make an accursed sinner, who in a spirit of penitence wetted the feet of Jesus with her tears, dried them with her hair, covered them with kisses, and moistened them with ointment? Here we must remember that the history of a woman who was accused before Jesus of many sins, as well as that of the woman who anointed him, formed part of the most ancient evangelical traditions. The Gospel of the Hebrews is said to have contained it, and Papias also to have given it.* Of the sinful woman in Luke it is expressly said (ver. 47), that her many sins were forgiven; on the other hand, she is not really accused to Jesus, but the Pharisee only thinks within himself that if Jesus had been a Prophet he must have known what sort of a worshipper he had got. But we find in the fourth Gospel an account, which is indeed attacked by criticism,† but which is, if not originally a component part of this Gospel, very ancient.

It is the sketch of the adulteress (viii. 1—11), a woman who is expressly accused before Jesus of only one sin in which she had been caught, and was taken by him under his protection.

It is clear at once that a narrative of this kind, if Luke had it before him in the Gospel of the Hebrews, must have been especially welcome to that disciple of Paul; and quite as much so that he could not be satisfied with it in the form in which we now read it in the Gospel of John. In this account the woman appears throughout as passive; she does not seek Jesus, but is dragged to him by others; moreover, while she

---

* See Euseb. Hist. Eccl. iii. 39, 17.

† See, *e.g.*, Ewald, The Johannine Writings, i. 270. On the other hand, its genuineness is defended by Hilgenfeld, The Gospels, p. 285 ff.

stands before him she performs no act of any kind, but her accusers, Pharisees and Scribes, avail themselves of the opportunity to put a captious question to Jesus, who disarms them by appealing to their own consciousness in a manner which, if looked at from an historical point of view, is extremely improbable. It was absolutely necessary for Luke, in accordance with his point of view, to represent the impulse of the sinful woman for salvation as an independent one, her approach to Jesus as spontaneous. The profligate son, though forced by necessity, had still formed his own resolution to return to his father, had done so, and confessed his sin; Zaccheus, the chief publican, had climbed a tree from eagerness to behold Jesus; the Publican in the Temple, praying for forgiveness, had beaten his breast. So also the sinful woman must have exerted herself in some way or other to obtain the indulgence which Jesus shewed her. Such exertion might be considered as having been involved in the anointing; and as the woman who is said to have performed this was not named by the older Evangelists, nor anything else more definite stated about her, a combination of the two narratives was the less difficult, as the description of a man or woman as a sinner had, in the spirit of the Gospel, nothing degrading in it, repentance being assumed. But as an humble sinner, the woman was not to approach the head, but only the feet of Jesus; the first thing with which she wetted the latter must have been her tears of repentance; she could not have considered her hair as too good to dry the feet of the Lord, which she had bathed with her tears, nor her lips to touch them with kisses, nor the most precious oil wherewith to anoint them; all features which serve the purpose of illustrating, in the most striking manner, the proud omission on the part of the Pharisaic host of the corresponding duties which courtesy required. In connection with this, the speeches which are here interchanged, not between Jesus and his disciples, but between him and the Pharisaic host, have for their subject, not the expenditure of the ointment, but the character of the woman who anoints. While the Pharisee regards her as a person of abandoned character, and one who degrades even Jesus by her approach, Jesus represents the Pharisaic self-righteousness as the source of want of love, the forgiveness of sins claimed by the sinner and granted by him as the source of humble love, in a parable which in many respects may be looked upon as the counterpart to the parable of the King who reckons with his servants (Matt. xviii. 23—35). In both there are two debtors, the one with a larger, the other with a smaller debt: only that in Luke both are indebted to the same creditor; in Matthew, one of the servants to the king, the other to his fellow-servants. In Matthew, the servant to whom, at his request, the king* has forgiven the larger debt, refuses to forgive the smaller to his fellow-servant, and is consequently set up as an example to be avoided: in Luke, conversely, he to whom much is forgiven is also he who loves most (that is, the creditor who has forgiven him the debt, as nothing is said of any one who was indebted in turn to him), and it is only said of him to whom little is forgiven, or who, like the self-righteous Pharisee, thinks he has little occasion for forgiveness, that he will love little.

We have, therefore, here a group of five narratives, the middle one of which is, 1, that of Matthew and Mark of the unknown woman who at a supper at Bethany had anointed the head of Jesus, had been censured by the disciples for her extravagance in doing so, and defended by Jesus. On the extreme left of this narrative stands, 2, that in the Gospel of the Hebrews about a sinful woman, who was accused before Jesus, and by him (probably, as we no longer have the original narrative) dismissed uncondemned, with the recommendation to sin no more; on the extreme right,

* Here both parables coincide also in expression. Matt. xviii. 25 : μὴ ἔχοντος δὲ αὐτοῦ ἀποδοῦναι—. Luke vii. 42 : μὴ ἐχόντων δὲ αὐτῶν ἀποδοῦναι—.

3, that of Luke about the two sisters Martha and Mary, one of whom receives Jesus in her house and serves him industriously, while the other sits listening at his feet, and is defended by him against the censures of her sister. The first and second of these histories is combined by Luke, 4, in his narrative about the sinful woman who anoints the feet of Jesus; the first and third, by John, 5, in his narrative about Mary's anointing him, only that he has, at the same time, out of the fourth composite narrative of Luke, about the anointing by the sinful woman, introduced the features of the anointing of the feet and the drying with the hair, as suitable to the sensitive character of his Mary of Bethany.

85. The Passover, and Institution of the Last Supper.

The meal at Bethany was of importance to the Christendom of the earliest period, on account of the anointing of Jesus which had taken place at it, as an anticipative compensation for the non-payment of that honour to him after his death. So also was the Passover which he had eaten at Jerusalem with his followers shortly before his death. This was because there was a connection between it and the memorial meal, the repeated celebration of which formed the real centre of the life of the Church in the first ages of Christianity.

So important an event required, above all, a corresponding introduction. The Founder of the Supper of the New Covenant must, it was supposed, even in the mode in which he arranged the Supper (Matt. xxvi. 17—19; Mark xiv. 12—15; Luke xxii. 7—13), have shewn his high omnipotence. In the same way as, when his entering the capital in a manner corresponding to his dignity was under consideration, he had only to send his messengers, who had only to mention the need of the Lord, in order to persuade the chief inhabitant of the neighbouring village to give up his beast of burden for his use, so on this occasion he has, according to Matthew, only to send his disciples to a friendly citizen of the capital, with the announcement that the Lord intends to keep the Passover at his house with his disciples, in order to obtain, without delay, the use of the required room all ready for his purpose. Now even in this, as there is no reason for supposing any previous arrangement with the owner, in the sense of the Evangelist there is something miraculous implied, whether that miraculous element is to be understood to have consisted in the magical power of the word of Jesus, or in an arrangement of Providence in his favour. We have the miraculous element, even without taking into account the difficulty, if not the impossibility, there would naturally be, considering the press of strangers at the time of the Passover, in finding on the morning of the first day of the feast a place in the city disengaged for the evening.

There was, however, an obvious inducement to bring forward the miraculous element in a more palpable form, as this history of the engagement of a room resembled very closely the model of that of the ass for the entrance into Jerusalem. That this was the case we see in Mark and Luke, in the circumstance that in their description Jesus is represented as sending, not, as in Matthew, his disciples generally, but, as he does for the ass, two of them only (according to Luke, Peter and John); then, as in the first case, the two messengers are to find an ass bound; and as formerly Samuel had foretold to Saul that, as a proof of his gift of prophecy, he should meet certain persons, some of them bearing food and drink (1 Sam. x. 2 ff.), so in the two middle Evangelists, Jesus here foretells to the two disciples that when they came into the city, they will be met by a man with a water-pitcher, whom they are to follow into the house into which he enters, and to ask the master of the house, in the name of the

Teacher, for the room in which he can eat the Passover with his disciples; upon which the man will shew him a large upper room, already provided with seats; and there they are to arrange the feast: all of which turns out accordingly.

The fourth Evangelist has omitted the whole of this history, as he has that of the entrance. In the case of the latter, he represents the ass as being found by Jesus, without any more definite statement of the mode or the manner. In this case he represents a feast as being prepared, without saying where and how (xiii. 1 ff.). But is the meal of which he speaks really the same with that described by the Synoptics? It seems not; for while the Synoptics describe their meal expressly as that of the Passover, John gives the clearest indications that the meal he describes was a meal *before* the Passover, and instead of the institution of the last Supper, which the Synoptics represent as taking place during the time of eating the meal, John speaks of a washing of feet which Jesus performed upon his disciples during that time.

According to Matthew, on the first day of unleavened bread, the disciples go to Jesus, with the question, "Where wilt thou that we prepare the Passover for thee?" and then, when the room has been engaged, it is said further that Jesus sat down with the twelve (Matt. xxvi. 20), according to Luke (xxii. 15) declaring that he had greatly desired once more to eat that Passover with them before his Passion. Here then we have the Passover, which, according to the ordinance of Moses (2 Mos. xii.), was to be eaten on the evening of the 14th of Nisan.* The evasion which assumes that perhaps Jesus, whether foreseeing that his death was to occur the following day, or in compliance with a custom required (only unfortunately not capable of being proved) by

---

* According to the Jewish method of beginning the day at six o'clock in the evening, the time appointed for eating the Paschal lamb belonged properly to the fifteenth of Nisan, as the beginning of this high festival; but, as in the above passage, it is, in the ordinary phraseology, reckoned to the fourteenth.

the excessive number of visitors to the feast, enjoyed the feast a day too soon, is contradicted not merely by Luke, who describes the day as that on which the Paschal lamb must be killed (xxii. 7), but in fact by Matthew as well, when he speaks of the "first day of unleavened bread," which, according to the Mosaic ordinance (2 Mos. xii. 15, 18), was the 14th, and certainly not the 13th of Nisan.

On the other hand, not only is there no hint whatever in John that the meal in question was the Passover, but when it is said (xiii. 1 ff.) that Jesus, conscious on the one hand that his end was near, and on the other of his exalted dignity, did at a Supper this or that *before* the Passover, the meal spoken of cannot have been the Passover, but must have been an earlier one. And when the order given by Jesus to Judas to do what he does quickly, is interpreted by the disciples to mean that Jesus commissioned him to buy what the society might want *for* the feast (xiii. 29), the feast, and especially that of the Passover, was still to come; for all sorts of things had to be bought for it; and that this was not yet over is most unquestionably clear from the fact that on the next morning the Jews refuse to enter into the prætorium of the heathen, so as not to pollute themselves, but to be in a condition to eat the Passover (xviii. 28).

If, however, in consequence of the manner, so obviously different, in which the Synoptics on the one hand, and John on the other, describe this meal, an attempt is made to distinguish two meals, one of which, with the washing of the feet, took place on the 13th, the other, with the Supper,* as the Passover, on the 14th Nisan, we are immediately convinced from other circumstances that, on the contrary, both parts refer to only one meal. For according to John as well as according to the Synoptics, it is during this meal that the

---

* Thus, *e.g.* Hess; more lately, among others, Röpe, Historico-critical treatise, to prove that the Supper of the Feet-washing, John xiii., is not identical with that of the Passover (1856).

treason of Judas is foretold by Jesus, and during it, or at all events immediately after its close, the denial of Peter likewise; and moreover the latter is spoken of by John, who is supposed to describe the earlier meal, as a thing that is to take place before the next cock-crow (xiii. 38). This datum shews at the same time, what indeed is clear enough without it, not only from the introduction of the Johannine narrative, which represents the washing of the disciples' feet as the last proof of Jesus' love for them, but also from the farewell addresses and the departure to the place of arrest, which are connected with it, that John as well as the Synoptics intends to describe the last Supper of Jesus with his disciples. But as this one and the last meal of Jesus in the Synoptics is as plainly the Passover-meal itself as it is in John, a meal on the evening before, we have here a contradiction as entire as a contradiction ever was, and in which one side must be wrong.*

The fact that there are still theologians who in the face of this plain statement still deny the contradiction, clearly shews that in theology a standard prevails totally different from that of simple truth; and the further fact that in the endeavour to get rid of it they set to work in opposite ways, one

---

* The following table will shew the relation between the two descriptions, and also the course of events in the Passion-week:

Day of the Month and Feast according to the Synoptics.	Day of the Week according to all the Evangelists.	Day of the Month and Feast according to John.
14. Nisan. Evening.	Thursday. the	13. Nisan. Supper.
15. Nisan. First Feast-day. Passion	Friday. and	14. Nisan. Death of Jesus.
16. Nisan. Second Feast-day. Jesus	Saturday (Sabbath). in the	15. Nisan. First Feast-day. Grave.
17. Nisan. Third Feast-day. In the	Sunday. Morning	16. Nisan. Second Feast-day. Resurrection of Jesus.

party seeking to draw over the Synoptics to the opinion of John, the other John to that of the Synoptics, others to find the one account as well as the other possible,* only shews that they are induced to attempt the solution, not by any of the texts on either side, but by that extraneous interest which is indifferent as to which side has to give way, provided both are brought under one roof, *i.e.* the historical credit of both is saved. That neither may be wrong, one of the two must submit to the greatest wrong, *i.e.* the violent distortion of their plain words and unmistakeable opinion. Here runs the boundary-line between those theologians with whom we can still treat intelligently, and those whom we must leave to themselves, and to the principle in the service in which they have enlisted.

By this, however, we do not mean that all those theologians who recognise in this point the contradiction between the synoptic account and that of John, have thereby rid themselves of every prejudice. For if it is asked which of the two sides is supposed to be right and which wrong, the faithful adherents of John range themselves around their master, who cannot be wrong, because then they themselves, with their modern faith pinned upon him, would be wrong. That is a consideration as untrue and erroneous as any; historical testing is a court of justice which has to find its verdict unconcerned about possible consequences. If the fourth Gospel cannot prove its own credibility from its own evidence in behalf of itself, the verdict must and will be given against it, whatever may be the amount of displeasure and embarrassment thus caused to modern theology.

Following this principle, if we test the two contradictory accounts, that of the Synoptics, according to which the last Supper of Jesus was that of the Paschal Supper, on the

* The first by (among others) Wieseler, Chronological Synopsis, p. 334 ff.; the second by Weizel, The Christian Passover of the Three First Centuries, p. 315 ff.; the third by Schleiermacher in his Lectures on the Life of Jesus.

evening of the 14th, and the day of his death the day of the Paschal feast, the 15th of Nisan, is at all events the oldest. It is admitted, indeed, that all our three first Evangelists wrote after the destruction of Jerusalem, but used sources in which, to a certain extent, much more ancient Palestinic traditions about Jesus were found. Moreover, in the dispute as to the celebration of the Passover, which in the second half of the second century repeatedly broke out between the Church of Asia Minor and that of Rome, the custom of keeping the 14th Nisan as the day on which Jesus ate the Paschal lamb with his disciples, by the celebration of the Supper on that day, appears as the ancient tradition in support of which the people of Asia Minor appealed, in particular, to the example of the Apostle John. Meanwhile their opponents also, in order to justify the observance of the Easter Supper, without reference to the day of the month, on the day of the Resurrection, *i.e.* on the Sunday, and not before, appealed to the tradition of the Church, the dispute was, like all regular ecclesiastical disputes, not of an historical but of a dogmatic character.* Clinging to the 14th Nisan as the day of the Jewish Passover was looked upon in later times as Judaism, disregard of the day was considered as identical with releasing Christianity from Judaism; hence we see shortly after in the Eastern Church the men of progress, as for instance an Apollinaris of Hierapolis, and later still a Clemens of Alexandria, on the side of the Romish observance. To establish this, it was now said that Jesus celebrated the Supper on the day before the Passover; he did not eat the Paschal lamb; but while the Jews were eating it

---

* With regard to this dispute, compare Euseb. Eccl. Hist. v. 24; Chron. Paschal. Alex. ed. Bonn. i. 13 ff.; Baur, Critical Examination of the Canonical Gospels, p. 334 ff.; Christianity of the Three First Centuries, p. 156 ff.; Hilgenfeld, Paschal Dispute of the Ancient Church (1860); Canon and Criticism of the New Testament, p. 219 ff. Besides these, critical treatises by both authors in Zeller's Theological Annuals and Hilgenfeld's Journal of Scientific Theology.

he was subjected to the Passion; he was, indeed, himself the real and true Paschal Lamb, the Son of God, of whom the Lamb had been but the unessential type. This was the chronological realisation of the notion already suggested by the Apostle Paul (1 Cor. v. 7), that Christ, our Passover, was sacrificed for us; but the same thought also lies at the bottom of the account of the fourth Evangelist. Jesus ate no Paschal Supper before his Passion, but represented in his own person the Paschal lamb: for on the same day and during the hours during which the typical Paschal lambs were being slain on the altars of burnt-offering in the court of the Temple, he was shedding his life-blood on Golgotha as the true Lamb of God.* Apollinaris, about A.D. 170, refers to this account of the fourth Gospel, at the same time drawing attention to the fact that the opposite view, which appeals to Matthew (if not modified, as Apollinaris seems to have done, according to John), brings the Gospels into discrepancy with each other.

We may thus penetrate John's motive for giving the representation which he does; we understand why he placed the last Supper of Jesus on the day before the Paschal Supper, and the death of Jesus on the day of this Supper, and consequently antedated by one day the account of the older Evangelists: it was the endeavour, most intimately connected with his point of view from first to last, to represent Jesus at the culminating point of his ministry as no longer taking part in the bygone Jewish festival, but as laying the foundation of a new religion by substituting his own death for it.

Easy, however, as it is to see how, according to this, the fourth Evangelist may have given an unhistorical account of these matters, it is in the same degree difficult to assume

---

* I avail myself here of the striking words of a very orthodox theologian, Krafft, Chronology and History of the Four Gospels, p. 130. It is perhaps this typical relation that induced John (xii. 1) to place the Supper at Bethany, at which Jesus was anointed for his death, on the sixth day before the Passover, *i. e.* the 10th Nisan, on which, according to 2 Mos. xii. 3—6, the Paschal lambs were selected. Comp. Hilgenfeld, Gospels, p. 298; Ancient Christianity, p. 40.

that the Synoptics can be right in their chronology. The Passover, indeed, presents no difficulty, but, all the more, what is said to have taken place during the night and on the next day. That the Sanhedrim, on a night so sacred as that after the eating of the Paschal lamb, and on a day so sacred as was the following first day of the feast, should have not only sent out armed servants for the arrest of Jesus, but have undertaken personally to form a court, to go through the trial, to pass judgment, and lay an accusation before the Procurator, and then have induced the Romans to execute the sentence of death on such a day—all this is extremely improbable. Servants indeed, though it is not expressly stated that they were armed, are represented by John as having been despatched by the High-priests and Pharisees to seize Jesus on the principal day of the feast of Tabernacles (vii. 45, comp. 32), and, according to Acts xii. 3 ff., Herod imprisoned Peter during the days of unleavened bread, though he certainly intended to defer his condemnation and execution until after the feast. We are very imperfectly informed as to the arrangement of the judicial system of the Jews in reference to their Sabbatical Calendar and that of their festivals, as Josephus on this point says very little, and the statements in the Talmud are in many ways obscure and also contradict each other. Thus we learn from it, indeed, on the one hand, that the Sanhedrim met on the Sabbath and feast-days, but not in its usual place: but it is not said that these meetings were for the administration of justice; nay, the administration of justice is spoken of elsewhere as one of the things forbidden on the Sabbath. But as regards the execution of a sentence, we have a statement of the Rabbi Akiba preserved from the time of Hadrian: Whoever says anything against the scribes is taken up to Jerusalem at the time of one of the three great festivals, in order to be then put to death, that the people may take warning. It is not, indeed, said that the execution was carried out on the very day of the feast; but there is less difficulty in connection with this, as the sentence, at all events, was executed by the Romans.*

It is, however, further maintained that, independent of everything else, the account of the Synoptics is inconsistent with itself, as they describe the day of the execution of Jesus by an expression which contradicts their own assumption that it was the first and greatest day of the Passover, and that consequently the preceding Supper was the Paschal Supper. They describe it (Matt. xxvii. 62; Mark xv. 42; Luke xxiii. 14) as the preparation day, or the day before the Sabbath; but it is objected that the first day of the Passover, having, like all other first days of the festivals lasting several days, itself the rank of Sabbath, could not have been called so, and that this description must have been transferred from an older representation, according to which the day of the execution of Jesus, as is said in John, was not the first day of the feast, but the day before. It is to this circumstance, they maintain, that the statement of Luke refers, that the women prepared spices and ointments on the evening of the burial, and rested, according to the Law, over the following Sabbath (xxiii. 56). Had the day of the death and burial been the first day of the Passover, they could not have occupied themselves with the preparation of spices on it any more than on the Sabbath following it; and it is only in John, it is said, that the haste to take the body down from the Cross in the evening with reference to the sanctity of the following day, has any real meaning, as in his account the day of execution is the day before the Passover, and so the following day the first day of the Passover. But, even in John, the day of execution is described as the preparation day, not for the Passover, but for the Sabbath (xix. 14), and the reason that

---

* Comp. on this subject, Bleek, Contributions, i. 140 ff.; Gfrörer, The Sanctuary and the Truth, p. 197 ff.

is given why the next day should not be desecrated, is, not that it was the first day of the feast of the Passover, but that it was a Sabbath (xix. 31), and it is only by the addition of the words that that day was a high day, *i.e.* especially sacred, that its character as being at the same time the first day of the feast is alluded to. If, therefore, we see in the fourth Gospel, in which the Sabbath is also the feast-day, its character as the Sabbath predominating, that Gospel stands in this respect on the same ground as the three former, who, of the two days placed in juxtaposition, consider the second, the Sabbath, as the more sacred, and it is obvious to suppose that at that time in similar cases it was so considered, and indeed it quite corresponds to the spirit of late Judaism to attach such importance to the Sabbath above everything else. At all events, as Bauer rightly remarks, what was or was not consistent with the custom of the Jews at that time, must have been better known to the author of the first Gospel, who stood in so close a relation to Judaism, and still closer to the Palestinic sources of history, from which he took his own, than to us at the present day. If, therefore, he did not hesitate to assert that Jesus was condemned and crucified on the first day of Easter, we may fairly be satisfied with this statement.

It is in the same circumstance which induced the fourth Evangelist to antedate the last Supper of Jesus by a single day, and out of the Passover Supper to make a Supper the day before, that we have to look for his reason for making no mention, on the occasion of the Supper which he does describe, of the institution of the last Supper (Matt. xxvi. 20—29; Mark xiv. 17—25; Luke xxii. 14—20). That the Supper was known to him as a Christian rite, would be a necessary assumption, even if it were not clear from his sixth chapter that it was so; but the persuasion also that it was instituted by Jesus himself on the occasion of his own last Supper, was already in the days of the Apostle Paul so general throughout Christendom, that it must have been known to the author of the fourth Gospel even without the Synoptics. But upon the point of view of the fourth Gospel, the last Supper of Jesus could in no way have been represented as a Passover Supper. Quite as little, upon the same point of view, could he be supposed to have instituted THE Supper on the occasion of it, if the last was not to appear as an offshoot of a Jewish custom. It might indeed be said that it could not appear so if the last Supper of Jesus was placed on the evening *before* the Passover: the fourth Evangelist, having so placed it, might confidently represent Jesus as instituting the Supper during that meal. But, as is clear from the description of the synoptic Gospels, the institution of the Supper by Jesus was, in the conception of the most ancient Church, so closely connected with the Passover, that a last Supper of Jesus, or even any Supper at all to which that institution was appended, would always have been looked upon as a Passover, and whoever did not wish to acknowledge the Supper as having been instituted on the occasion of the Passover, would have had to represent it as not having been instituted at a Supper at all. And in that case it might have been not instituted in any ritual form at all, but only invested with a symbolical meaning, as is actually done in words in the sixth chapter, but with typical miracles in the account of the gifts of wine and bread found in the Gospel. Thus the Supper was indeed unmistakeably intended and founded by Jesus, but founded not in a real and material manner, but in that mystico-ideal way which is peculiar to the Gospel of John, and not in connection with the Jewish custom of a feast, but as something new, in which the exclusion of the old was taken for granted.

This last point is brought out by the fourth Evangelist in a manner which might seem at first sight as tending again to a connection with the usages of the Jewish Passover. Christ having died about the time when the Paschal lambs were slain, and his bones not having been broken as being those of the true Paschal lamb (of which further on), one of the soldiers pierced his side with a spear, and immediately there flowed thereout blood and water, that the Scripture might be fulfilled which says, "They shall look on him whom they have pierced" (John xix. 33—37 ; comp. Zech. xii. 10). They had pierced, that is, the Son of God, whose blood is drink indeed (John vi. 55), not merely in the spiritual but also in the material sense at the Supper; on which occasion the water which flowed with the blood from the wound in the side, beside its reference to the water of baptism, might at the same time refer to the water which according to the custom of the earliest Christians used to be mixed with the wine of the Supper.* While, therefore, in the synoptic Gospels, Jesus partakes of the Jewish Passover, and founds the last Supper in connection with its usages, in John he dies as the true Paschal Lamb, that is, as the Son of God, who yields himself for the sins of the world, and pours forth from his wounded side the drink of life, typified indeed by the bloody sacrifices of the Jews, but which now for the first time, at the Christian Supper, is really and truly present.

86. The Feet-washing, with the Announcement of the Treason and the Denial.

If, however, according to the representation of John, neither the Paschal lamb was eaten at the last Supper of Jesus, nor the Supper of the Lord instituted, then was the form deprived of all its proper meaning; for the announcement of the treason and the denial, which was all that remained, was not sufficient to maintain it in its original importance. But the author of the fourth Gospel did not wish entirely to dispense with it, partly because it had obtained

---
* Justin Mart. Apol. i. 65 ff.

that importance in the Christian tradition, partly because it might serve as a desirable foundation for the farewell speeches which he wished to introduce into this portion of his narrative. He was obliged, therefore, to consider of a substitute; if possible, one of such a description that, on the one hand, like the distribution of bread and wine, it bore the character of a symbolical act, and on the other stood in close connection with the loving and farewell speeches which he proposed to add in this place. According to his general practice, he took a survey on this occasion also of the synoptical accounts before him, to see whether they did not present some material of which he could make what he wanted, and, as he had frequently done before, he found material of this description in Luke. This Evangelist, certainly most strangely, in describing the dispute of the disciples as to which of them it was to whom the allusion of Jesus as to his future betrayal referred, had thought of that other dispute of the disciples about the question which of them was the greatest, and he had thus represented that dispute about precedence, which Matthew more suitably places earlier, as breaking out over the last Supper (Luke xxii. 24 ff.; comp. Matt. xx. 20 ff.). On this occasion he represents Jesus as saying, among other things, that, in opposition to the custom of the world, he that is greatest among them shall be as the younger; and he that is chief as he that doth serve. "For whether is greater, he that sitteth at meat, or he that serveth? Is not he that sitteth at meat? but I am among you as he that serveth." In another passage of the same Gospel this comparison is expanded into a regular parable, the reward of those whom Christ on his return shall find in a proper moral state being represented by the image of servants whom their lord when he returns home at night finds watching. "Verily, I say unto you," it is said here, "that he shall gird himself, and make them to sit down to meat, and will come forth and serve them" (Luke xii. 37). Now these images are actually brought upon the scene in this passage by the fourth Evangelist, as he represents Jesus as girding himself and assuming the character of a servant in the presence of his disciples, and then at the conclusion adding the moral, that if he, their Lord and Teacher, has done this to them, they should also do the same to one another, as the servant is not greater than his lord, neither he that is sent greater than he that sent him (xiii. 4—16). But he does not, like the master in the parable, assume the character of the servant by offering them meat, but by a still more menial service, that of washing their feet, which at the same time, by the purification effected by it, carried with it a further symbolical meaning. And as a clear indication that by this narrative the Evangelist intends to fill up the gap caused by the omission of the institution of the Supper, he represents Jesus as performing the washing of the feet likewise as an act which is to be repeated in the society, for he describes him as declaring to the disciples that as he has washed their feet, so are they to wash the feet of each other hereafter; that he has given them an example which they are to imitate. And these expressions, indeed, in the mind of the Evangelist are only meant symbolically (comp. moreover 1 Timoth. v. 10), but still have an intentional resemblance to those of Paul and Luke: "This do, as oft as ye shall drink it," &c. &c.

It would be, on natural grounds, quite possible that Jesus should have entertained suspicions of the unfaithful disciple, and even expressed them, but the Evangelists represent him as foreknowing and foretelling the treason of Judas in a supernatural manner (Matt. xxvi. 21—25; Mark xiv. 18—21; John xiii. 18—20), and indeed they do so for a reason which must have induced them to represent the case so, even if it were not historically true. This dogmatic reason why Jesus must have been supposed to foretell the treason, and must have foretold it at table and nowhere else, we learn from the fourth Evangelist. With reference to the former, he puts into the mouth of Jesus the words (xiii. 19): "Now I tell you before it come, that, when it is come to pass, ye may believe that I am he." In these words the motive is disclosed which is the source of all those pretended prophecies of their own fate, especially if it is an unhappy one, which appear in the mythical history of great personages. The unhappiness, the ill-success in the life of a man of God, is always an offence, inasmuch as the natural assumption is that he who is beloved by God, is sent by God, will also be advanced by God, and this offence has to be set aside, the negation of the high commission, which appears to be involved in the unhappiness has again to be negatived. Such a negation is implied by the man of God foreknowing and foretelling the unhappiness which is to befal him. He can only know it through God, who by communicating this unhappiness to him marks him as one who stands near him, and indicates at the same time that the unhappiness which he causes him to know beforehand, is his own providential arrangement, and does not stand in contradiction to the lofty position of his ambassador. Moreover, inasmuch as our ambassador from God knows his evil fate beforehand, and does not attempt to escape from it, but on the contrary, acquiescing in the ordinance of God, calmly meets it, he appears in presence of that fate as not merely suffering but independent; it does not appear to be an external power which oppresses him, but a suffering which he has undertaken with the consciousness of the higher object which he has in view.

Now, in the misfortune which overtook Jesus, there appeared to be involved a special ground of offence, inasmuch as that misfortune was produced by the treason of one of his own disciples. If a familiar friend could betray him to his enemies, it must have been because that familiar friend saw nothing particular in him; and if he retained so false a friend near him, he cannot have penetrated the mind of that friend, and, consequently, cannot have been possessed of any superior knowledge. On the other hand, his adherents were possessed with the conviction, first, that their Master did penetrate the mind of the traitor, and, moreover, as the fourth Evangelist exaggeratingly assures us, even from the beginning (vi. 64). In the second place, rank ingratitude on the part of a messmate was already prefigured in reference to the Messiah in the life of his ancestor David (2 Sam. xv. 16), and foretold in the passage of the Psalm (xli. 9): "Yea, mine own familiar friend, in whom I trusted, which did eat of my bread, hath lifted up his heel against me." In this passage, which only the fourth Evangelist expressly brings forward, but upon which the whole account must have been formed from first to last, is involved the motive for representing Jesus as having foretold the treason of Judas actually at table. The exact words of the passage in the Psalms gave less occasion for this; the expression, "which does eat of my bread," indicates a relation of dependency, a bond of gratitude, violated by the unfaithful friend; but John quotes, "he that eateth bread *with me;*" the Christian tradition saw in the passage of the Psalm the violation by the traitor of the sacred law of hospitality foretold. In the case of such applications and imitations, everything is taken as literally as possible, and realised to the senses as much as possible. If the Messiah says, "he that eateth bread with me," he must have said it just while they were both eating bread together. But if he said it during the time of eating, it was said most suitably on the occasion of that eating which immediately preceded the performance of what was foretold. But this last occasion of eating was the Supper of the Passover, at which the bread was sopped in a dish with broth; so Jesus says, not simply, "he that eateth bread with me," but "he that dippeth his hand into the dish with me" (in Luke, less definitely, "the hand of him that betrayeth me is with me on the table"). At first sight this would be only a periphrasis for social fellowship; the expression "with me" would merely mean, during the same eating out of the same dish, so that among the twelve companions of Jesus no one in particular was indicated; Jesus might indeed have himself known the traitor, but not have thought good to name him, leaving it to the disciples to consider and ask who it could be. In Mark and Luke the thing is thus left in suspense. Matthew goes further, and represents Judas as being definitely pointed out as the traitor. We cannot but be surprised at his not employing the act of the dipping for this purpose, and representing him as being declared by Jesus to be the traitor who dips his hand into the dish simultaneously with himself; the mode in which the thing is done, by Judas asking at last whether it is he, and Jesus answering at once Yes, has something awkward and improbable about it, which the two middle Evangelists do not seem to have liked.

The fourth Evangelist has displayed greater dexterity in this passage. It is of course to be taken for granted that his Logos Christ must now have proved by the most accurate description of the person of his betrayer, that knowledge of him which he had from everlasting. In this he goes with Matthew, but he goes on a way of his own. He does not neglect the opportunity for a more definite description which the dipping of the hand in the dish afforded him. But a simultaneous dipping was not definite enough for him. He was to be the traitor for whom Jesus dipt, and to whom he gives a sop. Besides, in the fourth Gospel all this is quite differently connected. This last Supper appeared to the author of the account the most favourable opportunity for exalting the Apostle in whose name he wrote, and, with him, the whole spiritual tendency which he had in view. Here, if anywhere, a situation was given for representing his friend John as the bosom-disciple, the confidential friend, from whom the Master kept nothing secret. As the Son of God lies in the bosom of his Father, the poor Lazarus, after his departure, in Abraham's bosom, so John, as the disciple whom Jesus loved, lies in the bosom of Jesus (according to the Oriental custom of lying at table); and the natural result was, that in the painful uncertainty as to which of them it could be of whom Jesus spoke as him that should betray him, the rest turned to the bosom-disciple, and begged through him for the solution from Jesus. Peter is represented as the disciple who conveys the inquiries of the disciples, not immediately to Jesus, but to the bosom-disciple—this chief of the Apostles is compelled expressly to subordinate himself to John—and in this fact one of the inmost tendencies of the fourth Gospel is exposed: it is precisely with the relation of these two Apostles and the two forms of Christianity, one of which was connected with the name of Peter, the other with that of John, that the Gospel is concerned. And because only the latter disciple is intended to appear as the one who was acquainted with the inmost thoughts of Jesus, he is here represented as the one who could alone question him about his secret.

Judas makes an offer to the rulers of the Jews to deliver his Master into their hands. Matthew and Mark allege as the motive for this, the reward of money. In Luke the act is introduced with the remark that Satan had entered into Judas, also called Iscariot, one of the twelve (xxii. 3). This is so represented by John, that in the prophecy above mentioned, Jesus expressly declares that one of the twelve is a devil (vi. 70); at the beginning of the narrative of the last Supper this expression is moderated to the effect that the Devil put it into the heart of Judas to betray Jesus (xiii. 2); now on occasion of the sop being offered to him by Jesus, it is said (ver. 27), that, after the sop, Satan entered into him. The sop, therefore, given to the traitor by Jesus becomes to him a curse, and notwithstanding that in the Gospel of John the sop is not the bread of the Supper, we cannot help remembering the warning of Paul (1 Cor. xi. 27—29), that whoever eats of the bread or drinks of the cup of the Lord unworthily, eats and drinks his own condemnation : the idea of the Supper which the Evangelist would have wished here to keep at a distance, in accordance with his plan, appears nevertheless to have penetrated his mind involuntarily.

Thus in the fourth Gospel the malignant purpose of the traitor appears to be assisted by an act undertaken by Jesus with a different object. And he is expressly urged on to the execution of his design by the expression of Jesus (ver. 27), "What thou doest, do quickly." In these words Bretschneider* has discovered an exaggeration of the synoptic account. The other Evangelists say that Jesus was conscious of the intention of the traitor, and did not prevent its being carried out, but John, he observes, represents him as having even hastened its execution. The object is clear: the courage of Jesus, his elevation above all sorrow that man could bring upon him, appeared in so much a clearer light if he not only did not attempt to avoid the sword drawn against him, but met it with a brave push home. We shall shortly find the scene in Gethsemane also remodelled by the fourth Evangelist in the same spirit.

Of the occurrences at the last Supper of Jesus we still have remaining only the announcement of the denial of Peter. This, however, is placed by Mark after the conclusion of the meal, on the way to the Mount of Olives, and only Luke and John represent it as taking place while the Supper is still going on (Matt. xxvi. 30—35 ; Mark xiv. 26—31 ; Luke xxii. 31—34; John xiii. 36—38). The course of it is in all four accounts essentially the same. On a somewhat arrogant assertion of Peter to the effect, in the two first Evangelists, that even though all men are offended in Jesus, or separated from him, *he* will not be offended; in the two others, that he is ready, for his Master, to go to prison or to death, or to give up his life for him,—Jesus foretells to him that on this very night, before the cock crow, Peter will have denied him

* Probabil.

thrice. That at that critical time Peter was guilty of a weakness which looked like a denial of Christ, we may, in accordance with the unanimous tradition of the Evangelists, be willing to believe, and the more so in proportion as the statement was opposed to the deep feeling of reverence with which the chief of the Apostles was regarded in Christendom at the earliest period; it is also extremely probable Jesus might sometimes meet with a word of caution the exaggerated self-confidence of the disciples which might shew itself on different occasions; but that this was done so immediately before the consequences stated to have followed, and in this exact form, is the more doubtful in proportion as there is no mistaking the legendary elements in the cock-crow and the number three applied to the acts of denial. In Mark we see the poetical impulse advancing a step further: this advance is shewn by the circumstance that he alone thinks it necessary to count the number of cock-crows as well as the number of denials: before the cock crows twice Peter will have denied him thrice—a cold idea indeed, and one which received no further notice.

SECOND GROUP OF MYTHS.

THE AGONY AND ARREST OF JESUS.

87. The Agony at Gethsemane. Relation of the Fourth Gospel to this History.

There is a resemblance between the foreknowledge and foretelling of the treason and denial and that foreboding of his suffering which the three first Evangelists attribute to Jesus and represent as gaining expression in words and action in the scene at Gethsemane (Matt. xxvi. 36—46; Mark xiv. 32—42; Luke xxii. 39—46). Notwithstanding the elevation of his moral character, notwithstanding his resignation to what the task undertaken by him imposed upon him, Jesus might still have had to undergo a severe inward struggle when his terrible fate presented itself to his mind as unavoidable, and its bursting upon him as every moment possible. But the statement that this struggle, as represented by the Evangelist, occurred at the last moment before the fatal close, has an appearance more of poetry than of history, and the events of the scene itself as described by the Synoptics leave us in no doubt as to the unhistorical character at least of the details.

An agony of Jesus before his Passion is also spoken of in the Epistle to the Hebrews. It is said of Jesus (iv. 15), first that we have in him not a high-priest which cannot be touched with the feeling of our infirmities, but who was in all points tempted like as we are, yet without sin. Then, further on (v. 7), "Who in the days of his flesh, when he had offered up prayers and supplications, with strong crying and tears, unto him that was able to save him from death, and was heard in that he feared; though he were a Son, yet learned he obedience by the things which he suffered." The allusion to such a scene as that in Gethsemane is here more certain than that the synoptic account of the Temptation is referred to in the other passage of the same Epistle (iv. 15, comp. ii. 18); but still the germ of such a reference may be seen in the latter passage, and in the later evangelical descriptions the two scenes of the Temptation and of the Agony in the Garden were treated as parallel pieces. This is seen in the fact that in the statement of Matthew, which is the most original of all, who is followed by Luke in the history of the Temptation, and in that of the Agony by Mark, the struggle of Jesus consists, on each occasion, of three courses.

On this occasion it is not in the remote wilderness, but in a garden on the Mount of Olives, in the immediate neighbourhood of Jerusalem, where Jesus appears often to have passed his nights during the festival, that he is attacked, not from without by the personal Tempter, but in his inmost mind by the terrifying foreboding of his Passion and violent death. He is not, this time, quite alone, as he was before with the Devil in the wilderness, but, though in a solitary place outside the city, he has his disciples, with the exception of the traitor, with him. But of these, according to Matthew and Mark, he orders the majority to stay behind, so as to prevent the mystery of the panic and agony of the Son of God from being witnessed by any but the small and exclusive triumvirate he selected from the college of Twelve. They are to watch with him in his distress, but are unable to do so: the moment he departs from them a little in order to pray, he finds them, when he sees them again, fallen asleep, and has to rouse them again to watchfulness; they had penetrated the profound meaning of what was taking place before them quite as little as on the Mount of the Transfiguration, where Luke likewise describes them as falling asleep.

In the history of the Temptation, the Devil is represented as having thrice approached Jesus, on each occasion with a different temptation, and as having been every time repelled by him with a different text of Scripture. So, here, Jesus is thrice compelled by his internal agony to pray his heavenly Father to turn away his suffering, always, however, reserving the Divine pleasure, to which at last he resigns himself with filial submission, and meets courageously and decisively the inevitable suffering. Matthew does indeed on the second occasion vary the prayer of Jesus a little, and in a manner suited to more entire and complete resignation; then, on the third, represents the same speech as being repeated which Mark does on the second. This shews that from first to last the sacred number three was as much a matter of importance as the general contents of the prayer, *i.e.* that the narrative arose dogmatically, not historically.

Luke omits the number three of the disciples, and also the number three of the prayers of Jesus, as in the history of the Temptation Mark omits the number three of the separate temptations. But this only arises from his having something else to communicate which intensifies and exaggerates the narrative. After, that is, having repeated the prayer of Jesus in the same terms as Matthew and Mark, he represents an angel as appearing from heaven to strengthen him, then Jesus as becoming terrified, and praying so earnestly that his sweat fell like drops of blood upon the earth. The two cases might have been expected to have been reversed; but it would seem that the account preferred by Luke should be understood to mean that the appearance of the angel was intended to provide Jesus with sufficient strength to resist the subsequent mental attack, which was to be more violent than any which had preceded. Having thus described, not indeed three acts of Jesus, but still three separate factors, simple prayer, strengthening by the angel, struggling prayer with bloody sweat, the third Evangelist agrees with the two first in taking Jesus back to the disciples, when he repeats to them the command to pray which he had given them at the very first, at the same time censuring them for their sleepiness.

The whole of this history is wanting in the fourth Gospel, in the same way as the histories, resembling it in so many points of view, of the Temptation and Transfiguration of Jesus. The reason is still the same: it is that the Logos Christ of the Johannine Gospel was once for all elevated above the sphere of trials of this kind. The Jewish Messiah, as the Lord of the world to come, might put himself in competition with the Devil as Lord of this world, as with an equal, but not so he who came from heaven, who was above all; external brightness of the countenance, and a meeting with the Lawgiver and Prophets of the Jews, might be a glorifying of the synoptic Christ—anything of this character would only have reduced the Christ of John within narrower limits; fear of death, lastly, prayer that it might be averted, as the author of the fourth Gospel saw in death rather the glorifying of Jesus, and even the need of strengthening by an angel—

all this would have been, in the view of this Gospel, an absolute degradation of Christ.

Moreover, even if there was anything in these histories that might have been useful for the purpose of the Evangelist, he would feel the less inclined to allow it to escape from his pen in proportion as he found such matter firmly rooted in the evangelical tradition. It has already been pointed out how skilfully he preserved the essential meaning of the history of the Temptation, by adopting from Luke the notion of looking upon the Passion of Jesus as an attack of Satan. But he was able to relieve the two scenes of the Transfiguration and the Agony of their offensive elements in the most simple manner, and harmonise them with the peculiar spirit of his own Gospel by combining them together. His Jesus glorifies himself (as he was glorified at the transfiguration) in and through his life, and in his Passion he knows himself and shews himself to be glorified : thus is the Jewish materialism of the synoptic history of the Transfiguration, as well as the excess of the emotional and passionate element in the synoptic Agony, corrected.

Even in the Synoptics, the history of the Transfiguration stands immediately after an announcement of Passion and Death, with which Jesus, induced by a speech of Peter, connects the warning (Matt. xvi. 25 ; Mark viii. 35; Luke ix. 24): "Whosoever will save his life shall lose it; but whosoever shall lose his life for my sake, the same shall save it." The same thought meets us in the mouth of the Johannine Christ, after he had spoken first of his transfiguration, then of his death (xii. 23 ff.), in words almost identical (ver. 25): "He that loveth his life shall lose it; and he that hateth his life in this world shall keep it unto life eternal." And further on he says (ver. 26): "If any man serve me let him follow me. . . . . If any man serve me, him will my Father honour:" as he had said in connection with the synoptic announcement of the Passion before the transfiguration, "If any man will come after me . . . . let him follow me . . . . for whosoever shall be ashamed of me before this generation, of him shall the Son of Man be ashamed, when he shall come in his own glory, and in his Father's, and of the holy angels" (Matt. vi. 24; Mark viii. 34, 38; Luke ix. 23, 26); the corresponding passage to which is found in another place (Matt. x. 32): "Whosoever, therefore, shall confess me before men, him will I confess also before my Father which is in heaven."

These speeches in the fourth Gospel were occasioned by the fact that during the last visit of Jesus to the feast, after his solemn entrance into Jerusalem, Greeks who had come to worship at the feast, *i.e.* heathen who were inclined to Judaism, and perhaps were proselytes of the gate, were anxious to see Jesus, and for that purpose applied to the Apostle Philip, and he, in company with Andrew, acquainted Jesus with this (xii. 20 ff.). Upon this Jesus, without further noticing the wish of the Hellenes, says, "The hour is come that the Son of Man should be glorified;" and in what follows, his death is described as the necessary transition to this result. We have here one of those cases which enable us to see to the bottom of the peculiar character of the Johannine Gospel. On the point of view of the synoptic Gospels, the glorifying of the Messiah is connected at the Transfiguration with a meeting with two ancient prophets of the Jews; in the fourth, it is occasioned by the arrival of the Hellenes, *i.e.* of the heathen. The believers of the heathen world are the ripe fruit which the grain of wheat falling into the earth produces (ver. 24); but the perishing of the grain, the death of Jesus, is the necessary condition of this; and the speaker, therefore, now plunges into the thoughts suggested by this image, and connects with it the texts above quoted about gaining and losing life, about his servants following him and honouring him. This idea, that the death of Jesus is the necessary transition between his earthly pilgrimage and his glorification in the heathen world, suggests to the Evangelist the possibility of combining, in the scene to which the approach of the Hellenes gives rise, features out of the history of the Transfiguration with features out of that of the Agony in the Garden. Jesus confesses that he is shaken in his inmost soul by the thoughts of death that have arisen in him; but the Evangelist, as if wishing to correct the synoptic narrative, in which Jesus is represented as praying the Father to let the cup, or according to Mark (ver. 35, whom in this instance also the fourth Evangelist follows), the hour, pass away from him, represents his Jesus as putting to himself the question, "And what shall I say?" (in nearly the same words as in Mark), "Father, save me from this hour?" (No, I will not say so, for) "for this cause came I unto this hour."* In another passage also a corrective allusion to the synoptic prayer in Gethsemane is hardly to be mistaken. In John, Jesus subjoins to the order given to Peter the question (xviii. 11), "The cup which my Father hath given me, shall I not drink it?" How appropriate, in a Gospel intended for readers of Greek cultivation and accustomed to the ideal of Stoic apathy, a correction of the synoptic account in this very place was, is proved by the ridicule and censure which from Celsus downwards so many heathen opponents of Christianity have poured forth upon the notion of Jesus trembling in Gethsemane.†

It corresponds perfectly to the point of view of the Johannine Gospel, that the philosophical Emperor Julian, in considering the account of the agony, looked upon the feature of Jesus, as a God, having needed strengthening by an angel as particularly absurd. Our Evangelist might have omitted

---

* Even if the words, "Father, save me from this hour!" are regarded not as part of the question, but as a real prayer, still the attack passes over incomparably more quickly and easily than in the Synoptics.

† See the expression of Celsus and Julian, as well as those taken from the Gospel of Nicodemus, in Vol. ii. p. 429 of my Critical Treatise on the Life of Jesus, fourth edition.

this feature, and with the less hesitation, as Luke was the only one of his synoptic predecessors who had introduced it; but it was safer to make it unavailable for an opponent by representing the difficulty that arose upon it as a consequence of a misunderstanding. In those moments, he says, of most profound emotion, a higher Being did certainly speak to Jesus; but it was not an angel but God himself that so spoke; and he did so, not because he was obliged to strengthen Jesus, but as Jesus had prayed, not for strength for himself, but that the Father might in him glorify his own name, the heavenly voice only communicates this affirmative assurance of the accomplishment of this glorification; while of the surrounding multitude, those who were completely uninitiated and dull of comprehension took the voice of God for thunder, the half-awakened for an angel speaking with him.

But as, by the derivation of the heavenly voice from an angel, in John, there arises a connection between this scene and that in Gethsemane, as described in Luke, it is, on the other hand, in and for itself, taken from the synoptic history of the Transfiguration. In that history it was out of the cloud of light, or, according to the expression in the second Epistle of Peter (i. 17), out of "the excellent glory," that the voice sounded. In John there is no mention made of a visible appearance, but the glory is adopted into the words of the voice, which does not, as the history of the Transfiguration, describe Jesus as the beloved Son of God, whom the disciples are to hear, but only speaks of the glorifying which has already been vouchsafed to him, and shall still be vouchsafed. But even thus this sign appears too material for the inward and spiritual relation of the Logos Christ to the Father; as between these two Beings there was no occasion for such a request on the one side, such an appearance on the other, and therefore in this passage it was considered necessary that Jesus should declare expressly (ver. 30), as he had declared at the raising of Lazarus, that it is only on account of the surrounding multitude that he thanks the Father for the granting of his prayer.

The scenes of the Transfiguration, and of the Agony of Jesus, being thus combined in the fourth Gospel, they disappear as separate histories, and consequently the places in which they stand respectively in the three first Gospels stand vacant. A solemn conclusion of the Galilean ministry of Jesus, such as is formed in the synoptic Gospels by the history of the Transfiguration, was not wanted in that of John, because in it there is no such lengthened continuity of the sojourn of Jesus in Galilee, but from first to last there is an interchange between his stay there and his sojournings in Judea and Jerusalem. The Synoptics place the scene of the Agony between the last Supper and the arrest. But John required nothing of the kind. Jesus, as represented by him, had no need to struggle for courage and presence of mind on the field of battle; he must have brought there both these qualities with him. Moreover, before being torn away from his followers by the hostile power, it was necessary to represent him as initiating these persons, who had hitherto been children in understanding, by a lengthened address, into the depths of his mind, especially to familiarise them with the idea of his death, and the salutary effects of it, to make them generally of ripe age, and instead of disciples and servants, friends and fellow-labourers. This could not be done on the Mount of Olives, where the attack of the enemy was every moment to be expected, but only on the peaceful occasion of the last Supper: moreover, it supposed on the part of Jesus a calmness of mind which could not be disturbed, with which he was capable of meeting the violence of his enemies, without any fresh mental struggle. The battle, therefore, must have been already fought, and the corresponding scene, though, in accordance with the point of view of the whole Gospel, of a less violent character and less highly coloured, be transferred to an earlier place, preceding the last Supper. Every attempt to insert, in John, the synoptic Agony between the farewell speeches of Jesus from the 14th to the 17th chapter, and the approach of the traitor with his followers at the beginning of the 18th, is an attack not merely upon the moral elevation, but also generally upon the manly firmness of the character of Jesus. If, according to this, the mere thought of the suffering that awaited him was able once more to throw him back into so violent an inward struggle, it would have been a mere empty boast, or at all events a deficiency in self-knowledge, to have asserted beforehand as he does (xvi. 33) that he had overcome the world and its sorrows. It is manifest that the composer of the Johannine farewell speeches, especially of the High-priestly prayer in chap. xvii., had quite as little notion of an Agony having afterwards occurred, as the synoptic narrators of this Agony have of their Jesus having stood before upon the elevation of that prayer. One account does not presuppose the other; they are drawn from quite different points of view; they are quite incompatible representations; but in their present form neither of them can be looked upon as historical, and all we can say is that they are both fictitious, one being only the more simple in its conception, the other shewing more reflection and conscious purpose.

But that, even in these farewell speeches, the fourth Evangelist has only worked up and expanded the materials handed down to him by his predecessors, is clear from the constant coincidence of what he represents his Jesus as saying with the synoptic utterances of Jesus. And here we may notice, that it is a law which marks the spiritual peculiarity of the Evangelist, that when he modifies the thoughts and expressions of Jesus by additions of his own, and makes them approximate to his own form of thought and expression, he is very successful in bringing them into connection with the speeches which are the result of pure invention: when, on the other hand, he leaves them in their original form, then the discrepancy between them and his own form of thought, or his inability to transport himself out of the latter into the mode of thought and expression of the synoptic Jesus, not seldom causes him to introduce original utterances of this kind in the wrong place. This incapacity, of which we become aware as soon as he attempts to bring what is foreign to the character of his mind into connection with his singular and peculiar mode of description, is so little at variance with the dexterity of the same writer when he carves for himself, that, on the contrary, we see that both the one and the other are results of a nature thoroughly subjective and plunged deep into this subjectivity.

The synoptic section out of which especially the fourth Evangelist helps himself in these farewell speeches, is the speech in Matt. x., containing the instructions to the Apostles. The Johannine farewell speeches are indeed speeches containing instructions, only that they are delivered here, not on the occasion of his sending them forth during his lifetime, but of their taking upon them the Apostolical office after his impending departure. Even on the occasion of the scene with the Hellenes which immediately precedes the farewell Supper, we found texts out of this speech of instructions applied, as the speech about loving and hating life, or gaining and losing it, which at first sight we could not but suppose to be taken from the announcement of the Passion in Matt. xvi. 25, is also found with an unimportant variation in the speech of instructions (x. 39). Moreover, it was from this speech, as was mentioned above, that all is borrowed that Jesus says in the fourth Gospel at the last Supper on occasion of the feet-washing, to the effect that the servant is not greater than his master, he that is sent than he who sent him (John xiii. 16; Matt. x. 24). If these synoptic sayings are not badly introduced in connection with the Johannine description, the same cannot be said of those words of Jesus, likewise taken out of the speech of instructions (x. 40; John xiii. 20), that he that receiveth whomsoever he sends receiveth him, and he that receiveth him receiveth him that sent him. These words are pieced on after the announcement of the treason, without any other apparent connection than that he had the famous speech out of Matt. x. floating before his mind, and presenting some resemblance to that above quoted, and wished likewise to introduce it as aptly as he could. He succeeded incomparably better with the consolatory speech of Jesus (Matt. x. 19 ff.), which says that if his disciples are put upon their trial they are not to trouble themselves as to what they shall say, for it will not be they who speak, but the Spirit of their Father will speak in them. This text is made by the fourth Evangelist to a certain extent the theme of his farewell speeches, but he introduces his idea of the Paraclete, and thus gives to the original thought totally different applications. Hence we have here only isolated resemblances, but always suitably introduced (as John xiv. 26, xvi. 13, &c.); but the text is never fitted in in the original form which it bears in the synoptic.

There is another saying of Jesus, not out of the speech of the instructions, but out of the synoptic narrative of the Agony, which the fourth Evangelist endeavoured to preserve in its original form, but has only been able to do so with the ill success which usually attends him in such cases. It is the courageous challenge of Jesus with which Matthew (xxvi. 46) and Mark (xiv. 12) conclude this scene: "Rise up, let us go; lo, he that betrayeth me is at hand." He did not wish to lose this, as it harmonises with his endeavour to represent the suffering of Jesus as voluntarily undertaken. But he was unable to make use of the scene from the Agony, as we have already seen; and so much of it as he could make use of he was obliged to introduce in an earlier place; so he introduces this speech also in an earlier place. The most natural course would have been to put it at the end of the farewell speeches, as a challenge to leave the Supper-room and the city, and to go out to the Mount of Olives; and that the Evangelist intends to give it this meaning is clear from the alteration which he makes in it. Instead of making Jesus say, "Rise up, let us go," &c., he represents Jesus as saying, without mention of the traitor, "Arise, let us go hence" (xiv. 31). But for the conclusion of his farewell speeches, the Evangelist had intended to introduce a prayer of Jesus, in which he represented him as ascending from the speeches which he had made so far to the address to his heavenly Father; after this, no address to the disciples could follow without weakening the impression; if the speech was still to find a place, it must have been uttered sooner. Then it was in reality a matter of indifference when it was uttered; as the challenge would in no case have an immediate result, it might be introduced where a point of connection seemed to offer itself. But that was where Jesus represents the suffering that awaited him as an attack by the Prince of this world, who could, however, have no power over him; the courageous call upon the disciples appeared to be suitably introduced here, and thus the synoptic description intensified. In the latter it was applied only to the traitor; in the fourth Gospel it is the Devil himself whom Jesus goes to meet with courage so exalted. It is indeed strange, but not more so than much in the fourth Gospel, that after this encouragement the farewell speeches go on just the same as if it had never been spoken.

88. Arrest of Jesus.

In the three first Gospels, the approach of the traitor does not take place until after the conclusion of the Agony and the courageous call to the disciples. In the fourth Gospel, in which the history of the Agony in this place is dropped out, the first thing that occurs, after Jesus with his disciples has arrived in the Garden on the other side of the brook Cedron, is the approach of the traitor. According to Matthew and Mark, he comes with an armed multitude, despatched by the High-priests and elders of the people. With this multitude Luke associates the High-priests and elders themselves, together with the chiefs of the guard of the Temple; John, a company of Roman soldiers, and, as it was night, though the night of the full moon, he puts into their hands, besides the weapons, torches and lanterns (Matt. xxvi. 47 ff.; Mark xiv. 43 ff.; Luke xxii. 47 ff.; John xviii. 1 ff.).

It was a tradition in Christendom that Judas served as guide to the people who arrested Jesus (Acts i. 16), and this office of guide was generally understood to imply that he not only pointed out to the officers of the Jewish hierarchs the way to the place where Jesus was, but also, by means of a kiss, indicated to them his person, with which they were before unacquainted. The fourth Evangelist has nothing about the kiss; on the contrary, he represents the whole of what the traitor had to do as consisting in pointing out the spot where Jesus was at that time to be found, stating also how Judas was enabled to know it; for the Jesus described by John is known without being pointed out. According to the Synoptics, the traitor goes up to Jesus and gives him the kiss agreed upon, upon which, after a reproachful question to the unfaithful disciple, Jesus is seized by the constables. In John, as soon as the people make their appearance in front of the garden or garden-house, Jesus, with a supernatural foreknowledge of all that should come upon him, meets them with the question, Whom they seek? and on their answering, Jesus of Nazareth, he declares that he is that person; to which the Evangelist, as if wishing expressly to spare the traitor his kiss, adds the remark that Judas also stood with the people to whom Jesus thus made himself known, and they consequently required no further indication of his person. In this distinction, that according to the one account Jesus is pointed out by another and delivered to his enemies, according to the other he makes himself known and surrenders himself into the hands of his enemies, is involved again the whole of the distinction between the fourth Gospel and the older ones. The Logos Christ, he who had said of himself that no man takes his life from him, but that he himself lays it down of himself, that he has power to lay it down and has power to take it up again (John x. 17), he must prove this on this occasion also when he is passing into the power of his enemies ; he is not to be supposed to have waited till a third person said, This is he, but must himself have said at once, I am he. Jesus at the same time wished to save his disciples, and in this wish the Evangelist discovers the fulfilment, not, as on other occasions, of an Old Testament prophecy, but of some words of Jesus himself, that is of the speech which he had put into his mouth in the High-priestly prayer (xvii. 12), in a spiritually moral sense, that of those whom his Father had given him (Judas excepted), he had lost none ; a double interpretation of the same speech, agreeing perfectly with the double interpretation of which the whole of this Gospel is capable.

Moreover, by the turn which he gave to the affair, the fourth Evangelist gained yet another object. What was implied by the kiss of Judas, This is he, could produce no other effect upon the people except that of causing them to arrest him. On the other hand, if Jesus came forward to meet them with his, *I am he*, the scene was prepared for one of those effects which rhetorical writers were fond of introducing in the history of a Marius,* of the orator Antony† and others, when the hired assassins were said to have sheathed their swords, or run away, at the word or the look of the

---

* Velleius, Hist. Rom. ii. 19, 3. † Valer. Max. viii. 9, 2.

great man. Our Evangelist goes still further; he represents the people not merely as going back at the word of Jesus, but as falling to the ground. He repeats the words, I am he, three times (ver. 5, Jesus said unto them, I am he—ver. 6, As soon as he had said unto them, I am he—ver. 8, I have told you that I am he); and this shews that he lays particular stress upon them. They were the same words with which Jesus, when walking on the sea of Galilee, had tranquillised the terror of the disciples (John vi. 20; comp. Matt. xiv. 27); the faith or the confession that "I am he," is repeatedly set up by the Johannine Christ as the end to which he wishes to lead his followers (viii. 24, xxviii. 13, 19). In the words, "I am he," therefore, the whole fulness of what Christ is, the whole divinity of his personality, is contained; thus, when spoken by him, they operate as a supernatural talisman. The expression gets this meaning from the Old Testament: "See now that I, even I, am he, and there is no god with me: I kill and I make alive; I wound and I heal; neither is there any that can deliver out of my hand." "Ye are my witnesses," says Jehovah on another occasion (Isaiah xliii. 10 ff.), "that ye may know and believe that I am he..... I, even I, am the Lord; and beside me there is no Saviour." The expression is, therefore, originally an expression of God himself; and as the fourth Evangelist puts it into the mouth of Jesus, and represents it as producing the effect which on other occasions the countenance of God or some other celestial being produces, he also thereby raises it far above the position which it occupies in the Synoptics.

In Matthew and Mark the sword-cut inflicted by one of the disciples comes after the officers have laid their hands on Jesus; in Luke and John it comes before. This is a point in which the growth of legend and fiction comes most clearly into view. All the Evangelists are agreed that the ill-timed courage of one of the attendants of Jesus cost the servant of the High-priest an ear; but neither Matthew, nor Mark who here follows him, says which of the two ears it was; Luke and John are the first to tell us that it was the right one: in a picturesque scene of this kind legend cannot bear any uncertainty. Then we learn from the two first and the fourth Evangelist simply that the servant had lost his ear, not that he had got it again; only Luke assures us that Jesus healed it with a touch. How could the charitable physician with miraculous powers, who had removed so much evil, leave this unremoved, when it had been inflicted, if not by him, at all events on his account? Possibly the servant of the priest appeared (to the fourth Evangelist) unworthy of the miracle, or the miracle too trifling for this closing portion of the life of Jesus. Lastly, the three Synoptics are unable to give the name either of the disciple or the servant; only John knows that the name of the latter was Malchus, and that the former was Peter. Thus in the history of the Anointing only he knew that the woman who anointed was Mary of Bethany, her heartless censor Judas: he thought this act of anointing as appropriate to the character of Mary, the bestowal of the censure to that of the traitor, as the sword-cut to that of Peter. And indeed, in a double sense, the act might be called a courageous act; but the courage was wrongly exhibited, and rested upon a grievous error of the disciple as to the true destiny of Jesus. Hence even in Matthew the sword-cut of the unnamed disciple was followed by a reproving caution of the Master: but it exactly fitted in with the plan of the fourth Evangelist to expose Peter, especially in the place of a disciple without a name, to a censure pronounced by Jesus, assuming that the censure applied to something which did not contradict the traditionary character of Peter. In order to connect this feature firmly with the name of Peter, he subsequently, on the occasion of the denial, describes the servant who maintains that he saw Peter in the garden with Jesus as a relation of the one whose ear

Peter had cut off (xviii. 26); but then the servant would scarcely have said merely, Did I not see thee in the garden with him? but, Thou art the man who cut off my cousin's ear; and Peter, if conscious of the act, would scarcely have trusted himself in the palace of the High-priest. Of the words of reproach in Matthew, the fourth Evangelist only adopts the command to the disciple to put up the sword into the sheath; the threat that they who take the sword shall also perish by the sword, he seems to have found incompatible with the crucifixion of Peter (xxi. 18 ff.); finally, what Jesus says in Matthew of the more than twelve legions of angels which he had only to pray his Father for in order to render him assistance, were he not obliged to fulfil the Scripture and his destiny—John had to represent him as proving this in act. For if, according to him, Jesus caused the armed men to fall to the ground by a word, it was obvious that it would have been an easy thing for him to save himself if he had chosen, without legions of angels, by the divine power which dwelt in him.

While Matthew and Mark console themselves for the arrest of Jesus like a thief with the predictions "of the Prophets" (perhaps the passage in Isaiah liii. 12, which had been quoted by Luke earlier, xxii. 37), they see in the flight of all the disciples the fulfilment of the prophecy of Zechariah (xiii. 17), which Matthew represents Jesus as reminding them of on the way to the Mount of Olives (xxvi. 31). Whether the feature of the young man who in terror leaves the linen cloth behind with which he was covered and flees away naked (Mark xiv. 51 ff.), is due to tradition or to the imagination of the second Evangelist, or whether a particular meaning is concealed behind it, is a question which it might be difficult to decide.

THIRD GROUP OF MYTHS.

TRIAL AND CONDEMNATION OF JESUS.

89. THE TRIAL BEFORE THE HIGH-PRIEST AND THE DENIAL OF PETER.

Jesus, by the authorities of his own nation, whose Messianic Saviour he proposed to have been, was condemned as a criminal, was delivered up to the Roman Procurator, and immediately executed by the punishment of crucifixion. This fact was the terrible negation by which hope and faith on the part of his adherents who belonged to this very nation appeared to be for ever annihilated. If they were to be revived, this could only be done by that annihilating negative being in turn itself negatived. This was done in the first instance by the production of faith in the resurrection of Jesus. If death had put an end to his life, his resurrection put an end to his death—death was swallowed up in victory. But the death and the tortures under which it took place, the accusation and the condemnation, the disgrace and the shame through which the supposed Messiah had passed, remained; they could not be obliterated out of the memory of men, even of believers in Jesus, could not therefore be denied, but must have a turn given to them in the construction put upon them, such that they should lose their negative meaning, that if possible they should become supports of the faith, their negative value positive, their marks of shame signs of honour. This might be done in different ways, and from this point of view we have to consider the discrepancies between the evangelical accounts of this portion of the life of Jesus.

All the Evangelists agree in admitting that Jesus was pronounced guilty of death by the Jewish authorities (Matt. xxvi. 57, xxvii. 1; Mark xiv. 53, xv. 1; Luke xxii. 54—71; John xviii. 12—30). The two first represent the trial of

Jesus as taking place in the night, Luke not until the next morning, when also the two first state that the formal resolution of the Sanhedrim was taken. In connection with this, Luke describes the denials of Peter before, the two others after, the trial of Jesus, and both parties, Luke on the one hand and Matthew and Mark on the other, place differently and describe differently the ill-treatment which Jesus experienced during these hours. But these are accidental, or at least unimportant discrepancies. Then comes the question as to how the fact of the condemnation of Jesus by the supreme power of his country was made harmless for the faith?

In the first place, it is said that the condemnation was the result of false testimony. Matthew and Mark tell us that the Sanhedrim made exertions to suborn false witnesses, many of whom came forward, but, according to Mark, their evidence proved to be useless by reason of mutual contradiction. At last, according to Matthew, two came forward stating that Jesus said he could destroy the Temple of God, within three days build it up again, or, according to Mark, build within three days another not made with hands. The observation of Mark, after having stated that the substance of what each said was so identical, is superfluously apologetic. It has been already explained how far this testimony, which may indeed have been brought forward at this time, was false, and how much of it was true. The third and fourth Evangelists make no mention of such testimony in this place, but the substance of it was not unknown to either of them. According to Luke, something of the same kind was subsequently alleged against Stephen, but there also as false testimony (Acts vi. 14); John seizes the enemy's weapon boldly by the point: yes, Jesus did really say, not indeed that he would himself destroy this Temple, but that if *they* were to destroy it, he would restore it again in three days; but in this he did not, as the stupid Jews thought, speak of their Temple of wood and stone, but — of the Temple of his body! (ii. 19—22).

A second expedient by which the original Christian tradition nullified the effect of the accusation and condemnation of Jesus, was the industriously repeated statement that to the question of the High-priest as to what the false witnesses said of him, as subsequently before Pilate, he gave no answer (Matt. xxvi. 63, xxvii. 12, 14; Mark xiv. 61, xv. 5; Luke xxiii. 9; John xix. 9). If Jesus gave no answer, it shewed that he did not recognise the jurisdiction of the court before which he had been brought; but, what is the principal theory, he thereby shewed himself to be the Lamb who was led to the slaughter and opened not his mouth, as the sheep who is dumb before his shearers, *i.e.* as the Servant of God, or, according to Christian interpretation, as the Messiah, of whom the prophet Isaiah had prophesied (liii. 7). So to the question as to whether he is the Son (or Servant) of God, he makes no reply, but solemnly declares himself in all form, referring to Ps. cx. 1 and Dan. vii. 13 ff., to be the Messiah; and in the fact that now this is looked upon by the High-priest and the Sanhedrim as a capital crime, there was involved, according to the Christian view, a third, and, so to say, a self-contradiction of their sentence. If they condemned him because he maintained himself to be what he really was, they did in fact pass judgment not upon him but upon themselves, upon their strong blindness, upon their obstinate unbelief.

The insults and abuse which Jesus was hereupon compelled to endure from the servants, or even from the Jewish dignitaries themselves, are differently described by the Evangelists, but mockery, blows, stripes, and spitting in the face, are alleged by all: these things also had been prophesied by Isaiah in a passage capable of Messianic explanation (l. 6): "I gave my back to the smiters, and my cheeks to them that plucked off the hair; I hid not my face from shame and spitting;" by this also and by the calm resignation with which he bore it, he proved himself to be that which his blinded enemies would not recognise in him

The weakness of the chief of his disciples in denying him, is only a discredit to him and to the frailty of human nature, and is immediately repented of by the Apostle with the bitterest remorse; but even this denial becomes rather an evidence of the supernatural character of Jesus by means of the prophecy which he gave of it, and the accuracy with which the result corresponded to his prediction. That the narrators are only concerned with the triple denial, in accordance with the prophecy of Jesus, we see by the discrepancies which they admit in reference to persons, place, and circumstances. In connection with it, the double crowing of the cock in Mark is evidently a feeble refinement; but in Luke the look of Jesus at the disciple when the cock crowed is an effective feature, which is indeed in point of place and circumstances as improbable, historically, as its legendary origin is intelligible. For what Matthew, and Mark after him, represent subjectively as the vivid awakening of Peter's recollection of the prophecy of Jesus by the crowing of the cock, becomes in Luke objectively a look from Jesus penetrating his inmost soul. A peculiarity which John exhibits in this place is connected with a tendency of his Gospel already sufficiently well known to us, and is, in particular, a parallel case to the turn which he gave, on the occasion of the last Supper, to the inquiry of the disciples after the traitor. In the same way as, according to his account, instead of applying immediately to Jesus, the disciples there apply through Peter to the favourite disciple as spokesman, so here Peter, whom the others represent as simply entering the court of the palace of the High-priest, is introduced by that "other disciple," who is thus represented as an acquaintance of the High-priest; accordingly an opportunity is taken here also of exalting the supposed author of the Gospel at the expense of the chief of the Apostles.

In the famous chronological passage of the third Gospel (Luke iii. 1 ff.), the author of the fourth had found two High-priests, Annas and Caiaphas, for the year in which the Baptist appeared, and taken such good notice of this statement, which was of itself erroneous and inaccurate, that by a still greater mistake he always calls Caiaphas, when he speaks of him in the history of the last year of the life of Jesus, the High-priest for that year (xi. 49, xviii. 13), as if he had changed with Annas, whereas, after Annas had been deposed by the Roman Procurator Valerius Gratus, and some other persons had been invested with the High-priestly office for a short time only, his son-in-law Joseph Caiaphas held it for a series of years, especially during the whole Procuratorship of Pontius Pilate. Now it was the more obvious for the later Evangelist, on an occasion on which the High-priest was supposed to have something to do, as on the trial and condemnation of Jesus, to give that other (supposed) High-priest something really to do, as he thus had an opportunity at the same time of representing Jesus as having been repudiated and maltreated by two Jewish High-priests; as Luke, conversely, but with a similar purpose, represents him as having been found innocent by two judges, neither of them belonging to the Jewish hierarchy, that is, by Herod as well as Pilate. That he had no particular sources of information at his command with regard to the trial of Jesus before Caiaphas, betrays itself also in the fact that he makes the main substance of it, introduced only by a question of the High-priest as to his disciples and his doctrine, to consist in the appeal of Jesus to the publicity of his ministry, which the Synoptics had put into his mouth on the occasion of his arrest (Matt. xxiv. 55; Mark xiv. 48; Luke xxii. 52 ff.). He then says nothing whatever of the trial before the real High-priest, to whom he represents Jesus as being sent by Annas. This is remarkable, and must remain unintelligible until we observe that, with his usual object in view of making Jesus play as important a part

THE TRIAL BEFORE THE HIGH-PRIEST.

as possible from first to last, he had already anticipated the two points which, according to the two older Evangelists, were brought out at this hearing of the case. In the first place, he had brought in the speech about the destruction and rebuilding of the Temple on the occasion of the first visit of Jesus to a feast (ii. 19); in the second place, the assurance that henceforth they shall see the Son of Man sitting at the right hand of power and coming in the clouds of heaven, had already, according to the fourth Gospel, been given by Jesus to Nathanael, on meeting with his first disciples, in similar words (i. 51), from henceforth they should see the heaven open, and the angels of God ascending and descending to the Son of Man.* Even of the condemnatory sentence of Caiaphas it may be said that the Evangelist had anticipated it, not only in speaking of the Council of Blood (xi. 49 ff.), but also again (xviii. 14), where with reference to this narrative he had described Caiaphas as him who gave counsel to the Jews that it was expedient that one man should perish instead of the whole people. All that was left was the "Yes" pronounced by Jesus in answer to the question as to whether he was the Christ, the Son of God; but the fourth Evangelist did not choose to represent the Jesus of his Gospel as thus confessing himself at once to be the Messiah of the Jews. Thus he passes over the hearing before Caiaphas with a summary statement, representing the denial of Peter as taking place in the court of Annas, and the result of the trial being the condemnation of Jesus, he passes on to the following process before Pilate.†

* On each occasion, ἀπάρτι ὄψεσθε.

† The English translation of the aorist ἀπέστειλεν by the pluperfect "had sent," which is undoubtedly erroneous, gives a totally different impression of the order of events from that which is here assumed by Strauss on the authority of the Greek text, rightly interpreted.—*Tr*.

90. THE DEATH OF THE TRAITOR.

There was a difficulty, capable of being turned to the disadvantage of Jesus, in the fact that he had been delivered by one of his disciples into the hands of his enemies. This difficulty the ancient Christian legend had, as we have seen, attempted from the first to set aside by representing this treason as having been foreknown and foretold by Jesus, and even prophesied in the Old Testament. It had even deprived beforehand the denial of Peter of its sting by such a prediction on the part of Jesus; but it had also done the same subsequently by the heartfelt repentance which it represented Peter as exhibiting. A subsequent repentance of a similar kind was all the more requisite in the case of Judas' treason, in proportion as the guilt of it exceeded that of Peter: in this case simple repentance was not enough, the repentance must become despair; nay, whether he repented or not, the traitor must be absolutely overtaken by the divine vengeance.

That a traitor should feel remorse, that he should even perish either by his own hand or by an accident, is possible and has happened in other cases; but our New Testament accounts with regard to the death of Judas point, in their discrepancy, not to a fact, but to different Old Testament passages and types which have been connected with one fact at the most, a fact moreover which probably has no connection whatever with the traitor. According to Matthew (xxvii. 3—10), Judas, when he heard that Jesus was condemned (and we cannot indeed understand how he could be surprised at it), cast down his reward for treason in the Temple into the hands of the High-priest and elders with the confession that he had betrayed to them innocent blood; and they, Judas having hanged himself from despair, bought from a potter for the money, which as being the price of blood they could not put into the treasury of the Temple, a field to bury strangers in. This field, says the Evangelist, on account of the blood of Jesus which clung to it, was called up to his own days the Field of Blood. According to the Acts, on the contrary, when, on the occasion of filling up the place of the traitor in the College of the Apostles, Peter is speaking of his end (i. 16—20), he had not restored the recompence for his sin, but bought with it, we are not told from whom, a piece of ground, upon which he shortly after ended his days, not by suicide, but by a fall which burst his body ;* an accident which, becoming known all through Jerusalem, gave to the piece of ground the name of Aceldama, or the Field of Blood, according to this, therefore, from the blood of the traitor. These two narratives have nothing in common but the sudden death of Judas and the name of a piece of ground at Jerusalem; the first of which, that the traitor could have come to no good end, was a postulate of the Christian consciousness; the other, that there was at Jerusalem a piece of ground of that name, is possible, but it need not have anything to do with the traitor; even if it had not, the Christian legend might still bring the ground of blood into connection with the man of blood.

Now, as regards the narrative in Matthew, we may observe that death by hanging, which is represented to have been the end of Judas, is especially the traitor's death in the Old Testament. Of Achitophel, the unfaithful adviser of David, who had betrayed this ancestor of the Messiah to Absalom, it is said (2 Sam. xvii. 23), "He arose, and gat him home . . . . and hanged himself," exactly as of Judas, "He departed, and went, and hanged himself." Achitophel, indeed, did not do this from remorse, but because he saw that his treacherous but clever design had not succeeded: he had intended to destroy David, and now foresaw his own destruction, which he anticipated by suicide. Judas saw that the

* Luther indeed translates πρηνὴς γενόμενος, Acts i. 18, like ἀπήγξατο, Matt. xxvii. 5, "hanged himself," which is clearly a mistake.

Son of David had been destroyed by him, and this threw him into despair.

This, according to the narrative of Matthew, is not the first thing, but is preceded by an act of repentance, the restoration of the reward for his treason and the confession of his guilt. Even the remorse of Judas was a thing which from a Christian point of view would have been inferred even though nothing was historically known about it, and an authority for the expression of it by throwing the money into the treasury of the Temple was supposed to be discovered in a passage of a prophet. Matthew quotes Jeremiah, but what he quotes is from Zechariah (xi. 13); and the mistake of the Evangelist comes from this, that this potter who is spoken of in this passage as he translated it, reminded him of the famous oracle about the potter in Jeremiah (xviii. 1 ff.). In the oracle of Zechariah, Jehovah appoints the prophet as a shepherd of the people; but he, soon disgusted with his thankless office, demands his pass or his dismissal. Thirty shekels of silver are given to him, and Jehovah commands him to throw the *goodly* price, at which he (Jehovah in his representative) was prized at of them, into the treasury; upon which the prophet takes the thirty pieces and casts them into the treasury in the house of Jehovah. Now if Judas had really got thirty pieces of silver for his treason, the application of this passage would naturally have forced itself upon men's minds; but I believe that it did so force itself apart from any corresponding reality, and that the thirty pieces of silver given to the traitor are taken from this passage. A contemptibly low price at which a shepherd sent by God, and in the last resort Jehovah himself, was prized by the ungrateful people, could not fail to suggest the price, at all events proportionably low, for which the best and truest shepherd of the sheep had been sold by his betrayer (Heb. xiii. 20; 1 Peter ii. 25); and if that price was found in the passage of the prophet fixed at thirty shekels of silver, it was that passage, and no historical information, that was the source on the authority of which Matthew—observe, Matthew only, who brings forward the passage, and in doing so coincides* in a remarkable manner with the Greek translation of it even in the words of his narrative—fixed the reward of the treason of Judas at that sum. The distinction indeed is not to be overlooked, that what in the passage of the prophet is a reward for service, is in the evangelical narrative pay for a purchase; consequently, while in the passage of the prophet there are only two parties, the hirer and the hired, there are here three, the buyer, the seller, and the subject of the sale; there the party hired gets the pay, while here, not the party sold, but the seller, receives the price. It is therefore said in the first passage that the party hired and so ill paid, *i.e.* the prophet, did at the command of Jehovah throw his reward, the thirty pieces of silver, into the Temple. In the passage of the Gospel, this could not be done by the person sold, but only by the seller, that is, the traitor, for he had received the pieces of silver. But as applied to him, the feature gave an excellent proof of his repentance, inasmuch as casting the money received into the Temple was the same thing as casting it at the feet of the guardians of the Temple, the High-priests and elders, from whom he had received it as the price of his treason.

But Matthew goes on to say that the High-priests were unable to put the money restored to them by Judas, as being the price of blood, into the treasury of the Temple, and that they bought for it a potter's field, and in reference to this he appeals directly to the prediction of the prophet. Whence the Evangelist gets the field we shall probably discover hereafter; but the potter himself he likewise took from the passage in the prophet, only not from its real meaning, but from an ancient misunderstanding of it. The place into which,

* Zech. xi. 12, according to the translation of the LXX.: καὶ ἔστησαν τὸν μισθόν μου, τριάκοντα ἀργυροῦς. Matt. xxvi. 15: καὶ ἔστησαν αὐτῷ τριάκοντα ἀργύρια.

according to Jehovah's command, the prophet was to cast his scanty pay and did so cast it, is indicated in the Hebrew text by a word which, with the vowel points usually marking it, would mean a potter, but would be thus absolutely devoid of sense: with other vowel points it may mean the treasury, and thus it must undoubtedly be understood. But the evangelical narrator adhered to the ordinary reading with its potter. But it is said further in the passage of the prophet that he cast the thirty pieces of silver into the house of God, after which there follows, as a more accurate description of it, the word which *we* translate by treasury, *i.e.* the treasury which was in the Temple, but the Evangelist by potter, nothing of the kind being there. The casting into the Temple, therefore, cannot have been the same thing with casting to the potter, and so the Evangelist made two acts of the proceeding, distributing likewise these two acts between different persons. He who cast the pieces of silver into the Temple was, according to him, the traitor; the money was brought to the potter by the High-priests, who did not choose to have in their treasury the price of blood. But for what did they bring the money to the potter? As the price of a piece of ground which they bought from him as a burying-place for strangers, and to which the name of the Field of Blood continued to cling from the money for which it was bought.

The Evangelist cannot have taken this piece of ground from the passage of Zechariah, as there is there no trace of such a thing; on the other hand, it reminds us of what is said in the Acts of the end of the traitor. This narrative, though differing so much in other respects, coincides with that of Matthew in this particular, that it also speaks of a piece of ground, which, however, the traitor bought himself, and not for a burying-place for strangers, but for his own purposes, and not from a potter. Now it is easy to see whence the author of the narrative got the piece of ground, for he tells us himself. He finds in the circumstance of the traitor having come by his death immediately after the purchase of it, the fulfilment of the prophecy, Ps. lxix. 26, "Let their habitation be desolate; and let none dwell in their tents." This is one of the pretended suffering Psalms of David, which were applied in Christendom at an early period to the suffering of the Messiah. Out of it (ver. 22) is taken the vinegar mixed with gall which is said to have been given to Jesus to drink upon the cross, and another passage of the same Psalm (ver. 10) is quoted in the fourth Gospel, as fulfilled in the purification of the Temple undertaken by Jesus (ii. 17). The punishments there threatened to the enemies of the speaker, admitted, if the Psalms were understood in a Messianic sense, of an application to the opponents of Jesus generally, the party among the Jewish people that were hostile to him, but in a most especial manner to him who had sinned most grievously against him, the traitor. Now if his habitation (piece of ground on which he dwelt) was to be desolate, he must first have had one, and where could he have got it but from the reward of his treason, which was now visited upon him by the desolation of the piece of ground which he had bought with the price of it? But if his habitation were made desolate and uninhabited, he, the inhabitant of it, must have died._ The wish that his enemies should be blotted out of the Book of Life, was also expressed against them in the same Psalm (ver. 29); and in another Psalm likewise quoted on this occasion (cix. 8), by the author of the Acts, it is said, "Let his days be few." But that the premature death of the traitor could not have been a natural one, was in part assumed as a matter of course, in part announced in that Psalm which threatened his habitation with desolation._ Let, it is said (ver. 23), "their table become a snare before them;" just as in the Acts of the Apostles it is said of Judas, that he fell headlong and burst asunder in the midst, and all his bowels gushed out—because, we may suppose, he had at his own table fed himself up into fatness on the pay which he got for his treason.

That the traitor's body swelled to an enormous size, was in Christendom a very ancient tradition, noticed even by Papias.* It is said that he became so fat that he could not pass through a space large enough for a waggon, and of this assertion another writer made out a story (thus legends of this kind grow), that he was crushed by a waggon meeting him, so that his bowels gushed out. Dropsy was said to be the cause of this enormous size, and especially the head and the eyelids of the traitor were said to have swollen to such a degree that he ceased to be able to see out of his eyes. Here the blindness might be merely a colouring given to the picture, dropsy only an assumed cause of the swelling, and the latter an assumed cause of the bursting; as we read, however, in one of the Psalms to which the author of the Acts of the Apostles appeals in speaking of the fate of Judas, the following words recorded against the enemy (cix. 18), "Let his cursing come into his bowels like water, and like oil into his bones," we have the dropsy, and in the words of the other Psalm (lxix. 24), "Let their eyes be darkened that they see not," we have the blindness prefigured in the Old Testament.

If the double tradition with regard to the end of the traitor could thus arise in the Christendom of the most ancient period without anything historical being known about it, the only question that remains is, whether the piece of ground, as to the purchase and name of which the two accounts, otherwise so different, agree, is not to be considered as historical. But it is only in the statement that there was near Jerusalem a piece of ground called the ground or the field of blood, that the two accounts do really agree; each taking its own way in bringing the facts into connection with Judas and his treason. One represents it as having been bought by

* The passages are quoted in my Critical Discussion on the Life of Jesus, ii. p. 400 ff., note 19 and 20.

Judas himself, the other by the High-priests; the one says it was named from the blood of Jesus clinging to it, the other from the blood of the traitor gushing out upon it. The bond, therefore, between the traitor and the ground has no tenacity, but the ground takes an independent position, *i.e.* there may have been a piece of ground near Jerusalem which, Heaven knows why, had the name, nay, perhaps have been used for burying strangers in; this piece of ground with its awful name the Christians claimed for the traitor, but the mode of bringing it into connection with him was not settled; the author of the narrative in the Acts looked upon it as the desolate habitation of the traitor, the writer of the first Gospel saw in it the object for which the blood-money restored by the traitor had been paid to the potter. And it is not here necessary to assume that the field came by its reference to the potter in consequence of the clayey nature of its soil; it was enough that in consequence of the name of Field of Blood it came by its reference to the traitor, with whom the potter was connected by reason of the false interpretations of the oracle of Zechariah.

91. The Trial before Pilate and Herod.

Until the days of the destruction of Jerusalem and later, and consequently during the period during which the substance of the narratives of the synoptic Gospels was forming, the real enemies of the youthful Christianity were found in the Jews of the old belief. On the other hand, Romans and Greeks shewed themselves to be partly indifferent, partly even capable of belief, or at any rate, apart from local or transitory obstacles, such as the persecution of the Christians under Nero, tolerant. Up to the date of the composition of the fourth Gospel, the conflicts with the power of the Roman

Government had indeed increased, but were infinitely outweighed by the extent to which the conversion of the heathen had proceeded; in consequence of which the Greco-Romish world was looked upon as the real and proper field for the spread of Christianity, and the Jews continually more and more as an obstinate and abandoned multitude. Now as Jesus at the conclusion of his life had come in contact with both powers, Judaism and Heathendom, the hierarchy of his own nation and the civil power of the Romans, it is natural that the conditions prevailing in both directions in Christendom generally, and in separate circles of it at the time of the composition of the several Gospels, should also shew themselves in the description of this portion of the history of the life of Jesus.

That Jesus was put to death by order of the Roman Procurator is certain;* there is no trace of his having given immediate or personal offence to that officer by his ministry; there is, therefore, every probability in favour of the representation given by our Gospels, that the Jewish authorities, being themselves deprived of the power of life and death by the Romans, endeavoured to gain over the Roman Procurator for their purposes, by bringing the man whom they wished to destroy for hierarchical reasons, into suspicion with the Romans on political grounds. The political character of the Jewish idea of the Messiah made it possible to do this. Jesus had recognised this idea as applicable to himself only hesitatingly, and with a disavowal of its political side; but the people, and even his own disciples, had up to that time taken the less notice of this disavowal in proportion as it was unintelligible to them. So much the more easy was it for the Jewish authorities to represent to Pilate in a politically dangerous light the success which Jesus met with in gaining followers among the people, the concourse which attended

* Tacit. Annal. xv. 44.

his lectures, the homage which had been given to him on his entrance into the capital. So far, therefore, the evangelical account has all historical probability in its favour.

But if Pilate lent them his support, the inference from this will be, that they had either really convinced him of the dangerous character of Jesus, or that he himself was convinced that his own interest called upon him, in this instance, to comply with the wishes of the Jewish leaders. In the first case, he may indeed at first have doubted of the guilt of Jesus, but not until the last have had a conviction of his innocence; in the second, he would at all events not have proclaimed this conviction publicly, as he would thereby have placed himself unnecessarily in a bad light, and counteracted his object of deserving the gratitude of the Jewish authorities, by exciting their disgust. However probable, therefore, may be the evangelical account as to the mode in which the Jewish hierarchs contrived to gain the Roman Procurator to their side, it is highly improbable in respect of all which they represent Pilate as saying or doing in order to declare loudly and solemnly his conviction of the innocence of Jesus. And as we may observe how, during the period of the formation of our Gospels, Christendom was continually turning away from Judaism with disgust, and to Heathendom with hope, we see the source from which the unhistorical element became here amalgamated with the evangelical narratives.

When, in the two first Evangelists, Pilate, on Jesus being brought before him, immediately puts to him the question as to whether he is the King of the Jews, this is perfectly natural, provided only we assume that the accusation of the Jewish authorities, not mentioned until after, consisted in the allegation that he had said he was. Luke, more appropriately, and more correctly illustrating and bringing forward the political side of the Messianic idea, puts these accusations first, stating that the Jews accused Jesus before Pilate of misleading the people, and dissuading them from paying tribute to Cæsar. On this accusation of the Jewish authorities Jesus was silent, and to this question of the Procurator only gave the monosyllabic reply, "Thou sayest it," without further explanation. Now this might indeed, as being a fulfilment of the prophecy about the lamb that suffered without opening its mouth, edify the Christians, but would scarcely gain favour for Jesus with the Romans, which, however, is said to have been the result. And even succeeding Christians might on this occasion have expected some expression of Jesus having reference to his position to the political side of this Messianic idea, such as the fourth Evangelist does not hesitate to introduce.

On the whole, this Evangelist has worked up the whole scene before Pilate with especial care. Even at first, in order to keep in sight the Passover, as being immediately at hand, he represents the Jews as not entering into the judgment hall, but Jesus as being led into it. Then Pilate, when he wishes to question Jesus, goes in, and when he wishes to speak with the Jews, comes out, and at last brings Jesus out with him. Thus the scene gets a dramatic, not to say a theatrical character, though indeed to the question as to who is supposed to have given to the Evangelist, who stood with his countrymen outside, a description of the conversations between Jesus and Pilate in the interior of the judgment hall, the answer is almost impossible. The representation given by the fourth Evangelist, even at the very first, will give as it were the key to the judicial drama that follows. The Jews having sent the prisoner in to Pilate, Pilate comes out and inquires the accusation, which they give him. Their reply, rude almost to absurdity, that if the man had not been a malefactor, they would not have delivered him to the Procurator, is only intelligible by supposing that it was given in order to bring out both Pilate's demand that they should judge him according to their law, and also their rejoinder, which was necessary to explain that they did not possess the privilege of putting criminals to death. It was of importance to the Evangelist to introduce this notice, because it was only in consequence of this circumstance that the prediction of Jesus with regard to his death, that it would consist in a lifting up from the earth (xii. 32, viii. 28) could be fulfilled, inasmuch as in the Jewish code the punishment of crucifixion did not appear; but for a crime such as Jesus was accused of, the Jewish punishment would rather have consisted in stoning (3 Mos. xxiv. 16, 23). But when he hereupon represents Pilate as going to Jesus and putting to him the question in the same terms as those of the Synoptics, and also as abruptly, whether he is the King of the Jews, we still do not know, notwithstanding all preliminary explanation, whence Pilate is supposed to have got this question, as the Jews had not told him what their accusation against Jesus was; the explanation, therefore, which has been continued up to this point, the object of which was to shew the incompetence of the Jews to inflict capital punishment, and consequently to suggest a reason for the crucifixion, here breaks off, and a new one begins, the purport of which is to expound the supermundane nature of the kingdom and kingly dignity of Jesus, and which ends in the question of Pilate, What is Truth? Jesus had said that he was a King, in so far as he had been born and come into the world to bear witness of the Truth. Upon this Pilate asks, What is Truth? In the same way at an earlier period, when Jesus spoke of the exaltation of the Son of Man, the Jews had asked, Who is this Son of Man? (xii. 32; comp. viii. 28)—consequently this is one of those questions arising from misunderstanding or no understanding at all, by which the fourth Gospel loves to illustrate the sublimity of the thoughts and utterances of its Christ, the notion of "Truth" being as much connected with fundamental ideas of a specially Johannine character, as that of the Son of Man is with those of Christianity in general.

When, after this conversation, the fourth Evangelist represents Pilate as coming out and declaring to the Jews that he finds no guilt in the accused, there is here at any rate better reason for his doing so, than in Luke, where it is simply unintelligible how Pilate, when Jesus had refused all further explanation, with the exception of the dry expression, "Thou sayest it," could declare his conviction of his innocence. The express declaration of innocence in this passage is taken by John almost word for word from Luke; for the two first Evangelists have in this place nothing of the kind, nor anything anywhere in this form. But in their description there now comes in the episode of Barabbas, which John represents as following that declaration of innocence, and which, finding it so firmly rooted in the ancient Christian tradition, we must consider on the whole to be historical. But whether Pilate, as the Evangelists represent, proposed to adopt the custom at the Passover of releasing a prisoner, as an appeal from the fanatical priesthood to the unprejudiced populace, and by contrast with a robber and murderer to facilitate the redemption of Jesus, and whether he did this so earnestly with repeated proposals, is indeed another question. And that he, when this attempt had failed, improvised the scene of washing his hands, and thus solemnly testified to the innocence of Jesus, acquitted himself of the blood "of that just man," and laid the responsibility of it upon the Jews—all this is only exceeded in improbability by the statement that the assembled Jewish populace took, as solemnly, this responsibility upon themselves, and expressly laid upon themselves and their children the guilt of the blood of Jesus. This representation, which is peculiar to the first Gospel, is manifestly made up altogether out of the Christian consciousness of a later date, which saw in the fearful end of the Jewish state and nation the execution of vengeance on those children whose fathers had shed the blood of Jesus. What their own interest required was, to have as it were official testimony to the innocence of their Christ, and this they foisted upon Pilate. But it is impossible that he could care so much for a Jewish enthusiast, which at the best he considered Jesus to be, that if he did not find it advisable to save him, he would have made an exposure of his own weakness and cowardice by so solemn a declaration of his innocence.

The first Evangelist does to a certain extent suggest a motive for this interest of Pilate in Jesus by a feature likewise peculiar to him, in the warning, that is, which he represents as being addressed to him by his wife, while actually sitting on the judgment-seat, to have nothing to do with that just man, for she had suffered many things in a dream that day because of him. On reading of this warning dream of Claudia Procula, as the legend soon after called Pilate's wife, who does not remember the pretended dream of Calpurnia, Cæsar's wife, on the night before the murder, and her prayer to her husband not to go out that day; and who would not be in a condition, remembering on the one hand this universal belief of the period, and on the other the personal inclination of the Evangelist for suggestive dreams which we recognise even in the history of the infancy, to form a judgment upon this narrative of this writer?

These two narratives, of Pilate's washing his hands and of his wife's dream, are simply passed over by the abridging Mark, while Luke and John seek to substitute for them other features producing a similar effect. Even before the digression about Barabbas, and immediately after Pilate's declaration that he can find no guilt in the silent prisoner, Luke has a statement (xxiii. 6—15), in making which he stands as much alone as Matthew does in that of the washing the hands—the statement as to the leading away of Jesus to Herod. He connects it with what precedes by saying that the Jews maintain their accusation against Jesus by asserting more particularly that he stirs up the people from Galilee up to the capital of Judea; whereupon Pilate seizes upon the word Galilee, and sends the Galilean to the Governor of his district, that is, the Tetrarch Herod Antipas, who was likewise present in Jerusalem during the feast. Luke has already made preparations beforehand for the statement. In the passage (ix. 9) in which during the ministry of Jesus in Galilee he mentions the attention which the fame of the miracles of Jesus excited in the mind of Herod, he concludes with the remark, peculiar to himself, that Herod wished to see him. It is to this wish that allusion is now made in the joy which the Prince feels at having him at length in his presence; and as on the former occasion the miracles were the cause for which he wished to see him, so now also he hopes to witness some miracle done by him. But as his wish is not fulfilled, inasmuch as Jesus meets all Herod's questions as well as all accusations of the chief priests and scribes who remained with him with persistent silence, the disappointed Prince with his men of war resort to ridicule, and finally he sends back the accused to Pilate arrayed in a gorgeous robe. In and for itself, this account contains nothing that might not have really happened as it is told. Neither is anything proved against its historical character by the fact of its being peculiar to Luke. But we must add, that it contains no matter whatever of its own. Nothing is stated about the questions of Herod or a sentence passed by him, and the mockery, together with the gorgeous robe, is only taken from the subsequent passage which follows the judicial sentence of Pilate, where the two other Synoptics have these features, and they are omitted by Luke. Lastly, we see most plainly the object which the narrative has in view, and so we become distrustful of its historical character. Jesus having been brought back from Herod to Pilate, Pilate appeals in support of his earlier judgment to the fact that now neither Herod nor himself find in him any guilt worthy of death. That is, the innocence of Jesus is to be attested by two judges, neither of whom could be said to be prejudiced in his favour, and of whom one was a heathen, and the other, though a Jew, still not a priest; as, on the other side, the fourth Evangelist represents Jesus as being rejected not merely by one, but by two, Jewish chief priests.

But there is another way also in which the third Evangelist attempts to increase the weight which, on the part of the Roman Procurator, is thrown into the scale of the innocence of Jesus. According to the narrative of the two first Evangelists, Pilate, after the failure of the attempt to substitute Barabbas, caused Jesus to be scourged and led away to crucifixion. Here, therefore, the scourging appears, according to the custom of the Romans, to be only an accident preliminary to crucifixion. But according to Luke, the Procurator repeatedly offers to substitute scourging, as the lighter punishment, for crucifixion, hoping thus to spare Jesus the heavier; but the Jews reject his offer, and insist upon putting Jesus to death (xxiii. 16, 22 ff.). If the motive for Luke's preference of this distinguishing feature is not clear in itself, it can hardly fail to become so in comparing the fourth Gospel, where Pilate performs what in Luke he merely offers, ordering Jesus to be really scourged (xix. 1), not, as in Matthew and Mark, as an introduction to the crucifixion, but in order to prevent it, that is, to persuade the hard-hearted Jews to desist from their demand for the punishment of death, on beholding the piteous countenance of the sufferer under the lash. It is on this account that the Evangelist here brings in also the mockery of the soldiers, the clothing with the robe of purple and the crown of thorns,—events which the two first Evangelists represent indeed as coming after the scourging, but when Jesus had been already sacrificed by the Procurator, while in John they are intended to serve the purpose of strengthening the claims to compassion expressed in the countenance of Jesus, and thus, if possible, of averting from him the extreme punishment. When, then, Pilate has brought forward to the Jews their victim, thus accoutred, with the words, Behold the man! and they, untouched even by this, persist in their demand for his crucifixion, Pilate on the one hand has done all that was possible to save Jesus, and on the other his Jewish opponents have shewn a hardness of heart such as is not seen in the description of any other Gospel.

In all the Synoptics, after the failure of the attempt to substitute Barabbas, Pilate yields, and commands Jesus to be led away to crucifixion. The fourth Evangelist represents him as still persevering in the effort to save Jesus. Hence it becomes an object for him to shew how the Jewish hierarchs set about attempting to persuade him to reverse his decision (xix. 6—16); and thus at the same time the process of his resistance is prolonged, and the cunning obstinacy of the Jews is more palpably realised. At first, the endeavour of Pilate to save Jesus receives a fresh impulse from the statement of his opponents that Jesus had professed to be the Son of God. In this the Jews see a crime worthy of death; but the heathen, on hearing it, is stated to have been penetrated with a feeling, however dark and mysterious, of the real state of the case. Then comes in the allusion of Jesus to the higher power, without which the Procurator could have had no power over him (comp. Rom. xiii. 1), a hint of higher responsibility which can but increase the hesitation of the Roman. But now the Jews play their best card, for, connecting what they say with the conversation at the beginning about the kingly office of Jesus, they represent the disinclination of Pilate to condemn the pretended king as disloyalty to the Emperor. The Procurator, then, having long resisted on good grounds the urgency of the Jews, at last yields to the lowest motive of personal interest, and against his better knowledge too, as he must from his former interview with Jesus have been well aware that his prisoner only professed to be a king in a sense which could not possibly bring him into collision with the Cæsar. Certain it is, that the process of the condemnation of Jesus is here represented exactly in correspondence with the feelings of later Christendom, but scarcely with reality. For Pilate could only have acted as he is represented here to have acted from motives of profound sympathy with Jesus. And it certainly is not easy to see from what cause these feelings should have arisen in the Roman, though it is very obvious how the Evangelist might be induced, from his own Christian consciousness, to attribute them to him.

FOURTH GROUP OF MYTHS.

CRUCIFIXION, DEATH AND BURIAL OF JESUS.

92. THE CRUCIFIXION.

Jesus ended his life upon the Cross; he endured the most ignominious of criminal deaths. Thus, according to traditional Jewish ideas, he lost all claim to recognition as the Messiah. The disciples, and those of the Jews who were led by them to believe in Jesus, modified their ancient Jewish conceptions in accordance with that fact, adopting into *their* idea of the Messiah the characteristic of his Passion as an intercessory sacrifice, of his death as an expiatorial one. This, within the circle of Jewish ideas, was only possible by passages being pointed out in the writings of the Old Testament, in which the sufferings and violent death of the Messiah appeared to be spoken of. There were in reality none of this description; but the servants of Jehovah in Isaiah, spoken of collectively in the singular, and individual pious persons, were represented as the victims of manifold sufferings, tortured even to death, and apparently abandoned by God, and to find the Messiah in such passages was the easiest thing in the world in the then state of scriptural interpretation among the Jews at the time. Now if at the time when men begun, in the interval between his death and his return in the clouds of heaven, to look back upon the past life on earth of Jesus the Messiah, the evangelical narrator encountered the problem of rendering an account of the most untoward event in his history, his crucifixion, it was natural that he should, in the attempt to solve it, bear firmly in mind those passages out of the Old Testament, and, taking feature by feature, point out that with all the contempt and suffering which Jesus bore, still nothing whatever had happened to him but what had long since been prophesied in the Old Testament as destined to occur to the Messiah—nothing consequently but what fell in with the scheme of Providence to save the people of Israel and all believers by the suffering and death of the Messiah. In the description, therefore, which the Evangelists give us of the course of events on the occasion of the crucifixion of Jesus (Matt. xxvii. 32—56; Mark xv. 21—41; Luke xxiii. 26—49; John xix. 17—30), we shall expect to find, *a priori*, a mixture of historical recollection and modification of the statements according to alleged prophecies in the Old Testament.

The first feature of the evangelical narrative to be noticed is, that when Jesus went forth to the place of execution his cross was borne by a man of Cyrene, Simon by name, who, according to Mark and Luke, was just coming from the country (Matt. xxvii. 32; Mark xv. 21; Luke xxiii. 26). In this statement the three first Evangelists agree, and the silence, or rather the contradiction, of the fourth, involved in the assertion that Jesus carried his cross himself (xix. 17), will not, in and for itself, make us doubt its truth, for we may well suppose that to the mind of the latter the statement of the Synoptics might seem to be an anomaly which he must have considered it his duty to get rid of. What, from his point of view, could be conceived more perverse than to introduce a substitute for the purpose of bearing the cross in the place of the Lamb of God who bore the sins of the world, of him who, himself as a Mediator for mankind, had taken upon himself suffering and death upon the Cross? If this substitution were made in the case of bearing the cross, why should it not have been carried out also in the death? and indeed Basilides the Gnostic is said to have taught that Simon was crucified in the place of Jesus.* Away then, the Evangelist might have thought, with the false substitute; and thus he represented Jesus as one who as he bore our sorrows, so also bore his own cross. If, according to this view, the synoptic account is not to be shaken by that of John, still a glance into the motive of the Johannine representation places us in a point of view where the question arises whether, after all, the synoptic statement also might not owe its origin to a similar dogmatic motive. The Cross of Christ, when the first offence arising from it had once been conquered, soon became the fundamental symbol of Christianity. For a man to take upon himself the cross of Christ was identical with following his example, and the call to do so was put into the mouth of Christ in the words (Matt. xvi. 24), "If any man will come after me, let him deny himself, and take up his cross and follow me." Figurative speeches of this kind always brought with them the temptation to those who read, or those who heard them, to understand them literally, as referring to a real external occurrence; but the cross of Jesus could in reality have been borne after him when he was going to the place of execution; and it was certainly not unnatural for the imagination of the first Christians to set up at this moment a first bearer of the cross who, though forced by others to become so, did not, in accordance with the precept of Jesus in the Sermon on the Mount, refuse the office, but took the cross upon him, and, as Luke says, carried it after Jesus. Quite as natural was it, if, as may well have been the case,

---

* Iren. Adv. Hær. i. 24, 4.

the cross of Christ was really borne by another to the place of execution, just for the sake of that symbolical meaning, to retain this feature, together with the name of the man who bore it; and the agreement of the three Synoptics, not only in the name, but also in the statement as to the home of the bearer of the cross, will always approve itself as favouring the latter assumption.

There is another occurrence that takes place on the way to the place of execution, described only by Luke; this is that much people, and especially women, lamenting his fate, followed Jesus; he however bid the daughters of Jerusalem to weep rather for themselves and their children, on account of the terrible days which in a short time would come upon their city (Luke xxiii. 27—31). It is common to all the Synoptics to represent the destruction of Jerusalem as a punishment for the guilt of the inhabitants towards Jesus, but Luke displays an especial tendency to do so. Thus he, and he alone, represents Jesus as weeping over the city on his approach, because by her blindness she is bringing upon herself and her children the misfortune of the siege and her destruction (xix. 41—44). The features whereby Luke represents Jesus as describing the future fate of Jerusalem, are taken from the great farewell speech, where, in Luke as well as in the other Synoptics, Jesus says (xxi. 23), "Woe unto them that are with child, and to them that give suck in those days!"—as here, "The days are coming in which they shall say, Blessed are the barren, and the womb that never bare, and the paps which never gave suck:" and the wish which they shall then utter, that the mountains may fall upon them and the hills cover them, is borrowed almost literally from Hosea x. 8.

After the arrival of Jesus at the place of execution, nothing is more important for the two first Evangelists than to shew how two Old Testament prophecies have been fulfilled in him. First, says Matthew, with all simplicity (ver. 34), they gave him vinegar to drink mixed with gall, and when he adds that after Jesus had tasted it he would not drink it, this seems less extraordinary than that anything of the sort should have been offered to him. Moreover, Mark cannot help considering it incredible, and therefore he converts the vinegar and gall into wine and myrrh (ver. 23), and thus gains a connection with the Jewish custom of intoxicating beforehand, with spiced wine, malefactors who were to be put to death.* It is possible that he thus hit upon the true state of the case, and that such wine was really offered to Jesus, but refused by him, because he did not wish to be intoxicated; but then the second Evangelist could only have guessed at this fact, for what was before him in Matthew was not anything that really occurred, but only a prophetic feature out of one of the two Psalms, which, together with the extract from Isaiah liii., forms, as it were, the programme according to which the whole history of the Crucifixion in our Gospel s is drawn up. In the Christendom of the most ancient times, the two Psalms xxii. and lxix. were considered, as we have repeatedly had occasion to remark, erroneously indeed throughout, as prophecies of the sufferings of the Messiah, and thus all the features in them, in so far as they had not been already applied, provided only that they suit the situation, are brought in and adapted to it. One of these features is the thirst and the allaying of it by a disagreeable potion. "My tongue cleaves to the roof of my mouth," complains the composer of the one Psalm (xxii. 16): that of the other (lxix. 21) says: "They gave me also gall for my meat, and in my thirst they gave me vinegar to drink." Matthew, instead of putting gall into the meat, which could have no place at the crucifixion, mixes it with the drink, and thus brings out the vinegar with gall, representing it as being offered to Jesus

* See the reference in my Life of Jesus critically discussed, ii. p. 514, note 15.

before the crucifixion, perhaps because he knew that on these occasions an intoxicating mixture was sometimes offered, while Mark is the first to bring the description into perfect harmony with the established custom.

But as the gall always created a difficulty, another theory kept only to the vinegar, which, according to the Psalm, must have been offered to Jesus the Messiah. Moreover, this vinegar presented itself in connection with an historical custom; it was mixed with water, and the Roman soldiers on marches and other expeditions drank it so mixed, and therefore at that time the soldiers who were under orders to be present at the crucifixion would have had it at hand. But as, according to the passage in the Psalm, the Messiah had vinegar given him to drink "for his thirst," or as, according to the other Psalm, his tongue cleaved to the roof of his mouth, the theory which omitted the gall, and held exclusively by the vinegar, put off the supplying of the latter to a later period, when the prolonged hanging on the cross might be supposed to have excited a more severe thirst. Then Luke, still thinking of the soldiers' drink, represents the vinegar as being offered by the soldiers in a spirit of mockery (ver. 36); while John, just at the last moment, and immediately before the decease of Jesus, represents some of the bystanders, with, as it appears, a good intention, as dipping a sponge in vinegar and applying it to his mouth upon a stalk of hyssop (ver. 29). All this, a clear proof of the source of the statement, is prefaced by the words to the effect that Jesus said, "in order that the Scripture might be fulfilled: I thirst," by which only the fulfilment of the passage in the Psalm already mentioned can be meant. Besides this offer at a later period of vinegar alone, the third and fourth Evangelists say nothing whatever of vinegar and gall or myrrh-wine being offered to Jesus quite at first; while, on the other hand, Matthew and Mark, as usual, and as in the case of the loaves and fishes, that nothing may be lost, have incorporated with their Gospels the history of the giving of vinegar in both the forms which it had taken. The second time they represent, as John does, that the vinegar was given in a sponge : an agreement in a feature not taken out of the Psalm, in which we may see the trace of an historical source, but quite as much also only of a custom at crucifixions. On the other hand, the stalk of hyssop, which appears only in John, *i.e.* the same Evangelist who sees in the crucified Jesus the true Paschal Lamb, reminds us of the Mosaic ordinance with regard to the blood of the lamb, in which, likewise, the hyssop plays a part (2 Mos. xii. 22).

After a brief mention of the crucifixion, which had in the mean time been completed, the two first Evangelists now hurry on to the second feature out of these passion-Psalms fulfilled in Jesus—a feature which the two other Evangelists do not allow to escape them (Matt. xxvii. 35 ; Mark xv. 24 ; Luke xxiii. 34; John xix. 23 ff.). The sufferer of the 22nd Psalm had, among other things, complained (ver. 18), "They parted my garments among them, and cast lots upon my vesture." This feature also may possibly have been realised in the case of Jesus, as, according to the Roman law, portions of the clothing of persons executed became the spoils of the executioners. But that in this place the Evangelists drew not from a historical source but solely from the passage in the Psalm, though this is expressly quoted only by the fourth, is clear from this, that each of them describes the occurrence exactly as he understood the passage in the Psalm. Any one understanding it correctly was aware that in the second half of the verse neither a different act nor a different subject was spoken of from those in the first, but that what was said in the first was only more accurately defined in the second. The passage was thus understood by the three Synoptics, most clearly by Mark, and so he tells us that the soldiers divided the clothes of Jesus among them, casting lots for them, which Mark explains to mean that they cast lots which piece each was to have. On the other hand, the fourth Evangelist understood the passage wrongly, as if it spoke first of a division of the clothes and then of a casting of lots for the coat, as two different acts about two different objects, and he tells us accordingly that the soldiers (whose number he limits to four) divided among themselves the other clothes, *i. e.* the upper garments, without the use of the "lot," and then cast lots for the under garment (this being what he understands by the χιτών in the passage in the Psalm), not wishing either to apportion it directly to one of themselves, or to spoil the unseamed garment by rending it. Exactly as above in the passage of the Prophet about the ass and the foal of the ass; only that here Matthew and John change places—the misunderstanding, this time, is as much on the side of the latter as before on that of the former. Whether the fourth Evangelist gave this turn to his narrative with the intention at the same time of alluding, under the figure of the unseamed vesture of Christ, as under that of the untorn net (xxi. 11), to the unity of the Church, of the one flock under one shepherd (x. 16), is an hypothesis that can only be put in the form of a question.

It must have been an especial consolation to the faithful historian of the crucifixion, that exactly those points which made this history so painful to the Christian conscience, the disgrace and the contempt of the crucified Messiah connected with that crucifixion, were so definitely foretold in the Old Testament as he now learnt to understand it. In the passion-Psalm (xxii. 7) it was said, "All they that see me laugh me to scorn; they shoot out the lip, they shake the head;" what wonder if now, as the Synoptics tell us (Matt. ver. 39 ff.; Mark, ver. 29 ff.; Luke, ver. 35 ff.), the passers-by, or the spectators, together with the elders, mocked the crucified Jesus and shook their heads at him? Even their mocking speeches are given by Matthew almost in literal agreement with the passage in the Psalm: "He trusted in the Lord that he would deliver him; let him deliver him, seeing he delighted in him" (ver. 8): "he trusted in God; let him deliver him now, if he will have him." Now in the Psalm the speakers are described as bulls, dogs, lions, and unicorns, *i.e.* as outrageous sinners: however fitting, therefore, it is on the part of the Evangelists to put these speeches into the mouths of the Jewish opponents of Jesus, it is quite as unlikely that men, learned as they were in the Scriptures, should really have used the words of that Psalm, which, as they must have remembered, were the speeches of godless sinners. It is more probable that they should really have uttered those words which are not taken from the Psalm, but have reference to the particular circumstances of Jesus; as, for instance, the ridicule at the man who saved others but cannot now save himself, and the demand that the pretended Son of God and King of Israel, the mighty destroyer and rebuilder of the Temple, should now prove his exalted nature by descending from the cross.

In connection with this mention of the King of the Jews in the mocking speeches first of the High-priests and Scribes, then of the soldiers, on the occasion of the giving of the vinegar to drink, Luke speaks of the Superscription on the Cross (xxiii. 38; the other Evangelists had made mention of it earlier, Matt. xxvii. 37; Mark xv. 26; John xix. 19—22), the main point of which was this very description of Jesus as King of the Jews. Luke first, and subsequently John, state prominently that the superscription was written in three languages, Greek, Latin, and Hebrew; both of them, the follower of Paul as well as the author of the Gospel of the Spirit, see in this circumstance a foreshadowing of the fact that the words of this supposed King of the Jews shall be spread abroad in the Grecian and Roman world far beyond the range of Judaism. Besides this, the latter gives to the title of Jesus as King of the Jews, a turn such that all the ridicule that might be connected with it became harmless as far as the Christians were concerned, and fell upon the Jews themselves.

They felt, says John, mortified by this title being given to a crucified malefactor, and begged the Procurator to change it; but he adhered to what he had written; and so the fact remains that the Jews crucified their King, and that therefore he that was crucified is no longer King of the Jews, but the Son of God and Saviour of the world, in which character he is recognised by the Christians who have been initiated into the profound doctrines of John.

Luke and John mention as quite at the beginning what Matthew and Mark do not introduce until much later, that two transgressors, thieves, according to the two first Evangelists, were crucified with Jesus, and, moreover, in such a position that he occupied the intermediate place between them (Matt. ver. 38; Mark, ver. 27 ff.; Luke, ver. 32 ff.; John, ver. 18). Moreover, we read in Mark that by this circumstance was fulfilled the prophecy which he quotes (Isaiah liii. 12): "He was counted among the transgressors." In Luke (xxii. 37), the same passage had been quoted by Jesus himself at the close of the last Supper, as one which had yet to be fulfilled in him by the fact of his being arrested as a transgressor. Mark, or whoever interpolated this verse into his Gospel (for the genuineness of it is doubtful), saw in the words of the prophet a definite prediction of the crucifixion of Jesus between two malefactors; a circumstance so little alluded to in the passage, even for the most arbitrary explanation, that we can hardly look upon the feature of these two men being crucified with Jesus as one that could be elicited only out of the passage of the prophet. It may have been historical, but still welcome to the Evangelists on account of this supposed prophetical reference. A further use of it also is made by them, each after his own fashion. Matthew and Mark represent the two wretches as joining in the general chorus of contempt which sounds around the crucified Messiah; Luke's ear is finer, and can distinguish between the two voices. Only one really joined and mockingly called upon Jesus, if he is the Messiah, to save himself and both of them; but the other, better disposed, rebukes his fellow, and not merely recognised Jesus, but also begged him, when he returned in his kingdom, consequently in the character of the Messiah, to remember him (ver. 39 ff.). Here then we have a criminal, who undoubtedly came now for the first time into contact with Jesus, understanding without preliminary instruction the doctrine of a suffering and dying Messiah. This doctrine Jesus had up to that time vainly tried to make his disciples comprehend. Now that this should have been so is as unintelligible as the motive is self-evident which influenced the author of the third Gospel or his representative to give this additional colouring to the feature of his joint crucifixion with the two criminals. In the blasphemy uttered by a condemned criminal, the ignominy of the crucified Messiah had reached its lowest point. In this fact naturally lay the inducement to represent him as gaining additional glory from this very humiliation. Especially was this the case with a writer who had given an especial colouring to the general evangelical feature of the friendship of Jesus with sinners. The statement that the malefactor on the cross was converted and believed, was completely in the spirit of the parable of the Prodigal Son, of the narrative of the anointing by the sinful woman. Hence the third Evangelist adheres so far to the traditional account as to leave one of the two criminals maintaining his character for mockery and contempt, and contrasts with him the other as a repentant and faithful sinner favoured by Jesus. Thus he obtained a contrast that was, in and for itself, very effective. It has been surmised by Schwegler* that Luke, in his account, intended to typify by the two abjects the opposition between the relation of the Jews and the Heathen to Christianity, the obstinate unbelief of the one, the faith, combined with repentance

* The Post-Apostolic Age, i. 50. Comp. Baur, Critical Investigation of the Canonical Gospels, p. 512. Volkmar, Religion of Jesus, p. 332.

and a desire for salvation, of the other. This is indeed an acute conjecture, but again one of those which cannot indeed be forgotten, nor, on the other hand, maintained and affirmed as a proved result.

93. The Words on the Cross.

In the answer of Jesus to the repentant criminal, we have already touched upon one of the words on the Cross, of which there are, traditionally, seven enumerated. That is the number, if the accounts of all the Evangelists are combined. But, taken singly, no one has so many. Matthew and Mark have each only one, and both of them the same; Luke three, but different from these two; John the same number, but again those of which none of the three former know anything. And if we could now ask each of the Evangelists separately, we do not know what the two first might say to the words on the Cross of the two others; of the third it is probable, and of the fourth beyond doubt, that they would have rejected, with a protest, the expression which the two first put into the mouth of Christ, the crucified.

This expression is the well-known one, "My God, my God, why hast thou forsaken me?" which both the Evangelists give in the original Aramaic, in order to make intelligible the confusion which they represent as having been connected with it (Matt. ver. 46 ff.; Mark, ver. 34 ff.). It is well known that these words are the beginning of the 22nd Psalm, and thus on the point of view of the two first Evangelists it is quite what might be expected, that after a series of objective features mentioned in this passion-Psalm have been pointed out as having been fulfilled by the crucified Jesus, the introductory verse of it which describes the subjective feeling of the person who speaks in it should now be adopted by Jesus himself, and thus his entire suffering be declared to be the fulfilment of the prophecy contained in the Psalm. Such appeared to the two first Evangelists to be the case; in them the passage put into the mouth of Jesus is not much more than a quotation; but if we look to Jesus, and the tone of feeling of which these words, if he spoke them, must have been the expression, it will require, not merely in the case of the Man-God of ecclesiastical doctrine, most arbitrary assumption to make a feeling of abandonment by God conceivable in him,* but even we upon our purely human point of view should be afraid of derogating from the spiritual and moral elevation of Jesus, if even at this crisis of most profound suffering we were to attribute such a feeling to him. For by it would be implied the supposition that he had made and now discovered a mistake in himself and his work and his own conception of both, as he must otherwise have recognised in the very death which had now overtaken him personally, the true and real way to the triumph of his cause which he had long foreseen. Even the third Evangelist, with his loftier conception of Christ, was dissatisfied with that expression, and it was perhaps for this very reason that he heightened the description of the agony in Gethsemane, that every symptom of weakness might be at an end with that scene, and for all that followed only calmness and elevation remain. To the fourth Evangelist, conversely, the scene in Gethsemane was insupportable: a mental perturbation, under which, however, his confidence in God was never for a moment lost, was the most that he felt to be conceivable for his Logos Christ, but a feeling of abandonment by God was absolutely excluded by the fundamental idea of his personality.

That exalted state of mind which under the most extreme personal suffering, so far from losing the command over

---

* Comp. my Life of Jesus critically discussed, ii. 429 ff.

itself, has still room for sympathy with others, and even for the authors of the suffering, is represented by the third Evangelist as being realised by his Jesus even in the very first words which he represents him as uttering while, as it appears, he hung upon the cross, "Father, forgive them; they know not what they do" (xxiii. 3, 4); an expression harmonising not merely with the command to love enemies, but with that feeling of charity which embraces all, makes the best of everything, and which has been described to us above as the fundamental feeling of Jesus; though it must not be overlooked that the Evangelist did undoubtedly intend to exhibit in this place, as realised in Jesus, what Isaiah had said of the Servant of Jehovah, that he, while numbered among the transgressors, bore the sins of many, and made intercession for the transgressors (Isaiah liii. 12). A similar feeling is exhibited by the second of the expressions on the cross in Luke, the assurance to the believing malefactor that he, even before the second coming of the Messiah, should be with him in Paradise on that day (ver. 43). In the third and last, the Crucified does indeed remember himself, but in a form entirely opposed to the complaint of abandonment by God, in an expression of the most trustful resignation, immediately before his decease: "Father, into thy hands I commend my spirit" (ver. 46). A similar prayer, and a similar intercession for his murderers, is put by Luke in the mouth of Stephen, whom he represents generally in a different point of view, as an image of Jesus (Acts vii. 59 ff.); but the words are taken out of Psalm xxxi. 6, and literally according to the Greek translation.

The fourth Evangelist takes the words which he finds in the third, as the last words of Jesus, and applies them as a formula to indicate his death, representing him as bowing his head, and giving up his spirit (to his Father), having first said, "It is finished" (xix. 30). Just for the reason that these were supposed to be the last words of Jesus, a different turn had to be given to the giving up of the ghost, from that in Luke; but why should these be the last words of Jesus? Even the expression on the cross that precedes the last, the expression "I thirst," is introduced by the fourth Evangelist with the words that Jesus uttered it because he knew that now all was finished, that also this passage in the Scripture about the thirst, and giving vinegar to drink, might be fulfilled in him (ver. 28 ff.). Consequently it was the completion of his work, which had been announced indeed beforehand by Jesus in his High-priestly prayer (xvii. 4), but which was now in reality at hand, on the one hand, and the complete fulfilment of the prophecies referring to him, on the other, which John intended to represent as being spoken of by the dying Jesus: perhaps also in connection with the description in Luke, according to which Jesus, as has been already said, had declared before going out to the Mount of Olives, that like everything that had been written of him, so also must the prophecy in Isaiah liii. 12 be now fulfilled in him (xxii. 37). But this reference to fulfilled Scriptures is a different thing in John to what it is in Matthew; the fulfilment of the prophecies in Jesus is, as we see in this very passage, at the same time the fulfilment of his work, the solution of the problem of the incarnate Logos, with which his pilgrimage on earth has an end and his glory begins; in the place of his limited human ministry, the mission of the Paraclete comes in.

The two expressions on the cross in John, hitherto considered, are connected with circumstances of which the other Evangelists also make mention; the third, or, in point of time, the first, refers to a situation of which, with exception of himself, no other reporter knows anything. According to Matthew (xxvii. 55 ff.) and Mark (xv. 40), the crucifixion was viewed only by a number of women, the Galilean companions of Jesus, among whom Mary Magdalene, Mary, the mother of James and Joses, and the mother of the sons of Zebedee, or, in Mark, Salome, are mentioned by name; the Twelve they suppose not yet to have re-assembled again after the flight which followed upon the arrest of Jesus, though they represent Peter as venturing with doubtful courage into the court of the palace of the High-priest. In Luke there is no doubt that among "all the acquaintances" of Jesus whom he represents as viewing the crucifixion, in company with the women, the Twelve also are comprised (xxiii. 49): but they, like women, only place themselves timidly at a distance. On the other hand, in the fourth Gospel (xix. 25 ff.), there appears, together with the two Marys, the Magdalene and the other, here called the wife of Cleophas, instead of the mother of the sons of Zebedee, the mother of Jesus himself, and with her the beloved disciple, whom the Evangelist foisted in with Peter, in the court of the High-priest, in order to represent him here as being the only one of the disciples present at the cross of Jesus. And moreover he places him, and with him the women, so close to the cross, that the Crucified can speak a confidential word to them. We do not require to know the substance of what was said, to enable us to guess at once that this arrangement would agree with that cleverly-laid plan which the fourth Evangelist follows with regard to the beloved disciple whom he chooses as the patron of his work. However, the substance of the speech of Jesus is this, that he recommends the favourite disciple to his mother as her son, her, to the favourite disciple as his mother, and he, as the Evangelist observes, from that hour takes her to himself. According to the Acts (i. 14), the mother of Jesus, after his decease, together with the other women, kept with the Eleven and the brethren of the Lord. It is well known that among the first Peter, among the last James, was pre-eminent, and if John came in as a third man (Galat. ii. 9), he was still, as he appears mostly in the synoptic combinations of the same three names, only the third and not the first. Here, on the other hand, he appears not merely as the first, but as the only one, and, by the declaration of Jesus, is brought into a perfectly exclusive relation not only to his mother, but also to himself. As the personage who steps into the place of Jesus with his mother, he is raised far above all other Apostles, Peter not excepted; as the younger son, as it were, of Mary and the survivor of Jesus, he is, as Baur acutely observes, the Brother of the Lord, and indeed, according to the whole character of the Gospel, the spiritual Brother, with whom the natural Brother, so alien to the spirit of Jesus, cannot be compared. Moreover, this narrative, like so many others apparently peculiar to the fourth Gospel, is only a modification of a well-known synoptic one. When, on one occasion, during the delivery of a lecture, the mother and the brothers of Jesus were announced to him, he asked, "Who is my mother, and who are my brothers?" Then he pointed or looked at his disciples with the words, "Behold my mother and my brethren!" (Matt. xii. 49; Mark iii. 34). This figure cannot be mistaken in the Johannine expression on the cross: "Woman, behold thy son! and (disciple) behold thy mother!" only that here, not all the disciples, but the favourite disciple exclusively is brought into the fraternal relation with Jesus.

94. The Miracles at the Death of Jesus.

About the sixth hour, *i.e.* as the Jews counted the hours from the dawn of day, about midday, all the Synoptics represent a darkness as coming on, and continuing until the ninth hour, *i.e.* till three o'clock in the afternoon (Matt. xxvii. 45; Mark xv. 33; Luke xxiii. 44 ff.). According to Mark, who fixes the beginning of the crucifixion at the third hour, *i.e.* at nine o'clock in the morning, Jesus had then been hanging on the cross for three hours; according to Matthew and

Luke also, he had then been hanging for some time, but how long they do not say.

The darkness, which is only described more definitely by Luke as a darkening of the sun, cannot, at the time of the Easter full moon, have been a natural eclipse of the sun; and indeed the addition of all the reporters to the effect that it extended over the whole earth, points to a miraculous event. In proportion as the appearance of Jesus had been of importance, must nature have put on mourning for him. Such was the taste of the age; the sun, according to the then existing Roman legend, had done the same on the occasion of the murder of Cæsar* and before the death of Augustus.† The darkening of the sun about the time of Cæsar's murder is indeed described to us as part of the dull and gloomy character of the whole year,‡ so that we see how a perfectly natural phenomenon, continuing for some time, and thus accidentally coinciding with that event, might be pressed into the service of superstition and flattery: but the phenomenon was soon looked upon as a real solar eclipse,§ and moreover to have coincided to the day and hour with Cæsar's murder, as, according to the three first Evangelists, the darkness is said to have coincided with the hour of the death of Jesus. Modern theologians eulogise the fourth Evangelist for sparing them such a system of prodigies; it is, certainly, too objective for his mode of thinking and feeling, only we are, unfortunately, compelled to say, too natural; moreover, for the glorifying of the death of Jesus he has in his mind quite other things; whether they are, for us, more edifying, is a point that will be discussed in its proper place.

---

* Virgil, Georg. i. 463 ff. Ovid, Metam. xv. 785 ff., represents the darkening of the sun, and other things which Virgil describes as coming after the murder, as preceding them in the character of prodigies.

† Dio, cap. lvi. 29. ‡ Plutarch, Cæs. 69.

§ Servius on the passage of Virgil.

The darkness, then, lasts three hours; then, about the ninth hour, Jesus, in Matthew and Mark, utters the lament about being forsaken by God, and after the drink mixed with vinegar has been offered to him, his death follows, accompanied by a loud cry, to which Luke ascribes the words discussed above (Matt. xxvii. 46—50; Mark xv. 34—37; Luke xxiii. 46). After this, Matthew, and the same event was also said to have been connected on the occasion of Cæsar's death with the darkening of the sun,* represents an earthquake as taking place; but he also, in agreement with the two other Synoptics, reports the occurrence previously to this of an event still more far-fetched, which is, that the curtain of the Temple, without doubt that which separated the Holy of Holies from the Holy, was rent in twain from top to bottom (Matt. xxvii. 53; Mark xv. 38; Luke xxiii. 45). A sudden bursting open of closed doors often appears in the legends of those times as a prognostication of approaching misfortune; Cæsar's murder, the deaths of the Emperors Claudius, Nero, Vespasian, even the destruction of the Temple at Jerusalem, are said to have been announced in this way.† Calpurnia, the night before the murder of her husband, saw in a dream the gable of the house fall down: so the Hebrew Gospel had a similar feature on the occurrence of the death of Jesus, representing, not that the curtain of the Temple was rent, but that the roof of it fell in.‡ The *Recognitions* of Clement§ give to the rending of the curtain the meaning of a lament at the approaching destruction of the Temple; but the fact that it is only the curtain on which the prodigy is displayed, appears to point in a different direction. The Apostle Paul, alluding

---

* Virgil, as quoted, v. 475 ; Ovid, as quoted, v. 798.

† Sueton. Jul. 81. Nero, 46. Vespas. 23. Dio Cass. lx. 35. Tacit. Histor. v. 13.

‡ Hieron. Ep. 120, ad. Hedib. § i. 41.

to the cover which Moses put over his face, declares that through Christ a veil is taken away which so long as the Old Testament system lasted was spread over heavenly things (2 Cor. iii. 13—18); and the Epistle to the Hebrews connects a similar thought with the curtain of the Temple. Under the Mosaic system of religion, the priests had access only into the Holy Place, and the High-priest alone, once a year, into the Holy of Holies, with the expiatory sacrifice of the blood of beasts; Christ, it was said, had once for all by means of his own blood entered into the space within the curtain, into the Holy of Holies in the heavens, and in doing so had become the forerunner of Christians, and had opened for them also the entrance to it (vi. 19 ff., ix. 1—12, x. 19 ff.). In this representation of the Epistle to the Hebrews, the existence of our evangelical narrative is manifestly not assumed; for if the author of the former had known anything of a rending of the curtain of the Temple, he would not have omitted to make use of this circumstance, so closely connected with his line of thought. We could not, indeed, maintain, conversely, that the evangelical narrative was derived from the description in the Epistle to the Hebrews; but if we take this last in conjunction with the expression of the Apostle Paul, we see a group of thoughts and images current in that most ancient Christianity which arose out of Judaism, and which, after this had been used long enough as mere comparison, must at last have settled down naturally into a narrative like that which we have before us.

With all these miraculous events—darkness, earthquake, rending of the curtain—our first Evangelist's appetite for miracles was not yet satisfied. With the earthquake, peculiar to himself alone, he connects the splitting of the rocks (ver. 51), as the tempest in which Jehovah had once passed before Elijah on Mount Horeb had rent mountains and shattered rocks (1 Kings xix. 11). But on this occasion the splitting of the rocks is only a means adapted to produce the next feature with which the Evangelist is properly concerned, which is, that on the decease of Jesus the graves also opened, that out of them there came forthwith many bodies of saints that had fallen asleep, resuscitated, who after the resurrection of Jesus came into the Holy City and appeared to many (ver. 52 ff.). It has already been mentioned above that the accounts of raising the dead in our Gospels are nothing but pledges given to itself by the faith of the Christendom of the earliest period, that Jesus, not having performed in his lifetime the Messianic raising of the dead, will so much the more certainly perform it on his second coming. Attention was also drawn to the disproportion between the guarantee and that for which it was to be the guarantee—a disproportion consisting in the fact that the dead raised by Jesus during his life on earth had returned only to earthly life, to die a second time, while under the Messianic resurrection the dead were to be raised in glorified bodies to immortal life; added to which was the small number of those isolated evangelical cases of resurrection which was quite incommensurate with the number of those for whom they were to answer. To compensate for this double deficiency, a case was desirable in which a larger number of dead, and these not men liable to die a second time, but as risen saints, should have come forth out of their graves. Moreover, the idea of such a resurrection was involved in the expectations of the Jews and early Christians; it was supposed that at the coming of the Messiah, a selection only, in the first instance, of the most pious Israelites was to rise in order to participate with him in the joys of the kingdom of the millennium; and then, and not until this period had elapsed, the remaining masses, good and bad, to undergo a searching trial.* The Christian theory, indeed, as we find it in the Revelation of John (xx. 4 ff.), transplanted the resurrection of the pious also to the time of Christ's second coming, but it was always useful for the

* Gfrörer, the Century of Salvation, ii. 276 ff.

strengthening of the faith if a sample of this resurrection had been given during his first presence upon earth. If it was asked at what moment of it, the choice might waver between the moment of his death and that of his resurrection; for though his victory over death and the grave had not yet come to light in the latter, still it was only by his yielding to death that it had been made possible, and thus Matthew divides, as it were, the occurrence between the two. The opening of the graves, and the resurrection of the saints that slept, takes place at the moment of the death of Jesus, when the earthquake and the splitting of the rocks in consequence furnished a point of connection; but their coming forth, and their appearance in Jerusalem, does not take place until Jesus also had arisen, who was always to be considered the first-born of the dead (Col. i. 18; Revel. i. 5), the first-fruits of them that slept (1 Cor. xv. 20).

In conclusion, the imagination of the early Christians represents the effects produced upon the bystanders by all these prodigies with which it surrounded the death of Jesus, to have been exactly that which it endeavoured itself to express. Of those bystanders, the least prejudiced must have been the executioners themselves, the Roman soldiers with their Captain, who, as heathens, were certainly not prejudiced beforehand in favour of Jesus, nor, as Jews, against him, and according to Matthew (ver. 54) they declared the impression made upon them by the earthquake and the other extraordinary circumstances in words to the effect that he whom those events concerned was truly the Son of God. In Luke (xxiii. 47), where there is no earthquake mentioned, and only at the last the departure with a loud-spoken prayer, the emotion of the Captain (the soldiers are not mentioned here or in Mark) appears to be produced only by this edifying end, and his words only declare that this, certainly, was a righteous man. Mark (xv. 39), instead of the prayer aloud, has only a loud cry; and as, on the other hand, in giving the words of the Captain, he follows, not Luke, but Matthew, his statement seems a strange one, that when the Captain saw that Jesus departed with such a cry, he declared himself convinced that this man was the Son of God. Whether from this we are to understand the meaning of the second Evangelist to have been, as has been surmised, that as evil spirits ordinarily went out with cries, so here the cry indicated the departure of the divine spirit of the Messiah from his body, or whether he considered this cry which so struck the Captain, when taken in connection with the early approach of death, at which he represents Pilate also as being surprised, as a sign that Jesus quitted life spontaneously, before death came in the course of nature—this is a point which can scarcely be decided. Of the prodigies which Matthew represents as ensuing on the death of Jesus, Luke (with Mark) omits all, with the exception of the darkness and the rending of the curtain. But he contrives to give a more perfect idea of the impression which was made upon the bystanders, by representing not only indeed the Roman officer, the heathen, as "giving honour to God" by an unextorted testimony in favour of Jesus, but the Jewish multitudes as conscience-stricken, and beating their breasts, and consequently as returning home not without repentance and self-condemnation.

95. The Spear-stab in the Side of Jesus.

Of all these events, either objective or subjective, the fourth Evangelist, as has been already remarked, has nothing whatever. They appeared to him, not so much unimportant, as of an external, exoteric character, in comparison with what he had to tell (xix. 31—37). Perhaps also he was here following immediately in the tracks of Mark. Mark says (xv. 42—45), that when, on the evening of the day of execution, Joseph of Arimathea begged Pilate to give him the body of Jesus (of which hereafter), the Procurator expressed surprise at his being already dead, and did not grant the prayer until the officer had assured him that death had, in fact, taken place some time since. Now it is indeed possible, as has been said, that Mark only thus intended to draw attention to the fact that the death of Jesus had occurred not in a natural but in a supernatural manner; but the circumstance in question might also be understood as an attempt to prove the reality of the death of Jesus, and for this the assertion of the officer might be considered as insufficient. If Pilate had reason to doubt whether the death of Jesus had really taken place in a natural manner, at the time when they thought of taking him down from the cross, he would, as might be supposed, take care to reduce the death to a certainty, or at all events to authenticate it.

That with this object something more was done with Jesus than what was implied by the mere crucifixion, would also appear probable to our Evangelist from another point of view. John, as the author of the Revelation, had said (i. 7), that when Christ comes hereafter with the clouds, every eye shall see him, even those who have pierced him, and all kindreds of the earth shall wail because of him. Here the passage in Zechariah (xii. 10) is applied to Jesus and his crucifixion. In this passage in the Prophet, indeed, he that was pierced was Jehovah, consequently the stabbing or piercing was understood merely figuratively, of mental mortification; but the Apocalyptic writer elsewhere also transfers names and attributes of Jehovah to Christ, and what was here said of Jehovah appeared to be much more applicable to the suffering Messiah. The piercing, accordingly, referred by the author of the Revelation to Jesus, there being no hint of a stab in the side in his work any more than in the Synoptics, was understood by that writer of the piercing of his hands, and perhaps also of his feet, with nails at the crucifixion. But not only the Hebrew word in Zechariah, but also the Greek word used in the Revelation, might seem to imply more than this. In fact, it generally meant piercing with a sword or a spear. If such a word was used in the prophecy, another reader, who took prophecies literally (and that the author of the fourth Gospel did so, we know from the account of the division of the clothes), might suppose that according to this Jesus might have been pierced not merely with nails in the extremities, but that his body also must have been pierced with a spear or a sword. Supposing him, then, to have been thus further pierced, this must have been done when he was already dead, and then, it was supposed, the only object could have been to make his death at all events certain.

But were such special arrangements necessary for this purpose? Why was Jesus not left with his two fellow-criminals simply to hang upon the cross till all were dead? According to the Synoptics, this *was* the case with Jesus; and he could, accordingly, be at once taken down: whether the two criminals also were dead when they were examined and taken down likewise, is not said, inasmuch as it had nothing to do with the point in question. According to Mark, death took place remarkably early in the case of Jesus; it was not very probable that it was so with the two others. Consequently the fourth Evangelist represents them expressly as still living. But why were not they at all events simply left hanging longer on the cross, till the next day, or even the day after? This was against the law of Moses, which ordained that bodies of persons crucified should be taken down before sunset (5 Mos. xxi. 23; comp. Josh. x. 27), and we may assume that this ordinance was respected in time of peace even by the Romans. Add to this, on the present occasion, that the following day was the Sabbath, and moreover, according to the Johannine reckoning, a particularly solemn Sabbath, that is the first, not (as in the Synoptics) the second, day of the

Passover. Now if the two criminals were still alive towards evening, an opportunity was given for hastening their death by the application of some special process. If a fatal stab with a spear was selected for this purpose, and the measure extended for the sake of certainty to Jesus, who was already in appearance dead, then there resulted on the one hand the wound prophesied by Zechariah, and on the other all the certainty that could be desired that, if Jesus was not already dead, this wound had killed him outright.

But with the body of Jesus not merely, as it was supposed, must something have been done, but also something have been omitted, namely, the breaking of the legs. He was not only he whom they pierced, but also the Lamb of God, especially the Paschal Lamb sacrificed in his death, and of this Lamb it was said in the law, "Not a bone of him shall be broken" (2 Mos. xii. 46). This, indeed, according to the Synoptics also, was not done to Jesus; but why was it then so expressly said that it was not to be done to the Paschal Lamb, and consequently also not to Jesus, if it might not have been very easily done to him, and was only not really done in consequence of a particular arrangement? Such a danger threatened him when the bones of his fellow-sufferers were broken; and as they were still alive, and it was necessary to do something with them in order to render possible the taking down of the bodies before evening, this might properly have been the breaking of their legs with clubs, not indeed in immediate connection with the crucifixion, but because it was customary among the Romans as a punishment for slaves, and was followed by death from mortification, if not immediately, at all events with certainty. The Evangelist rests the fact of Jesus being spared this process upon the ground that the soldiers commissioned to perform it found the victim, who was on the cross and who had died in consequence of the crucifixion, already dead. If indeed their eyesight did not satisfy them, and if they considered

Jesus to be like the two others, at all events probably still alive, it is not clear why they did not, as they were now on the spot, extend the breaking of the legs to him as well. Meanwhile, as they certainly found him in a different condition from the others, and the breaking of the legs was not completed with a single blow, like the stabbing with the spear, a tolerable reason was thus found for a change of proceeding, and at the same time what was dogmatically desirable, namely, the spear-stab instead of the leg-breaking, was also historically introduced.

Now, therefore, one of the soldiers pierced Jesus in the side as he hung there apparently dead, and what was the result? There came out blood and water. That, indeed, as every expert will tell us, can in no case have come out; for if the blood was still flowing in the body of Jesus, either from death not having yet taken place, or only a short time before, nothing but blood would have come; if it had ceased flowing, nothing whatever would have come; and even the water from the pericardium, supposing this to have been touched by the spear, and its fluid had not, as might have been expected, exuded into the cavity of the chest, it must in the first case have mixed undistinguishably with the blood, and, in the other, have appeared without any blood at all. But the Evangelist assures us that he himself saw the blood and water gush out (ver. 35). He does not, indeed, say so directly, but only that he who saw it bare record, and that his record is true, and he knoweth that he saith true. By this HE, the Evangelist understands the beloved disciple, the only one of all of them whom he places at the foot of the cross; this disciple, as the author of the Revelation, had testified (i. 7) that Jesus was pierced; and as he, according to his own declaration (Rev. i. 2), had only testified what he had seen (by which the author indeed meant his own prophetic visions), the Evangelist concluded that he must also himself have seen the wound with the spear and its consequences. Now the

Evangelist, as has been explained above,* considered himself as spiritually identical with the beloved disciple and author of the Revelation; what the latter had seen with the eyes of the body, *he* had seen with the eyes of the spirit; or rather, what he himself thought he knew in the spirit, he assumed the Apostle must have seen in the body.† "They shall look upon him whom they pierced," said the prophecy, and the prophecy must have been fulfilled. Him whom they have pierced they shall behold, *i.e.* they shall see that he was not a mere man, but the incarnate Word; and they shall see it plainly by the result of the spear-wound, by that which will gush out from that wound. Had only blood flowed out, then he that was pierced would have appeared to be only a mere man; something must have flowed out at the same time; and what else can this have been but that which the death of Jesus was to bring to his followers, namely, the Spirit under a visible sign? But the visible sign of the Spirit is water. Man must be born of water and the Spirit, if he is to come into the kingdom of God (John iii. 5); Jesus had given an assurance that if a man believed in him, streams of living water should flow out of his body, and, according to the explanation of the Evangelist, he had said this of the Holy Spirit, which those who believed in him should receive, but not until he had himself been glorified (vii. 38 ff.). It was, therefore, the pouring out of the Spirit, the communication of the new religious life, of which the death of Jesus was the condition, that the Evangelist spiritually beheld in the blood and water that gushed out of the wound in the side of Jesus. Whether he looked upon the gushing out of water and blood as at the same time a proof of death, or the spear-wound of itself appeared to him sufficiently so, in either case this side of the question was subordinate to its symbolical significancy. And accustomed as

* Vol. I. pp. 144, 149 ff.
† Compare, for what follows, Baur, Critical Investigations, p. 215 ff.

he is to see one thing in another, the idea in different reflexes, it is very possible that in speaking of the water and the blood he, like the author of the first Epistle of John (v. 6) and the ancient Apollinaris, was thinking also of the two Christian mysteries, Baptism and the last Supper; and again, in the case of the latter, of what was common in his time, the mixing of the sacramental wine with water.

If there is any passage in which the peculiarity of the fourth Evangelist shews itself to the utmost, it is this. It is impossible not to see his eagerness for the inward and the spiritual, but this goes hand in hand with a propensity for what is most objective, most material in form: his profundity excites our admiration, but his language is sometimes that of fond conceit. When the three first Evangelists, at the death of the Messiah, represent the sun as being darkened, the graves as opening, the curtain in the Temple as being rent, we see in all this fables indeed, but still such as claim our attention, and place us in the state of mind in which they originated; but when, on the other hand, the fourth Evangelist considers all this as not worth telling in comparison with what he imagines, that blood and water flowed out of the wound in the side of Christ—when this is his first and principal thought at the death of Jesus, when he sees in it the most profound mystery of Christianity, in corroboration of which he appeals to Moses and the Prophets, to eye-testimony and the truth of this eye-witness—we have so little sympathy with such a mode of viewing things, it seems to us so extravagant, that we have a difficulty in even comprehending it.

The Johannine narrative of the spear-wound which was inflicted on Jesus on the cross, betrays itself also to be an unhistorical interpolation by the fact that in the synoptic Gospels it is, in the first place, not implied, and in the second, to a certain extent, absolutely excluded. In none of them does Jesus, after his resurrection, as he does in the fourth

Gospel, shew the wound in his side to the disciples. But we cannot rest much upon this, because it is only in Luke that the shewing of the hands and the feet—and that without any definite reference to the marks of the wounds—is spoken of. But it is clear that in Mark the description of the course of events after the decease of Jesus implies that the body of Jesus continued hanging quietly on the cross until in the evening it was given up to Joseph in compliance with his prayer. Here it might occur to any one that omission is not exclusion. But the case is represented differently in Luke and Mark. According to John, Pilate, at the request of the Jews, had given orders to break the bones of the crucified men, and to take them down. If, therefore, Joseph came afterwards, he must have found the body of Jesus taken down already. According to Luke (ver. 53) and Mark (ver. 46), on the other hand, Joseph himself took the body down from the cross. It is clear, therefore, that these Evangelists do not assume any order to have been given by Pilate, or any taking down from the cross by the soldiers. But that Pilate, as Mark tells us, when Joseph made his request to him, should have expressed surprise at the death of Jesus having occurred so soon, and have seen in this circumstance a ground for hesitating to grant his request immediately, would be perfectly impossible if he had already given orders for the breaking of the bones with a view to the taking down from the cross.

But what is most extraordinary is, that the fourth Evangelist's own narrative does, one might say, exclude the account of the breaking of the bones.* He himself, after having mentioned it, continues as if he had not mentioned it. That is, he continues, as the Synoptics continue, immediately after the account of the death of Jesus: that then Joseph of Ari-

* De Wette draws attention to this in his Manual of Exegesis, in speaking of the passage (fourth edition), p. 282 ff. It is only from partiality for John that De Wette satisfies himself with the explanation that the ἄρῃ and ἦρε, ver. 38, mean simply the carrying away of the body, having meant, in ver. 31, the taking down from the cross.

mathea begged Pilate to be allowed to take down the body of Jesus, that Pilate granted his request, and that Joseph took the body. Consequently he speaks as if Pilate had not already ordered the taking down of the bodies of the crucified men; he falls into this difficulty because, after making his interpolation, he again adheres to the synoptic narrative, but by falling into it he shews that this portion of his history is nothing but his own interpolation.

96. Burial of Jesus.

It was naturally of great importance to the earliest Christian consciousness that the honour of burial should have been paid to the body of Jesus. Even Paul mentions it as a tradition that Jesus was buried (1 Cor. xv. 4); but in saying this he only wishes, as a preparation for what is said immediately afterwards of his resurrection, to establish that the body of Jesus went under the earth. In itself this might have been done only in the manner which was usual among the Jews in the case of persons executed, by his being taken down from the cross, and covered over with soil in the burial-place of other criminals. The Romans, however, as was remarked above, if the relatives announced themselves as coming to apply for the body of a person who had been executed, were accustomed to give it up to them for burial. And according to the Evangelists, such a person did really announce himself to Pilate in a rich man of Arimathea, by name Joseph, who belonged to Jesus as a disciple (Matt. xxvii. 57 ff.; Mark xv. 42 ff.; Luke xxiii. 50 ff.; John xix. 38 ff.

A rich man—these are the first words of the most ancient reporter, Matthew; he only adds incidentally that the rich man was also a disciple of Jesus. Luke and Mark forget the rich man in the honourable councillor, and whatever else they make of Joseph; while John seizes on the discipleship, and, in his favourite style, makes it a secret one, from fear of the Jews. But in other cases, wealth, in a good sense, is not of so much importance to the Evangelists: why does the first reporter so industriously put it forward here? The rich man had a tomb which he had had hewn for himself in the rock, and in which he now laid the dead Messiah. But it was in his death that the Messiah was brought into connection with the rich in Isaiah. With the rich, indeed, in a bad sense, as it would appear when it is said (liii. 9), "He made his grave indeed with the wicked, and with the rich in his death;" in which words, the rich being taken as synonymous with the wicked, a prophecy of a dishonourable burial might be proved. But the association with the wicked, the being numbered with the transgressors, was considered to have been already fulfilled in Jesus by his apprehension and crucifixion (Luke xxiii. 37; Mark xv. 28): thus the rich remained for his burial, he must have been laid in the tomb of a rich man, and this rich man not a godless, but a God-fearing man, who, believing in the Messiah, gave up his tomb to the murdered Christ.

The tomb of the rich man must have corresponded to his wealth on the one hand, to its lofty purpose on the other. A man in high position is addressed thus in Isaiah (xxii. 16):*
"What hast thou here, and whom hast thou here, that thou hast hewed thee out a sepulchre here, as he that heweth him out a sepulchre on high, and that graveth an habitation for himself in a rock?" This, indeed, was said rebukingly to a proud-minded man; but of the righteous man also it was said in the same Isaiah (xxxiii. 16), that he shall dwell on high in munitions of rocks, or, according to the Greek translation, in caves of rocks; then, consequently, even a God-fearing rich man might have hewn for himself a tomb in a rock, and the question as to whom he has here that

* Reference is made to this passage by Volkmar, Religion of Jesus, p. 257.

he does this, might be answered by a reference to the body of the Messiah, for whom he was there preparing a resting-place. But in order to correspond to its lofty purpose, the tomb must be a new one, not as yet polluted by any corpse, as it was not considered right that any man should have previously ridden on the ass which the Messiah used on his entrance into the capital. In the two other Synoptics, both the "wealth" of the man, mentioned in the passage in the prophet, as well as his relation with regard to the tomb, namely, that he himself had had it hewn for him in the rock, is omitted; still their meaning undoubtedly is that it was his property; and in John the connection is completely broken, and the new tomb in which Jesus is to be laid is selected, not because it belonged to Joseph, but because it was near to the place of execution, and a burying-place close at hand was desirable on account of the near approach of the festal Sabbath. Thus this feature serves the purpose of the fourth Evangelist, enabling him, as it does, to make still more palpable the pressure of time on that evening of the burial, which furnishes him with a reason for what is so important to him, the breaking of the bones in reference to the wound with the spear.

According to the three first Evangelists, after Joseph had taken the body of Jesus down from the cross, and before he laid it in the tomb in the rock, he rolled it in a linen cloth. Matthew adds that the linen cloth was clean, meaning probably that it had not been used before. In Matthew's account this is all; he knows nothing of anything further being done or intended to be done. No embalming was, to his mind, required, because a few days before, at the supper at Bethany, Jesus had been embalmed by the woman with the costly spikenard, with a view, according to Jesus' own explanation, to his burial. This account is likewise in Mark and John; Luke, as we have seen, gives it in a very different form, and so entirely without reference, either of time or otherwise, to the passion and death of Jesus, that he might at first feel sensibly the want of embalming on the occasion of the burial of Jesus. But as the more ancient tradition, as it is found in Matthew, contained nothing of the kind, Luke also represents it, not as having been really done, but only prepared, on the Friday evening by the women. They, he says, buy the necessary spices, but defer the embalming itself until after the Sabbath, that is, until the Sunday morning (Luke xxiii. 56, xxiv. 1). Though Mark, like Matthew, has the preliminary anointing shortly before the Passion, still that which was subsequently intended, as he found it in Luke, is welcome to him, only he thinks it more simple to defer the purchase of the spices until after the Sabbath has elapsed; as this ended before six o'clock on the Saturday evening, the women did not consider it necessary to trouble themselves with the purchase so soon as the Friday evening before six o'clock, especially as time pressed, but it was time enough to do this on Saturday, and so to proceed with the embalming early on the following morning (xvi. 1). But as, when the women came to the grave on Sunday morning, Jesus had already risen, the materials for embalming the body were no longer of any use; but as in Matthew, so also in Mark and Luke, it ended in his not participating in this honour. This was considered by the fourth Evangelist as intolerable; he therefore changes the mere intention to embalm, spoken of by his two predecessors, into one actually performed, and represents the body of Jesus as being wrapped, not merely in a linen cloth, like Matthew, but in linen clothes with the spices (xix. 40). But to his mind the women were physically unable to convey these spices. How could they carry the hundred-weight of myrrh and aloes which the Evangelist considered necessary for the embalming of the Son of God? For this purpose a man was required, who was also at hand in Joseph, or at all events in his servants. But Joseph had already performed his part in begging for, and taking down from the cross, the body of Jesus, and the fourth Evangelist had still another personage in reserve, of whom Joseph reminded him, likewise an eminent, though secret, disciple of the Lord, Nicodemus. It appeared to the writer to be quite appropriate to represent, as coming forward here for the third and last time, this man who had already twice appeared in his narrative in important situations.

All the Evangelists agree in stating that the sepulchre in the rock, in which the body of Jesus was laid, was closed with a stone rolled to the entrance. According to Matthew, it was a large stone; in Mark, the women going out take counsel as to who will roll away the stone for them from the mouth of the sepulchre; consequently they assume it as a difficult thing to do. While, however, the other Evangelists are satisfied with this closure, Matthew represents the stone as being in addition sealed by the High-priests, and the sepulchre as being guarded by a watch stationed there by Pilate at their request (xxvii. 62—66).

For when, in the earliest times of Christendom, the preaching about the resurrection of Jesus had taken the form that his sepulchre was found empty on the second morning after his burial, it was met by the unbelieving Jews with the allegation that it was found in this condition, not because its inmate had come out of it restored to life, but because his corpse had been stolen out of it by his disciples. This Jewish legend in opposition to the Christian, gave rise to a second Christian legend in opposition to the Jewish. If the Christian solution was to satisfy the problem, it must, on the one hand, make the stealing of the body impossible, and on the other, account for the denial of the resurrection on the part of the Jews. The stealing away of the body was impossible if the sepulchre was watched. Consequently the High-priests and Pharisees must go to the Roman Procurator and beg him to secure the sepulchre. But what in the world could move them to make such a request? What could the sepulchre signify to them, so long as they knew that he who had been laid in it was dead? They remember, they say, that that crucified deceiver did in his lifetime predict his resurrection after three days; they do not believe in a fulfilment of this prediction, but they are afraid lest his disciples should steal the body, and in connection with the prophecy give out that he has arisen. So the High-priests must have remembered speeches of Jesus of which his disciples, at the time of his death, can have known nothing whatever (else how could they have been so despairing?); they must have foreseen the rising up of the faith in the resurrection of Jesus, which is absolutely inconceivable: the Christian legend attributed to them the Christian belief of later times, only in the form of unbelief.

Pilate immediately grants them the watch, and orders them in addition to guard the grave as well as they can. He is right in doing so; a watch may be bribed, hocussed, and what they ought to protect be carried off. So they seal the stone that closes the mouth of the sepulchre, as formerly Darius had sealed the stone at the mouth of the lions' den, into which he caused Daniel to be thrown to prove whether his God would save him from the lions (Dan. vi. 18). Were they not, then, antitypes of Christ in the sepulchre—on the one hand, Jonas in the belly of the whale; on the other, Daniel in the lions' den?

Thus did the Christian legend establish the impossibility of the stealing of the body, alleged against the Christians by that of the Jews; but, under the circumstances, how could this Jewish legend originate? It was a matter of course for the Christian legend to assert that when the resurrection of Jesus occurred, an angel descended from heaven, and, shining like lightning, rolled away the stone from the sepulchre with a violent earthquake, that seals and watches availed nothing, and that the latter in particular fell down like dead men (Matt. xxviii. 4). And according to that legend, the watch reported the fact truly to the High-priests (ver. 11). The real High-priests and Elders would have considered such a report to be false, and have insisted upon an investigation, which must have elucidated the truth that the watchmen had slept, or had allowed themselves to be bribed, and the body to be stolen. The High-priests and Elders of the Christian legend, on the contrary, look upon the report of the miraculous resurrection of Jesus as true, and give them money to declare that to be false which the real dignitaries must have considered the truth, which the watchmen had motives for concealing, and they for elucidating by an investigation. The fact is, therefore, as stated above; the Christian legend attributes to the Jewish authorities the Christian belief, leaving them at the same time, as enemies of Christ, their unbelief; *i.e.* they believe in silence that Jesus returned miraculously to life, but still they would not recognise him as the Messiah, but persevere in their opposition to his cause. Thus the origin of the Jewish legend was indeed explained, but awkwardly enough, and only for the Christians, who, starting from the same assumptions, did not notice the contradictions involved in the attempt at explanation.

But the legend is, undoubtedly, very old, and the fact that Matthew alone has it, does not prove that he is more fabulous or later than the others, but, on the contrary, that he lived nearer to the country and to the period of the origin of this legend, which for his successors, writing later, and not in Palestine, had no longer the same interest. Still, as it had already existed, they might perhaps have adopted it, had it not stood in the way of another circumstance which was more important to them. This circumstance was the intention of the women to embalm the body of Jesus after the Sabbath had elapsed. If the sepulchre was sealed by authority and watched by Roman soldiers, and the women knew of it, as all Jerusalem, especially all the nearest connections of Jesus must have known of a measure so remarkable and so publicly taken, they could not hope to get there with their spices; but as they must have hoped to do this, in order to be able seriously to undertake the anointing, that obstacle must not stand in their way. If for these reasons the two middle Evangelists omitted the episode of the watching and sealing of the tomb of Jesus, still with the fourth Evangelist it did not stand in the way of the embalming, which they had undertaken on the Friday evening, but, together with the motives for it, the legend was too far removed from the whole point of view of that Evangelist for him to adopt it again.

FIFTH GROUP OF MYTHS.

RESURRECTION AND ASCENSION OF JESUS.

97. HISTORY OF THE RESURRECTION.

We have already in the first Book been obliged to treat at length of the Resurrection of Jesus, in consideration of its historical importance, as without faith in it a Christian Church could scarcely have been formed. We endeavoured to answer the question as to the reality that lies at the bottom of the tradition, *i.e.* how the belief in the fact can have arisen among the disciples of Jesus. We did this partly by following the indications of the New Testament writings, partly by examining the analogy presented by similar phenomena in the mental life of men. In doing this we have already discussed many individual points in the Evangelical accounts, as well as the summary statements of the Apostle Paul; it only remains to realise the gradual growth of the myth under this head, *i.e.* to shew how the accounts of the appearances of the risen Jesus form a series which is continually progressing from the visionary to the palpable, from the subjective to the objective. For this purpose we must take one by one the narrative portions into which the Evangelists divide the history of the Resurrection. In doing this, we will begin with the journey to the grave on Sunday morning, though this narrative (Matt. xxviii. 1—10; Mark xvi. 1—11; Luke xxiv. 1—12; John xx. 1—18) cannot have been formed until after single appearances of the resuscitated Jesus had been described, and it is for these also that we would now find a starting-point.

According to Matthew, then, that journey to the sepulchre is performed by the two Marys, her of Magdala and the other who is described by Mark as the mother of James and Joses. Matthew describes, not merely, as the other Evangelists do, what happened to the women at the sepulchre, but he also informs us of what had taken place before they came there; how, that is to say, an angel, shining like lightning, had descended from heaven, rolled the stone from the sepulchre, and how the terror of the guards laid them for dead upon the ground. It is this very point, that of the watch, of whom Matthew alone makes mention, which supplies the motive for his thus depicturing the action of the angel: he wished to shew how the watchmen were set aside; the other Evangelists had no occasion to do this, as they omit the watch altogether. When the women came to the grave, they see the angel sitting upon the stone that had been rolled away; this angel gives them the account of the resurrection of Jesus; shews them the now empty place where he had lain, directs them to communicate this message to the disciples, with the intimation that they are to go to Galilee, where they will see him. Then, Jesus himself having met them on the way back to the city, and repeated this commission, they (as must be supplied from what precedes and follows) execute their commission, and the Eleven, though all doubt in their minds is not satisfied, enter upon their journey to Galilee.

In Luke, apart from some unimportant variations, as for instance two angels within the sepulchre instead of one outside, the chief discrepancy between his description and that of Matthew lies in this, that the disciples have not to be sent to Galilee, because Luke places the appearance of Jesus, when risen, altogether in Jerusalem and the neighbourhood. But in order not entirely to omit the mention of Galilee from the well-known words of the angel, the women are reminded how Jesus, "while still in Galilee," prophesied to them his death and his resurrection. But Luke abstains from adopting out of Matthew the premature appearance of Jesus himself to the women on their return home; he had to avoid the instructions to them to go to Galilee, and at the same time he wished to give the factors in a more simple form, how that the risen Jesus is first announced by the angels to the women, by them to the disciples, and then, and not before, comes upon the scene in his own person. Hence it is that, on the women communicating to the disciples the message of the angels, he lays so much stress upon the unbelief of the former, an unbelief which is not to be removed until the appearance of Jesus himself and the infallible proofs given by him of his actual resurrection. In Luke, the message of the women cannot have put the disciples in motion to go to Galilee, as it contains no instruction to that effect; instead of this, it moves Peter to go in a different direction, that is, to the sepulchre, the emptiness of which, and of the linen clothes lying in it, it was desirable to represent as being attested by a man: meanwhile it was not necessary that anything beyond surprise should result from Peter's seeing these things, as the disciples are not to attain to belief in the resurrection of Jesus until they have had satisfactory proof of it.

Mark, in his account, follows Matthew throughout in all essential points. He represents the news of the resurrection of Jesus, together with the instructions to the disciples to go to Galilee, as being communicated by an angel to the women. On the other hand, we not only miss in his account the meeting with Jesus himself, but the women fail to follow the direction of the angel, as, from fear (it is not exactly evident of whom or of what), they do not venture to say anything to any one of the appearance which they have seen. And when Mark at this point (ver. 9), as if neither the resurrection of Jesus nor any information about it had been given to the Magdalene with the other women, all at once goes on to say, that when Jesus was risen early the first day of the week, he appeared first to Mary Magdalene—this mode of beginning over again in the middle of the narrative is certainly strange enough to lead us to give all attention to the circumstance that the concluding section of Mark (xvi. 9—20) is wanting in two of the best MSS. of the Gospels, and was, according to statements of great antiquity, wanting in several others which are no longer extant. Only it cannot but strike us as extraordinary that these MSS. contain the eighth verse, in which the inconsistency of the account with itself begins.* In ver. 7, the angel, as in Matthew, gives to the women a message to be taken to the disciples. And the meaning must originally have been, that, as in Matthew, the women imparted this message with joy. But, if they had given it, the disciples would certainly, as in Matthew, have gone to Galilee, and this, in Mark, they are not supposed to have done, as he, with Luke, represents the appearance of the risen Jesus as taking place, not in Galilee, but in Jerusalem and the neighbourhood. It is, therefore, the sudden veering of the Evangelist from Matthew to Luke which so strangely closes the lips of the women in ver. 8; and now, as we shall see more in detail, all that follows from ver. 10, being taken from Luke, is in part abridged, in part expanded; only the ninth verse, together with the appearing of Jesus to Mary Magda-

* Volkmar, Religion of Jesus, pp. 100 ff., 104.

lene, seems rather to be taken from John (xx. 11—18). This, if our results so far with regard to the dates of the two Evangelists are correct, would be in favour of the assumption that in the concluding section of Mark we have a later and unauthentic addition. But at all events the notice of the devils that had been driven out of Mary comes, not from John, but from Luke (viii. 2); as also the statement that the disciples did not believe the account of the Magdalene, for John says nothing of it, but Luke does say (xxiv. 11), that when the women told the disciples of the appearance of the angels, they looked upon the account as idle tales, and did not believe it. Thus, after all, the appearance itself might be taken out of Matthew, who also represents Magdalene with the other Mary as having the first appearance of Jesus on their return from the grave after the appearance of the angel; only that Mark, perhaps from another source, from the use of which possibly the abrupt re-commencement may be explained, limited the appearance to Magdalene alone.

From these accounts before him, the fourth Evangelist cautiously selected and sagaciously carried on what was available for his own point of view. Luke had distinguished with great accuracy the separate factors of the publication of the circumstances of the resurrection; John goes still further in doing so. In Matthew, the women see, on first approaching the sepulchre, the angel sitting outside on the stone that has been rolled away (in Mark they find him after entering the open sepulchre); Luke represents them, after entering the sepulchre, as first missing the body of Jesus, and then says that immediately after the two angels stood by them and explained all to them. John distinguishes still more accurately between these two factors. Mary Magdalene, whom he represents as coming forward alone at this juncture, as Mark does in the second section of his narrative, must be kept for a time to the negative proposition that the body of Jesus is no longer there; she has to go into the city with this intelligence to Peter, whose journey to the sepulchre, with its result, which is likewise little more than negative (mere wonder), seemed to have a more suitable connection with this, than, as in Luke, with the account of the angel's message already received. But John represents Peter, not, as Luke does, as going alone to the sepulchre, as little as he had represented him on an earlier occasion as going alone into the palace of the High-priest. On both occasions he associates with him the "other disciple," and this other disciple is no other than, professedly, himself. Moreover, two disciples, going in conjunction, had been already suggested to the fourth Evangelist by the third. Immediately after the journey of Peter to the sepulchre, occasioned by the message of the women, Luke tells of the journey undertaken the same day by two disciples, one being named Cleophas, whom Jesus joined, not being at first recognised (xxiv. 13—35); a non-recognition which Mark, who likewise mentions the circumstance, though only summarily, explains by a change in the figure of Jesus (xvi. 12). This feature, as well as the further one that Jesus censures their want of understanding in not having gained out of Moses and the Prophets the notion of the suffering Messiah, we shall subsequently find applied in his own way by the fourth Evangelist.

So Peter and the other disciple go together to the sepulchre, and the mode in which each of them has his part weighed out to him, apparently equally, in which every pound put into the scale of the one is immediately balanced by another put into the scale of the other, and at last an overweight brought out in favour of one, that is, the favourite disciple—the description of all this is, as has been already pointed out, one of the most manifest proofs of the artful calculation with which the Evangelist set to work in the composition of his Gospel. Both disciples ran together, and are, therefore, equalised at first. But the other disciple runs fastest and comes to the grave before Peter—consequently gets an advantage over him. But, like Peter in Luke, here the other disciple stoops to look into the sepulchre only from the outside, and sees the linen clothes lying without going in; so the latter is immediately done by Peter, who comes after, and who in Luke does not do it. He looks more accurately, and observes the linen clothes indeed lying in one place, but the napkin with which the head of Jesus had been covered not lying with them, but wrapped together in a place by itself: now, therefore, Peter has an advantage over the other. Upon this the other disciple also goes into the sepulchre—but what good now does Peter's earlier entrance do him, what good all the external observation which he had made at the moment, if they did not help him to that which he who arrived at the sepulchre first, but only entered it last, now attained, namely, to see and to BELIEVE? Faith brought about by sight is not, indeed, faith in the highest sense; but the disciples could not have this yet, for, as the Evangelists remark, they, like the travellers to Emmaus in Luke, were still without the understanding of the Scripture, *i.e.* the knowledge that in it the death and the resurrection of Christ were predicted as something necessary. This true faith could only be given to the disciples by the imparting of the Spirit, which had not yet taken place; but the other disciple attained to such faith as was then alone possible, and thus was established afresh his precedence over the chief of the Apostles, *i.e.* of the spiritual and Johannine over the carnal, Petrine, Christianity.

It was the observation of the Magdalene which the fourth Evangelist divides into its two component parts, keeping first to the negative, the not finding of the body of Jesus, and sending her with this result to the two disciples, that had occasioned their journey to the sepulchre. Now he represents the Magdalene also as appearing again at the sepulchre, and bringing up the other and positive part of her observation. As in Luke, Peter, and in John at first the other disciple, she only stoops into the sepulchre, without, like the women in Luke, going in; but, like them, she also sees now, not one, but two angels, and, moreover, at the head and foot of the place where the body of Jesus had lain. The address of the angels to the women in Luke, introduced by a question, is expanded by the fourth Evangelist into a question by the angel and an answer by Mary, and now he seizes upon Matthew and Mark in order to represent an appearance of Christ as being granted to her after that of the angels. But like the two travellers in Luke and Mark, so neither does she at first recognise the Lord, but, the sepulchre being situated in the garden, thinks at first that he is the gardener, though soon, being more spiritually-minded than they, she recognises him, not by the outward act of breaking bread, but by his addressing her as "Mary," consequently by his word of mouth. Hereupon we are most expressly reminded of Matthew by the caution given by Jesus to Magdalene, "Touch me not;" this command being unintelligible unless we remember in the first instance what Matthew tells of the women; that on being met by Jesus on the way back, they fell down before him and seized his feet. Here, in Matthew, Jesus forbade them to fear, and sent them to his brethren with the instruction to go to Galilee, where they were to see him. In John, like the angel in the Apocalypse (xxii. 8 ff.), he commands Mary not to offer him, as yet, the divine worship implied by falling at his feet, as he has not yet ascended to his Father, to whom, however, he will ascend immediately.*

---

* The fact of his exaltation not being yet complete, appears to me a sufficient ground for Jesus not yet accepting divine honours; that he had risen merely as a man, and that, as Hilgenfeld assumes, the Logos did not unite with him again until after his ascension to the Father, I am as unable to reconcile with the Johannine conception of Christ, as, above (§ 77), Hilgenfeld's explanation of ἐνεβριμήσατο τῷ πνεύματι.

Upon receiving from the two Marys the report of the appearance of the angel and of Christ, the Eleven in Matthew start upon their journey to Galilee, and repair to the hill which Jesus had appointed, and where he immediately appears to them (xxviii. 16—20). This, in Matthew, with the exception of the preliminary meeting with the women, is the only appearance of the risen Jesus. It cannot, indeed, be assumed that he may not also have heard or read of many others; but as in the case of the speeches of Christ he combined into a great mass what had been said on various occasions, so also now he combines the essential substance of several visions in one grand appearance before the assembled Eleven. As in these appearances the main point is to convince them of the reality of the resurrection of Jesus, they generally begin with doubts. Thus, in this instance, some of them doubt; but Jesus approaches nearer to them, announces himself to them as him to whom all power is given in heaven and on earth, and communicates to them his last injunctions and promises. How and by what means he satisfies their doubts is not said.

Here there was a place left vacant for later hands to fill up the evangelical history. Luke had represented Peter, on the receipt of the report of the women, as going to the sepulchre and returning home surprised: with this statement he interweaves the narrative of the travellers to Emmaus: when these last, having returned to Jerusalem, go in to the disciples, they receive intelligence of an appearance of the risen Jesus seen by Simon, of which there is no definite information given, but which reminds us of the statement of the Apostle Paul, 1 Cor. xv.;* and as the travellers were giving an account of what they had seen and heard to the assembled disciples, Jesus stood in the midst and saluted them. The first impression was terror, as they thought they saw a spirit; whereupon,

---

* Of the appearance to James, also mentioned by Paul (ver. 7), there is an apocryphal trace in a passage of the Gospel of the Hebrews: see above, p. 402.

HISTORY OF THE RESURRECTION. 411

to prove that it was he himself and not merely a spirit without flesh and blood, Jesus offered to allow them to touch his hands and his feet; and as even then there was a remnant of unbelief, though only in the form of joyful surprise, he asked for something to eat, and consumed before their eyes a piece of broiled fish and honey-comb (xxiv. 38—43), having, as it seems, on the occasion of the appearance at Emmaus, vanished in the very act of breaking the bread before he had himself partaken of it.

Mark appears to combine this narrative with that of the last appearance of Jesus, inasmuch as he represents him as shewing himself for the last time while the disciples are at table, without taking part in the meal himself (xvi. 14). But the fourth Evangelist touches up the account in his own way (xx. 19—29). First and foremost, as in the case of Mary Magdalene's journey to the sepulchre, he separates the factors. On the occasion of the appearance, as Luke describes it, belief and disbelief, terror and joy, are mixed up together. John, in the same way as he there makes two journeys of one, the first of which gives a negative result, and only the second a positive one, so here he makes of one appearance two, at the first of which he represents only joy and faith as coming to the surface, while he reserves the sediment of doubt for a particular second appearance in order to change it by a process all the more thorough into faith. And as in the former case, out of several women, he selected one Mary Magdalene, and made her, like another Mary of Bethany, the representative of the most heartfelt, most personal relation of faith and love to the Lord, so now he provides himself with a vessel for that doubt which Luke ascribed to the disciples without distinction, in the person of Thomas, who had already been brought into prominence by him in a similar manner.

It is not, however, merely in these main points that the Johannine narrative appears copied from that of Luke, but feature by feature the resemblance may be traced. Thus, in the latter, a supernatural entrance is indicated by the expression (ver. 36), "while they so spake, Jesus stood in the midst of them," as well as by the terror which the sudden sight of him occasioned. But in John this indication is strengthened by the feature of the doors having been shut, and a regular determination not to understand the Gospels correctly is required in order to agree with Schleiermacher in assuming a natural opening of the doors. The addition that it was from fear of the Jews that the disciples closed the doors of the room in which they met, is said indeed to be the immediate motive for this measure, and is consequently intended to make the statement as to the closed doors all the more credible; but at the same time it looks as if in this also the Evangelist had had in view the separation of two features that are united in Luke. In his account it is the appearance of Jesus which causes the disciples fear as well as joy; John refers their fear to the hostile Jews, in order to reserve only the joy for the appearance of Jesus. The expression, "Peace be with you!" which, in Luke, Jesus utters on entering, is in him nothing but the well-known Hebrew formula of salutation; but in the mode in which, in John, Jesus repeats the words, having before in his farewell speeches spoken to the disciples of the peace which he leaves to them, which they were to have in him (xiv. 27, xvi. 33), and in the mode in which he accompanies the words with breathing upon them and communicating the Holy Ghost, we see even this formula charged with the more profound and pregnant meaning of the fourth Gospel.

The risen Jesus comes through closed doors, but still he is not a spirit; he may be touched, but still has not a material body. We cannot, indeed, conceive such a combination, but the Evangelists could, and John as well as Luke has framed his description upon it. In Luke, however, Jesus offers to the disciples his hands and his feet: instead of this, in John it is his hands and his side. In Luke, nothing could be said of the latter, because he knows nothing of a wound in the side; and this time they are only shewn to them, not offered, as in Luke, to be touched, as John in this case also separates the factors that are combined in Luke, and reserves the stronger proof for the later appearance, which is intended to overcome doubt.

In order to supply a motive for this second appearance, it was necessary that at the time of the first, one of the Eleven should have been absent. This one was Thomas, who on former occasions (xi. 16, xiv. 5) is described as a person slow of apprehension. It was necessary that he should not have been satisfied with the report of his colleagues, and have made it a condition of his belief in the resurrection of Jesus that he should himself see him and feel the marks of his wounds. Luke speaks only indefinitely of the hands and feet as having been shewn to the disciples by Jesus in order to convince them of his corporeality; it may, indeed, be supposed, but it is not said, that the marks of the wounds were also to be taken into consideration: in John, the marks of the wounds were prominently brought forward, flesh and bones not being mentioned; perhaps to the mind of this Evangelist the mention of them might seem too material, and he imagined a body which still preserved the visible traces of wounds received as honourable scars, and could even be touched, but without having regular flesh and bones—a conception which we, indeed, cannot now realise, but may attribute all the more confidently to the author of the fourth Gospel. So, eight days after the first appearance, Thomas finds his condition fulfilled; the disciples are assembled a second time, and now Thomas is with them; again the doors are shut, Jesus passes without hindrance through them, stands with the salutation of peace in the midst of them, and now calls upon Thomas to apply the required test. He does so, and immediately, being fully convinced, he worships Jesus as his Lord and his God;

but is compelled to hear from him who had immediately before called upon him to be not unbelieving but faithful, the censorious words: "Because thou hast seen me, thou hast believed; blessed are they that have not seen, and yet have believed."

On these words, which close the historical narrative of the fourth Gospel, for what follows is only a concluding formula, the whole of the two-sided character, the whole of the sensuous supersensuousness of that Gospel, is distinctly stamped. That is declared to be true faith which requires no sensuous proof—as before no signs and miracles, so here no sight or touch; but why then is it that precisely in this Gospel far more stress is laid than in any other on such sensuous proof? why is it that here the proofs of the resurrection, as before the miraculous narratives, are exaggerated? If proofs of this kind have no value, why is a description of them given? And if they are only valuable for unbelief, in order to change it to belief, why are they told by the Evangelist, whose belief is so profound, with a sympathy which proves that even to him they were valuable? He, indeed, who lived some time after, and who was no more present than Thomas, when on the evening of the day of the resurrection Jesus came in to the assembled disciples, might also, like Thomas, have once doubted, and in order to be able to believe, have wished to have, as he had, sensible proof. If so, then he had renounced the wish for what was impossible, had got faith without sight; and he must have supposed that others instead of him, that the disciples who lived with Jesus had been able to obtain these sufficient proofs, that a John had seen blood and water flowing out of the side of Jesus, that a Thomas had put his fingers into the marks of the nails, his hands into the wound in the side of Jesus. When, therefore, Baur limits the meaning of this scene with Thomas to this, that all this seeing and touching, this materiality and palpable corporeality, proves nothing in favour of the faith in the resurrection of Jesus, unless this faith is established in itself as something certain and necessary, that therefore material and empirical faith must* always have absolute faith as its foundation— this, apart from its far too philosophical formalization, is only as true as the opposite, that in the sense of the fourth Gospel pure spiritual faith has, as its assumed foundation, faith resting upon sensible proof, or that it was in the mind of the Evangelist one and the same act to believe without having seen signs himself, and to conceive these signs as having been seen by others.† The mode in which, from this point of view only, the origin of a work like the fourth Gospel is conceivable, scarcely requires especial notice.

The fourth Evangelist, having described at greater length the application of the test of sight and feeling, conceived that the necessity for the proof from eating of the reality of the resurrection of Jesus was superseded. Perhaps, too, it was not to his mind, as being, like the flesh and the bones, of too material a character. The author of the supplement repeats this proof, working it into that strange chain of narrative in which we have already found echoes of the narrative of the miracles of the draught of fishes and the feeding, the attempted walking on the sea and triple denial of Peter, of the rite of the last Supper, and the breaking of bread at Emmaus, as well as of the rivalry in believing between the two Apostles, Peter and John, at the sepulchre of Jesus. Early in the morning, Jesus asks the disciples who are engaged in fishing on the Sea of Galilee, whether they have any meat, and on their giving a negative answer, bestows upon them the rich draught of fishes; tells them, however, to breakfast off the broiled fish and bread which was already lying on the shore, and himself distributes both to them (xxi. 1—14). Thus in this place, as well as in the whole chapter, all the particulars are very

* Critical Investigations, p. 229.
† Such is also Hilgenfeld's opinion, Gospels, p. 321 ff., note.

ambiguous and obscure; but as the risen Jesus does not, as at Emmaus, vanish after the breaking of bread, but the meal proceeds in his presence, we may assume that he also partook of it himself.

If up to this point, together with the repetition and modification of one or two miraculous accounts and a proof of the resurrection, the object of the narrative was at the same time the further regulation of the relation between the Apostle Peter and the Apostle John, from this point (ver. 15—25) forward its purpose is that exclusively. In the first place, by the triple interrogatory of Jesus to Peter, whether he loves him (more than the other disciples do), and then, when the latter has thrice affirmed this, on the last occasion with some pain, by the thrice repeated command of Jesus to feed his sheep, the triple denial of Peter is partly censured, partly forgiven, and the Apostle is confirmed afresh in his office of chief shepherd; then, from the well-known event, the death on the cross already alluded to* in the Gospel (xiii. 36) is predicted; and finally, the circumstance which appeared to place John below him, that it was not granted to the beloved disciple to glorify God by a martyr's death, is turned to the advantage of the latter over Peter. Peter is to follow the Lord in the martyr's death, but of John the Lord had said, if he would that John should remain until his coming again, what did that concern any one else? It is possible that this legend arose in Asia Minor in consequence of the great age which the Apostle John reached, in the sense that he would live to see the second coming of Christ: on John's death,

---

* On the whole this scene with Peter (xxi. 15—19), is only a further description of the conversation between Jesus and Peter, xiii. 36—38. There, Jesus had spoken of his departure to a place whither his disciples could not follow him; then Peter asked whither he is going, and Jesus answered that whither he is going Peter could not follow him then, but he would follow him afterwards. There is no doubt that it is implied in these words that the Apostle is to suffer the same death as his Lord. Then follows the prediction of the denial, to which reference is made in c. xxi.

the prediction thus understood had become untrue—hence our author attempts to bring it back into its original form, in what sense is uncertain; whether, that is, he laid the stress on the word "If" (as merely conditional), or understood by the word "Coming," something different from the visible return in the clouds, or, finally, by the word "Tarry," something different from surviving in the body;* it is, after all, his object to involve the matter in a mysterious and sacred obscurity. But as there follows immediately upon this statement the explanation that this was the disciple who testified to these things, and wrote this (ver. 24), it is possible that by "his tarrying" until the coming of Christ, the duration of this his writing, the continued validity of the Gospel of the Spirit contained in it, may be understood.

98. THE ASCENSION.

When we consider the visions which the different adherents of Jesus, male and female, thought they had had of him after his resurrection, and the legends which soon attached themselves to these visions as matter already existing, it was, as we have seen above, unavoidable that persons should look back and ask themselves when and how this new and higher life of him who had been crucified begun; *i.e.* that the conception of the resurrection of Jesus, his coming forth from the sepulchre on the third or some other day, should arise and be invested with the traditional decoration of an angelic appearance. And now it might be said that the equally necessary result of viewing the matter from the opposite side of the question, as to the close of this new condition, was the conception of the ascent to heaven of him who had arisen

---

* Perhaps a removal to Paradise, there to be exalted until the return of Christ. Comp. Hilgenfeld, The Prophets Esra and Daniel, p. 63 ff.

after one or after forty days. But the circumstance of our finding the account of the ascension only in two Evangelists, while that of the resurrection is common to all, shews us at once that the necessity in both directions was not the same. For the new life of Jesus must indeed have had a beginning, as he had certainly been dead; but an end it need not necessarily, nay could not have had, as his life was immortal. Or a conclusion was required for the life on which Jesus had entered through the resurrection only when it was considered a mere intermediate condition; but originally it was not so considered, or considered so in quite a different relation from that in which the ascension afterwards made its conclusion.

For it was held that the next epoch in the life of the risen Messiah would be his return at the end of the present period of the world. He was to come again from heaven, but, according to the most ancient Christian conception, he did not wait forty days after his resurrection to enter into it, but entered into it at the time of his resurrection. At all events, he had appeared to the Apostle Paul, and even if the ascension is not supposed to have taken place until forty days after the resurrection, this would be much later, consequently from heaven, and yet the Apostle places the appearance as being of a similar character, in the same category with those which the older disciples had had, presumably during those forty days; he conceived therefore the latter appearances also as coming from heaven. Matthew also stands upon this point of view. Indeed, the first appearance of Christ, which he represents as being granted on the morning of the resurrection to the women returning from the sepulchre, is so far obscure as that we do not know whether we are to suppose Jesus as having already descended from heaven, or, as on the occasion of the first Johannine appearance, on the point of ascending there. Then, when he shews himself on the mountain in Galilee to the Eleven, stating that all power is given to him in heaven and on earth, he manifestly comes from his Messianic investiture, and this (comp. Dan. vii. 14) can only have taken place in heaven. That the exaltation of the Messiah up to heaven did not exclude his constant and future operation upon earth, we see from the closing declaration of Jesus in Matthew (ver. 20), that he is with his disciples for ever, even to the end of the present period of the world; *i.e.* during the very term during which he will be really dwelling in heaven, and before he returns from thence to the earth again he will be, with his invisible ministration, in company with his followers; and it followed, as a matter of course, that he could not be prevented occasionally and in an exceptional manner from sometimes shewing himself to them in a visible form. It was in the character of preliminary exhibitions of this kind, preliminary, that is, not to the ascension, but to the second advent, that Paul looked upon the appearances of Christ granted to himself as well as to the older Apostles, for which therefore no limit of time was laid down, and which might have taken place just as easily years as days after the resurrection.

But now it came to pass that the immediately expected return of Christ was longer and longer delayed, while, on the other hand, the billows of excited mental life became calmer and calmer. The appearance granted to Paul remained the last of its kind; the gates of heaven which had received the ascended Christ had closed, and were not to be opened again until the end of the world for his glorious return. If from that troubled time, in which men vainly longed to see one of the days of the Son of Man (Luke xvii. 22), they looked back to those blessed days when the resuscitated Christ had revealed himself to his followers on the open highway and in the closed room, on the sea and on the mountain, had eaten with them and drunken with them (Acts x. 41), that seemed quite another time, between which and that which followed a great gulf was fixed. He could not then, as he had now done, have retired into heaven; he must, after coming forth from the grave, have stayed a time on earth, have vouchsafed his presence to his followers for a time before withdrawing from them for the long period which was to intervene before his future coming again. Thus naturally arose the conception of an interval between the coming forth of Jesus from his tomb and his ascent to heaven, of a period during which he that had risen, though concealed from the multitude, walked upon the earth, in order to announce himself to his followers as the risen Messiah by separate appearances before finally separating from them.

This sojourn of the Risen One on earth could only have lasted as long as the object of it required. This object was to make his resurrection known and certain to his followers, and to give them their last instructions and promises. This might be done in a short period. It might possibly be done in one day. The other conception did not require such haste. As it brought Jesus upon the place of his Messianic glory at the very moment of his resurrection, it might represent him as appearing upon earth at such intervals as he pleased. Thus in Matthew the appearance of Jesus upon the mountain in Galilee must be supposed to have taken place long enough after the resurrection, to give time to the disciples to return back from Jerusalem to Galilee, which in any case required several days. But if the celestial glory of the Messiah was withheld from him after his resurrection until he had finished all that remained for him to do with those whom he left behind, then haste was required for these things. It was also very possible, inasmuch as to the glorified body of the risen Jesus space no longer opposed any limits. Thus in Luke he shews himself first to the two disciples on the road to Emmaus, and accompanies them into the village, which is distant three hours from Jerusalem, and when they come back into the city he has not only appeared already to Simon, but introduces himself immediately after into the assemblage of the Eleven and the other disciples, whom he immediately led out towards Bethany in order to make them witnesses of his visible ascent to heaven (xxiv. 50—53). All this manifestly takes place on the day of the resurrection, and the circumstances are similarly represented in the abbreviated description of Mark (xvi. 14—20), the whole of whose concluding section indeed is too confused to admit of a definite idea being gained out of his account alone. For as he represents Jesus as appearing to the disciples while they are sitting at table, giving them his instructions and promises, and then after these speeches being carried up to heaven, the consequence is, that if we were to take him strictly at his word, we should have to entertain the very strange idea of an ascension out of the room.

If then, after the Messiah had thus passed from death to life, there was a strong inducement not to detain him too long from the final goal of his career, to shorten as much as possible the intervening state between his resurrection and his exaltation to heaven, still there was another motive which must have operated with ever-increasing influence in an opposite direction. Reports had gradually spread of so many appearances of Jesus after his resurrection, that it constantly became more difficult to conceive them as having all taken place in one day. Taking into account those only of which the Apostle Paul makes mention, to Peter, then to the Twelve, then to five hundred brethren, then to James, then to all the Apostles, there would, even with these, have been too many for one day, the requisite opportunities and situations considered. Even the object of these appearances, the conviction and instruction of the disciples, could not, on a nearer view, appear to have been attainable so quickly; neither disbelief nor stupidity could have yielded at a blow, and the imagination itself felt the necessity of introducing longer intervals. The closeness to each other of these two opposite views is shewn to us in the remarkable fact that one and the same writer, in the half of his work that was written first, has, in his description, followed the one view, and in the latter half the other. Luke, who in the concluding chapter of his Gospel implies that Jesus rose to heaven on the very day of his resurrection, speaks in the introduction to his Acts of the Apostles of forty days, during which he appeared to the Apostles after his resurrection, shewing himself alive by many kinds of proofs, and speaking to them of the kingdom of God, and it is not until the expiration of forty days that he represents the ascension as taking place. Whether this notion obtained currency in the interval between the composition of the first and second of his works, or he himself felt an inducement to imagine it, the motive can only have lain in the necessity of providing the requisite interval for the numerous appearances of Christ current in the legend, and for the great revulsion in the ideas of the disciples supposed to have taken place during this interval. The limitation of this space of time to forty days exactly was involved in the Jewish symbolism of numbers, a symbolism which had already become Christian as well. For forty years the people of Israel was in the wilderness, the same number of days Moses had been in Sinai, for forty days he and Elijah had fasted, for the same length of time Jesus had sojourned in the wilderness without meat and drink before the temptation; for forty days long Ezra was said to have retired into solitude with his five scribes, in order to devote himself to the restoration of the holy Scriptures that had been consumed by fire, before he was withdrawn from earth.* Thus it was that for the period during which the risen Christ was teaching his disciples about the kingdom of heaven (Acts i. 3), the number forty (naturally of days, not years), which was traditional for intervals of this kind,

---

* 4 Esr. xiv. 23 ff. Comp. Volkmar, Introduction to the Apocrypha, ii. 288; Hilgenfeld, Prophets Esra and Daniel, p. 71.

presented itself as a matter of course. The appearance of Christ presented to the Apostle Paul could not indeed come within even this extended period; but it was clearly described by himself as a supplementary one, as something out of due time (1 Cor. xv. 8 ff.); and the object of a special distinction to Paul could only be served by Christ condescending to appear once more from heaven in order to gain the Apostle to his side.

Moreover, there is one point in which these accounts, differing as they do with regard to the close of the earthly walk of Jesus, harmonize with each other, even that of the fourth Gospel not excepted, which we must speak of in particular further on. It is, that they put into the mouth of the departing Jesus certain ordinances and promises, which, however different they may be in the different Gospels, coincide nevertheless in certain main points. The commission to preach the doctrine of Christ to all nations is common to all the synoptic accounts (Matt. xxviii. 16—20; Mark xvi. 15—18; Luke xxiv. 44—49; Acts i. 4—8). That Luke does not, as the two others do, mention baptism, is accidental; but when what Mark in later phraseology describes as preaching the Gospel, Matthew expresses in the Jewish-Christian legal form that the disciples are to teach all mankind to observe everything that Christ has commanded, Luke, more in the spirit of Paul, that they are to preach in his name repentance and forgiveness of sins—in these discrepancies the peculiarities of the different writers, so noticeable also elsewhere, are not to be overlooked. It has been already remarked that the destination of the Gospel for all people, *i.e.* the admission of the Heathen also into the new kingdom of the Messiah without any other condition than that of baptism, was a view which had by no means presented itself to the disciples of Jesus so soon after his departure, and modern criticism has come pretty generally to the conclusion that the common baptismal formula, as unheard of elsewhere in the New Testament as it is customary in the later language of the Church, "in the name of the Father, and of the Son, and of the Holy Ghost," is due to the hand that put the last touches to our Gospel. As on the occasion of Jesus meeting with the two travellers to Emmaus, so also in this, the concluding scene immediately before going forth to the ascension, it is, in the view of Luke, a matter of especial importance that Jesus lays before the disciples the right understanding of the Scriptures, and points out to them in the Old Testament the doctrine of the passion and death of the Messiah; the only possible condition under which the disciples could firmly continue to believe that their crucified Master was the Messiah, being their conviction that such a fate had been already prophesied for him in the Old Testament. The other event which the departing Jesus announces in Luke to the disciples is that pouring out of the Spirit in the capital which they had to look for, and which it was already part of his plan to describe in the second division of his work. The account of Mark of the last words of Jesus to his disciples stands in unfavourable contrast with these two. After mentioning the command to baptize, and pointing it with a promise and a threat, he names, as the signs which are to characterize believers, the power to cast out devils, to speak with new tongues, to lift up snakes, to drink deadly poison without harm, to heal the sick by laying on of hands; features which, with the exception of the last but one, are taken out of the Gospels and Acts of the Apostles (ii. 4 ff., xvi. 16—18, xxviii. 2—10); but are here in part generalized, in part multiplied, by the introduction of the extravagant feature of drinking poison, in a way which shews us at how early a period in the Church a superstitious feeling directed only to signs and wonders begun to smother the genuine spirit of Jesus. If we imagine a Christian travelling about with pretended credentials of this kind in the heathen world of that period, we should have exactly one of those jugglers upon whom Lucian pours out his satire, not without a side-glance at Christianity.

Matthew now concludes his Gospel with the distinct spiritual perspective opened by the promise of Jesus to be with his followers until the end of the world. The two middle Evangelists subjoin the visible concluding act of the ascension. The statement of Mark, indeed, as has been already observed, is so indefinite in point of locality and details, that we might even doubt whether he really means a visible ascension or not; but he indicates all the more definitely whence he gets the whole conception. When he says (ver. 19), "So then after the Lord had spoken unto them, he was received up into heaven, and sat on the right hand of God," he could not himself have meant that any one saw this last proceeding, but he took it out of the passage in the Psalm (cx. 1): "The Lord said unto my Lord, Sit thou on my right hand until I make thine enemies thy footstool." This passage, obviously admitting of a Messianic application, and which moreover Jesus was said to have applied to himself (Matt xxvi. 64; Mark xiv. 62), required for its literal fulfilment the exaltation of the Messiah to heaven, and thus, at the conclusion of his earthly pilgrimage, Jesus must have ascended into heaven.

The narrative of Luke is more full and more vivid, especially in the second edition, corrected and enlarged, of his account of the ascension, the Acts of the Apostles. At the conclusion of his Gospel (xxiv. 50—53), he says that Jesus led his disciples out to Bethany, and while he was here giving them his blessing with uplifted hands, he departed from them and ascended into heaven, whereupon the disciples fell down and worshipped, and returned full of joy to Jerusalem. According to the introduction to the Acts of the Apostles (i. 4—12), Jesus collected the Apostles once more upon the Mount of Olives (at the foot of which Bethany lay), and while he was giving them his last commissions and promises, he was taken up; and a cloud received him out of their sight. They looked after him as he moved from them on the cloud into heaven, and while they were so engaged, there stood by them two men in white apparel (*i.e.* angels, like those described at the tomb), who interrupted their gazing by the assurance that the same Jesus which was taken up from them into heaven, should so come again in like manner as they had seen him ascend into heaven. We need only reverse this in order to discover how, as before in the case of Mark, this conception of the visible ascension of Jesus arose. As the Messiah was to come again hereafter, so must he now have gone away; but according to Daniel, he was to come in the clouds of heaven, so also must he now have ascended on a cloud into heaven.

In the Old Testament two especially holy men, Enoch and Elijah, had already been miraculously removed from the earth; but the departure of the first is not described as visible (1 Mos. v. 24; Sir. xliv. 16, xlix. 16; Heb. xi. 5), and the ascent of the latter with its fiery chariot and its fiery horses (2 Kings ii. 11; Sir. xlviii. 9), was not in accordance with the milder spirit of Jesus, and was, generally, too materially described. There was but one feature that could be taken from this antitype, the feature which Luke (Acts i. 9) brings into prominence, that Jesus was taken up *before the eyes of the disciples*, inasmuch as Elijah had connected the transference of his spirit to his disciple with the condition that Elisha should *see* him ascend. The first Saviour, Moses, who is elsewhere so often typical of the second Saviour, had died, according to the Old Testament, a natural death, and only been buried by Jehovah in an undiscoverable place (5 Mos. xxxiv. 5 ff.); on the other hand, we find in Josephus a narrative about his end which bears a striking resemblance to our history of the ascent to heaven.[*] On the mountain to which Deuteronomy already took him before

[*] Antiq. iv. 8, 48.

his death, Moses makes first the people, and then the elders, stay behind; and while he is taking leave of Joshua and the High-priest Eleazar, a cloud suddenly stands over him, and he vanishes in a deep hollow. This narrative, which he undoubtedly took from the later rabbinical tradition, a narrative the object of which was to place the Lawgiver by such an end upon an equality with Enoch and Elijah, Josephus endeavours to reconcile with the simple statement in the fifth book of Moses, that he died, by the remark that Moses wrote the latter intentionally, that no one might venture to say that on account of his extraordinary virtue he had joined the Godhead; a turn in which a side-glance of the Jewish historian at the deification of Christ, which was already beginning in his time, might be found.

Now, if from this point we take a parting look at the fourth Evangelist, we appear to find him at the conclusion of the evangelical history, not, as on other occasions, the foremost in introducing unhistorical modifications, but standing on the same ground as Matthew does, inasmuch as the brilliant concluding scene of the ascension is wanting both in him and Matthew. This may surprise us in the case of an Evangelist to whose exaggerated conception of the divinity of Christ such a scene might seem particularly suitable—of a Gospel in which it might appear to be particularly required as a literal fulfilment of many speeches of the Christ described in it about his ascension into heaven, his return into his glory with the Father (vi. 62; comp. iii. 13, xvii. 5). If the composer of this Gospel had really before him the account of the ascension, it might have been supposed that he could not have avoided adopting it, though modified in his own way; and as he has not done so, we might have concluded either that he wrote earlier than either of them, or that he rejected their account, if he knew of it, on purely historical grounds, because he was aware, as an eye-witness, that nothing of the kind had taken place. But in point of fact, he has adopted it, modified in his own way; and the fact that he has not adopted it in the form in which it was presented to him in Mark and Luke may be so perfectly explained from the spirit and scheme of his Gospel, that there is no necessity for attributing to him any historical motive, such being altogether foreign to him.

The fourth Evangelist, we might say, goes to work with the departure of Jesus to heaven in the same way as he did with his coming from heaven. The latter had been thrown by his predecessors into the form of the begetting of Jesus by the Holy Ghost, and though the Logos-idea of John required a different turn, still a corresponding representation might have been given of the entrance of the Logos into the womb of Mary. But the fourth Evangelist entirely passes over the begetting and birth of Christ, and is satisfied with referring to his exalted origin, partly in his prologue, partly in various passages of the speeches uttered by Jesus. Exactly in the same way with the ascension of Jesus into heaven, he represents him as sometimes alluding to it in his speeches, but does not himself describe it as a visible occurrence. But that the Evangelist does assume this occurrence as having actually taken place, is perfectly clear from the scene with the Magdalene above described, where Jesus speaks of his ascending to the Father, not as having actually taken place, but immediately to take place. Attention has also been already drawn to the fact that John here follows Matthew, only that it comes out more definitely in him than in Matthew, that it was not before, but after, this first appearance that the risen Jesus ascended into heaven. But as in Matthew the appearance of Jesus on the mountain in Galilee assumes the ascension to heaven as an event that had already occurred, so also in John does the appearance to the disciples with closed doors. For the communication of the Spirit by breathing upon them, could not, according to the view of the Evangelist, be accomplished until Jesus was glorified (vii. 39); but his glorification was not complete until after his departure to the Father. The fourth Evangelist, in representing this communication of the Spirit as having been made personally by Jesus on the day of his resurrection, places himself in opposition to the third, who, in his Acts of the Apostles (chap. ii.), represents this communication as not having taken place until fifty days later, after Jesus had already taken his departure from earth. In this case also, as well as in that of the ascension, he avoids the external sensible occurrence which Luke makes of the pouring out of the Holy Ghost; the soft aspiration appeared to him more spiritual, and in particular more in accordance with the spirit of Christ than the storm and the fiery tongues in the narrative of the Acts; moreover, the Paraclete, supposing Jesus to have communicated it himself by breathing upon his disciples, appeared to come in more definitely as his continuing representative.

But, besides this omission of the ascension, there is another point in which, at this concluding moment, the fourth Evangelist is connected with the first. The speech of Jesus after breathing upon the disciples (ver. 23), "Whosesoever sins ye remit, they are remitted unto them, and whosesoever sins ye retain, they are retained," reminds us of his words in the first Gospel (xvi. 19, xviii. 18), which are represented, indeed, in the fourth as having been uttered on an earlier occasion. The words are, "Whatsoever ye shall bind on earth shall be bound in heaven; and whatsoever ye shall loose on earth shall be loosed in heaven." Here the change which the fourth Evangelist makes in the speech might be explained by reference to the dispute as to the veniality of certain sins, which, as we see from the Shepherd of Hermas, begun to disturb the Church early in the second century.

In consequence of this avoidance of the visible ascension, the fourth Gospel has this feature in common with the first, that, like the latter, or even more than the latter, it dispenses with its proper conclusion, so that an opening was left for the addition of an appendix (in chap. xxi.), and this too after its own properly concluding scene, the appearance of Jesus to the disciples who were assembled with closed doors, has received a supplement in the appearance, eight days later, in favour of Thomas. But this very supplementary scene concludes with a speech which opens a perspective extremely suitable for the conclusion of the Gospel, and resembling that which is opened by the concluding expression in Matthew. The words, " Blessed are they that have not seen and yet have believed !" are spoken not merely to Thomas, but in his person to all men who should come to faith in Christ without the possibility of seeing; they are the legacy of the Johannine Christ to his Church, a legacy which has still its meaning for us, only indeed in the sense of that expression of Lessing, a sense wrapped for our Evangelists in thick and mystic clouds. The expression is to the effect that accidental historic truths can never form the proofs of necessary truths of the Reason.

99. CONCLUSION.

This principle is important to us, now that we have arrived at the conclusion of our critical process, in proportion as we are penetrated with the conviction that our historical knowledge of Jesus is defective and uncertain. After removing the mass of mythical parasites of different kinds that have clustered round the tree, we see that what we before considered branches, foliage, colour, and form of the tree itself, belonged for the most part to those parasitical creepers; and instead of the removal of them having restored the tree to us in its true condition and appearance, we find, on the contrary, that they have swept away its proper foliage, sucked out the sap, crippled the shoots and branches, and consequently that its original figure has entirely disappeared. Every mythical feature added to the form of Jesus has not only obscured an historical one, so that with the removal of the first the latter would come to light, but very many have been destroyed by the mythical forms that have overlaid them, and been thus completely lost.

It is not agreeable to hear and therefore is disbelieved, but whoever has seriously examined the subject and chooses to be candid, knows as well as we do that few great men have existed of whose history we have so unsatisfactory a knowledge as we have of that of Jesus. How much more clear and distinct, beyond all comparison, is the figure of Socrates, which is four hundred years older! It is true, indeed, that of the history of his youth and education we likewise know but little. But we know accurately what he was in his mature years, what he attempted and what he effected; the figures of his disciples and friends stand out before us with historic clearness; with regard to the causes and the course of his condemnation and the facts of his death we are perfectly informed. And though a few anecdotical additions are not wanting, his biography has continued free, in the main, from that mythical matter under which the historical figures of many ancient Greek philosophers, Pythagoras for instance, have been, like the figure of Jesus, almost smothered. This preservation of his image, in the case of Socrates, is due to the circumstance of his having lived in the most cultivated city of Greece, at the most brilliant period of intellectual enlightenment, and when literature was most flourishing. And several of his pupils were also distinguished writers, and in part made their teacher the immediate subject of their works.

Xenophon and Plato.—On mention of these names, who does not think of Matthew and John, but how unfavourable for the two last is the comparison! In the first place, the authors of the Memorabilia of Socrates, of the two Convivia, of the Phædo, &c., were actual disciples of Socrates; the authors of the first and the fourth Gospels, on the contrary, were no immediate disciples of Jesus. With regard to the above-mentioned writings of the two Athenians, we should have required no external evidence to be preserved; we should still have recognised them as the works of contemporaries and personal acquaintances of Socrates. In the case of the two Gospels, however ancient, however consistent the testimony for their apostolic origin might be, still one should put no faith in it, as it would be contradicted by the plainest primâ facie appearance of the books themselves. In the next place, the exertions of the two writers about Socrates are directed throughout to setting plainly before us his peculiar character and value as a man, as a citizen, as a thinker and educator of youth. This, too, our two Evangelists do after their own fashion. But this is not enough for them. Their Jesus is assumed to have been more than man; he is assumed to have been a miraculous man, begotten of God, and even, according to one of them, the Divine Creative Word incarnate. Hence, in their description, there not only runs parallel with the activity of Jesus as a teacher a series of miracles and develop-ments of miraculous destiny, but this miraculous element is an ingredient in the doctrine itself which they put into his mouth, so that they represent Jesus as saying things about himself which it is impossible that any man of sound under-standing should have said. In the third place, Plato and Xenophon agree in all essential points in what they say about Socrates. There is much which they report in similar terms; several features, peculiar to one, do still, when taken in con-junction with those which the other supplies, unite admirably in one image; and if Xenophon, as regards the philosophical spirit of Socrates, as often falls as much below his subject as Plato with his arbitrary inventions soars above it, and puts Platonic speculations in the mouth of Socrates, the two de-scriptions easily correct each other by a comparison of the two writers, and have no tendency to mislead, because that of Xenophon is evidently the result of naturally inadequate power to grasp his subject, while Plato in his Socratic Dialogues makes no claim to the character of an historical writer. How irreconcilable, on the other hand, is the Christ of Matthew with that of John, and how solemnly the author of the fourth Gospel, in particular, protests the truth of his reports, we have seen. But everything that distinguishes the accounts that have reached us about Jesus from those about Socrates, in respect of historical admissibility, to the advantage of the latter, has its roots in the difference of times and nationalities. With the clear atmosphere and brilliant light of Athenian cultivation and illumination, in which the image of Socrates is seen by us so plainly, is contrasted the thick and murky cloud of Jewish error and superstition, and Alexandrine fanaticism, out of which the form of Jesus looks at us and is scarcely to be recognised as human.

It may be said, and has often been said, that all that is unsatisfactory in the evangelical biographies of Jesus is richly compensated for by the fact that we still have before us his work in the Christian Church, and may now draw our inferences from this work to its originator. Thus, of Shakespeare, for instance, we know but little that is historical, and much that is fabulous is asserted of him; we do not, however, allow this to disturb us much, as his compositions enable us to restore in perfect distinctness the figure of his personality. The comparison would be appropriate if we had the work of the Prophet of Galilee at first hand, as we have those of the British poet. But the former has passed through very numerous hands—of persons who have had no scruple to interpolate, to omit, and to change in every way. The Christian Church, even in its earliest form as it appears in the New Testament, was moulded by so many other factors as well as the personality of Jesus, that any inference from it to him must be most uncertain. Even Christ the risen, upon whom the Church was founded, is quite a different being from what the man Jesus had been, and it was upon that conception of Christ the risen that not only the conception of him and his earthly life, but also the Church itself, was so moulded that it becomes a very doubtful question whether, if Jesus had returned about the time of the destruction of Jerusalem, he would have recognised himself again in the Christ who was at that time being preached in the Churches.

I do not think that the case is so bad as has lately been maintained, as that we cannot know for certain of any one of the texts which are put into the mouth of Jesus in the Gospels whether he really uttered it or not. I believe that there are some which we may ascribe to Jesus with all that amount of probability beyond which we cannot generally go in historical matters, and I have endeavoured above to explain the signs by which we may recognise such. But this probability approaching to certainty does not extend far, and with the exception of the journey of Jesus to Jerusalem and his death, the facts and circumstances of his life are unfavourably situated. There is little of which we can say for certain that it took place, and of all to which the faith of the Church especially attaches itself, the miraculous and supernatural matter in the facts and destinies of Jesus, it is far more certain that it did not take place. But that the happiness of mankind is to depend upon belief in things of which it is in part certain that they did not take place, in part uncertain whether they did take place, and only to the smallest extent beyond doubt that they took place—that the happiness of mankind is to depend upon belief in such things as these, is so absurd, that the assertion of the principle does not, at the present day, require any further contradiction.

100.

No! the happiness of man, or, speaking more intelligibly, the possibility of fulfilling his destiny, developing the powers implanted in him, and thus participating in the corresponding amount of well-being—it is impossible—and on this point the saying of Reimar is an everlasting truth—it is impossible that this can depend on his recognition of facts into which scarcely one man in a thousand is in a position to institute a thorough investigation, and, supposing him to have done so, then to arrive at a satisfactory result. But, as certainly as men have a common destiny, attainable by all, so the conditions also of reaching it, *i.e.* independent of and before the exertion of the will in the direction of the object, the knowledge of that object must be given to every man, and that knowledge cannot be an accidental acquaintance with history coming from without, but must be a necessary knowledge attainable by reason, such as every man can find in himself. This is the meaning of the profound saying of Spinoza, that for the purposes of happiness it is not in any way necessary to know Christ after the flesh; but that the case is different with that eternal Son of God, namely the Divine Wisdom, which appears in all things, especially in the human mind, and in Jesus Christ appeared in a pre-eminent degree. Without this, he says, no one can attain to happiness, because it alone teaches what is true and false, good and bad.* Kant, like Spinoza, distinguished between the historical person of Jesus and the Ideal of humanity pleasing to God, involved in human reason, or in the moral sense in its perfect purity, so far as is possible in a system of the world dependent upon wants and inclinations. To rise to this ideal was, he said, the general duty of men; and though we cannot conceive of it as existing otherwise than under the form of a perfect man, and

* In Letter 21.

though it is not impossible that such a man may have lived, as we are all intended to resemble this ideal, still that it is not necessary that we should know of the existence of such a man or believe in it, but solely that we should keep that ideal before us, recognise it as obligatory upon us, and strive to make ourselves like it.*

This distinguishing between the historical and the ideal Christ, that is, the exemplar of man as he is destined to be, and the transferring of beatifying faith from the first to the second, is the unavoidable result of the modern spiritual development; it is that carrying forward of the Religion of Christ to the Religion of Humanity to which all the noblest efforts of the present time are directed. In this the world sees an apostacy from Christianity, a denial of Christ. This view rests upon a misunderstanding, for which the modern expression, perhaps also the mode of thought of the philosophers who made this distinction, is partly responsible. For they speak as if the exemplar of human perfection at which the individual has to aim had existed in the Reason from the first. So that they would seem to imply that this exemplar, *i.e.* the ideal Christ, might have been present within us as much as it is now if a historic Christ had never lived or worked. But this is by no means really the case. The idea of human perfection, like other ideas, was imparted to the human mind only, at first, in an elementary shape, which gradually reaches its perfection by experience. It exhibits a different conformation in different nations, varying according to the natural character, the conditions of their climate and history, and admits of our observing a progress in the course of history. The Roman conceived of man as he ought to be, differently from the Greek, the Jew differently from both, the Greek, after Socrates, differently from and unquestionably more perfectly than before. Every man of moral pre-eminence,

---

* Religion within the Limits of Pure Reason, second chapter, first section, p. 73 ff. of the second edition.

every great thinker who has made the active nature of man the object of his investigation, has contributed in narrower or wider circles towards correcting that idea, perfecting or improving it. And among these improvers of the ideal of humanity, Jesus stands at all events in the first class. He introduced features into it which were wanting to it before, or had continued undeveloped; reduced the dimensions of others which prevented its universal application; imported into it, by the religious aspect which he gave it, a more lofty consecration, and bestowed upon it, by embodying it in his own person, the most vital warmth; while the Religious Society which took its rise from him provided fo. this ideal the widest acceptance among mankind. It is true, indeed, that this Religious Society originated in quite other things than the moral significance of its Founder, and did anything but exhibit this in its purest form: in the only writing of our New Testament which perhaps comes from an immediate disciple of Jesus, the Revelation of John, there lives a Christ from whom little is to be gained for the ideal of humanity; but the features of patience, gentleness, and charity which Jesus made predominant in that image, have not been lost to mankind, and are exactly those from which all that we now call Humanity might germinate and grow.

Meanwhile, however high may be the place of Jesus among those who have shewn to mankind most purely and most plainly what it ought to be, still he was not the first to do so, nor will he be the last. But as he had predecessors in Israel and Hellas, on the Ganges and the Oxus, so also he has not been without followers. On the contrary, that exemplar has been, after him, still further developed, more perfectly finished, its different features brought into better proportion with each other. It cannot be overlooked, that in the pattern exhibited by Jesus in his doctrine and in his life, some sides being finished to perfection, others were only faintly sketched, or not indicated at all. Every point is fully developed that has reference to love towards God and our neighbour, to purity in the heart and life of the individual: but even the life of man in the family is left by the Teacher, himself childless, in the background; his relation towards the body politic appears simply passive; with trade he is not only by reason of his calling unconcerned, but even visibly averse to it, and everything relating to art and enjoyment of the elegancies of life is absolutely removed from his range of view. That these are important defects, that we have here an one-sidedness before us which is grounded partly on Jewish nationality, partly in the circumstances of the time, partly in the special relation of the life of Jesus, no one would attempt to deny, inasmuch as no one can deny it. And the defects are not merely such that only the finishing details are wanting, while the ruling principle is given; but as regards the State in particular, trade and art, the true idea is wanting from first to last, and it is a fruitless undertaking to attempt to decide upon the precepts or after the example of Jesus what the action of man ought to be as a citizen, what his conduct in connection with the enrichment and embellishment of existence by trade and art. On these points something was wanting that required to be supplied from the circumstances of other times, other states and other systems of cultivation. And what was wanted was found in part by looking back upon what Greeks and Romans had accomplished in these respects, in part in what was reserved for the further development of mankind and its history.

But all these defects in what was given by Jesus will be best supplied if we start with considering what *was* given as a human acquisition—human, and therefore capable of improvement and requiring it. If, on the contrary, Jesus is considered as the God-man, as the pattern form introduced among mankind of universal and exclusive applicability, any attempt towards giving this pattern greater perfection must naturally be repudiated—its one-sidedness and imperfection must be made the rule—and all those aspects of human action which are not represented in it must be either declined or simply regulated externally. Nay, inasmuch as by the side of or above the moral example set by Jesus he himself stands as the God-man, belief in whom, apart from and before the recognition of that pattern image, is the duty of man and the condition of his happiness, then that upon which everything depends is thus degraded into the second class, the moral greatness of Jesus is crippled and its first operation prevented, even the moral obligations which derive their authority from being involved in the conditions of human nature are represented in the false light of being positive commands of God. Therefore the critic is convinced that he is committing no offence against what is sacred, nay rather that he is doing a good and necessary work, when he sweeps away all that makes Jesus a supernatural Being, as well meant and perhaps even at first sight beneficial, but in the long run mischievous and now absolutely destructive, restores, as well as may be, the image of the historical Jesus in its simply human features, but refers mankind for salvation to the ideal Christ, to that moral pattern in which the historical Jesus did indeed first bring to light many principal features, but which as an elementary principle as much belongs to the general endowment of our kind, as its improvement and perfection can only be the problem and the work of mankind in general.

THE END.

PRINTED BY C. GREEN & SON, 178, STRAND.

www.ingramcontent.com/pod-product-compliance
Lightning Source LLC
Chambersburg PA
CBHW032136010526
44111CB00035B/592